W9-CMR-638

WOMEN, SCIENCE AND MEDICINE 1500–1700

WOMEN, SCIENCE AND MEDICINE 1500–1700

MOTHERS AND SISTERS OF THE ROYAL SOCIETY

EDITED BY
LYNETTE HUNTER *&*
SARAH HUTTON

SUTTON PUBLISHING

First published in the United Kingdom in 1997 by
Sutton Publishing Limited · Phoenix Mill
Thrupp · Stroud · Gloucestershire · GL5 2BU

British Library Cataloguing in Publication Data
A catalogue record for this book is available from the British Library

ISBN 0 7509 1334 7 (case)
ISBN 0 7509 1343 6 (paper)

Cover illustration: Alethea, Countess of Arundel, *by Antony van Dyck (by kind permission
of His Grace The Duke of Norfolk).*

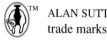

ALAN SUTTON™ and SUTTON™ are the
trade marks of Sutton Publishing Limited

Typeset in 10/12 pt Baskerville.
Typesetting and origination by
Sutton Publishing Limited.
Printed in Great Britain by
WBC Limited, Bridgend.

CONTENTS

LIST OF ILLUSTRATIONS

LIST OF CONTRIBUTORS

Reid Barbour is Bowman and Gordon Gray Associate Professor at the University of North Carolina at Chapel Hill. His publications include *Deciphering Elizabethan Fiction* (1993) and *English Epicures and Stoics: Ancient Legacies in Early Stuart England* (Massachusetts Studies in Early Modern Culture). He is currently working on a book about religious imagination in the age of Charles I.

Margaret P. Hannay is Professor of English at Siena College. She is the author of *Philip's Phoenix: Mary Sidney, Countess of Pembroke* (OUP, 1990) and is currently editing *The Collected Works of Mary Sidney Herbert, Countess of Pembroke* with Noel J. Kinnamon and Michael G. Brennan for Clarendon Press.

Frances Harris is a curator in the Department of Manuscripts at the British Library. She has recently published *A Passion for Government. The Life of Sarah, Duchess of Marlborough* (Oxford University Press, 1991). She is currently working on a study of John Evelyn and Margaret Godolphin.

Lynette Hunter is Reader in Rhetoric at the University of Leeds and Gresham Professor of Rhetoric. She is currently researching civic rhetoric in the Renaissance period and its bearing on gender and politics. Her work ranges from food history to contemporary literature and theory, to bibliography and textual editing. Her most recent work is *A Rhetoric of Situated Textuality: Taking the Feminist Critique of Science to Aesthetics* (forthcoming 1998).

Sarah Hutton is Reader in Renaissance and Seventeenth-Century Studies in the Faculty of Humanities, Languages and Education at the University of Hertfordshire. Her publications include *New Perspectives on Renaissance Thought* (edited with John Henry, Duckworth, 1990) and a revised edition of Marjorie Nicholson's *Conway Letters* (Clarendon Press, 1992). She is currently working on a book-length study of Anne Conway.

Rob Iliffe is Lecturer in the History of Science and Technology in the Centre for History of Science, Technology and Medicine at Imperial College, University of London. He has published a number of articles on the history of science in the early modern period and is preparing a book-length study of the relations between theology and natural philosophy in the early career of Isaac Newton.

Margaret Pelling is currently University Research Lecturer and Deputy Director of the Wellcome Unit for the History of Medicine at the University of Oxford. Most recently she has edited, with Hilary Marland, *The Task of Healing: Medicine, Religion and Gender in England and the Netherlands 1450–1800* (Erasmus Publishing, 1996). She is completing a volume of her essays on early modern health and medicine to be published by Longman and a monograph on unlicensed medical practice in London, to be published by MacMillan.

Hilary Rose is a feminist sociologist of science. She is Professor Emerita of Social Policy at the University of Bradford and is also attached to the Institute of Education, University of London. Her most recent book is *Love, Power and Knowledge: Towards a Feminist Transformation of the Sciences* (Polity, 1994). She is currently working on a book which explores the geneticization of culture and society.

Elizabeth Tebeaux is Professor of English at Texas A & M University and Professor of Managerial Studies at Rice University. She has published on the history of tecnical communication in the English Renaissance and is currently pursuing research on English technical writing from 1641–1700. Her most recent monograph is *The Emergence of a Tradition: Technical Writing on the English Renaissance, 1475–1640*, published by the Baywood Publishing Company.

Frances Willmoth is currently based at Cambridge University Library and is affiliated to the Department of History and Philosophy of Science at the University of Cambridge. After completing her doctorate on Sir Jonas Moore (published in 1993), she is the current editor of the correspondance of the first Astronomer Royal, John Flamsteed, *The Correspondance of John Flamsteed* (Institute of Physics Publishing, Bristol and Philadelphia, 3 vols: 1995, continuing). Her research interests include practical mathematics, maths education, surveying and cartography, as well as the history of astronomy.

Adrian Wilson works in the History and Philosophy of Science Division, Philosophy Department of the University of Leeds and is researching provincial voluntary hospitals in eighteenth-century England. He is the author of *The Making of Man-midwifery: Childbirth in England, 1660–1770* (UCL Press, 1995) and has edited *Rethinking Social History: English Society and its Interpretation, 1570–1920* (Manchester University Press, 1993).

FOREWORD

Hilary Rose

FROM HOUSEHOLD TO PUBLIC KNOWLEDGE, TO A NEW PRODUCTION SYSTEM OF KNOWLEDGE

Just over a quarter of a century ago second wave feminism burst into existence primarily, but not only, in the countries of late capitalism. As the Women's Liberation Movement, this entered a tumultuous political canvass of old and new movements demanding the liberation of colonial peoples, black people, the working classes, students, the poor and, as the ecological movement developed, Nature herself. Women now sought to become the subjects rather than the mere objects of history, to make themselves socially and politically visible, to take themselves out of nature and into culture. This immense project of turning the world upside down simultaneously demanded that the subject of enquiry was changed – the proper study of mankind was no longer man, but woman

The search for knowledge about women looked both into the everyday lives of women in the present and to the history of women in the past. The absence of previous serious cultural and political reflection on women's lives gave an intense energy to the task of finding the answers to the question of who were 'we' as contemporary women? What did we think and feel about our lives, our bodies, the social order, indeed the entire cosmos? Then we wanted to know who were our foremothers, what did they think and feel? Who were these culturally invisible figures whom we believed must, like us now, have been there in the past, but who were, as the socialist feminist historian Sheila Rowbotham (1973) put it, *Hidden From History*. Rowbotham herself sought to recover the history of women in the socialist and labour movements; others began to recover the equally well hidden history of women as writers, artists, musicians, healers, and scientists.[1]

Sometimes this task was carried out by women working in particular fields seeking to recover the lost history of their precursors and sometimes through the systematic work of feminist historians. It was through reading the writer Virginia Woolf that I learnt about Aphra Behn. For those of us interested in women in the history of science the pioneering text of the historian Laura Osen's *Women in Mathematics* (1974) taught us about Hypatia, Agnesi, the Marquise du Châtelet, Sophie Germain and the great Sophia Kovalevskaya.

The canvass of time (AD 375–1935) covered in Osen's short book is something of a heresy in the history business, and speaks of that early need to challenge the conspicuous absence of women scientists in the 2,000 year master narrative of the masculinist origins and history of western science. Such an encyclopaedic approach formed a crucial first response to the cultural erasure of the contribution of women. Subsequently there were to be other equally grandiose interruptions to that pale and androcentric narrative of science: Africa not Athens was claimed as the cradle of science, post-colonial had joined feminist voices in decentring the story. Even though this post-colonial strand largely set itself to reinsert the contributions of black men into the narrative, and so far says rather little about the contributions of black women, it has none the less served as an ally of the feminist critique of science. At the same time within feminism these alternative grand narratives have given way to rather more detailed accounts of contemporary women scientists.

Contemporary accounts can draw on rich archival material and on interviews with the subjects and their collaborators. Building such accounts is a very different exercise from constructing narratives of women in antiquity or even women interested in understanding and manipulating nature in the early modern period. That the women under scrutiny in these chapters are visible at all is remarkable. For however much the historian longs to reconstruct the past faithfully the availability or lack of archival material sets profound constraints. Research ingenuity plays its part in surmounting these problems as in the retrieval of the London women doctors from legal records. Who gets to write records, whose records are kept and whose thrown away are shaped by historical context, in which gender, as well as access to cultural and financial capital, plays a powerful part. We are left grateful that the unknown J.W. had the imagination to posthumously publish Elizabeth Grey's work, even though his motivation can only be guessed at.

Further discussing 'science' and 'technology' in these past contexts is not a simple matter of taking current usages of these terms and laying them onto the past to determine who produced knowledge and who manipulated nature. Instead these biographical studies illuminate how both science as knowledge and technology appear as new social practices and how particular people are culturally authorized to engage in these innovatory activities

When the experimental laboratory (or rather its precursor, for the 'laboratory', like the 'scientist', was a concept awaiting invention) was located in the private home of the reasonably well to do or the aristocracy, such as that of Mary Sidney, the domestic technological resources which fed this emergent chemistry and biology and medicine drew on the empirical knowledge and technological know-how developed in the kitchen and the still room. Both these domestic spaces were the terrain of women, and were the location of knowledges such as those concerning food preservation and the production of household chemicals, for the care of the sick. Such household knowledges were part of the expected competencies of women, recognized as crucial in a housewife but simultaneously as of no wider public value outside that domestic context. As herbalists or pharmacists women held, transmitted and developed extensive empirical knowledge of the healing properties of plants and other substances. Yet as we see in these chapters, it was men who prepared the herbalist texts for printed publication, although this required that their target, the domestic healer, was literate. To find that women were also surgeons and doctors provides a context for the midwifery skills of an Eleanor Willughby, and suggests that this was a period when the gender division of labour was undergoing more negotiation and change than has been recognized.

In one obvious sense this world of household knowledge has largely disappeared. The ever-expanding array of industrially made products has rendered such knowledge redundant. Yet this disappearance is both recent and over a short period of time. My grandmother, a country woman, would use fresh cobwebs to hold a clean wound together, and fresh hot urine to ease the pain of chilblains. Today as we approach the end of the twentieth century there are counter currents, for there is something of a return to household knowledge taking place, the absolute hegemony of scientific medicine is yielding to a widening appreciation of the diversity of healing knowledges. No one is surprised by the woman friend who cares effectively for the minor ailments of her children and herself with homeopathy, but who also turns to chemotherapy for breast cancer.

Nor has this present recognition of the limits of western science been only a matter for individuals searching for a more holistic medicine: the huge corporations of the pharmaceutical industry are currently putting significant resources into 'ethnoscience'. In the past the ethnosciences, those knowledges of nature developed by indigenous peoples, were simply ignored or plundered. By contrast, in today's post-colonial context there is some protection offered to the intellectual property rights of indigenous knowledge holders. Thus a contract between the Chinese government and Glaxo Wellcome, monitors Glaxo Wellcome's study of Chinese herbal remedies. These are seen as the source of unquestionably powerful therapies, with corresponding market potential, but whose mode of action is ill-understood within the conceptual framework of western science.

Such contemporary negotiations should sharpen our recognition of the range and depth of women's household knowledge in this early modern period, together with its appropriation and reconstitution as public knowledge by men. It is of course an absurd point, but no one offered these women contracts acknowledging their intellectual property rights, which tells us as much about the history of the ownership of knowledge as it does about the history of women.

Thus these biographies remind us both of the continuity of empirically based knowledge of nature from the pre-modern to the beginnings of modernity, but also of the processes of the separation of this knowledge from its embeddedness in everyday domestic life to a production system of knowledge set culturally apart. With the usual clarity of cultural hindsight we can see this process of separation and appropriation from everyday life as integral to the formation of modernity, namely the construction and cultural recognition of abstract disembodied knowledge. Nor was this delight in abstraction to be equated solely with the masculine, as the scientific concerns of Hutchinson, Conway and Cavendish show. But for these women it is also a matter of social position; the women doing abstract disembodied science were aristocrats, and their lives like those of their male counterparts were nearer to the library than women of the middling classes.

The lives of the early modern women documented here demonstrate that science and technology is not some fixed category but is continuously historically constructed and reconstructed. A subtle division of labour between the women points to the different lives of women in the middling classes, and the aristocratic women. Women in the middling classes with their closer relationship to household production, tended to be stronger on empirical knowledge: the doctors, midwives and the food technologists. While yet another group who tended to be closely connected to men involved in the new public production system of science (Howard, Boyle, Evelyn, and Flamsteed), were centrally part of the new theory-driven experimentalism. Given the closeness between the scientific project of these women and the new public knowledge, and their personal family relationship to the founding fellows of the Royal Society, their exclusion is all the more remarkable. What complex and fast-changing cultural and political currents produced such Janus-like behaviour on the part of men such as John Evelyn or Robert Boyle? What went on in the minds of these men so that the wife or the sister was at one moment their intellectual confidante and at the next, the Other, to be excluded from the new public knowledge?

In the case of women scientists in the twentieth century the supportive role of the women's colleges and the informal networks among women have come more clearly into view. Thus Bedford College, never a scientific or educational power house, and casually erased by the combination of first a modernizing Labour government and then an economizing Conservative government, educated more women fellows of the Royal Society than any other institution.[2] The crystallographer and Nobelist Dorothy Crowfoot Hodgkin, who with Florence Nightingale was one of only two British women ever to have been awarded the Order of Merit, was very conscious of the crucial support given by her Oxford women's college. Informal networks among women were critical too. When Marie Curie fled Paris because of the newspaper furore over her love affair with a divorcing colleague she came to England, sheltering anonymously in the house of Hertha Ayrton, a sister physicist and feminist.

I want to recall the biographies of women scientists written in the early years of the Women's Liberation Movement, for these were written under the sway of the powerful slogan 'the personal is political'. I take the slogan as a vivid political precursor developed by a hugely creative social movement, to the social post-modernist attention to complexity, diversity and situatedness. Such a slogan made it possible to see really nasty things that the potent cultural self-representation of science as disinterested, democratic and open to all who would faithfully follow her procedures, effectively hid. Thus it was the biography of a woman scientist published in 1975 which dramatically changed the cultural and political understanding of the women in science issue. The argument changed: it was not that women in science (even in the mid-twentieth century) had simply been ' forgotten', and could be put back into the record by politely recalling them to notice, but that there was clear evidence that women's contribution to science could be, and had been, systematically erased by grossly competitive and self-seeking men. This painful understanding of just how badly men scientists could behave, in direct conflict with that widespread conception of the democratic disinterested community of scientists, arrived with Anne Sayre's story of the disgraceful treatment of the brilliant crystallographer Rosalind Franklin whose x-ray photographs had made possible the model of the double helical structure of DNA. The personal story of Franklin was to become the icon for the politics of misogyny in science.[3]

The bare bones of the story are that the crucial photographs were taken by Franklin's London colleague Maurice Wilkins, without either her knowledge or permission, to show to his collaborators Jim Watson and Francis Crick in Cambridge. While the key papers published in *Nature* included one by Franklin and her colleague Gosling, her crucial contribution to the DNA story was from thenceforward systematically written out, not least by the DNA model builders. A cruel premature death had removed her from consideration for the Nobel prize awarded to Watson, Crick and Wilkins. But what was truly shocking was that in their acceptance speeches two of the three Nobelists neglected to mention the contribution of their dead colleague and the third was niggardly.

Sayre was a writer, and through her husband David, who was also a crystallographer, had become friends with Rosalind Franklin. When Franklin died at thirty-eight from cancer, Sayre as friend and a writer with access to those many decent crystallographers who knew a serious injustice had been done, set herself to put the record straight. The outlines of the scandal are today so widely known that few people know how they know, thus a science editor, who might be expected to know better, suggested recently that I write a biography of Franklin as it would 'make a great story'. He seemed quite surprised when I suggested that it was because there already was a brilliant biography that he knew of Franklin at all. Without Sayre, her ill-treatment would be known only to the crystallographers and the historians. Yet I am not sure that the cultural erasure of Franklin is not taking place all over again. This year saw the republication of *The Double Helix* whose author, the Nobelist Jim Watson, is still treated with unquestioning deference.

In similar vein the representation of the DNA story at the Science Museum, London erased Franklin's contribution until the anger of the crystallographic community forced the museum to acknowledge her contribution. Key among those setting the record straight has been Aaron Klug, currently President of the Royal Society. In his own Nobel acceptance speech Klug again put Franklin into the crystallographic narrative and indeed keeps her memory bright, recently lecturing on her at the National Portrait Gallery. But it was Sayre's book which corrected the record within the wider culture, even if today I have an uncomfortable doubt about how well feminism has been able to make the correction stick.

Though not a selfconsciously feminist text, Sayre's book was written in the context of the flowering of the Women's Liberation Movement. As such it both echoed and constructed the rising awareness of women that to work in science is to work in an especially masculinist world. Further this world of science was portrayed as not simply unfriendly, but as a place where men are the gatekeepers and only they can dictate whether the contribution of any particular woman is to be recognized. As the historical work of recovery continued, the accounts of men appropriating the work of women became a distressingly routine feature of the women in science narrative The failure of the Nobel committee to recognize Liese Meitner's contribution to physics, alongside her prize-winning collaborator Otto Hahn in 1944, was a not dissimilar scandal. That Meitner, like Franklin, was also Jewish in that terrible epoch, was alas by no means just a memory when Franklin was working in the immediate post-war period and served to intensify their disadvantage.[4]

More recently the award of a Nobel prize to Hewish for discovering a quasar when it was his graduate student Jocelyn Bell, now Professor of Physics at the Open University, who actually carried out the empirical work of identification, generates scepticism as to whether the gatekeepers have changed their practices despite their audible expressions of concern. Accounts of actively egalitarian men scientists who go out of their way to secure the recognition of women colleagues, like Mitlag Leffner for both Kovalevskaya and Curie, are still precious exceptions.

For that matter, despite various expressions of concerns and policy initiatives to promote women and girls, in science at both national and international levels (from the UK government report *The Rising Tide*, the expression of concern by the European Union and the UNESCO report on *Gender and Science* produced for Beijing alike) there still is a glass ceiling for women in science. At the elite levels the statistics show a disturbing resistance to change. There have been just ten women science Nobelists over the course of the century (and almost the same number of women literary Nobelists, so any naive hope that literature is more feminine and friendly should be suppressed). Even though Marie Curie received not one but two Nobel prizes, neither the French National Academie des Sciences would admit her, nor would the Royal Society elect her a foreign fellow, though her husband and joint prize-winner, Pierre, was deemed electable by both. Nor do current statistics describing the recognition of women by the scientific and engineering elites suggest an outbreak of equality. Thus the current figure for the US National Academy of Engineering gives 42 women in a total membership of 1,893; while the older National Academy of Science has 103 women out of a total of 1,848 members. In Britain, the 1990 figure for the Royal Society was 39 women out of a total of 1,098 Fellows

Yet the matter of the under-representation of women only came under question with feminism. Thus while the distinguished sociologist of science Robert Merton noted that the majority, some 60 per cent, of the founding Fellows of the Royal Society were Puritans, a valid and interesting point, he ignored or took for granted the much more astonishing phenomenon that all the Fellows were men. Just how astonishing this was only comes into cultural visibility when we read the biographical accounts of women in science in these foundational years. In these chapters we see that not only were a minority of elite women hives of scientific activity, but that numbers of these women were part of the family and intellectual circle of the men who were to elect themselves as the founding fathers of the Royal Society. How did such men reconcile themselves to membership of a family circle that included brilliant creative women, and establish this exclusive club for the new 'masculine thought'. The defence that men, because they had access to systematic instruction, were necessarily better qualified than all women, cuts little ice. For not all the founding fellows were Newtons and Boyles; numbers showed more modest competence. So the question of just how they justified themselves in excluding for example the brilliant Margaret Cavendish is pertinent. Of course they could and did label her 'mad', and a good deal is made of her 'inconsistency'. Cavendish herself knew the price of the education of an autodidact and in *The Blazing World* grants herself the systematic education for which she longed. For that matter the highly intellectual Christina of Sweden, today an icon of Scandinavian feminism, was similarly labelled 'eccentric', and Watson successfully labelled Franklin as 'difficult'. Even without the perjorative labels, many contemporary women scientists pressing against the glass ceiling still lack the positive qualities that men seem only to be able to see and reward in other men.

We see other sad continuities. Mary Evelyn clearly felt that to maintain her acceptability to the men she culturally valued it was necessary to distance herself from the Duchess of Newcastle, even though it was Mad Meg's circle which was in good part her cultural lifeline. Today a similar phenomenon repeats itself. Academic women who have benefited from the outspoken angry criticism of an earlier generation of feminists, simultaneously both benefit and distance themselves from that anger in order to retain their acceptability to men. By contrast men scientists have Teflon coats. There seems little risk of negative labels sticking and harming their reputations. Newton's extraordinary theological writings do not affect his place as the father of classical physics, neither does Einstein's exploitation of the mathematical skills of his first wife Maria Milic, nor his neglect of their psychotic son dent his quasi saintly image. Even Jim Watson's appalling account of his competitiveness, his womanizing among the Cambridge au pairs, his denigration of Franklin, is seen just as boyish liveliness.

While unfashionably I want to insist on the commonalities, and above all the power of men as gatekeepers throughout the early to late modern, even post-modern period, there are important differences too. In the early period discussed by the chapters in this book, indeed well into the mid-twentieth century, women's access to the practice of science and to recognition turned very precisely on individual men linked to them by men from their family of origin or by marriage. It is not by chance that the chapters tell us in detail about whose daughters these women are, and of their marriages, their social and intellectual circles. What is new is the emphasis on the presence of women in those circles, the clever aunts, the gifted mothers and the learned grandmothers. We are invited to see a happy reversal of Galton's Hereditary Genius where talent only ran on the male side, women being merely the empty vessels of biological reproduction.

For these well- and high-born British women with intellectual ambitions, the option of entering a nunnery and its intellectual life was pre-empted by Henry VIII, and the universities were closed to them until the nineteenth century. They were denied the university education open to equivalent Italian women and they did not have access to any precursors of the seventeenth-century Parisian salons, unless we see the fluid 'circle' as its less geographically defined counterpart. British women with intellectual ambitions in this period had neither mainstream or alternative culturally defined spaces and places. Instead their participation in these intellectual activities required supportive men intimately linked to them.

Having secured by marriage, or felicitously having been born into a domestic context where women's intellectual capacities were nourished, ambitious women could secure an education by their membership of some informal intellectual and social 'circle', the door to that circle typically having been opened by a father, husband or even brother. But while the acquisition of intellectual accomplishments could be seen as an enhancement to the woman's marriageability (John Evelyn loved Mary's books before he saw her), the systematic development of that knowledge, above all creating new knowledge, required minimally an indifferent or tolerant, but better still, actively supportive husband. Although such figures were crucial in securing access to networks, which could include some of the greatest scientists of the age, for ambitious women to maintain their place in these networks often required great tact. Few had the freedom that Mad Meg secured for herself by marrying into one of the most powerful aristocratic families in England.

Arguably these scientific ladies, experimenting before the separation of work and home in the production of knowledge, had one advantage – more permeable barriers. The institutional separation, a process spread over many decades and at different rates for different fields and disciplines, worked to exclude women. Those fields of science which became large scale, funded extensively by state and industry (for example chemistry in the nineteenth century and physics in the twentieth), were also the most hostile to women. It has been the craft areas of science (today astronomy and primatology) where women have achieved more.

Biology was relatively late to leave the home. The novelist Naomi Mitchison recalls helping her brother and father (the Haldanes) in their laboratory in the Oxford family house in the early years of this century. And in the 1940s under the growing weight of Italian fascism, the biologist Rita Levi Montalcini, eventually to be made a Nobelist in the 1980s, had a laboratory in her family palace. As the home and work separation in the production of science came to fruition in the mid-twentieth century it was accompanied by the biggest dip in the percentage of trained women PhDs, and was only reversed by pressure from feminism.

But as the relentless pace of technological change not least in the production of knowledge continues, the home-based computer and electronic communication once more close the gap. Whether this offers new possibilities for women or imposes near sweatshop conditions on different groups of women depends on larger questions surrounding the changing political economy of science. These changes are profound, leading science and technology policy analysts speak of nothing less than 'a new production system of knowledge'. What they are trying to get at in this dramatic language is the restructuring of the production system. It is not only that the state has given way to industry as the chief investor in scientific research, but that the university as the old location of fundamental research, is increasingly the site of new hybrid forms of production. These new hybrid forms bring industrial and academic researchers together. The interesting question becomes: how is the knowledge increasingly produced by industry and these new hybrid forms to be culturally understood?

Certainly the increased commercial emphasis on secrecy looks to weaken the conception of science as public knowledge. Where the old Baconian public knowledge enabled its producers to claim the ability and the right to 'speak truth to power', few today are prepared to grant 'the disinterested language of truth' to the new knowledge production system when interests are so manifestly at stake. The outlines of the new production system of knowledge emerging at the millennium are still shadowy. Some of us think that the discourse is changing, so that the new words of 'expert' and 'trust' are replacing the old words of 'scientist' and 'truth'. It is even harder to see what part gender plays in this restructuring. While I have not enough space to do more than hint at the complexity and turbulence of the contemporary knowledge production system, it makes a rich historical location for looking back at the foundational years of modern science through the new lenses provided by the painstaking accounts of the lives of these women. The story of gender at the 'birth of modern science' has become a good deal more complex.

Notes

1 Normally I speak of science as 'wissenshaft' or 'tiede', that is the whole of systematic knowledge; here because these biographies are of women interested in natural phenomena I use the narrower Anglo-Saxon convention of science as natural science.

2 I am grateful to the Bedford-educated Patricia Clarke FRS for this point.

3 Later, Evelyn Fox Keller's biography of Barbara McClintock in some senses replaced Sayre's biography as the definitive narrative. I have difficulties with the popular reading of Keller, with McClintock as the unrecognized intuitive loner, for McClintock was a highly established and recognized scientist, who was not an isolate but lived with a close woman friend. That both McClintock and her immediate colleagues distanced themselves from the Keller biography, whereas Sayre's biography was supported by much of her research community, gives us further food for thinking about biographies and audiences.

4 The popular television film *The DNA Story* cast Jeff Goldblum, which with his stereotypically Jewish looks, massively muddied the historical waters. Watson, Crick and Wilkins, whatever their actual religious beliefs, came from the dominant Christian culture. In the 1950s when there were quotas for Jews to be admitted to public schools and when Jews were routinely excluded from golf clubs etc., this miscasting hides the problem of anti-Semitism.

WOMEN, SCIENCE AND MEDICINE: INTRODUCTION

Lynette Hunter and Sarah Hutton

The years between the founding of Gresham College in 1597 and the founding of the Royal Society in 1661 were critical years in the emergence of modern science. The developments that took place in science in this period are often referred to as the Scientific Revolution, though, latterly, the concept of a revolution in the history of science has come to seem less appropriate as historians of science have begun to note the Renaissance antecedents of many aspects of seventeenth-century science.[1] Whether or not one accepts the revolution model of the emergence of modern science, the seventeenth century was, indeed, a time of new ideas, new theories, new methods of enquiry. The old Aristotelian synthesis of knowledge and the scholastic system of learning had been definitively discredited by the new astronomy of Copernicus and Kepler, and the new mechanics of Galileo. The field was open for new theories to replace the old, and there were plenty of contenders to fill the void.

While Bacon was hailed as their inspiration and precursor by many proponents of new methods of investigating nature,[2] the contribution of other innovators should not be overlooked. Among these, Descartes made a serious claim to being the true heir of Galileo, by applying the principles of the new mechanics to the domain of philosophy. In the 1640s and 1650s Cartesian physics was the main contender to fill the gap left by the demise of Aristotelianism. Descartes proposed a philosophical system which appeared to account convincingly for the phenomena of the universe. His was, however, a system which was arrived at deductively by *a priori* reasoning from first principles rather than inductively, that is *a posteriori*, via experimentation. In so far as Descartes sought to account for all natural phenomena in terms of the size, shape and location of particles in motion, he subscribed to a form of kinematic physics known generically as the mechanical philosophy. Another version of science based on such principles is, of course, to be found in the work of Thomas Hobbes. The important theoretical contribution of figures we nowadays think of as philosophers rather than scientists is itself a reminder that the term 'science' was not yet fixed in its modern sense, but retained its Latin meaning of 'knowledge' in general, even as the term came to denote the more specialized field of knowledge and method of enquiry that it has today. When discussing early modern science it is often more helpful to employ the term still in use in the seventeenth century for the body of learning pertaining to astronomy, chemistry, physics and biology, namely 'natural philosophy'.

It is also important to remember that even after the establishment of the Royal Society, the method of enquiry into the nature of things that we nowadays call scientific was still in the early stages of development. At the time of the founding of the Royal Society, observational techniques and experimentation which had developed from the medieval technical practices of many trades working with physical, chemical and biological material were certainly established as viable, indeed necessary, for investigating the operations of nature. But the principles of experimental methodology were still in the course of elaboration. Some areas, notably pneumatics, lent themselves more easily to experimental observation than others. Some experiments worked in theory but were impossible to conduct in practice – a famous example is Blaise Pascal's hydrostatic experiment which required a man to sit submerged in 20 feet of water balancing a tube of mercury on his knee.[3]

Furthermore, as the heterogeneity of the contributions to early modern science suggests, science was not yet established as an agreed practice, a particular procedure for investigation and discovery. The picture of natural philosophy in the mid-seventeenth century was more complex, more confusing, more contested, than the scientific method that emerged from it might suggest. This alone explains why, in looking for women's contribution to science in the early modern period, we should not expect to find so many prototypes of modern scientists, so many disregarded Madame Curies patiently compiling their data by observation and experiment in accordance with clearly laid-down principles of verification. From well before the early modern period women had participated substantially in what was then called 'oeconomics', which referred to the primary economic unit of the family within the local community.[4] Their largest field of work was maintaining the household and its contribution to the community. This involved the practice of what we would now think of as physical and organic chemistry, as well as all aspects of preventive medicine and of pharmacy.[5] The technology with which they worked became a fundamental part of the emerging experimental methodology, and was being practised concurrently with refinement of that methodology in the name of natural philosophy. At the same time, the intellectual ferment and the challenge of new ideas and new patterns of thinking in the seventeenth century may well have been a factor in enabling women to participate in the intellectual debates of the period. The evidence is that among educated women many wholeheartedly embraced the new learning of the time.

The emergent state of science in the seventeenth century is not the only explanation for the difficulties encountered in investigating the contribution of women. In conventional history of science, the contribution of women appears statistically insignificant – notwithstanding the key contributions of figures such as Marie Curie, Dorothy Hodgkin and Rosalind Franklin. Feminists have been quick to point out the pitifully small numbers of women scientists.[6] This fact appears to suggest that there is something essential to science which is (and was) hostile to women. Even if we were to rewrite the history of science to incorporate women, it is difficult to shake off its negative picture: simply to 'add women' means iconizing the exceptional few, so reinforcing the negative picture of science in general. Moreover, the further back in time one goes, the harder it is to find a woman who fits the definition of 'scientist'. The Enlightenment can at least offer Madame du Châtelet, but can we really call her nearest equivalents, the *salonistes* of the seventeenth century, 'scientists', for all the interest shown by some in cosmology and new philosophy? Or should we be looking elsewhere? Or are we working with an uninstructive definition of the scientist? Is it not anachronistic to impose a modern definition on an earlier period, especially one when, as we have already observed, there was neither consensus on the nature of science nor a practice of enquiry identifiably equivalent to modern science?

Whether by accident or design, we have inherited a 'story of science' which is organized around the achievements of 'great' scientists who happen to be men. The 'great men' account of the history of science also happens to be a model which excludes not just women but other social inferiors: the technicians of science, for instance, who made experiments possible; the journeymen whose practical involvement afforded a model for reorganizing methods of investigation. It is ironic that Bacon himself singled out applied sciences such as navigation and printing as examples of the advancement of learning, yet the navigators and machine designers who made the progress in these areas do not feature in the 'story of science'.[7] The chronological proximity of a technologist such as Hugh Platt, who had developed a concept of new knowledge surprisingly similar to that of Bacon,[8] and who yet remains virtually unknown today, poses an unresolved question about the complexity of class and communication in the history of science. Similarly, in the history of medicine, the learned practitioners and theorists receive notice, but the lowly healers and midwives, the mere 'mechanicks' of medicine are left out of account. It has too quickly been forgotten that women of the early modern period had a developed technical knowledge in order to perform their social and economic functions. They could also handle abstract theory. Even though they were not card-carrying scientists, or members of the Royal Society, in their domestic roles women of the sixteenth and seventeenth centuries had plenty to do which is relevant to the history of science. As Bathsua Makin observed in 1673,

> To buy wooll and Flax, to die scarlet and purple, requires skill in natural philosophy.[9]

Overlaying the antithetical model of science history that overlooks the contribution of women to the history of science are the debates in feminist theory which seek to address the question of whether science is and has been intrinsically biased against women.[10] Among those who have tried to answer this question by reference to the past, Evelyn Fox Keller and Carolyn Merchant lead the field.[11] A major problem with these studies is that the historical terrain which they have explored is itself restricted by the kinds of limitation of the traditional approach to the history of science just described. This underlines the urgency for new work of documentation. In trying to make visible women's involvement and to distinguish the factors which determine their exclusion or inclusion, we must be careful not to be imprisoned by the historical models we use. Instead of employing a historiographical approach which delimits the terrain so as to exclude categories of contribution, we need to examine a broad range of material, and avoid being constrained either by traditional or overly modern categories. In other words, to make women visible in the history of science we have to institute a rethink of the history of science itself.

A WAY FORWARD

The present collection aims to be neither comprehensive in its coverage nor definitive in its conclusions. Each of the studies presented here addresses, in one or more respects, the issues raised above. Together they offer a beginning point in the task of documenting and assessing the contribution of women in the history of science. Almost by definition, the women discussed constitute an excluded group, but, arguably, some are more excluded than others. It is, perhaps, easier to slot learned ladies such as Anne Conway and Margaret Cavendish (discussed by Sarah Hutton) into the familiar picture of the Scientific Revolution than to make space for 'mere factors and mechanicks' such as the lay-doctors and midwives of seventeenth-century London (the subject of studies by Margaret Pelling and Adrian Wilson). The apparently secondary relation of many women to their more famous husbands and brothers (as Frances Harris, Rob Iliffe and Frances Willmoth show) should not obscure the fact of the deep involvement in science of many women. A dominant theme is the relationship between women's involvement with scientific pursuits as a direct outcome of their social and domestic role, and the technical know-how and experience-based practice this brought with it. Competent housewifeliness, as Lynette Hunter shows, required skills in chemistry and medicine for even the most mundane of duties. Besides, as she argues in relation to Lady Ranelagh, as ladies became ladies of leisure, science too developed as the leisure pursuit of *virtuosi*.

While it is not always possible to document women's practising of science as a separate pursuit from 'Kitchin Physick', it is clear that many were sufficiently conversant with ideas on natural philosophy to engage in discussion. As economics, thought of as a valuable category of social recognition, expands from local community issues to embrace the finances of national capitalism, so too does scientific experiment move from the household to the academic societies in order to achieve recognition. The examples of Mary Sidney (discussed by Margaret Hannay), Mary Evelyn (discussed by Frances Harris) and Lucy Hutchinson (the subject of Reid Barbour's study), as well as the aforementioned Cavendish and Conway, testify both to a high level of education among certain sections of the female population, and to the differing responses over the period to their application of that education to natural philosophy. The period from 1550 to 1700 also marks significant changes in the attitude to women's *public* participation in science. Much of the work by the women discussed in this collection exists in manuscript alone; some was printed after they died; very little was published in their names during their lifetimes. Publication as 'literature' rather than as 'natural philosophy' was far more acceptable, and clearly limited female involvement in technical and scientific matters. Yet as Elizabeth Tebeaux's study of the literature and literacy of technology indicates, the additional 'secondary relation' of women to printed work is fundamental to all aspects of this volume. The one chapter which sits apart from the rest by virtue of its male subject is Sarah Hutton's study of Bacon. This is the nearest any of the studies comes to addressing the terms of the current debate on science and gender. That this should be so demonstrates the underlying impetus of this collection, which is a concern to begin to shift the emphasis on men and their activities in much feminist commentary on early modern science towards the contributions of women. The bibliography at the end of the volume does not purport to be either comprehensive or definitive. Rather, by providing a unified list of sources and studies cited by each contributor, we hope that it might serve as a starting point for further study of women and early modern science.

The origin for the present collection was a series of four lectures held at Gresham College in 1995. The present book is an acknowledgement both of Gresham's past role in the history of science and of its new orientation, four centuries later, when women have a role which they were denied at its foundation. This is in no small part due to the Provost incumbent since 1988, Peter Nailor, who died during the period when this collection of papers was being assembled. One result, among many, of his scholarly visions was the lecture series out of which the initial papers came. The college is now in the careful hands of Dr Andreas Prindl. Thanks are equally due to the Academic Registrar, Maggie Butcher, whose intellectual imagination encouraged the series in the first place and nurtured it into existence.

The administrative staff of the School of English, University of Leeds have been supportive beyond any expectation, as have the staff of the Brotherton Library, Special Collections. We would particularly like to thank and record the valuable work of Dr Mark Robson, who compiled the index, assisted with editing and carried out picture research.

Lynette Hunter and Sarah Hutton, 1997

Notes

1 The classic study is Rupert Hall (1983). For a revisionist view, see Pumfrey, Rossi and Slawinski (1991). The novelty of seventeenth-century science has also been called in question by recent studies which have demonstrated the longevity of the Aristotelian tradition; see Henry and Hutton (1990).

2 Webster (1975).

3 See Shapin (1994), pp. 339–40, which reproduces the illustration of the experiment from Pascal's *Traitez de l'equilibre* (1663).

4 There is a large number of printed texts from the period outlining this concept of 'oeconomy', most occurring within discourses on the concept of civil behaviour, and reaching a peak in the first twenty years of the seventeenth century. For example, see Richard Robinson, *A morale methode of civille policie* (London, 1576), Thomas Ridley, *A View of the Civile and Ecclesiastical Law* (London, 1607), Joseph Hall, *Salomon's Divine Arts of Ethickes, Politickes, Oeconomickes* (London, 1609), T. D., *The Dove and Serpent* (London, 1614), and Daniel Touteville, *St Pauls Threefold Cord* (London, 1635).

5 For an introductory list to these books, see L. Hunter (forthcoming).

6 Dale Spender (1982).

7 History of a science which focuses on the developments which prefigure modern science also rules out of account the explanatory theories and investigative practices that have fallen into disuse: the obvious example is alchemy – 'obvious' also because it is, to modern minds, clearly not a science. Yet that does not mean that alchemical investigative practices and practical knowledge did not feed into 'scientific' investigations of the natural world in the seventeenth century. On the interaction between alchemy, chemistry and medicine, see Clericuzio and Rattansi (1994).

8 See, for example, Platt's *The Jewell House of Art and Nature* (London, 1595).

9 Bathsua Makin (1673), p. 35.

10 The literature on feminism and science and the cognate topic of feminist epistemology is too vast to list here, but a serviceable bibliography of the subject can be found in Keller and Longino (1996). See also Harding (1986), Rose (1994), Tuana (1989).

11 Keller (1985), Merchant (1980), Schiebinger (1989).

1

THE RIDDLE OF THE SPHINX: FRANCIS BACON AND THE EMBLEMS OF SCIENCE

Sarah Hutton

They relate that Sphinx was a monster, variously formed having the face and voice of a virgin, the wings of a bird and the talons of a griffin. She resided on the top of a mountain, near the city of Thebes, and also beset the highways. Her manner was to lie in ambush and seize the travellers, and having them in her power, to propose to them certain dark and perplexed riddles, which, it was thought she received from the Muses, and if her wretched captives could not solve and interpret these riddles, she with great cruelty fell upon them, in their hesitation and confusion, and tore them to pieces. . . . This is an elegant, instructive fable, and seems invented to represent science, especially as joined with practice. For science may, without absurdity, be called a monster, being strangely gazed at and admired by the ignorant and unskilful. Her figure and form is various, by reason of the vast variety of subjects that science considers; her voice and countenance are represented female, by reason of her gay appearance and volubility of speech; wings are added, because the sciences and their inventions run and fly about in a moment, for knowledge, like light communicated from one torch to another, is presently caught and copiously diffused; sharp and hooked talons are elegantly attributed to her, because the axioms and arguments of science enter the mind, lay hold of it, fix it down, and keep it from moving or slipping away.

(Bacon, *The Wisdom of the Ancients*)[1]

Minerva by most writers was depictured in the shape of a young woman, of a liuely and fresh countenance, yet something threatening and angrie in hir lookes, her eyes were very fixe, assured and stedfast, and much like the colour of a blewish greene, or that of a troubled sea, and shee was armed complete at all peeces, with a long speare in one hand, & on hir other arme a shield or target, made of the purest Christall, on the top of her helmet was placed a garland, made of Oliue branches. . . . Touching the birth of her, it is written, that she was borne without a mother, and that shee issued and came forth into the world out of the head of Iupiter (according to the opinion of all the fantasticke Poets.) By which is meant & understood that all human knowledge and vnderstanding proceedeth from the superior and diuine guidance aboue, whereby these intellectuall parts become celestiall, and despisers of terrene delights . . . & she wore on her head a wonderfull rich helmet, all made and hammered of massie gold, which with the beauty thereof shined most gloriously, sending forth a most excellent lustre, and delicate transparencie. . . . Pausanias (speaking of the Athenians) sayth, That there was in that countrie a very stately, and curiously built Image of Minerua, which had engrauen on the top of the helmet the shape & forme of a Sphinx, and on both sides of it were cut out & carued the portraitures of two Griffins, which are held indeed to be neither beasts nor birds, but doe equally partake of both kinds, for they have the vpper part (as head, necke and wings) of an Eagle, and the rest of their bodies shaped to the true similitude of Lyons.

(Lynche, *Fountaine of Ancient Fiction*)[2]

The issue of whether science is hostile to women is a live one today.[3] One way of answering the question 'Whose science *is* it?' is to ask, 'Whose science *was* it?' and to examine the writings of key figures in the history of science for evidence of sexist bias. Perhaps the most persuasive such study is Evelyn Fox Keller's *Reflections on Gender and Science*, which is frequently cited as confirmation that science, as it has developed and is practised today, is a fundamentally masculine enterprise. On the basis of an analysis of Francis Bacon's use of metaphor, Keller concludes that Baconian science was distinctly masculine.[4] The metaphor at the root of this view comes from a short, incomplete tract entitled *Temporis partus masculus* (*The Masculine Birth of Time*). According to this, man will master nature (conceived as female) and make her his slave:

My intention is to impart to you, not the figments of my own brain, nor the shadows thrown by words, nor a mixture of religion and science, nor a few commonplace observations or notorious experiments tricked out to make a composition as fanciful as a stage-play. No; I am come in very truth leading you to Nature with all her children to bind her to your service and make her your slave.[5]

Bacon is not the only figure examined by Keller, but her analysis has deep implications for the history of science on account of the key position accorded Bacon as one of the fathers of modern science.[6] In respect of Bacon, Keller's argument also carries conviction because the gendered image of domination on which she focuses connects with the fact that Bacon frequently underlines a link between knowledge and power. The masculinity of the image of domination is apparently further underscored by the title of *Temporis partus masculus*, which trades on the paradoxical concept of a 'masculine birth', implying thereby that science as an activity eschews the female. Keller's argument for the masculinity of Baconian science is echoed in Genevieve Lloyd's argument for the masculinity of philosophical reason, which has served to reinforce Keller's argument in respect of science. In her account of Bacon in *The Man of Reason*, Lloyd emphasizes the motif of the domination of nature expressed through sexual metaphors. She argues that 'This metaphor of maleness is deeply embedded in philosophical articulation of ideas and ideals of reason'.[7] It is now almost a commonplace among feminists that Baconian science is masculine in orientation, and that this is revealed in Bacon's choice of sexual metaphors of oppression to describe its aims. Susan Hekman may be cited as representative of those who accept Keller's thesis. In *Gender and Knowledge* she gives an account of the 'sexual metaphors that dominate Bacon's work', and comments:

> that science has been defined as a masculine activity that women, because of the qualities associated with feminity, are incapable of, is obvious from the foregoing analysis of the work of Bacon and the tenets of the New Philosophy. Women, who are excluded from the sphere of rationality, are declared to be unfit to participate in the activity of science, the highest expression of rationality.[8]

This kind of assessment of Bacon has wide implications for science as a whole if Baconian science is considered as the prototype of modern science. Such a view of the position of Bacon in the history of science invites the construction of a masculine heredity of modern science that can be traced back to Bacon's gendered metaphors. The use, by Bacon's successors and admirers, of similar metaphors and the vocabulary of domination lends credence to the view that Bacon bequeathed to science a masculine mode of discourse. Henry Oldenburg is a case in point; he described the aims of the Royal Society as 'to raise a Masculine Philosophy . . . whereby the mind of man may be enobled with the knowledge of Solid Truths' (an example used by Keller).[9] Another example (though one not quoted by Keller) of the motif of science as domination is given by Robert Boyle. In his *Usefulness of Experimental Natural Philosophy* he says of 'the pleasantness of natural philosophy':

> the study of physiology is not only delightful as it teaches us to know nature, but also as it teaches us in many cases to master and command her.[10]

The Keller view of Bacon is not without difficulties. It rests on and reinforces the view that Bacon is the father of modern science. It is based on a narrow sample of Bacon's writings and his use of metaphor. And its conclusions pre-empt further questions of whether, why and how women were excluded from science, and what were the conditions of their involvement in it. In this chapter I should like to reopen the question of whether Baconian science is antithetical to women and I shall do so by placing Bacon and his writing in a broader

contemporary context than does Keller. In particular, I should like to situate
Bacon's use of metaphor within the larger field of his use of figurative language.
Twentieth-century readers do not share the body of presuppositions and
rhetorical strategies available to Bacon's contemporaries and on which he drew
to express himself. As a result we are not alive to many of the meanings which
were obvious to a Renaissance reader. From the perspective of the late
Renaissance, the significance of Bacon's metaphors appears very different from
the interpretations that seem obvious to post-modern readers. One consequence
of this is that it is not so easy to conclude that Baconian science is by definition
misogynistic. When Baconian science is situated historically, its relationship to
modern science appears more complex and uncertain than his critics usually
assume. As a result it is difficult to designate him the *fons et origo* of the perceived
masculinity of modern science.

BACON IN CONTEXT

Bacon was born into and made his career within the power-broking elite of
Elizabethan and Jacobean England. He grew up among highly educated
women. His mother, Anne Bacon (née Cooke), was famously learned. She was
one of only two women to have a herbal dedicated to her. Her sister, Mildred
Burghley, was described as running a university in her household. Recent
studies of his politics have emphasized his links with Tudor and, especially,
Stuart monarchy and its self-serving, autocratic political programme.[11] He
served as an MP under Elizabeth, and rose to become Lord Chancellor (in
1618) under James I. But to recognize Bacon's political interests is not
necessarily to confirm any sexist bias in his science. After all, we should
remember that Bacon's best hope of seeing his programme for the reform of
systems of enquiry implemented, both institutionally and in method, was royal
patronage. It is not accidental that *The Advancement of Learning* was dedicated to
King James I. If he was writing to persuade the king to adopt his proposals, he
had to write in terms that would appeal to a notoriously misogynistic king with
imperial pretensions. This does not mean that Bacon does not exhibit gender
bias in his choice of metaphors. But any such bias in his choice of tropes must
be put into the context of rhetorical strategy generally, and the type of political
power with which their author had to operate. Persuasion was a key part of
Bacon's decision to publish. Those whom he sought to persuade were the
political elite.

Furthermore, by education Bacon was trained in rhetoric, the art of
persuasion, which formed the basis of the humanist education then prevalent.
In the rhetorician's repertoire, metaphors are figures of speech which belong
with a whole range of oratorical/stylistic devices. In the late twentieth century,
we are perhaps guilty of an over-emphasis on the importance of metaphor –

for a whole host of reasons to do with the psychological and literary culture which we inhabit. It is true that Bacon's metaphors stand out because, on the whole, he is not given to figurative writing. But figures of speech are only one tool of rhetoric. There is more to rhetoric than metaphor, and metaphor is not the only means which Bacon uses to persuade – I shall return to this point later.

It is largely on account of his inductive method, and the experimental process of verification that goes with it, that Bacon has earned his illustrious position as patriarch of science. The image of Bacon as the prototype of the modern empirical scientist is very much the product of the nineteenth and twentieth centuries.[12] But should we accept without question his status as *a* or *the* father of modern science in the sense that he anticipated science as we know it? To her credit, Evelyn Keller recognizes that Bacon is not a modern *tout court*: she describes him as a 'transitional figure'. Nonetheless, even if we accept her account of Baconian metaphor, the only warrant for extrapolating her conclusion about Bacon to the rest of science is a 'story' of science which regards him, unproblematically, as the father of modern science.

Firstly, we too often take at face value the claims of the so-called 'moderns' of the seventeenth century that what they are engaged in is fundamentally new, and constitutes a clean break with the past. That is one reason why positivistic accounts of the history of science and philosophy begin with the seventeenth century. But these claims for novelty, even when they have some just grounds, serve to obscure the fact that the mind-set of people such as Bacon was deeply rooted in the thinking of their predecessors.[13] Bacon was, in many ways, not as original in his method as is claimed, and some of the subjects which he listed as legitimate topics for investigation would not be recognized as scientific now – for example, alchemy and 'Natural divinations'. Such elements in Bacon's survey of the state of learning are not trace elements of old dross surviving in the bright new gold of modernity, but germaine to his project of enquiry. Besides, those who accept the Keller thesis have not recognized that the metaphor of the domination of nature was not original to Baconian science, but is to be found among alchemists and hermeticists of the Renaissance.[14] Furthermore, in adopting it, Bacon was retailing a philosophical axiom going back to Aristotle, that the knowledge of causes gives power over the things caused. In respect of his 'scientific' credentials, Bacon has in fact been much criticized for his failure to understand the importance of mathematics in science, and for not supplying a hypothetical framework for his experiments. To give an example of the kind of difficulties faced by those who treat his science as a prototype of modern science: to positivists it is an unsoluble conundrum that the great Bacon rejected the work of another forefather of modern science, William Gilbert ('father' of electronics). Viewed in all its complexity, Bacon's 'science' is a very strange antecedent to contemporary science. We should, therefore, think twice before resting our critique of modern science in him, for in doing so we criticize a constructed image, further simplified for canonical purposes. Besides, the emphasis on Bacon as a key figure in the history of science is unduly nationalistic, part of a view of science which values the British contribution above any other European contributions.

And, while taking stock of the complexity of Bacon's 'scientific' enterprise, it is not inappropriate to ask whether there is anything intrinsic to his idea of science that supports the view that science is intrinsically anti-feminine. There is in fact much about Bacon's method that fits with the kind of models for more experientially adapted and pluralistic forms of science advocated by some twentieth-century feminists.[15] Among these we could mention Bacon's repudiation of monolithic systems of thought – his critique of philosophers such as Aristotle and Plato for being more interested in working out internally consistent systems than in providing a means to add to the sum of knowledge. Hand in hand with this goes his emphasis on the *practical* outcome of scientific enquiry. Not only should it be practical, but it should be for the good of society as a whole – the areas which he lists as desirable goals of science in *Magnalia naturae* are 'The curing of diseases counted incurable', 'The mitigation of pain', 'making new threads for apparel; and new stuffs; such as paper, glass &c.'.[16] Not only are the scientific achievements of King Solomon's House in *New Atlantis* for the benefit of society as a whole, but the enterprise by which they are researched and developed is a collective one. Furthermore, Bacon emphasized the provisionality of knowledge and its limitedness. And this is incorporated into his recommendations for the way scientific investigations are recorded and communicated: his emphasis on the *aphorism* as a unit which can be added to:

> the writing of aphorisms hath many excellent virtues. . . . For, first, it trieth the writer whether he be superficial or solid: for aphorisms . . . cannot be made but of the pith and heart of sciences; for discourse of illustration is cut off; recital of examples are cut off; discourse of connexion and order is cut off; descriptions of practice are cut off. So there remaineth nothing to fill the aphorisms but some good quantity of observation: and therefore no man can suffice, nor in reason will attempt, to write aphorisms, but he that is sound and grounded. . . . Secondly . . . particulars being dispersed do best agree with dispersed directions. And lastly, aphorisms, representing a knowledge broken, do invite men to inquire further. . . .[17]

This aphoristic model for the language of scientific enquiry corresponds almost exactly to another image Bacon uses to describe scientific investigation, namely as the production of 'knowledge that is delivered as a thread to be spun on' – a metaphor whose social connotations link it unmistakably to women.[18]

RHETORIC METAPHOR AND POWER

Bacon's preference for aphorism as the medium of scientific discourse did not mean that he was not adept at figurative writing. Although he used metaphor with discrimination, he did not eschew the device entirely. As already observed, his metaphors achieve distinctiveness from the fact that he does not use them very often; as a result they are thrown into prominence when he does. Although he uses metaphors discriminatingly, he uses a variety.[19] Nor is metaphor the only type of figurative writing he employs. In his remarks on literary style in *The Advancement of Learning*, he acknowledges the value of fiction (poesy) and reserves special commendation for a particular form of figurative writing, fables:

> Allusive or parabolical [poesy] is a narration applied only to express some special purpose or conceit. Which latter kind of parabolical wisdom was much more in use in the ancient times, as by the fables of Aesop, and the brief sentences of the seven, and the use of hieroglyphics may appear.[20]

Fables, writes Bacon, are an important means of expressing conceptually difficult points, which they serve 'to demonstrate and illustrate'. But they also function enigmatically, serving 'to retire and obscure . . . mysteries and secrets'.[21] The most elaborate example of Bacon's use of fable is his treatise *De sapientia veterum* (*The Wisdom of the Ancients*) published in 1609. Here Bacon turns his hand to an allegorical mode of writing to construct a set of myths which represent his ideas by adopting and adapting aspects of Greek mythology. To do so he draws on the emblematic literature of his time, interpreting particular deities from the Greek pantheon as symbolic representations of his own opinions: modern wisdom is presented enigmatically as if it were ancient learning. The body of wisdom contained in these fables comprises sub-celestial knowledge, that is knowledge of the physical world and knowledge of human kind. The fables applicable to the former include both allegories of particular doctrines which Bacon favoured (e.g. atomism, symbolized by Cupid in no. XVII) and allegories of the processes of learning and enquiry, science as an enterprise of discovery and system of knowledge. It is characteristic of the way that Bacon constructs his allegories that he does not use standard Renaissance interpretations of the mythographical images which he discusses. Rather, he provides his own, but these are developed from images and interpretations of the type found in contemporary handbooks of mythography. Indeed, the deities themselves are portrayed in accordance with the iconography laid down by the likes of Giraldi, Ripa and Cartari.[22] In these, the gender of the mythographical subject is usually (although not always) determined by the gender (in a grammatical sense) of the Latin noun: nature as *Natura* is female. Thus it is that intellectual activity and 'hard' sciences are standardly female, for example philosophy (*Philosophia*), knowledge (*Scientia*), medicine (*Medicina*), astronomy (*Astronomia*), mathematics (*Mathematica*), mechanics (*Mecanica*).

The allegorical images constructed by Bacon in *De sapientia veterum* do not admit of straightforward readings in which science, domination and masculinity are opposed to nature and feminity. For example, in the fable 'Proserpine or Spirit' he interprets Proserpine as the ethereal spirit and her husband, Pluto, as the earth with which it is united. In this partnership, it is the spirit, the female principle Proserpine, which plays the most significant role, and rules her husband Pluto.

> It is an honour justly attributed to Proserpine, and not to any other wife of the gods, that of being the lady or mistress of her husband, because this spirit performs all its operations in the subterranean regions, whilst Pluto remains stupid, or as it were ignorant of them.[23]

This is an androgynous image of nature, where the female predominates. If Bacon's image of nature is androgynous in 'Proserpine', in 'Pan' nature is symbolized by the male god Pan. In 'Atalanta' Bacon reverses the received gendering of the nature/culture dichotomy: nature is male, art female in this 'noble allegory of art and nature'. Nor is his use of gendered metaphor predominantly masculinist. His metaphors of spinning and weaving, for instance, describe the process of increasing knowledge by comparing it to an activity predominantly associated with women.[24] And on one occasion he uses a maternal image for natural philosophy (i.e. science), which he calls 'The Great *Mother* of the Sciences [who] has been reduced to their handmaid'.[25]

The topos of power over nature certainly occurs frequently in Bacon's writings.[26] But there are two important aspects of this which are too easily overlooked. First, the topos of power over nature is only once used by Bacon in conjunction with a metaphor of female subjugation: the infamous metaphor from *Temporis partus masculus*, quoted above, and on which Evelyn Fox Keller focuses. Bacon does, it is true, employ the image of marriage, on a number of occasions, to express the relationship between the natural philosopher and the natural world. But the enslavement image occurs in a treatise which is an incomplete, early work (*Temporis partus masculus* was written prior to 1603), and one which Bacon chose not to publish. Could he, perhaps, have decided that the line of argument and mode of expression were inappropriate both to his account of science and for the audience whom he would persuade?

Secondly, power certainly conveys the idea of domination. But in Bacon's use of the topos, there is a distinction to be observed between power as mere brute force and power as rule or *imperium*.[27] A striking representation of the *imperium* of science are the title-pages of *Instauratio Magna* (1620) and *Sylva sylvarum* (1627) which allude to an emblem of the Holy Roman Emperor, Charles V. This

Scienza (Science), from Ripa's *Iconologia* (1625), p. 589.

The title page from Francis Bacon's *Instauratio Magna* (1620).

emblem depicts the pillars of Hercules, which supposedly marked the division between the Old World and the New, the known with the unknown. The motto, *plus ultra* ('yet further'), contradicts the older *Ne plus ultra* ('no further') to convert the image from denoting limits to representing expanding horizons. Commenting on Charles V's emblem, Paolo Giovio takes particular note of its imperial dimension:

> In truth these Pillars with their mot [motto] (considering the good fortune in the happie Conquest of the West Indies, which eclipseth the glory of the old *Romaines*) doth satisfie the vewe, with the goodly subiect, and delighteth the minde of the considerate regarder, with the perfection of the soule annexed to it.[28]

Bacon's title pages appropriate this emblem to construct an image of scientific discovery which incorporates the heroic and imperial import of Charles V's *impresa*. In *Instauratio Magna* the ship of knowledge sails beyond the pillars of Hercules (the boundary marks of the then known world) towards the new world of science. In *Sylva sylvarum* a globe representing the intellectual world (*mundus intellectualis*) floats beyond the pillars of Hercules. The image is expressed verbally on several occasions in Bacon's writings, for example in his dedication to King James of the second part of *The Advancement of Learning* where it is directed in a most flattering way towards the monarch:

> For why should a few received authors stand up like Hercules' columns, beyond which there should be no sailing or discovering, since we have so bright and benign a star as your Majesty to conduct and prosper us?[29]

BIRTHS OF TIME

Bacon frequently uses the enigmatic expression, 'birth of time' to describe his proposed new natural philosophy. On at least one occasion, this birth is described as 'masculine' – in the title of *Temporis partus masculus*. In Renaissance mythography and emblem books, Time is indeed represented as having (though not giving birth to) a child. And the child of Time is Truth, normally depicted as a naked woman being rescued from error: hence the motif *Veritas filia temporis*, 'Truth the Daughter of Tyme, and there is nothing so secrete, but the date of manie days wil reveale it'.[30] In so far as Bacon believed that his new method of enquiry would yield truth, this emblematic motif is appropriate to it and his choice of expression, 'birth of time', should be read as an allusion to that tradition. His term 'masculine birth', with the emphasis on parturition, does not find an analogue in contemporary versions of the *Veritas filia temporis* motif. But there is an important clue in *De sapientia veterum*: in no. XXX, 'Metis, or Counsel'

Medicina (Medicine), from Ripa's *Iconologia* (1625), p. 413.

where Bacon invokes the myth of the birth of Pallas Athene from the head of Zeus, and adapts it as an allegory of counsel. In Bacon's version, Jupiter devours his pregnant wife Metis and then gives birth to Pallas Athene from his brain:

> he [Jupiter], perceiving she [Metis] was pregnant by him, would by no means wait the time of her delivery, but directly devoured her; whence himself also became pregnant, and was delivered in a wonderful manner; for he from his head or brain brought forth Pallas armed.[31]

The story of Metis resulting in the 'masculine birth' of Pallas is open to a misogynistic reading. But Bacon's interpretation suggests otherwise, for he emphasizes the interdependence of kings and their councillors, employing the metaphor of marriage to do so. The significance of Jove's ingestion of Metis is interpreted not as an act of violence and destruction but in terms of procreation. The counsel given to a king, 'is formed, as it were, in the womb of the council'. The monarch, however, takes credit for it ('so that the decree and the execution shall

Minerva armed with a sphinx on her helmet, in place of a crest, from Cartari's *Imagini* (1571), p. 361.

seem to flow from himself'). In doing so, he gives the counsel so taken the strength of his authority, and the appropriate image for advice thereby translated into decree is the goddess Pallas Athene: 'and as this decree or execution proceeds with prudence and power, so as to imply necessity, it is elegantly wrapt up under the figure of Pallas, armed'. In this way female counsel (Metis) is given male approval (Jove/the king) and re-engendered as female wisdom (Pallas Athene). But figured as Pallas, that wisdom is endowed with apparently male attributes (weaponry), which are in fact essential signifiers of the goddess Pallas.

The masculine birth of Pallas is a motif associated specifically with Bacon and his project for the reform of learning by his secretary, Rawley, who describes Bacon's writings as 'offspring of his brain . . . as Jove when he gave birth to Pallas'.[32] The Latin name for Pallas Athene is Minerva. In Renaissance mythography and iconography she represents intellectual prowess. She is, says Cartari, 'the renowned Goddess of prudence and inventress of all the arts' ('*stimata Dea della prudenza, & inventrice di tutti li arti*'). Or, as his English imitator Richard Lynche put it, 'Minerua [was] reuerenced and adored amongst them [the ancients], for the Queen of Goddess and Wisdome, Learning, and Knowledge'.[33]

As Cesare Ripa notes, Minerva's intellectual prowess is symbolized by her, helmet which, he says, represents the strength and wisdom of reason, that is '*prudenza nell'anima intelletuale*'.[34] Following Cartari, Lynche expatiates on the significance of Minerva's helmet:

> she wore on her head a wonderfull rich helmet, all made and hammered of massie gold, which with the beauty thereof shined most gloriously, sending forth a most excellent lustre, and delicate transparencie. *Homer* sayth, That by this helmet so infixed on her head, is signified, that the wit and policie of man (which alwaies resteth in the braine of the head) is (as a man may say) so armed, and at all times prouided & readie, that it defendeth the bodie from all eminent dangers, mischeefes, and inconueniencies, & that it doth shine & is made beautifull with vertuous & worthie works, studies of contemplation, and diuine meditations.[35]

Not only is Minerva, in Renaissance mythography, a personification of wisdom and intellectual acumen, but, as the mythographers remind us, she was born from the head of Jupiter or Jove. Hers was, in other words, a masculine birth.

> *Minerva* is called *Jupiters* daughter, to shew that wisdom and learning are Gods special gifts; she was begot of his brain, because the brain is the seat of wisdom and learning; without the help of women, because wisdom comes not by generation but by infusion, study and experience.[36]

The masculine birth of Minerva is commonly interpreted as the physical representation of her intellectual endowments. Writing within the same tradition half a century later, Alexander Ross concurs:

> Touching the birth of her, it is written, that she was borne without a mother, and that shee issued and came forth into the world out of the head of Iupiter (according to the opinion of all fantastick Poets.) By which is meant & understood, that all human knowledge and vnderstanding proceedeth from the superior and diuine guidance aboue, whereby these intellectuall parts become celestial, and despisers of terrene delights.[37]

Before dismissing this male-born Truth-*cum*-Minerva as a monster in nature, a perversion of nature's processes, apt image of a gendered nature/culture dichotomy, it is worth noting that in Cartari's description of Minerva he specifically rejects any misogynistic interpretation of the fact that Minerva is born without the aid of the female. He imputes such a misogynistic interpretation to Martian, who followed Aristotle.[38] Richard Lynche renders Cartari's defence of women thus:

> But *Martianus* interpretes it to the disgrace of women, (being indeed a great and sore enemie vnto all that sexe) but (his exposition being too seuere and rigorous in that behalfe) it shall not be pertinent further to declare it. Whose opinion also *Aristotle* himselfe something embraced, affirming . . . that as Minerua was borne without a mother, so all women generally are of themselues without wit, knowledge, secrecie or assured constancie: but such inuention proceedes onely of malice, and some other seed of rancour, which was indeed irradicated in his breast against that praise-worthie sexe. Wherein I dare in some sort contradict *Aristotle*, in that (it is apparent) that there are in the world women of as great spirit, wit, capacitie and setled resolutions as most men are, and are as eloquent in deliuery of their thoughts & as scholler-like in chusing fit and significant words, in composing and annexing their pithie, sententious, and well-placed phrases, as most men are whatsoeuer.[39]

It does not, of course, follow that Bacon drew on Cartari or Lynche, since the fable of Pallas/Minerva was well enough known and his application of it in the allegory 'Metis, or Counsel' does not derive from Cartari (though it is to be found in Giraldi). We cannot safely infer that Bacon's Truth-*cum*-Pallas bears the associations imputed to Minerva by Cartari. After all, Alexander Ross's interpretation later in the seventeenth century remains true to his Aristotelian (and consequently misogynistic) allegiances by omitting the defence of women to be found in his source.[40] The question of whether Bacon's mythographical metaphor, the brainchild Truth/Pallas, constitutes a negatively gendered image for his scientific enterprise cannot be answered without examining how it connects with his vocabulary of images, especially those chosen to represent his intellectual project. In this context 'Sphinx, or Science', no. XXVIII in *De sapientia veterum* is instructive.

SPHINX

In this fable, 'Sphinx, or Science', Bacon retails the story of Oedipus and the Sphinx, but interprets it as an allegory of the successful domination of nature by man. Sphinx is 'science, especially as joined with practice'. The Sphinx is a monster (see the quotation at the start of this chapter). Oedipus is the man who achieves success by investigating human affairs and the natural world. He is able to solve the riddle put to him because he doesn't act too hastily – this, in Bacon's account, is the significance of his lameness. The Sphinx, in Bacon's interpretation, is the knowledge (*scientia*) of nature and of human affairs which gives the knower 'two kinds of empire', that is dominion (*imperium*) or rule – underlined by the fact that Oedipus became king of Thebes as a result of interpreting the riddle. The two empires are 'the empire over nature, and the empire over man'. The former is natural philosophy, of which the 'true and ultimate end' is 'dominion over natural things, natural bodies remedies, machines, and numberless other particulars'.[41] The term translated variously as 'dominion' or 'empire', Bacon gives consistently in the Latin as *imperium*. The successful solver of the Sphinx's riddles is, like Oedipus, destined for rule/dominion/empire: '*ad imperandum natus est*'.[42]

The first thing to note is that Bacon is not using the term science here in our modern sense, though his usage covers what came to be science, namely natural philosophy. In 'Sphinx', 'science' (Latin *scientia*) signifies two branches of sub-celestial knowledge – specifically, knowledge of human kind and knowledge of nature. Secondly, at face value, this fable appears to give a negative image of the knowledge represented by the Sphinx. She is, after all, a monster ('science may, without absurdity, be called a monster'), and she is a female monster at that, and 'a virgin' as well. Moreover, the female characteristics on whose significance Bacon chooses to dwell all belong to a negative stereotype of woman as vain and garrulous:

> her voice and countenance are represented female, by reason of her gay appearance and volubility of speech.[43]

The Sphinx is, moreover, endowed with 'the talons of a griffin', which signify the way *scientia* controls the mind –

> sharp and hooked talons are elegantly attributed to her, because the axioms and arguments of science enter the mind, lay hold of it, fix it down and keep it from moving or slipping away.[44]

The Sphinx is not a subject that figures prominently in the iconographical handbooks of the Renaissance, though it does figure in the visual arts.[45] One representation of it of which Bacon may have been aware was that included in Paolo Giovio's *Imprese*. This work was translated by Samuel Daniel in 1585, but was printed without illustrations. He renders Giovio's mystical interpretation of the Sphinx as follows:

> . . . the *Aegyptian Sphinx*, which did interpret Riddle (*sic*) with abstruse and secret matters, and also that Serpent with his tayle in his mouth, which signifies time, with this *Gnome* [i.e. gnomon]: *Incerta animi decreta resolvet*.[46]

Giovio seems to have chosen the Sphinx here for its enigmatic associations.[47] In other Renaissance depictions of the Sphinx, it symbolizes ancient wisdom, notably the wisdom of the Egyptians, which was, after all, expressed enigmatically in hieroglyphs. A striking example of this is the image of the sage, Hermes Trismegistus, on the floor of Siena cathedral. In this two Sphinxes support the tablet containing the wisdom of Hermes, which is placed on the sage's left.[48]

Although it is not featured in its own right in Renaissance handbooks of mythography and iconography, the Sphinx does figure in them as an attribute. Notably, it is one of the defining symbols of Minerva, goddess of wisdom/intellectual prowess. In one of the possible depictions of Minerva's helmet, a Sphinx occupies the place of the plume. Ripa expounds the iconography of Minerva's helmet: '*I griffi, & la sfinge sopra l'elmo dinotano, che la sapienza ogni ambiguite resolve*'.[49] Giraldi, in *De diis gentium*, ascribes to Pausanias the description of Minerva where her iconographical signifiers include a Sphinx, griffins, a spear, and an image of Medusa on her breast-plate.[50] Lynche gives what he claims is the description by Pausanias:

> a very stately, and curiously built Image of Minerua, which had engrauen on the top of the helmet the shape & forme of a Sphinx, and on both sides of it were cut out & carued the portraitures of two Griffins, which are held indeed to be neither beasts nor birds, but doe equally partake of both kinds.[51]

The association of Minerva with the Sphinx is noted by other English-language mythographers of Bacon's time, including Alexander Ross and Abraham Fraunce.[52] Ross connects the Sphinx crest of Minerva's helmet to the veiled character of the wisdom she represents:

> They gave her a golden Helmet, sometimes with a Sphinx on the top of it, to shew that Wisdom is glorious and shining, and withal that wise men use not to babble out secrets: for it is wisdom in some things to play the Sphinx, and not divulge all we know to all men promiscuously. Christ himself spake some times by Parables.[53]

In representing *scientia* Bacon has, therefore, by means of a deft synecdoche, effected a redescription of Minerva/Wisdom as the Sphinx. Moreover, Bacon's Sphinx is equipped with the talons of a griffin, and the griffin is another of the defining symbols of Minerva. Together, Sphinx and griffin represent properties of the mind: intelligence or understanding. The Sphinx and griffin are, writes Cartari,

> animali feri, e terribili, se pure se ne trova . . . onde si puo conoscere quale guardia debba havere ciascheduno del proprio ingegno.[54]

And Minerva, as Cartari reminds us, was born from the head of Jupiter, without the aid of woman; hers was thus a 'masculine' birth. Moreover, as we have seen, Pallas, who figures in Bacon as another intellectual virtue, was designated Counsel by Minerva. Finally, the other 'masculine' birth to which Bacon alludes in the formulation, the 'birth of time' is that of Truth, the daughter of Father Time. What we have here, then, is a cluster of interrelated images, connected by cross-referencing to iconographic sources. Bacon does not directly transpose those symbols for his own use, but exploits the meanings associated with them to elaborate his own.

The redescription of wisdom as monster (Sphinx) instead of goddess (Pallas/Minerva) is open to interpretation as a misogynistic move: as a gendered image the she-monster is, arguably, a grotesque perversion of 'the renowned goddess of prudence and inventress of all the arts'. On this reading, science (which the Sphinx represents) can be construed as antithetical to the female. But Bacon's own interpretation of the Sphinx does not bear out this negative view. Although its human (female) face, talons and wings might suggest a harpy, with all the negative gender connotations of that image, Bacon does not pursue that analogy. Rather, he notes that the Sphinx is a monster in the eyes of its beholders, but only in the eyes of 'the ignorant and unskilful'. Its composite attributes are an image of variety ('her figure is various by reason of the vast variety of subjects that science considers';[55] that is, science in the sense of *scientia*, not modern science). And its griffin's talons are interpreted by reference to the wise words of Solomon:

> sharp and hooked talons are elegantly attributed to her, because the axioms and arguments of science enter the mind, lay hold of it, fix it down, and keep it from moving or slipping away. *This the sacred philosopher observed when he said, 'the words of the wise are like goads or nails driven far in'* [Ecclesiastes 12:11].[56]

Images carry with them the imprint of previous usage.[57] In this example, Bacon signals this by explicit cross-referencing to the wisdom of Solomon. In the case of the Sphinx: to the unwary ('ignorant and unskilful', as Bacon calls them) it is a monster. Before its riddles are solved, they are 'subtle and abstruse', but the wisdom they contain, 'being once made plain, intelligible, and common, it may be received by the slowest capacity'. To those conversant with mythographical traditions of the Renaissance, the Sphinx is a symbol of Minerva, goddess of wisdom. At first sight, the monstrous Sphinx is a puzzling mask, concealing yet also giving clues to meanings and associations that lie behind it – a classic case of 'veiled' truth. In its representation as Sphinx, knowledge (*scientia*) has become an enigma: perhaps appropriately for the mystery of nature to which it holds the key. Whatever ambiguities the twentieth-century reader may see in Sphinx/Minerva, Bacon's allegory of *scientia* is not one where male science can be said to transcend the feminine. Knowledge itself (*scientia*) is female, even if the knower (Oedipus) is male.

The reading of Baconian science as a masculine enterprise on account of his use of metaphor rests on privileging one type of metaphor over others. And most of Bacon's feminist critics cite just one metaphor, namely the metaphor of enslavement from *Temporis partus masculus* – a metaphor Bacon discarded when he abandoned the work. Studies of metaphor, especially sexual metaphor, can be illuminating. But, by concentrating on one such metaphor or group of metaphors at the expense of others, we learn less about Bacon than about the preoccupations and priorities of his modern readers. We perhaps betray more about our *fin-du-vingtième-siècle* concerns than we reveal about the coiner of a particular metaphor or his intellectual project.

POSTSCRIPT

Evelyn Fox Keller concludes *Reflections on Gender and Science* with an account of the microbiologist, Barbara McClintock. Keller shows how one scientist saw things differently from her peers and was finally vindicated by the success of her researches. Among the many features of the McClintock example, the sceptical distance she maintained between herself and the dogmas of science is remarkable: as she is reported as saying in Keller's study of her, 'trying to make everything fit into set dogma won't work . . . there's no such thing as a common dogma into which everything will fit'. Instead of coming to research with set ideas of what to find, she recommends that scientific researchers 'listen to the material' and 'let the experiment tell you what to do':

> much of the work done is done because one wants to impose an answer on it
> – they have the answer ready, and they want the material to tell them, so
> anything it doesn't tell them, they don't really recognise as there, or they
> think it's a mistake and throw it out. . . . If you'd only just let the material tell
> you.[58]

Is there perhaps a lesson for us here? If her counsel to scientists is applicable to historians and to feminist historians at that, we too should, in McClintock's words, 'hear what the material has to say'[59] – in our case the material is the data of history. To investigate the contribution of women to the history of science is to deal with a topic that historians 'don't really recognise as there'. Or at least this was until very recently the case. But there is still an enormous amount of work to be done. The problem for us is how to use the material without being imprisoned in our own conceptual constructs, or anyone else's for that matter.

Notes

1 'Sphinx or Science' from *De sapientia veterum* tr. J. Devey, in Bacon (1884), p. 253.

2 Richard Lynche (1599), sigg. Siij–T.

3 See, for example, Sandra Harding (1991), Evelyn Fox Keller and Helen Longino (eds) (1996).

4 Evelyn Fox Keller (1985). Keller's discussion has been instrumental in establishing a key role for the analysis of metaphor in determining the gender bias of science. Helen Longino, noting that feminists are faced with misogyny in scientific traditions, states, 'Models often have their start as metaphors. . . . What many feminists have pointed out . . . is the use of metaphors of gender ideology and social relations for natural processes and relations', 'Subjects, Power and Knowledge: Description and Prescription in Feminist Philosophies of Science', in Alcoff and Potter (1993), p. 101. Susan Bordo (1987), pp. 105 and 127n.; R. Berman, 'From Aristotle's Dualism to Materialist Dialectics: Feminist Transformation of Science and Society', in S. Bordo and A. Jaggar (1989), p. 226; Harding (1991), pp. 300–1. An important paper which predates this debate is Mary Hesse (1980). Also, Michèle Le Doeuff (1989).

5 Bacon, *The Masculine Birth of Time or Great Instauration of the Dominion of Man over the Universe*, in Farrington (1970), p. 62.

6 The other important element in her argument is her acceptance of Carolyn Merchant's thesis that more intrinsically female epistemes, like alchemy, were displaced by a masculine, mechanical model of nature that derived from Descartes and Hobbes; see Merchant (1980).

7 Lloyd (1992; first publ. 1983), p. viii. In her preface to the second edition Genevieve Lloyd notes that were she to rewrite the book, she would put more emphasis on metaphor.

8 Hekman (1990), pp. 115 and 120. The elision of two fundamentally different types of science, the Baconian and the Cartesian, is typical of the application of the argument in discussions like this, and probably owes much to the Merchant thesis. Susan Bordo is another who relies on Keller and Merchant to argue that Bacon's metaphors constitute a 'flight from the feminine'. She too makes a link with Descartes: Bordo (1987), pp. 104–5, 112.

9 Quoted in Keller (1985), p. 52.

10 *Some Considerations Touching Experimental Natural Philosophy* in Boyle (1744), vol. 1.

11 For example, Julian Martin (1991). On Anne Cooke Bacon, see Lamb (1985).

12 Antonio Pérez-Ramos, for example, argues that there have been 'fluctuations between different senses of Baconianism' and that Bacon has been 'misunderstood in a most radical way by his earliest followers in the Royal Society' (1986), p. 31.

13 For a very Renaissance view of Bacon, see Graham Rees (1975; 1977). Lisa Jardine (1974) underlines the Aristotelian framework of Bacon's idea of the sciences and of his general theory of knowledge.

14 Mary Tiles (1986) .

15 Harding (1991), Keller (1983), Rose (1994).

16 *Magnalia naturae* in Bacon (1974), p. 249. This selection is, admittedly, biased. The endeavours of Baconian science are not all so public-spirited, including as they do, 'Instruments of destruction, as of war and poison'.

17 *Ibid.*, 2.17.6–7. ed. cit., pp. 134–5.

18 *Ibid.*, p. 135.

19 For a discussion of his main metaphors, see Brian Vickers (1968).

20 Bacon, *Advancement*, 3.4.3.

21 *Ibid.*, 3.4.4.

22 L.G. Giraldi (1548), Cesare Ripa (1603), Vincenzo Cartari (1580). See Schebinger (1989).

23 *De sapientia*, p. 264. Devey has 'Pluto or earth', the Latin just 'Pluto'. He translates '*natura*' here as 'natural philosophy'. Bacon's interpretation is suggestive of Renaissance vitalism rather than the empirical corpuscularianism of the Royal Society.

24 For example, 'The mechanical arts draw little light from philosophy, though they do gradually enlarge the humble web woven by experience', *Cogitata et visa* in Farrington (1970), p. 73.

25 *Ibid.*, p. 77 (my italics).

26 Quite how frequently, in the case of *Novum Organum* can be discerned from Marta Fattori (1980).

27 This is a point Newton makes in the General Scholium to the third book of his *Principia*, when describing the power of God in the universe: Newton's God is a God of power, but as such, a God of Dominion, but 'Universal Ruler', who 'governs all things not as the soul of the world, but as Lord over all'. Newton tr. Motte (1936), p. 544.

28 Giovio (1585), tr. Samuel Daniel, sig. Biiii[9]. The imperial dimension was not lost on other commentators; see E. Rosenthal (1971; 1973). On the heroic dimension of Bacon's image, see John M. Steadman (1971).

29 See also *Cogitata et visa*, Farrington (1970), p. 76: 'Pillars have been erected beyond which progress is forbidden, and there is no ground for surprise that man does not achieve an end which he neither hopes nor desires'.

30 Meres (1598). The motif was familiar in Bacon's time, e.g. '*Time* (that . . . is the father of Veritie) cannot suffer hir to be hidden by any coloured fraud or deceit', Sir Thomas North (1570, ed. J. Jacob 1888), p. 212 and Thomas Peyton (1620), p. 73 and frontispiece. The motif derives from Aulus Gellius, *Noctes Atticae*, XII.11.7. It is discussed in Bing (1937), Wittkower (1937), Gordon (1939), and S. Iwasaki (1958). See also W. von Leyden (1958).

31 *De sapientia*, in Bacon (1884), p. 264.

32 '*propagine scilicet cerebri sui . . . instar Jovis, cum Pallada enixus sit*'; Rawley, '*Nobilissimi auctoris vitae*', prefacing *Instauratio Magna*, Bacon, *Works* (1854), vol.2, p. 277.

33 Lynche (1599), sig. Siij[v].

34 Ripa (1603), p. 453.

35 Lynche (1599), sig. Siij[3]. See Cartari (1580), p. 356.

36 Lynche (1599) , sig. Siij[v].

37 Ross (1648), p. 284.

38 Cartari (1580), p. 360. On Aristotelianism and misogyny, see I. Maclean (1980).

39 Lynche (1599), Siij[2–3].

40 'women for the most part are hinderers not furtherers of wisdom and learning: therefore she is said to be a perpetual Virgin, because men that live a single life have fewest avocations from the studies of wisdom and knowledge', Ross (1648), p. 284.

41 *De sapientia*, in Bacon (1884), p. 260.

42 In confirmation of the link between knowledge and power, Bacon claims that the emperor Augustus Caesar's signet ring bore an image of the Sphinx (*ibid.*, p. 260).

43 *Ibid.*, pp. 258–9.

44 *Ibid.*, p. 259.

45 See A. Chastel (1959), pp. 88–9; H. Demisch (1977).

46 Giovio (1585), sig. Giii⁹. In his *Diologo dell'imprese* (1559) Giovio notes:
'la Sfinge degli Egetti che su le intrerpretar gli euigmi e le cose abstruse cel tempo. . .' (p. 139).

47 Athanasius Kircher cites Clement of Alexandria to the effect that Sphinxes represent the
mysteriousness of divine and natural wisdom: '*Sphinges in sacris ponut, ad indicandum sermonem de Deo,
natura, similisque esse obscurum & aenigmaticum*', *Oedipi Aegyptiace* (1654), 3: 130. Later on he notes that
the Egyptians depicted Sphinxes not because they believed they or similar beasts existed but to
denote recondite things ('*ad connontanda reconditora mentis sensa*'), *ibid.*, p. 460.

48 This is reproduced as the frontispiece in Frances Yates (1964). See also p. 42. As Yates points
out, Pico della Mirandola states in his *Oration on the Dignity of Man* that the Sphinx signified the need
to veil mysteries from non-adepts (*ibid.*, p. 103). The Sphinx is established as a symbol of Egypt in
Ripa's iconography of the river Nile.

49 Ripa (1603), p. 54.

50 '*Simulachrum, inquit, auro & ebore constat, media eius galea sphingis species apposita, utraque vero galeae
parte gryphes sunt exculpti. Simulachrum stat, uesta podere, id est ad talos demissa: Medusae capite in eius pectore
inserto, & Victoria magnitudine quatuor cubitorum, in manu est hasta, ad pedes scutum iacet, uxta hastam draco, &
caetera*', Giraldi (1548), p. 467. The spear and the Gorgon's head are also symbols of Reason, another
female figure in the mythographical pantheon: both the images of 'Ragione' described by Cesare
Ripa (1603), for instance, have Medusa's head depicted on their armour and carry a spear (p. 453).
On the frontispiece of her *The World's Olio* (see p. 221 below), Margaret Cavendish is depicted flanked
by Apollo and a female figure bearing a spear with the device of the Gorgon's head. Given
Cavendish's intellectual interests, the latter can be interpreted as signifying either Reason or
Minerva.

51 Lynche (1599), Siij³.

52 Fraunce (1592), p. 40v. Fraunce's book was dedicated to Mary Sidney, Countess of Pembroke.

53 Ross (1648), pp. 285–6.

54 Cartari (1580), p. 360.

55 Bacon (1884), p. 258.

56 *Ibid.*, p. 259.

57 For a discussion of this in the case of philosophers borrowing images from one another, see
Le Doeuff (1989).

58 Keller (1985), p. 62.

59 *Ibid.*, p. 98.

2

WOMEN AND TECHNICAL WRITING, 1475–1700: TECHNOLOGY, LITERACY, AND DEVELOPMENT OF A GENRE

Elizabeth Tebeaux

Studies in English Renaissance and seventeenth-century writing have focused almost exclusively on literary, political, historical and religious works. However, the *Short-Title Catalogue* (Pollard and Redgrave, 1976–86) records a substantial number of other works which can be called 'technical writing'. These works on farming, military science, beekeeping, animal husbandry, medicine, estate management and navigation, to list just a few sample topics, illustrate the technologies of the Renaissance and instructions for performing work important to the daily lives of English people. Despite its abundance, such writing has been largely ignored as a tool for examining the development of English technical writing and the literacy levels of its readers. Yet these books flourished after the advent of printing and their numbers increased dramatically throughout the period 1550–1700. As for all publications, technical book production increased substantially during the last half of the seventeenth century.

Within this large assortment of 'how to' books are a number of technical texts for women – books on cooking, household management, needlework, medical treatment, midwifery, gardening, and silkworm production. These obscure works, many of which were extremely popular, if we use numbers of editions as an indicator, tell us a great deal about the technologies used by women in their homes and about working lives, their knowledge needs, about the development of technical writing as a distinct genre, and about the literacy level of women readers who are often assumed to have had poorer reading skills than men. While lack of records has made the extent of literacy for both men and women in Renaissance England extremely difficult to assess,[1] these technical books provide an as yet unexplored means of assessing men and women's reading ability while showing major milestones in the development of technical writing during the years when printed texts were reshaping language. These 'how to' books for women provide a microcosm for studying the close relationship between increasing knowledge, print technology that allowed textual containment of knowledge, and the development of literacy among women readers who were the target audience of these books. Technical writing emerged with the demise of the oral tradition as the major method of transmitting instructions for tasks necessary to the working lives of both men and women of the English Renaissance and the seventeenth century. However, these works have at least one additional value: they become a point of departure for understanding the changes in literacy among women during the second half of the seventeenth century. Many of the same kinds of popular technical book written *for* women during the Renaissance rather suddenly began to be written *by* women during the 1641–1700 period.

LITERACY, TECHNICAL WRITING AND WOMEN OF RENAISSANCE ENGLAND

Assessments of literacy in Renaissance England are at best nebulous, not only due to incomplete records but also due to lack of knowledge about education.[2] However, increases in the numbers of affordable printed books for men and women clearly indicate that literacy was expanding during the English Renaissance.[3] However, studies of Renaissance writing that focus on women's books have centred mainly on the lives and literary and religious reading by women of the upper classes.[4] Ezell moves beyond women's reading to discuss the writing by these upper-class women.[5] Her study suggests that these women were highly literate, having received education from private tutors. However, studies of women's reading and writing have focused on traditional religious and literary genres – poems, devotions, prayers, meditations and political polemic. Technical books and works on science have been largely ignored.

Thus, an examination of this new category of books – technical books for and by women – offers a unique opportunity for insight into the lives and minds of women during the Renaissance and the seventeenth century. As Hull commented in her description of the large numbers of guidebooks for women, many 'appear to be directed primarily to a middle-class audience, to women who perhaps had servants but who were not removed from the mechanics of household affairs'.[6] This observation is compelling, as studies of men's and women's literacy have suggested that literacy was the privilege of upper- rather than middle-class women and that within each class women were less literate than men. Education for women was usually assumed to be limited and 'confined to subjects which would fit them for the roles of wife and mother conventionally allocated to them'.[7] As Wrightson stated, education was valued only if it was socially and economically advantageous.[8] Campbell, in her study of the English yeoman, concluded that a fitting education generally included proficiency in needlework, management of domestic affairs, and instruction in basic reading and writing. While many yeoman records show that women were unable to sign their names, many more were unable either to read or write. To what extent women learned to *read* as part of their preparation 'as is fit and necessary for one of her degree and calling' remains uncertain.[9]

Thus, Hull's description of the place of guidebooks for women provides a new tool for assessing the literacy of women, particularly those of the non-elite classes, and for examining the development of English technical writing:

> With several notable exceptions (particularly fiction addressed to ladies of the court) the books for women appear to be written (or translated) for the less sophisticated and marginally educated women of the gentry or the growing commercial families. The emergence of a large group of women who could read in English probably helped to accelerate the use of English in print and the gradual decrease in the importance of the classical and French languages.[10]

An examination of a cross-section of technical books for women and then a brief discussion of the first technical books written by women during the 1641–1700 period yields a number of observations that expand current knowledge of the development of technical writing and the increase of literacy among women during the Renaissance:

(1) Expansion of knowledge, traditionally associated with the Renaissance, is reflected in the increasing sophistication of technical books for women throughout the 1475–1640 period. Increasing numbers of technical books and their increasing length by 1640 suggest that more knowledge was available and desired by readers than could be conveyed by oral transmission. Books that would be read and used for reference to perform essential tasks – books about cookery, silkworm propagation, beekeeping, medical diagnosis and treatment, and household management – included more information by the early seventeenth century than they had contained in the middle of the sixteenth century.

By the closing decades of the seventeenth century, many of these types of book were being written by women. The level of detail in content and the agility of style suggest that a growing number of women now possessed more than basic writing skills. These women writers must have assumed that their intended audience of women readers would be able to comprehend these books.

(2) The increasing quantity of technical instructions transmitted textually (rather than orally) led to the emergence of a plain style which foreshadowed modern technical writing style – common nouns and action verbs, subject–verb–object constructions, active-voice clauses. Writers of early printed technical books for women apparently realized that a difference existed between writing that would be used to enable the reader to perform a task and writing that would be read slowly and leisurely, such as fiction and religious works. The development of plain style throughout the sixteenth and seventeenth centuries, as revealed in these technical books, may have been enhanced by writers who saw the need for a style appropriate to conveying information and instructions – a

style that preserved the clear quality of spoken instructions and achieved directness and conciseness. Thus,

- prose replaced poetry as the medium for conveying technical knowledge after reading skills made memorizing of basic instructions unnecessary;
- oral residue (additive clauses and phrases) decreased in written text as the sixteenth century progressed;
- analytic style (periodic sentences, 'if' and 'when' clauses) merged with and finally obscured the additive style.

By the closing decades of the seventeenth century, this style was handled with equal skill by female and male technical writers.

(3) Contrary to existing conclusions about women's literacy, middle-class women readers had approximately the same reading comprehension skills as middle-class men. Differences can be found in books containing sections directed to men and to women. However, these differences occur frequently in length and extensiveness of content rather than in complexity or difficulty of style. While technical books for men have more content and more detail than technical books for women, this difference does not suggest that women were less literate.

Books that appeared after 1660 showed little variation in complexity of style. However, the absence of Greek and Latin allusions in women's books suggests that women still lacked opportunities for classical education.

(4) Technical books *for* women changed significantly during the 1500–1640 period; technical books written *by* women after 1640 sustained these changes. Such books for and by women, published from 1508–1700, increased in length, in technical detail, in level of expression, and in complexity of sentence structure. The disappearance of poetry as a means of conveying technical knowledge suggests that women became able to handle written prose and not just didactic lyrical presentations that could be easily memorized.

Ultimately, by isolating and examining these technical books for middle-class women we can show how increasing literacy and the development of technical writing were interrelated.

RENAISSANCE TECHNICAL BOOKS FOR WOMEN

A survey of the *Short-Title Catalogue* reveals a substantial number and variety of technical books for women, most of which can be grouped into seven major classifications: books of food and medicinal recipes, books on home medical remedies and procedures, books for midwives, books on silkworm production, books on agrarian estate management, books on gardening, and books on needlework.

BOOKS OF COOKERY AND HOUSEHOLD PHYSICK

The most popular technical books for women were 'books of cookery'. As Camden stated, over twenty different cookbooks were published, many in multiple editions before 1640.[11] Because extensively used books such as these may not have survived, we cannot estimate how many cookbooks existed.[12] However, the *Short-Title Catalogue* notes that of those of which we have extant copies, most enjoyed multiple editions. These small books were cheaply printed, as the poor quality of the type (English black letter) usually testifies. Most were random collections of recipes that often lacked divisions and classifications, although recipes for meats, breads, cakes, sauces, and preserves might be grouped together. By the closing decades of the Renaissance, these books separated recipes into distinct categories fully demarcated in the table of contents.

Cookbooks, which often included recipes for home medicinal preparations as well as food, provide an interesting window into changes in middle-class women's literacy, the advancement of cooking as a technology, and English style as a vehicle for this technology. For example, early Renaissance cookbooks showed less technical precision and organization of recipes than those of the late Renaissance and the seventeenth century, a characteristic which first suggests that cooking as an art had advanced. For example, a *Book of Cookery*, published by Pynson in 1500, provided several recipes for preparing meats. The style indicated the prevalence of the oral tradition: additive style, aggregative syntax rather than analytical, simple rather than detailed instructions – i.e. sight dominance was subservient to hearing dominance.[13] The simple listing of ingredients and the order in which they were used suggested that the recipe served as a means of aiding the woman's memory rather than of providing complete instructions that were to be learned by reading only. This earliest extant printed English cookbook contained recipes for basic foods. The recipes were simple and short:

for to make chckyns in Musy

To make chckyns in musy / take smale chckyns
chopped and boyle theym in swete broth and wyne and putte
therto percely and sage and powder of peper or graynes and
colour it with saffron / then take whyte of egges and ale
drawen through a cloth and put therto and styre it well
togeder and put thereto an unce of gynger and whan it
begynneth to boyle set it from the fire and serue it.[14]

Another important text in the cookbook category was the *Boke of Kervynge* (8 edns, 1508–1631), which was also included in at least five more editions of later cookbooks. The non-syntactical listing of items in many sections suggests that the written instruction was used as a memory prompt rather than as a source of specific instruction to be gained by reading only. The following excerpt shows the mnemonic style used in this very early English work. Like the *Book of Cookery*, its diction suggests that women readers, even in 1508, would have been capable of reading material that incorporated spoken language:

Seruyce.

Fyrste sette ye forth mustarde and brawne potage
befe motton stewed. Secande / swanne / capon / pygge /
venyson bake / custarde / leche and lombarde. Fruyter
vaunte with a subtylte two potages blaunche manger
annd gelly. For standarde venyson roste kydde fawne and
cony / bustarde storke crane pecocke with his tayle
hereonsewe bytture woodcocke partryche plouer rabettes
grete byrdes larkes / . . .[15]

In contrast, Murrel's *A Daily Exercise for Ladies and Gentlewomen*, published over a century later in 1617, provided precise instructions. While additive sentence structure was still dominant, the syntax was more sophisticated than that used in the *Book of Cookery* and exemplified some analysis rather than aggregation. Diction in both works suggests that the writer used words that would have been part of the common speaking vocabulary. The detail of these instructions suggests that they were intended to be read rather than to serve as memory prompts:

Strawberry cakes

Take a quart of very fine flower, eight ounces of fine
sugar beaten and cerfed, twelve ounces of sweet butter, a
Nutmegge grated, two or three spoonefuls of damaske
rosewater, worke all these together with your hands as hard
as you can for the space of halfe an houre, then roule it in
little round Cakes, about the thicknesse of three shillings one
vpon another, then take a siluer Cup or a glasse some
foure or three inches ouer, and cut the cakes in them, then
strow some flower vpon white papers & lay them vpon
them, and bake them in an Ouen as hotte as for Manchet,
set vp your lid till you may tell a undredth, then you shall see
the white, if any of them rise vp clap them downe with some
cleane thing, and if your Ouen be not too hot set vp your lid
again, and in a quarter of an houre they wil be baked
enough, but in any case take heede your Ouen be not too
hot, for they must not looke browne but white, and so draw
them foorth & lay them one vpon another till they bee
could, and you may keep them halfe a year the new baked
are best.[16]

As the art and technology of cooking developed, printed cookbooks became longer and more elaborate, their sentence structures more developed and their recipes more complex than those published in the first half of the sixteenth century. For example, other cookbooks appeared that provided instructions for a variety of household preparations – sachets, perfumes, dentrifices, cosmetics, desserts and confections – such as Platt's *Delights for Ladies, to adorne their Persons, Tables, closets and distillatories* (16 edns, 1599–1636) (see p. 36 below).

Because women were usually responsible for caring for the sick – family members, servants and perhaps neighbours – cookbooks often contained recipes for medicines in addition to those for foods. The *Short-Title Catalogue* records more books that combined 'cookery' with 'physick' than books devoted solely to recipes. As Hull stated:

> Rural household communities were largely self-supporting, and a woman was expected to know how to raise some of the food as well as how to prepare and preserve it. Housewifery frequently involved the supervision of a sizable staff and the role of mentor and doctor to a small community. Women delivered the babies, and they prepared 'cures' for every-thing from scratches to the plague.[17]

For example, *A closet for Ladies and Gentlewomen, Or, The Art of preseruing, Conseruing, and Candying* (10 edns, 1608–36) included recipes for 'Medicines, Salues, for Sundry Diseases'. A loosely classified collection of recipes, this little book featured instructions for preserving peaches, quinces, oranges, lemons and rose leaves as well as instructions 'For the Woormes', 'To stench bleeding at the Nose', 'To know whether a Child hath the Wormes, or no'. The style still exemplified additive qualities characteristic of the oral tradition, but cause–effect syntax is also present. The completeness of the instructions suggests that this work was also written to be read and used without additional oral aid:

To preserue Apricockes.

Take a pound of Apricockes, and a pound of sugar,
and claryfie your sugar with a pint of water, and when your
sugar is made perfect, put it into a Preseruing-pan & put
your Apricockes into it and so let them boyle gently, and
when they bee boyled ynough and your syrope thicke, pot
them andso keepe them. In like manner may you preserue a
Pear-plum.

To know whether a child hath the Wormes, or no.

Take a peece of white Leather, and pecke it full of holes
with your knife, and rub it with Worme-word, and spread

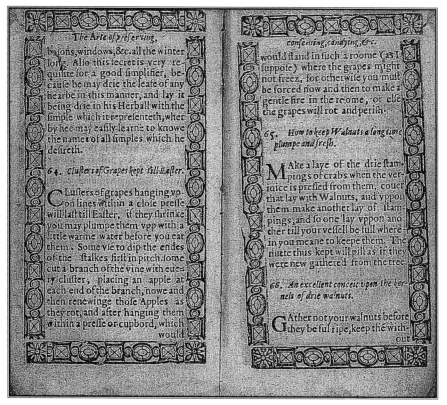

Pages from Henry Platt's *Delightes for Ladies* (1602).

honey on it, and starwe the powder of Alesackatrina, and lay it on the Childs Nauell, when he goeth to bed, and if hee haue the wormes, the plaster will sticke fast, and if he haue them not, it will fall off.[18]

The good Huswifes handmaide for Cookerie in her Kitchin (2 edns, 1594–7), as its subtitle suggests, contained *Manie principall pointes of Cookerie, as well how to dresse meates, after sundrie the best fashions vsed in England and other Countries, with their apt and proper sawces, both for flesh and fish, as also the orderly seruing of the same to the Table. Hereunto are annexed, sundrie necessary Conceits for the preseruation of health.* Partridge's *The Widdowes Treasure* (10 edns, 1582–1639), was another conglomeration of recipes for foods and medicinals: for example, 'For an Ague', 'For the Tooth-ache', 'To keepe Venison fresh a long time', 'To keep it from rotting after it is new slaine'.

Despite the variations in content and organization of these kinds of book, the style remained basically the same. Recipes might vary in technical precision – 'handfuls' to 'quarts' to 'cups', but the level of language and sentence structure remained fundamentally the same: concise, imperative clauses (direct address) connected in a loose, additive style. Cause–effect analysis ('if' and 'when' clauses) began to appear within larger additive structures by the end of the sixteenth century. However, all recipes were composed of common verbs and nouns used in daily language, as the previous examples illustrate.

The fact that these books of cookery and household 'physick' gave less emphasis to exact quantities than to ingredients and placed little emphasis on precise instructions for making and then using foods and folk medicines implies that these early cookbooks, like modern advanced cookbooks, assumed that women readers had a basic knowledge of cooking which they learned through oral transmission and from demonstration. The recipes themselves point to the fact that women had a reading knowledge of words that comprised their spoken vocabularies and that many of the recipes had been recorded as they had been dictated. Wright, Bennett, Levy, Laqueur and Houston have all suggested that, for middle-class readers particularly, the acquisition of literacy was ongoing. 'For many people, education in a school was only part of a much wider means of learning which encompassed the home, peer groups and work experience.'[19]

Perhaps the availability of cookbooks that textually embodied information as it had been orally transmitted aided in the development of literacy of women of the middle and yeoman classes. The growing numbers and variety of cookbooks support Thomas Laqueur's conclusion on this point: 'People did not become literate for this or that particular reason but because they were increasingly touched in all areas of their lives by the power of communication which only the written word makes possible.'[20] Reading skills, and later writing skills, allowed men and women to function more effectively in a variety of social contexts. While much information – both religious and practical – was still transmitted orally, textual embodiment of knowledge allowed quicker access to more information than readers could gain and remember through verbal instruction alone. Learning new tasks was no longer dependent only on person-to-person transmission of needed information. The growing availability of affordable texts and the ability to access these texts by reading opened up new opportunities for self-education.

MEDICINAL BOOKS

The extensive number of books containing food and medicinal recipes suggests that women could read material that was probably familiar to them from oral transmission and that recipes were written in a style that still reflected oral-based language patterns. However, the substantial number of medicinal books for home use suggests that women's literacy levels had increased dramatically from the middle years of the sixteenth century to the middle years of the seventeenth century. Most of these books employed a sophisticated, Latinate diction as well as complex sentence structures.

The *Short-Title Catalogue* records several books written for landowners, most likely manorial wives, who were responsible for the medical care of family members, servants and even neighbours. For example, Owen Wood's *An Alphabetical Book of Physicall Secrets* (1 edn, 1639) was a collection of remedies for a variety of conditions. Its sub-title indicates that men and women were assumed to possess a knowledge of pharmaceutical terminology and access to a variety of chemicals – *For all those Diseases that are most predominant and dangerous (curable by Art) in the Body of Man. Collected for the benefit, most especially of House-holders in the Country, who are either farre remote, or else not able to entertaine a learned Physician: as likewise for the help of such Ladies and Gentlewomen, who of charity labour to doe good.* The following excerpt indicates this required knowledge level:

Aches olde, the Cure.

. . .Take oyle of Turpentine d i lb, oyle of Bayes iii j,
Mace, Cloves, Nutmegs, Cinnamon ana i, oyle of
Spike i, Iuniper-berries vii j, Castor, Eusorbium ana i,
Brocksgrease iij, Mummy i d. digest them for one moneth
in horse-dung, then distill them artificially, and anoynt the
griese therewith.[21]

The fact that for some remedies no quantities were given suggests that they were still part of the oral tradition in which quantities were conveyed by spoken instruction and thus were already known to readers. As in the earlier medicinal and food recipes, ingredients, textually given, served mainly as memory prompts:

Ache in Bones or Ioyntes, the Cure.

Take black knots of the Ash tree in the Spring
time, grinde them small, and boyle them over a soft fire with
fresh Butter in an earthen pot sufficiently, then take them
from the fire, let them coole, and keepe them close stopped,
then take as many of Broome flowers in May, grinde them as
the other, then mixe them all together, and boyle them
againe with a quarter of a pinte of Malmsey, then keepe it to
anoynt the griese therewith.[22]

This work is particularly interesting because it illustrates from a Renaissance perspective O'Keefe's point that orality and literacy existed in a continuum and that increasing literacy allowed people to function with a more extensive, detailed level of knowledge than if they were forced to rely solely on knowledge that could be remembered.[23] As Owen Wood's book shows, the residue of orality continued to surface in printed texts which were attempting to capture in written language knowledge that had been orally transmitted.

Medical self-help books exemplify major milestones in the development of technical style. Slack suggests that readership of these small volumes ran the gamut from poorly trained practitioners, to men and women of the elite classes, to merchants, yeomen and their wives.[24] Thus, the style had to appeal to a wide variety of readers of varying educational and literacy levels. And this style was apparently successful. As Slack points out, vernacular medical texts comprised some of the most popular sixteenth-century literature. Many such books were printed regularly for fifty years and enjoyed over a dozen editions, partly because authors were well attuned to the requirements of their readers and adjusted their writing accordingly. Sir Thomas Elyot's *Castell of Health* (1595), with its guide to self-diagnoses, dietary advice and practical remedies became the prototype for many of these manuals.[25] In the Prohem, Elyot stated that his purpose was to provide background knowledge so that the patient might 'instruct his physician wherunto he may adopt his counsel and remedies'. Like other writers of medical self-help manuals, Elyot dealt with afflictions that affected men as well as women, such as gout, nosebleeds, coughs and haemorrhoids. While his style maintained the subject–verb–object clause structure found in the books of cookery and physick, Elyot used complex sentences – 'if', 'when', 'which' clauses – and Latinate diction in contrast to the more simple style of the basic medicinal recipes. The emphasis on the basic kernel, a characteristic of the first cookbooks, diminishes as the number of periodic sentences increased. The following excerpt appeared in the 1595 edition:

Of Hemeroydes or piles. CAP. 9

Hemeroides bee veynes in the fundament of whome
doe happy sundry passions, somtime swelling without
bleeding, sometimes superfluous blood by the purssance of
nature is by them expelled, and then bee they very
conuenient, for by them a man shall escape many great
sicknesses, which be ingendred of corrupted blood, or of
melancholie. Semblablie, if they bee hastilie stopped from
the course which they haue beene used to, thereby doe
increase the saide sicknesse, which by them were expelled,
as dropsies, consumptions, madnesses, frensies, and diuers
diseases of the head, and other sicknesses. . . . And if they
flow too much, there insueth feebleness, tearing of the body,
alteration of colour, great paines in the lower partes of the
bodie.[26]

Most of these self-diagnosis and treatment books also covered common illnesses and conditions peculiar to women. Highly popular (21 edns, 1557–1607) was *The Secretes of the Reuerend Maister Alexis of Piemont*. A fairly compact quarto, this work had four parts which increased in length with each addition. In the final editions, each section contained approximately a hundred and sixty pages and each part had its own table of contents. In a sense, this work encompassed most of the topics covered in other books for women – medical remedies, instructions for making inks and dyes, instructions for removing spots and stains, for glazing ceramics, for making perfumes and sachets and soaps. A survey of the topics in the four parts of this work provides a synopsis of household management – specific chores that women had to perform, the technologies involved, common ailments and problems encountered daily in running an urban or rural household. The author varied the amount of explanation for each topic. Instructions for making soap were allocated three pages of instructions mixed with detailed process description, while instructions for bee sting remedies were allotted only four lines. The writer apparently knew which topics women would be familiar with and which would require extensive explanation. This technical manual remains a clear precursor of the modern 'how to' manual in its style and arrangement of topics.

Another popular type of self-help medical books were the uroscopy books, such as *Here Beginneth the Seinge of Urynes* (13 edns, 1525–75). This book attempted to show readers how to diagnose health problems by analyzing the colour and density of their urine. Many of these books were arranged predominantly in lists and with simple active-voice sentences. Drawings of urinals served the purpose of the modern-day bullet and illustrate the earliest use of bullets in English printed books. The book contains an illustration describing women's urine and what the colour indicates (see p. 41 below).

BOOKS FOR MIDWIVES

Perhaps the most impressive book for women was Roesslin's *The Birth of Mankinde, otherwyse named the Womans Booke* (10 edns, 1540–1604), which was also the most popular English book for midwives throughout the sixteenth century. The preface stated that the work 'is nowe so plainely set foorth, that the simplest Mydwyfe which can reade, maye both underrstand for her better instruction, and also other women that haue nede of her help'. Divided into four books, it was perhaps the most technically advanced volume for women printed in the sixteenth century.

The first book provided a technical description of the female anatomy – nine verbal and correlating labelled drawings – to explain the location and function of the main internal organs as well as the reproductive and urological systems. In the technical descriptions the writer or translator was careful to avoid

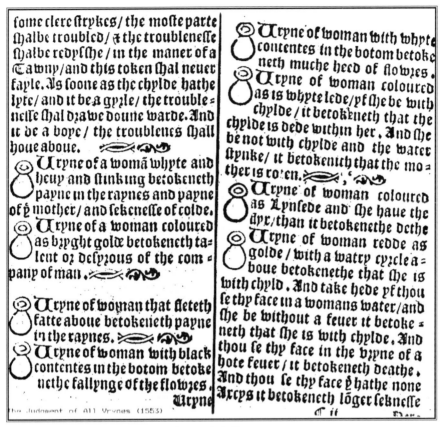

Pages from *Here Beginneth the seinge of Urynes* (1650).

extensive use of Latin medical terms, employing common English nomenclature so that the text could be read without an understanding of the Latin phrases. This shift indicates that as a technical writer, he realized the importance of writing to his readers' knowledge level. Most of the nine figures were plagiarized from Latin anatomical works which had been translated into English.

An illustration taken from the 1626 edition, showed 'the third fygure of women' (see p. 153 below). The following text explained the drawing. This popular midwives' instruction manual reveals that midwives had a higher literacy level than women who read the books of cookery and 'physick', that they had command of some Latin medical terminology, and that they were capable of reading and following semi-technical anatomical descriptions:

This present figure sheweth the Matrix or wombe, with the thinne couerynges
which do bynde it to *Peritonium*, cut foorth from the body, and the necke therof is
here so folded togther, and turned ouer, that the mouth or openyng of the
bottome of the Matrix doth herre manyfestlye shew it selfe. And we haue
lykewyse so opened the bottome and the necke of the bladder, that the holownes
of the same, with the insertion of the wayes of vrine, are here manyfestlye sene.

A The former face of the bottome of the Matrix, beyng not yet vndouered of
any pannicle.
BB The necke of the Matrix.
C A parte of the bottome of the Matrix, swellyng foorth into the vpper seate
of the necke of the Matrix, in maner of a Karnell.
D The mouth of the bottome of the Matrix.
EE A pannicle knitting the Matrix to *Peritonium*, and conteynyng his vesselles.
F The left testicle of the Matrix.
G The vayne and artire of feede.
H Portion of the feede vayne and artire, commynge to the vpper seate of the
bottome of the Matrix.
I A portion of the feede vayne and Artire comyng to the testicle.
K The vessell caryeng the seede from the testycle into the Matrix.
L The holownes of the bladder.
M The insertion of the wayes of the vrine.
N Here hangeth foorth a lyttle peece of the wayes of the vrine.[27]

That the literacy level of midwives improved from the middle years of the
sixteenth to the middle years of the seventeenth century is evident from an
examination of the style of a second book, written for both midwives and young
surgeons. *Child-birth, or, The Happy Deliverie of Women*, translated by James
Guillemeau, enjoyed two editions (1612–35). A lengthy work, just as *The Birth of
Mankinde*, the first three parts were dedicated to problems encountered during
pregnancy and childbirth. The final part, *The Nvrsing of Children*, was essentially a
book on how to care for young children and how to treat their diseases. It can be
described as a Renaissance version of modern guide books to infant care that also
included general paediatric methods. Like *The Birth of Mankinde*, *Child-birth*
assumed a high reading comprehension level. Spencer's study indicates clearly
that during the seventeenth century British physicians did not regard female
midwives as having much importance.[28] Views such as Spencer's are echoed in the
angry rebuttals of women such as Elizabeth Cellier and Jane Sharp (the latter was
the author of the first book for midwives written by an English woman). Both
women asserted the value and competence of women throughout history. Thus,
we can assume that Guillemeau's book was read by both male and female
midwives.

As Guillemeau's book indicates (see p. 169 below) indicates, the nurse was expected to read prescriptions and prepare them to treat common diseases such as French pocks. *Child-birth* even includes instructions for using surgical instruments, such as tongs, to remove a dead foetus from the womb.

BOOKS ON SILKWORM PROPAGATION

Books on silkworm propagation were definitely written with women readers as their target audience, as the propagation of silkworms was considered an exclusively female profession until the mid-seventeenth century.[29] Dale noted that even though the silkworm industry was not recognized in a definite guild, it was pursued on the lines of the craft guilds of male workers. The silkwomen accepted apprentices, employed workers, understood their own business transactions and were sufficiently organized to present petitions to the government.[30] These books are also significant because they illustrate the development of technical writing and the substantial literacy of silkwomen and professional people in general. For example, in discussing patterns of book ownership in England between 1560 and 1640, Clark noted that professional people often possessed the largest book collections. Clark reported that 'in the important textile centers of Canterbury and Maidstone those working in the silk and clothmaking crafts also tended to be above average in the ownership of books'.[31] The fact that women made an impact on the economy, as discussed by Todd and Prior, and that the demands made on them were considerable, suggests that a substantial literacy level would have been essential for their economic survival.[32]

The *Short-Title Catalogue* records at least five works relating to the propagation of silkworms. Three works on the topic revealed not only the nature of the work and the growth of related technology but also an increased stylistic sophistication that became associated with technical books. First, T.M.'s *The silkewormes, and their flies* (1 edn, 1599), which covered thirty separate topics, was written entirely in verse. Yet the verses covered such unpoetic subjects as propagation, dyeing, the value of the eggs, temperatures for keeping the eggs, time for hatching, collection methods, sickness, metamorphosis from worms into flies, preservation of eggs, and the uses of silken threads. Its ballad stanza suggests that it was written to be read to and then memorized by women who may not have been able to read. Because the information is conveyed through poetry, detailed content is limited:

> The first three weekes the tend'rest leaues are best,
> The next, they craue them of a greater size,
> The last, the hardest ones they can digest,
> As strength with age increasing doth arise:
> After which time all meate they do detest,
> Lifting vp heads, and feete, and breast to skies,
>   Begging as t'were of God and man some shrowde,
>   Wherein to worke and hang their golden clowde.

> But whilst they feede, letal their foode be drie
> And pull'd when Phoebus fact doth brightly shine,
> For raine, mist, dewes, and spittings of the skie,
> Haue beene ful of the baine of cattle mine:
> Stay, therfore, stay, til dayes-vpholder flie,
> Fiue stages ful from Easterne Thetis line:
> > Then leaues are free from any poysned feede,
> > Which may infect this white and tender breede.[33]

A second work, Stallenge's *Instructions for the Increasing of Mulberrie Trees, and the Breeding of Silke-wormes, for the making of Silke in this Kingdome* (2 edns, 1609) was published two decades after T.M.'s work. This little book is equally brief (thirteen pages) but reveals the shift to prose to convey instructions. Comparing the excerpt below with T.M.'s shows how prose was emerging as the best vehicle for explaining the silkworm processes. In contrast to the style of cookbooks and books of 'physick', the style here is more complex: clauses showed occasional periodic structures and embedded clauses within main clauses. This development of clause structure suggests that by the early years of the seventeenth century writers may have expected silkwomen to be able to read prose and not to need to rely on poetic embodiment of instructions:

> What ground is fit for the Mulberrie seedes, how the same
> is to be ordered, & in what sort the seedes
> are to be sewed therein.

The ground which ought to be appointed for this purpose, besides the naturall goodnesse of it, must be reasonably well dunged, and withall so scituated, as that the heate of the sunny may cherish it, and the nipping blastes of either the North winde or the East, may not annoy it: the choice thereof thus made, that the seeds may the better prosper, & come vp after they bere sowne, you shal dig it two foote deepe, breaking the clods as small as may be, and afteward you shall deuide the same into seuerall Beds of not aboue fiue foote in breadth, so that you shal not neede to indanger the plants by treading vpon them, when either you water or weeded them.

  The Mulberrie seedes you shall lay in water for the space of xxii houres, and after that you shall drye them againe half drie, or somewhat more that when you sowe them they may not cleaue together: thus done, you must cast them vppon the fore saide beds, not altogether so thicke as you vse to doe other garden seedes, and then couer them with some fine earth (past through a Siue) about half an inch thicke: In drye weather you shall water them euerie two dies at the farthest, as likewife the Plants that shall come of them: and keepe them as cleane from weedes as possibly you can.[34]

The third work, De Serres's *The Perfect Vse of Silk-wormes, and their Benefit* (2 edns, 1607–9), was one of the books read by the housewife.[35] Approximately one hundred pages long, this work provided much more extensive as well as detailed explanation and instructions for growing and harvesting silkworms. It includes some of the same diagrams used in the previous work on silkworm production, *Instructions for the Increasing of Mulberrie Trees*, but is much more technical than either of the two previous books. The textual level of this work clearly suggests that its audience possessed substantial reading skills. Sentences and paragraphs are noticeably longer than those in Stallenge's work.

> To gather the leaues for to be giuen to the Wormes.
> For the order which one is to hold in gathering the mulberry leaues, for the vvictuales of these creatures, consisteth the second article of this work, for to make the trees of a perpetuall seruice. It is to be noted, that to plucke off the leaues bringes great damage to al trees, oftentimes euen causing them to damage to al trees, oftentimes euen causing them to dye: but seeing that the Mulberry is destined to that, it naturally supporteth such tempest better than any other plant: yet neuerthelesse you must goe to it very retentiuely, for to disleaue the Mulberrie inconsideratlie is the way to scorch them for euer, to cause them miserably to die in languishment. Euery one confesseth that to gather the leaues with both hands, leafe after leafe, without touching the shoote, is the most assured way for conseruation of the trees. . . .[36]

Thus books on silkworm husbandry, just as cookbooks, medicinals and technical manuals on midwifery, showed (1) increasing technicality after the closing decades of the sixteenth century; (2) the need for increasing knowledge for women readers who pursued this profession; and (3) a concomitant rise in required language comprehension level. While the active-voice patterns of oral transmission remained, these were embedded in simple, compound, and then complex sentence structures. These books on silkworms provide a microcosm through which we can trace the development of technical writing style as language shifted from oral transmission patterns to silent reading patterns. Technology nourished this shift by making poetry an unsuitable medium for the expression of even more detailed information. By the second quarter of the seventeenth century, women interested in learning the silkworm business and the basics of silkworm propagation would probably have needed reading skills more advanced than those they would have received in petty schools.

BOOKS ON AGRICULTURE AND ESTATE MANAGEMENT

'How to' books on estate management – these included techniques for farming, gardening and animal husbandry – are particularly useful guides in observing the development of an English technical writing style and assessing the literacy of women whose husbands were successful merchants. As Wright noted, books on agriculture, 'the writings of Fitzherbert, Tusser, and Markham long remained popular' because London merchants, having made sufficient money to buy a country estate, bought these books to help them manage their new purchases and lead a successful rural life.[37] The works by the three authors mentioned by Wright – Fitzherbert, Tusser and Markham – contained sections for men and women that provide revealing examples for assessing the literacy of women and for tracing the shift from orality to textuality as this movement shapes the emergence of technical discourse by the third decade of the seventeenth century.

One of the oldest and most popular books on husbandry and household management of the English Renaissance was Thomas Tusser's *Five Hundred Points of Good Husbandry*. This work, written completely in verse, enjoyed twenty-one editions from 1557 to 1607 and included sections on farm management and 'The Points of Huswiferie'. Agricultural historians assume that this earliest printed farming manual was popular because it could be read easily by those with minimal reading skills and then read aloud to and memorized by people having no reading skills at all. In contrast to Markham's book, first published in 1614, Tusser's uses mostly folklore and basic instructions. Its simple content remained unchanged through its twenty-one editions. The simplicity of the content and its poetic medium may suggest why it was more popular with less sophisticated readers, both men and women, than works by Markham, whose output, written six decades later, exhibited a sustained commitment to factual discussions of farming and animal husbandry and assumed that those who used them would have adequate reading skills. Comparing Tusser with Markham suggests that technology and literacy – content and style – changed substantially between 1557 and 1614. While Tusser's work remained popular, an audience for a more sophisticated, technical approach to agriculture had emerged.

However, neither Tusser nor Markham assumed that women readers were any less literate than men readers. For example, Tusser's section on 'The Points of Huswiferie' began with an inventory of the usual day's chores, proceeded to observations on topics such as 'brewing', 'dinner matters', 'The good huswifelie Physicke', and 'The good motherlie Nurserie', and concluded with verses on how to keep the home happy. As the following excerpt from 'Malting' illustrates, Tusser's work was not popular for the quality of its poetry but more likely because of its reliance on the oral tradition to convey practical advice in easily memorized rhymed couplets. The poetry level is similar to T.M.'s work on silkworms:

Ill malting is theft,
Wood dride hath a west.
House may be so handsome, and skilfulnes such,
to make thy owne malt, it shall profit thee much.
Some drieth with strawe, and some drieth with wood,
wood asketh more charge, and nothing so good.

Take heede to the kell,
Sing out as a bell.
Be suer no chances to fier can drawe,
the wood, or the furzen, the brake or the strawe.
Let Gillet be singing, it doth verie well,
to keepe hir from sleeping and burning the kell.

Best dride best speedes,
Ill kept, bowd breedes.
Malt being well speered, the more it will cast,
malt being well dried, the longer will last.
Long kept in ill soller, (undoubted thou shalt.)
though bowds without number loose quickly thy malt.[38]

That technical writing emerged as a genre between 1557 and 1614 is clearly evident if we compare Tusser's book with Gervase Markham's *Countrey Contentments* (5 edns, 1614–33). This work contained two books, the first directed to male and the second to female readers. Both had detailed tables of contents. Book 1, entitled *The Hvsbandmans Recreations*, dealt with methods of caring for hounds; instructions for hunting hares and deer; instructions for breeding, training and riding horses; instructions for raising and caring for hawks and greyhounds; and instructions for shooting the longbow and crossbow, for bowling (croquet), and for tennis. Book 2, '*The English Hus-wife*' included remedies for various illnesses, instructions for kitchen gardens, recipes for salads, breads, meats, herb dishes, sauces, desserts, pastries and jellies; instructions for dyeing wool and spinning; instructions for growing flax and preparing it for spinning; instructions for dairying; and methods of brewing beer and ale.

'*The English Hus-wife*' differed from other books addressing similar topics in that it provided more explanation. Markham apparently assumed that his women readers, who had recently moved to the country, needed substantial process descriptions and instructions on some topics. Thus, the chapters on wool, hemp, flax and clothmaking, dairying, and brewing provided more explanation for the processes described than did the chapters on cookery and 'physick', topics with which city wives would already have been familiar. A comparison of the content development of each section suggests that Markham was sensitive to the level of detail that his women readers would need.

However, the style Markham used throughout '*The English Hus-wife*' does not indicate that he believed that his women readers were any less literate than his male readers. An examination of excerpts from Book 1 ('*The Husbandmans Recreations*') and Book 2 ('*The English Hus-wife*') below illustrates the similarity of style and presentation of content. This point becomes particularly significant for two reasons: (1) '*The English Hus-wife*' also appeared in at least three separate editions, a fact that suggests the continuing popularity of the work; (2) Markham, one of the most prolific authors of the 1475–1640 period, showed a remarkable ability to write romances and histories as well as 'how to' books. Each kind of work exhibits a different style, a fact that suggests that Markham realized that different readers and different prose genres required different styles.[39] However, like most Renaissance technical writers, Markham used a terse subject–verb–object arrangement within active-voice clauses. Nevertheless, by the second decade of the seventeenth century, the additive style used in books of cookery had been replaced by an analytic style embodying active-voice clauses.

From Book 1:

Best houres of feeding [hounds]

Now for the best times of feeding, it is held amongst all our best experience't *Huntsmen*, to be in the dales of rest early in the morning before Sunne rise, and in the euening at Sunne set; But in the daies of *Hunting*, you shall let them goes fasting out of the *Kennell*, and feed them as soone as you come home to the *Kennell*, or before in you a way homeward, if you haue anie horse flesh, or other carion readilie prouided; otherwise with such meat as you haue, so it will fill their bellies, for a *Hound* by no meanes would be pinched of his bellie after his labour, and thefore be sure if your meat be course to fil his guts well, if it be sweet, strong and comfortable, then less with serue him.[40]

From Book 2:

Gathering of seeds

Seedes must be gathered in faire weather, at the wane of the Moone, and kept some in boxes of wood, and some in bagges of leather, and some in vessels of earth, and after to be cleansed and dried in the sunne or shadowe; other some, as Onions, Chibols and Leekes, must be kept in their husks. Lastly, shee must knowe that it is best to plant in the last of the Moone, to gether grafts inn the last but one, and to graft two daies after the changes, and thus much for her knowledge briefly of Hearbes, and how shee shall haue them continually for her vse in the kitchin.[41]

Books such as Markham's support Hogrefe's observations that women had to be ready to assume a variety of roles. The number of instructional books dedicated to explaining how to perform many of these tasks and the multiple editions that many of these books enjoyed imply that women were able to read these books containing rather detailed prose analyses and that they readily made use of their husbands' books. In her assessment of 'Women as Manor Wives', Hogrefe concluded:

> No women, it seems, worked harder or needed more varied abilities – not even in the twentieth century – than the wives of the men who owned great manor houses or other great country estates. . . . When her husband was at home, the manor wife ate with him, sat by his side after the meal, discussed the management of the entire estate with him, and was both companion and business partner. In his absence she entertained his guests and, with the help of a bailiff or steward, directed the farming operations – the planting and harvesting of crops, the sale of produce, the care of animals, and the general welfare of the tenants.
>
> As mistress of the manor, she supervised the brewing, baking, and cooking; planned the butchering; ordered foods and other necessities not produced on the premises; carded, spun, and wove woollen cloth, prepared flax and made linen cloth; embroidered; directed the making of most garments worn by members of the household; and acted as doctor and surgeon for the family and for tenants who needed her services.[42]

This range of responsibilities – indicated in the wide variety of instructions presented in other books, such as Dawson's *The Good Huswifes Iewell* and Partridge's *The Widdowes Treasur* – would have also found useful Markham's *Cheape and Good Husbandry for the Well-ordering of all Beasts, and Fowles, and for the generall Cure of their Diseases* (1614). In addition to extensive instructions for choosing horses and treating their diseases, he also included the following sections: 'Of the Bull, Cow, Calfe, or Oxe', 'Of the Sheepe', 'Of Goates', 'Of Swine', 'Of Poultrie', 'Of Geese', 'Of Turkeyes', 'Of Water-Fowle, and others', 'Of Hawkes', 'Of Bees' and 'Of Fishing'. As he did in *Countrey Contentments*, Markham incorporated instructions with process explanation wherever he thought explanation was proper. *Cheape and Good Husbandry* illustrates what came to be the standard technical style of the early seventeenth century – active-voice clauses developed within complex sentences. His books exemplify some of the best early pieces of process description.

Perhaps the most remarkable estate management book, and a clear precursor of Markham's, was Fitzherbert's *The Booke of Husbandrie* (11 edns, 1526–98). This work grew in number of topics and extent of coverage, but the style was unchanged throughout its eleven editions. Fitzherbert's work differs from Markham's in range of content and extent of coverage. Its presentation suggests that women readers on estates had long enjoyed a substantial command of written English. While Tusser's work has extensive recourse to folklore, Fitzherbert's was the first technical book on agriculture and estate management. Both books apparently had substantial readerships, based on their sustained popularity. The differences in required literacy level suggest that differences in literacy within the English farming community were substantial, but that these did not occur along gender lines. While 75 per cent of Fitzherbert's book is directed to men, the final sections for women, located in the fourth book, reveal no difference in required literacy level from the sections directed to men. Fitzherbert views the care and feeding of poultry as the wife's responsibility and provides specific instructions. For example:

Chapter. 6.
Howe to choose the best Hennes for broode.
If you desire to make choyse of the best hennes for broode, you must in all poynts haue them of the same colours which I haue already shewed in the choyse of your Cocks, tlhough they neede not bee eyther so hie, or big of body. They must be large breasted and bigge headed, hauing a straight redde double comme, great white eares, and her tallons suen. The best kinde are such as haue fiue clawes, so that they be without spurres: for such as haue spurres will yield ye small profit, by reason that with theyr spurres when they sit they breake theyr egges.[43]

If we compare this excerpt with an excerpt from Book I, we can see no difference in level of required literacy. While Fitzherbert limited the role of women to caring and feeding poultry and managing the house, he did not seem to expect that they needed less information than men to perform their respective tasks. From the first book:

Chapter 20.
Of three diuers kinds of Manure, and which
is the best.
There be diuers sorts of Manures, and first of those that bee worst, as Swines dunge, which Manure breedeth and bringeth vp thistles, the scourings of Hay barnes, or Corne barnes, which bringeth vp sundry weedes and quirks, and rotten Chaffe, which diuers vse, but brings little good. The shoueling of highwayes and streetes is very good, chiefly for Barley. Horse dunge is reasonable. The dunge of all maner of Cattel that chew the cudde is most excellent. Doues dunge for colde ground is best of all, but it must be spred very thinne.[44]

BOOKS ON GARDENING

Technical works on gardening form a large category of books that, in contrast to those on estate management, illustrate important differences in women's and men's literacy as well as developments in technical writing. That gardening was an important vocation is attested by the substantial numbers of books on the subject recorded by *The Short-Title Catalogue*. Gardening as a vocation was a male occupation, as suggested by Hill's *The Gardeners Labyrinth* (5 edns, 1577–1608), which included detailed instructions and process descriptions of gardening and drawings of gardeners performing these tasks. The workers in these drawings were males who appeared to be employed in large estate gardens. The book, composed of 2 parts – 179 pages and 37 chapters – was detailed in its approach to gardening, as illustrated by the following chapter titles: 'The rare inventions for the defence of Seedes committed to the earth, that they may not be endamaged by byrdes, not creepyng things. Chap. 16'; 'Of the tymes of wateryng beddes, and what manner of water ought to be vsed for Plants, with the inuentions of Vesselles. Chap. 24'; 'Of the remouing of plants, with the breaking and slipping of sundry sets. Chap. 25'.

While botany as a field of study would not begin to emerge until the end of the seventeenth century, the extensiveness of this work reveals the importance of gardening for the English, the development of gardening as a technology, and the detailed methods for its successful practice. The following excerpt illustrates the complexity of the style, with its allusion to Latin authorities, periodic sentence structure, precise phrasing of section heads:

> What care and diligence is requyred of euery Gardener
> to these, What increase & commodities well laboured
> earth yeeldeth. Chap. 2
>
> The husbandman or Gardiner, shall enjoy a most comodiouse and delectable garden, whiche both knoweth, can, and will orderly dresse the same: yet not sufficient is it to a Gardener, that he knoweth, or would the furtherance of the garden, without a cost bestowed, which the workes and labours of the same require: nor the will againe of the workman, in doing and bestowing of charges, shall finally analyse, without he haue both arte and skil in the same. For that cause, it is the chiefest poynt in euery facultie and busines, to understand and know what to begin and follow: as the learned *Columella* out of *Varroniauus Tremellius* apatly vtterth. The person whiche shall enioy or haue in a readinesse these three, and will purposedly or with diligence frame to him a well dressed Garden, shall after obtayne these two commodities, as utilitie and delight. . . . [45]

In contrast to this work for male readers, another gardening book, Lawson's *A New Orchard and Garden* (5 edns, 1617–37), was divided into two parts, one for men and one for women. Its content emphasized that gardening tasks were assigned according to gender, as the work's sub-title suggests: *The best way for planting, grafting, and to make any ground good. for a rich Orchard. . . With The Country Housewifes Garden for hearbes of common vse, their vertues, seasons, profites, armaments, variety of knots, mydals for trees, and plots for the best ordering of Groundes and Walks.* The first part of *A New Orchard and Garden*, written for men, like *The Gardeners Labyrinth*, approached each topic in detail. For example, Lawson devoted over two pages to Chapter V, 'Of the Forme'. The following excerpt illustrates the style used throughout the first part:

> The goodnesse of the Soyle, and Site, are necessarie to the well being of an Orchard simplie, but the forme is so far necessarie, as the owner shall think meete for that kinde of forme wherewith euery particular man is delighted, we leaue it to himselfe, *suumcuiq; pulchrum.* The forme that men like in generall is a square, for although roundness, be *forma perfectissima*, yet the principle is good where necessitie by art doth not force some other forme. Now for as much as one principiyall end of Orchards is recreation by walks, and universallie walks are streight, it followes that the best forme must be square, as best agreeing with streight walks: yet if any man be rather delighted with some other forme, or if he ground will not beare a square, I discommend not any forme, so it be formall.[46]

In this section on 'Forme', Lawson included a labelled drawing, a Renaissance technical description of the form of an orchard and garden with its mazes (see p. 53 below).

In contrast, *The Coventrie Housewifes Garden*, included as Part II of *A New Orchard and Garden*, was much shorter (twenty-three pages compared with fifty-seven for Part I). Each section was limited to a page or only a short paragraph. Some topics were discussed in both Part I and Part II, such as 'The Soyle', 'The Site', 'The Forme'. Those in the housewife's section were less detailed. For example, 'Chap. III. Of the Forme', was allocated only one paragraph:

> Let that which is said in the Orchards form suffice for a Garden in generall: but for speciall formes in squares, they are many, as there are devices in Gardiners braines. Neither is the wit and art of a skilfull Gardiner in this skillful point not to be commended, that can worke more variety for breeding of more delightsome choise, and of all those things, where the owner is able and bestrons to be satisfied. The number of formes, Mazes and knots is so great, and men are so diuersly delighted, that I leaue euery housewife to her selfe, especially seeing to set downe many, had been but to fil much paper; yet left depriue her of all delight and direction, let her view these few, choise, new formes, and note this generally, that all plots are square, and al are bordred about with Priuit, Raisins, seaberries, Roses, Thorne, Rosemarie, Bee-flowers, Hop, Sage, or such like.[47]

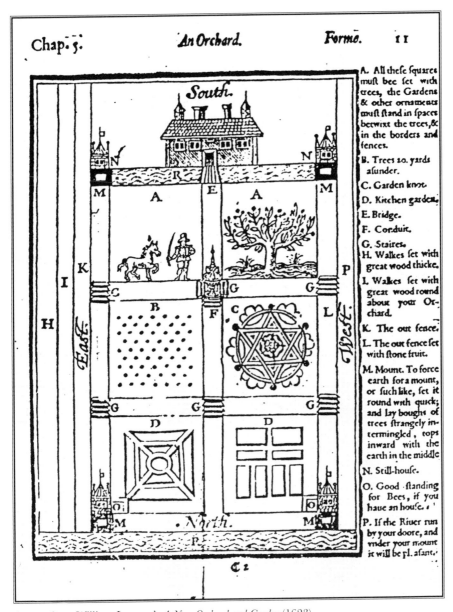

A page from William Lawson's *A New Orchard and Garden* (1623).

54   ELIZABETH TEBEAUX

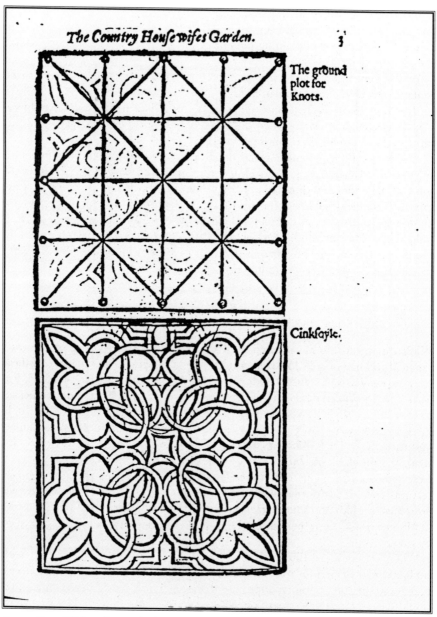

A page from William Lawson's *A New Orchard and Garden* (1623).

The accompanying drawing (see p. 54), gave configurations for mazes. A comparison of these two drawings would seem to indicate that women were in charge of designing and planting the mazes within the larger garden, which was the male gardener's province.

While the sections for men and women differed in extent of coverage, the sentence structures were similar. However, no Latin phrases were used anywhere in *The Coventrie Housewifes Garden*. This difference echoes the fact that during the Renaissance middle-class women did not receive education in Latin, which was taught in the all-male grammar schools.

A New Orchard and Garden, when compared to *The Gardeners Labyrinth*, also suggests that differences in gardening tasks were based on the physical strength some of these required. Women apparently pursued gardening on a smaller scale but still needed much of the knowledge required by full-time gardeners: knowledge of pests, means of planting various herbs, fruits and vegetables. Thus, reduction of information in *The Coventrie Housewifes Garden* may have been due to the diminished nature of women's work, as the level of the text itself does not reveal substantial differences in literacy.

TECHNICAL BOOKS BY WOMEN IN THE 1641–1700 PERIOD

While this discussion has focused on women's literacy as suggested by the wide range of technical books for women in the Renaissance, the relationship of these works to similar works published in the 1641–1700 period needs to be noted. *The Short-Title Catalogue* records no published technical books by women in the period 1475–1640. As Lynette Hunter reports in her study (see Chapter 4 below), only three women wrote 'how to' books on home medicine during the Renaissance, and these were not published until the 1650s. Two of these books, which are similar to the domestic 'how to' books written by Dawson, Platt, and Partridge, were directed to women who had the responsibility of caring for their families, servants and friends during illness. Elizabeth Grey's *A Choice Manual of Rare and Select Secrets* (1653) and Queen Henrietta Maria's *The Queen's Closet Opened* (1655), as Hunter notes, were the first books on home medicines and recipes published by women.

When we compare Elizabeth Grey's work, *A Choice Manual* (19 edns), with similar works written for women during the Renaissance, we notice that Grey's book contains more information about more topics, particularly topics that would have interested women. The writing style echoes that used by Partridge, Murrel, and Dawson, but is clearly superior to Dawson's in terms of narrative quality. The rugged style of Dawson, for example, contrasts with the more fluid one of Elizabeth Grey, whose writing shows the emergence of modern prose style.

From Dawson:

For to staunch bloud.
Take Bole armoniake, and Turpentine, and make a plaister, and lay it too, and take the mosse of the Vazelltree, and cast it into the wound and it will staunch foorthwith, and the longer that it is gathered the better it is. Also take a good peece of martimes Beefe out of the rouse, and heate it on Coales, and as hotte as yee may suffer it laye it threr to: also take the piece of leane salte Beefe, and let the Beefe bee of that greatnesse that it may fill the wounde, and lay it in the fire in the hotte ashes, til it be hotte through, and all hot thrust it in the wound, and binde it fast, and it shall staunch anon the bleeding, when a maister vaine is cut, and if the wound be large.[48]

From Elizabeth Grey:

For a sudden and violent bleeding at the nose.
Take an Egg-shell and burn it to a coal, then pulverize or beat it to a fine powder, and let the person snuff it up his Nostrils or take your two thumbs and press them hard against the Temples of the Bleeder, and you would admire how speedily it will divert the course of the blood. For those that are accustomed thus to bleed, let them make an ordinary Posset taking off the currd, let the juice of Liverwort beaten be added thereunto, and so drink morning and evening.[49]

Eight books of a similar nature were written by Hannah Woolley, who was a schoolmistress, governess and personal secretary of middle-class origins. Her books, all published during the 1670s, show a maturity of style – complex sentence structure within the loose style – along with sentences composed of additive clauses. Apparently assuming that her legitimacy as an author would be questioned, she opens with a short chapter explaining her qualifications for writing a guide book for women. In short, she provides a narrative resumé (see p. 57 below for the opening pages). Like many women, Woolley would seem to have felt the need to justify her qualifications for writing on her chosen topic.

As Patricia Crawford noted in her discussion 'Women's published writing 1600–1700', women 'were forced to write for publication because they knew that their experiences as women were different from those of men'.[50] One of Woolley's books, her 1675 work *The Gentlewomans Companion or, a Guide to the Female Sex*, illustrates her belief that her guide for women did differ in its point of view. However, Hannah Woolley clearly believed that her female readers would be able to handle the complex style and detailed discussion of the issues she presented. To judge by Smith and Cardinale's (1990) bibliography of women's writing in the

(10)

A short account of the life and abilities of Authoress of this Book.

I Would not presume to trouble you with any passages of my life, or relate my innate qualifications, or acquired, were it not in obedience to a Person of Honour, who engag'd me so to do, if for no other reason than to stop the mouths of such, who may be so maliciously censorious as to believe I pretend what I cannot perform.

It is no ambitious design of gaining a Name in print, (a thing as rare for a Woman to endeavour, as obtain) that put me on this bold undertaking; but the meer pity, I have entertain'd for such Ladies, Gentlewomen, and others, as have not received the benefits of the tythe of the ensuing Accomplishments. These ten years and upwards, I have studied how to repair their loss of time, by making publick those gifts which God hath bestow'd upon me. To be useful in our Generation is partly the intent of our Creation; I shall then arrive to the top of the Pyramid of my Contentment, if any shall profit by this following Discourse. If any question the truth of what I can perform, their trial of me I doubt not but will convince their infidelity.

The things I pretend greatest skill in, are all works wrought with a Needle, all Transparent works, Shell-work, Moss-work, also cutting of Prints, and adorning Rooms, or Cabinets, or Stands with them.

All kinds of Beugle-works upon Wyers, or otherwise.

All

(11)

All manner of pretty toyes for Closets.
Rocks made with Shells, or in Sweets.
Frames for Looking glasses, Pictures, or the like.
Feathers of Crewel for the corner of Beds.
Preserving all kind of Sweet-meats wet and dry.
Setting out of Banquets.
Making Salves, Oyntments, Waters, Cordials; healing any wounds not desperately dangerous.
Knowledg in discerning the Symptomes of most Diseases, and giving such remedies as are fit in such cases.
All manner of Cookery.
Writing and Arithmetick.
Washing black or white Sarsnets.
Making sweet Powders for the Hair, or to lay among Linnen.
All these and several things beside, too tedious here to relate, I shall be ready to impart to those who are desirous to learn.

Now to the intent I may increase your wonder, I shall relate how I came to the knowledg of what I profess. When I was fourteen years old, I began to consider how I might improve my time to the best advantage, not knowing at that age any thing but what reason and fancy dictated to me. Before I was Fifteen I was intrusted to keep a little School, and was the sole Mistress thereof. This course of life I continued till the age of Seventeen, when my extraordinary parts appear'd more splendid in the eyes of a Noble Lady in this Kingdom, than really they deserv'd, who praising my works with the appellation of curious pieces of

Hannah Woolley's *The Gentlewomans Companion* (1675).

seventeenth century, Hannah Woolley was one of the most prolific women writers and the most prolific provider of 'how to' books for women in the seventeenth century.

For example, Woolley's *Guide* contains more than 100 pages on conduct, proper bearing, fashion, recreation, marriage and management of servants, in addition to 60 pages of recipes, 100 pages of medicinal recipes and a final 100 pages focusing on more advice on managing servants. The work is not as well organized as works by Murrel and more particularly Partridge, who subdivided his books under types of food with separate headings for medical 'receipts', but better organized than Dawson's. We can almost see Woolley attempting to arrange her thoughts about areas for which women were responsible. The progression of the table of contents suggests that she wanted to be sure she included all the information that women might need to manage their lives. Ms Woolley states in 'The Epistle Dedicatory' that she has drawn from '*The Queens*

Closet; May's Cookery; The Ladies Companion; and my own *Directory and Guide*; Also, the second part of *Youth's Behaviour*' as well as other books she deemed proper and necessary.

Two other significant technical books written by women in the last half of the seventeenth century need to be mentioned: Jane Sharp's *The Midwives Book* (1671) and Elizabeth Cellier's *A Scheme for the Foundation of a Royal Hospital . . . for the Maintenance of a Corporation of Skillful Midwives* (1687). Elizabeth Cellier's *Scheme* is the first technical proposal written by a woman, a document that attracted fierce rebuttal by the College of Physicians. Ms Cellier then published an eight-page counterattack *To Dr. — An Answer to His Queries, Concerning the Colledg of Midwives* (1688) in which she justifies the skills of the midwives. Because they were women they were in a better position to judge the needs of women. Cellier argues from a broad feminist platform for the rights of women to continue to practise a profession in which women have dominated since before the golden age of Greek medicine.

Cellier's proposal is remarkable because it anticipates modern proposal format: introduction, statement of the problem, technical proposal in the form of an itemized list of needs and goals, argument for the plan, a method by which the plan would be paid for, and a conclusion that restates the merits of the proposal. The discourse in both of these works by Cellier (two of fifteen extant published items) shows superb command of both written English and argumentation.

Jane Sharp's *The Midwives Book* (1671), of which four editions are recorded by 1725, further underscores the problems that women were having in practising midwifery during the closing decades of the seventeenth century. Chapter 1 discusses the problems midwives faced due to their lack of formal medical education. She admits that women do not have the knowledge of medical terms that the physicians have, but she then states that the midwives possess the essential knowledge, that understanding 'hard words' is not important. This book, nearly 400 pages, suggests that Ms Sharp had read existing midwifery literature and brought together the information she deemed most important for the practising midwife.

As Crawford noted,[51] the number of books by women increased dramatically after 1640, but women's need to justify their competence, their right to publish in areas once considered the province of men, and their right to pursue midwifery as a profession all testify to the difficulties women faced in assuming new and active roles that surfaced during the Civil Wars in English society.

Smith and Cardinale's annotated bibliography of seventeenth-century women's writing effectively documents the rapid increase of published books by women after 1641. 'How to' books were well represented among these works which contained polemic and learned discussion on politics, theology, literature and even natural philosophy. Cookbooks written by women also started to appear. Perhaps the first collaborative cookbook, written and compiled by several women, appeared in 1653/4: *The Ladies Companion, or a Table furnished with sundrey sorts of Pies and Tarts . . . By Persons of Quality whose names are mentioned.* The ability of women to write as well as read had now taken a major step forward. Also evident is a growing confidence in what they chose to write and to publish.

TECHNICAL BOOKS AND ISSUES OF WOMEN'S LITERACY IN THE RENAISSANCE AND SEVENTEENTH CENTURY

This introductory study of technical books for and by women of the English Renaissance and the seventeenth century provides a microcosm for glimpsing (1) the emergence of technical writing in the first printed books in English; (2) the development of that writing as it reflected the growth of technology and the demise of the oral tradition; and (3) the development of literacy among women readers, the target audience for many of these books. Existing research has suggested that the numbers of women readers grew throughout the Renaissance and that men were generally afforded more opportunity to develop reading skills as the English grammar schools were limited to males. However, technical books, with their maturing style, and female target audience, provide a new perspective for tracking the growing literacy of women of the non-elite classes whose lives have often received less attention than those of women of the upper classes.

The relationship between the design of technical writing and the literacy level of its intended readers is a basic consideration for modern technical communicators; but the compelling fact, based on these Renaissance technical books, is that technical writing and literacy were equally intertwined during the sixteenth and seventeenth centuries. In addition, technical writing became more necessary for more people as the growth of knowledge made the dependence on its oral transmission less and less feasible. In adapting to the emergence of technology and the use of text to convey this technology to a widening audience, these early technical writers showed an impressive awareness of their *audience* – her content needs and her literacy level – and developed topics and chose their style accordingly. These numerous books also show the shift from poetic presentation to plain prose style with its emphasis on active-voice clauses, concrete verbs and nouns that reflected the knowledge level and needs of women readers.

The impressive numbers and editions of these works further reinforce Bennett's (1952) and Hull's arguments that the expansion of the book trade provides a revealing measure of the thirst for practical works, not just literary and historical works that would have appealed primarily to the upper classes. Hull noted that between 1475 and 1575, the 85 practical guides directed to women generated 290 editions.[52] As Bennett had stated earlier, printers knew that their economic success depended on the sale of books: 'The fifteenth century had seen the rapid growth of the manufacture of vernacular manuscripts to meet a great variety of needs, and from Caxton onwards, printers were aware of the desire of men and women for texts upon all kinds of practical matters.'[53] Crawford's work and then Smith and Cardinale's bibliography[54] allow us to see why women suddenly emerged as writers and to appreciate the ongoing difficulties they faced in daring to write and publish in genres in which they had remained silent until the middle decades of the seventeenth century. While Lynette Hunter argues that early women experimenters such as Elizabeth Grey wrote as a social activity, I would add the suggestion that these women also wrote what they knew and believed that other women needed to know. These early technical books by women indicate that they believed that their own perspective on women's needs, as they worked as domestic medical practitioners and home managers, was more appropriate than that of men.

Thus, technical writing as we know it today has a distinct and dynamic history that developed alongside the rich traditions of Renaissance and seventeenth-century literature. In both Renaissance and modern technical writing contexts, literacy as a demographic element cannot be separated from the character of technical writing as it emerged in both eras.

These technical books for women also show that from 1500 to 1700 an increasing number of women developed the ability to read printed texts which became more 'technical' and syntactically mature, and that such women apparently sought and achieved higher levels of literacy throughout this period. Technical guidebooks also reveal that women had significant responsibilities as manorial wives, and that these responsibilities may have influenced their desire and need to read as a means to learn to perform a variety of estate and household management tasks. Yet, these books also show that technologies persisted, such as needlework, that continued to be taught solely by oral transmission. Heavily used needlework books – such as *A Booke of Curious and strange Inuentions, called the first part of Needleworkes* (1596) and *A Book of Engraved Lace Patterns* (1605) – were composed solely of pages of exquisite drawings of lace patterns.

While the quality and extent of education for middle-class women of the sixteenth and seventeenth centuries have not been ascertained, the increasing numbers and sophistication of books for women clearly attest to the fact that women of all social levels, and particularly middle-class women readers, were learning to read. Perhaps many of the books for women allowed them the opportunity to learn reading skills beyond those received in the petty schools. The existence of large numbers of technical as well as social and religious 'how to' books supports the view that self-education through technical books was one of the most powerful forces at work in the English Renaissance.

Ultimately, while studies of records, diaries and literary works suggest that women were, on the whole, less literate than men, a study of technical books for women forces the assumption that a substantial number of women were readers and that women who did read did so with an expertise equal to that of men. This conclusion is substantiated by the sophistication of style and argument in technical books written by women after 1640. In short, these works do not suggest that middle-class women readers needed works that were particularly elementary in style or content at the close of the Renaissance. This observation further supports the position of Levy, Laqueur and Houston who consider that throughout the English Renaissance and the seventeenth century, literacy became incorporated into the structure of the popular culture.[55] Recognizing the importance of technical books for women shows that technical writing was very much a part of that culture, a part that enjoyed increasing demand leading to the emergence of technical writing as a distinct genre along with literature, religious polemic and books of political controversy.

Notes

1 Anglin (1980), Cressy (1980), Levy (1982).

2 Simon (1966), Stone (1964), Thomas (1986).

3 Bennett (1952), p. 20, Bennett (1965), pp. xiii–xvii, P. Clark (1976), Green (1979).

4 Wright (1931), Labalme (1980), Masek (1979), McMullen (1977), Bainton (1980), Bradford (1969).

5 Ezell (1987).

6 Hull (1982), p. 128.

7 Houston (1988), pp. 154–5.

8 Wrightson (1982), pp. 188–9.

9 Campbell (1983), p. 274.

10 Hull (1982), p. 138.

11 Camden (1975), p. 41.

12 Hirsch (1975), p. 11.

13 Ong (1982).

14 *Book of Cookery* (1500), n.p.

15 *Boke of Kervynge* (1508), n.p.

16 Murrel (1617), p. 4.

17 Hull (1982), p. 36.

18 *A closet* (1608), p. 4.

19 Houston (1988), p. 5. See also Wright (1958), Bennett (1952, 1965), Levy (1982), Lacquer (1976).

20 Lacqueur (1976), p. 255.

21 Wood (1639), p. 6.

22 *Ibid.*

23 O'Keefe (1990), p. 22, Ong (1982).

24 Slack (1979), p. 241.

25 *Ibid.*, pp. 239–43.

26 Elyot (1595), p. 95. See p. 252 for remedies.

27 Roesslin (1598), fol. xlviii.

28 Spencer (1927).

29 Unwin (1927).

30 Dale (1932–4), pp. 324–35.

31 Clark (1976), p. 101.

32 Todd (1985), Prior (1985), Clark (1976).

33 T. M. (1599), p. 55.

34 Stallenge (1609), p. B2.

35 Camden (1975), p. 44.

36 De Serres (1607), p. 25.

37 Wright (1958), p. 565.

38 Tusser (1580), n.p.

39 Tebeaux (1990).

40 Markham (1614), p. 18.

41 *Ibid.*, p. 41.

42 Hogrefe (1975), p. 59.

43 Fitzherbert (1598), Book 4, p. 149.

44 *Ibid.*, Book 1, p. 28.

45 Hill (1577), p. 4.

46 Lawson (1618), p. 12.

47 *Ibid.*, p. 2.

48 Dawson (1596), n.p.

49 Grey (1653), p. 32

50 Crawford (1985).

51 *Ibid.*

52 Hull (1982)

53 Bennett (1952), p. 54.

54 Crawford (1985) and Smith and Cardinale (1990).

55 Levy (1982), Houston (1988), Lacqueur (1976).

3

THOROUGHLY RESENTED? OLDER WOMEN AND THE MEDICAL ROLE IN EARLY MODERN LONDON

Margaret Pelling

Women in the early modern period are providing an increasingly important focus for exploring the interaction of stereotype and what might (without prejudice) be called *actualité*.[1] This process is vital for achieving a balanced view of women's contribution to medicine. Older women have a peculiar significance in this context, because of the strength of the stereotypes purporting to represent them. I have tried to explore some of these issues in recent work on physicians, gender, iconography and the caring role of older women, which I should like to cite as background and for further references bearing on this discussion.[2] In the present chapter, I shall take as my main source the records created by the College of Physicians of London in its attempts to control what it defined as irregular practice. However, I shall first present some iconographical material, by way both of setting the stereotypical context, and of underlining the links in the contemporary mind between women, old or of mature age, and medicine. The examples are from Dutch and Flemish material because the equivalent of genre painting hardly exists at this time for England. Since my case study is English, this is in a sense illegitimate, and it must also be admitted that most of my pictorial examples come from the mid-seventeenth century, just after the case study. This slight extension of boundaries can, I hope, be justified on the basis of the similarities and interrelationships between the two countries, including, during the sixteenth and seventeenth centuries, major exchanges of population. However, it is necessary also to bear in mind the differences, not least in social structure and pattern of urbanization – and, indeed, the factors which led to the existence of genre painting itself. Simon Schama's case for the peculiarity of Dutch culture is a persuasive one, and does, of course, make good use of pictorial material. Schama drew attention to the 'moral topography' represented by the wrinkled faces of old women in Dutch genre, but moved quickly on from this to consider the dichotomy between good and bad among younger women.[3]

A favourite contrast in Dutch painting was between youth and age. An example bridging historical and genre painting is a study by Rembrandt, possibly of Bathsheba at her toilet (see p. 65 below).[4] The young woman shows her flesh and holds flowers as a symbol of beauty and evanescence. The old woman crouching as she attends to the girl's feet shows features of age in the service of beauty: subordination, short sight, the performance of menial duties. However, she is at least free of the fatal temptations represented by Bathsheba. This contrast was not an uncommon one, especially where prostitution was being hinted at, but painters did of course show older women in their own right. Adriaen van Ostade (1610–85) has an old peasant woman leaning on her half door and chatting – a figure of the type recently celebrated by Marina Warner.[5] This woman has lost most of her 'femininity' in terms of appearance, but is defined by what she is doing. She is a reminder of the extent to which talk was seen as the woman's vice. However, Ostade's is not a negative image, although some social distance might be implied between observer and subject. This distance was greater in the work of Ostade's pupil, Cornelis Dusart (1660–1704), whose portrayals of peasants are closer to caricature (see p. 69 below). In one study he shows an old woman drinking; judging by her face, she does it habitually. Drinking is all she is doing, and she is not communicating with anyone. This can be seen as one view of the end of life, at least among the peasantry; it is worth thinking how far she approximates to the male equivalents who were more commonly depicted.[6] Contrasting with the work of both Ostade and Dusart are the portraits of older women in more prosperous households. Jan Lievens (1607–74), a close friend of Rembrandt, has an old woman reading; she looks comfortable, but shows the conditions of age: poor sight, thin or non-existent hair, sensitivity to cold.[7] Such images were perhaps intended to recommend to both young and old the best preparations for death – dignified acceptance, and the study of good works – although this woman has three books, rather than one Bible, possibly as a mark of burgher status.[8] She is alone, but self-sufficient and respectable, and not poor. She appears to be acquiring wisdom, if not actually wise already.

Older women also appear quite frequently in specifically medical contexts. Such images are part of a tradition of moral commentary of which genre painting was a development. Women appear as accomplices, and medicine as a subset of worldly folly and deceit.[9] Jan Steen (1625/6–79), painting in the middle of the seventeenth century, epitomizes the later history of the tradition of depicting folly associated with Breughel and Bosch.[10] Like many northern artists before him, Steen used the motif of a 'head-operation' to remove the 'stone' of stupidity. In one crowded scene including both sexes and most ages, an older female accomplice is centrally placed and actively assisting in the deceitful operation.[11] She appears to be gloating over the victim's foolishness and suffering, but then so do all the village observers. However, one could infer that while their turn might come to be victims, hers would not. Similar female participant/observers appear in paintings by the Flemings Adriaen Brouwer (1606–38) and David Teniers the Younger (1610–90), which seem to have as their

Rembrandt's *Study for Bathsheba*, etching (*c.* 1650).

background motifs the five senses (in particular, touch) and the ages of man. Socially, these figures seem to be between peasant and burgher; if there is an obvious male practitioner, he can be assumed to be a surgeon or barber-surgeon. Compared with Teniers' women, Brouwer's are rougher, gloat more obviously and are more obviously old. Although gloating observers of both sexes were regularly shown by way of underlining the folly of assuming exemption from the human condition, it is implied that the main participant/observer in 'medical' versions of these scenes was more likely to be a woman, normally an older woman, and that the humiliation for the patient was worse if it were a woman (most patients being male). The woman is not always unsympathetic, but is usually placed in a position implying knowledge or experience.[12]

Finally let us turn to a very specific genre, the 'doctor's visit' – recently discussed in great detail by Laurinda Dixon, who stresses interpretations focusing on hysteria or *furor uterinus*.[13] The elements and moods of different versions vary, but the constant features of the genre are the physician, the young girl as his patient, and the implication that the young girl is lovesick or pregnant. Almost as often there is a female attendant present, not always elderly but usually older than the sick girl (see pp. 78 and 81 below). There is much play on the theme of who realizes the nature of the girl's condition, and who does not – very often it is the doctor who does not. These pictures cannot be read off realistically in terms of status, dress or social relationships, if only because they use stereotypes from theatre. They do, however, reflect perceived attributes, as in satire. To take a 'straight' version first, one by Gabriel Metsu (1629–67) (see p. 73 below): the girl is centrally placed, she looks ill, her dog (emblem of dirt as well as of faithfulness) looks worried, the physician holding up the urine flask appears dignified and serious.[14] But this sobriety is balanced on the girl's left – the 'sinister' side – by a chamberpot, a urine basket, and a knowing old woman, whose gaze, directed at the doctor, is distinctly sceptical. It is the knowingness of the old woman, based on her experience and familiarity with the girl's body, which is crucial for the observer. The doctor almost looks a fool for not already being suspicious; on the other hand, his verdict will matter more than the old woman's, at least in the short term.

Steen (presumed to be the pupil of Ostade) produced many versions of this scene, most of them broad in tone. In one crowded example, the patient is hardly present: the focus is on the doctor obliviously writing his prescription, and the old woman leering knowingly into his face.[15] This old woman is intrusive rather than reticent, and her posture underlines the fact that the doctor has failed the test set for him. The old woman, on the other hand, is probably guilty of some kind of complicity leading to the girl's condition.[16] The message is underscored by the clyster held by the boy, the cupid over the door, and the picture of lovers on the wall. As in the Metsu version, the old woman approximates to the stock figure of Juliet's old nurse, and it would not necessarily be the case that even a burgher household would include a person of those duties and of that age. The old woman is representative rather than literal.[17]

Older women are presented as practitioners as well as participants or intelligent observers. The theme of the wages of sexual sin, which tends to pervade Dutch genre painting, also comes up in depictions of female practitioners.[18] In a painting by Quirijn van Brekelenkam (c. 1620–68) of a 'Kopster' or cupper, an older woman, yet again in spectacles, is bleeding a young girl dressed in the same fur-trimmed satin jacket as in the 'doctor's visit' paintings.[19] There is a candle to show evanescence, and possibly an owl in the cage to indicate folly; the bread in a basket on the table appears as payment in kind, but could also reflect a proverb about buns in ovens. Here, in contrast with the 'doctor's visit' scenes, it looks as if the woman practitioner knows (and the girl does not). This relatively subtle scene may be contrasted with the better-known, vulgar version involving a woman cupper, produced near the end of the century by Dusart.[20]

These examples are probably enough to show that, in spite of the richness of the genre depiction of medical scenes, the aim was in no way to depict the range or reality of medicine, just as, in the portraits of old women, realism is present but is in service to the moral message. The harping is on human folly, in particular sexual behaviour, and thereby the connections between old people, young people, and medicine. At the same time, such pictures would not work unless their content related to an existing set of attitudes, if not to daily experience. Certain features of older women come through very strongly – in particular their knowingness, their irrepressibility and even their ubiquity. Their knowingness is the more marked given that such women are rarely shown as having a social status equal to the other main characters present.

We now turn to a group of 'real' old women involved in medicine, whose reality is nonetheless also presented by a group of males of the emergent urban middle class: the physicians, many of whom are treated with even less respect by the Dutch painters than are the old women (albeit in the guise of theatrical figures).[21]

At a meeting of the College of Physicians of London held in January 1583, the Registrar noted that a discussion took place 'concerning the means by which we could prevent itinerant and inexperienced old women from practising medicine'.[22] The fellows at the meeting concluded that no one could more successfully deal with the matter than William Fleetwood, Recorder of the City of London. Fleetwood, of course, is best known for the reputation he gained through his *exposé* of the language, habits, categories and deceptions of the 'masterless men' of the period: the sturdy, vagrant, and begging poor. Fleetwood carried conviction by confirming contemporary belief in an underworld with its own organization and modes of operation, including the counterfeiting of disease.[23] Interestingly, the fulsome Latin letter which the college subsequently wrote to Fleetwood made no specific mention of women, referring merely to 'controlling a bold and ignorant multitude'; this may have been seen as a better

way of arousing Fleetwood's concern.[24] It is worth noting here the point, made
by Thomas, that of all age groups this period was most preoccupied with the
control of youth.[25]

The college wrote this letter at the beginning of its best-recorded and probably
most sustained attempt to control unlicensed medical practice in London. It did
not, of course, invent the idea that women, and old women in particular,
ignorantly intruded into medicine. This was a long-standing stereotype, which
occurs in previous legislation aimed at the regulation of practice or at the
suppression of abuses in a wide range of occupations. However, the records of the
college's attempts at prosecution offer what is probably a unique opportunity to
match the stereotype against reality – or, rather, that version of reality which the
college transcribed into its 'Annals' as a record of its side of a long series of semi-
legal confrontations. We shall also find evidence of another stereotypical view,
more annoying to the college than beneficial to women, but nevertheless
significant: that old women knew more, and did less harm, than academically
qualified physicians. Like the other, this stereotype does not necessarily survive
historical inspection, at least in so far as it presupposes a clear contrast between
men's and women's forms of practice.

The College of Physicians predated the Reformation, having been founded in
1518. It was designed by Henry VIII's physicians and their humanist associates
on the model of the medical colleges of the cities of Catholic Italy. Although it
pursued irregular practitioners earlier in the century – especially during the
epidemic decade of the 1550s – the college's records are limited and retrospective
until *c.* 1580. Over the ninety-year period from 1550 to 1640, the college pursued
a total of 714 different practitioners, some of whom it never even saw, and others
of whom it came to know only too well.[26] These practitioners are called irregular
for convenience, but a more accurate term would be non-collegiate, since a small
but significant proportion (7.3 per cent) were well enough qualified to go on to
become members of the college.[27] In other words, the college was an extremely
exclusive body, as well as being very small in terms of the population it served.
The population of London *c.* 1600 was approximately two hundred thousand;
the average membership of the college between 1580 and 1640 was thirty-one
(fellows only), of which up to half a dozen could be members *ex officio* as royal
physicians.[28] It must be stressed that, its small size notwithstanding, the college
was as concerned with illicit practice as with malpractice. It was as important to
its argument to establish that a practitioner habitually practised physic without
the college's permission, as it was to prove that he or she practised incompetently.
Proceedings against the allegedly incompetent (or deceitful) were, however, often
initiated by others, who hoped to find in the college a useful weapon in a battle
already started either against, or by, a practitioner. It should be emphasized that
the relationship between a patient and a practitioner tended at this period to be
contractual, albeit often verbal. Actions between the two parties, especially with

Cornelius Dusart's *Old Woman Drinking.*

respect to debt, were not uncommon. A major proportion of the college's irregular opponents were respectable surgeons or apothecaries who were not, in the college's view, entitled to extend their activities by practising inward medicine.

For women, of course, the situation was rather different. The number of those having formal occupational standing in a guild or company, even as the widow of a freeman, was already very small; women were automatically excluded from the universities, and therefore from the college; they had no institutional backing with which to defend their practice.[29] Many of the women pursued by the college illustrate an obvious paradox with respect to the history of female practitioners, which is that they were the least visible, but probably also the most ubiquitous. The first port of call in times of illness was, as it still is, the family or household. It is true that men were extremely concerned about both their own health and that of their friends and family, and that this concern readily slid into forms of practice, first within and then outside the circle of friendship and kinship, in a way which is more usually seen as typical of the work of women.[30] Nonetheless, it appears to be a historical constant that the bulk of health care – in particular what would now be called primary care – was left to the responsibility of women. The richest sources about individual women tend, predictably, to be the letters, diaries and recipe books kept by noblewomen and the wives of the gentry.[31] Such sources, which most often reflect rural conditions, are prone also to exaggerate the extent to which women's practice was a private or household concern, connected with avoiding the dangers of idleness, or with *noblesse oblige*. With the college records, much less is usually known about each individual, but the women concerned represent a broader and lower social range, providing rare glimpses into practice by women both below the level of the gentry and in an urban setting. Although often operating at modest levels, these women are also closer to the 'professional model' of the practitioner in that they were paid in money or goods for their services.[32] It is worth simply drawing attention to the existence of such women, since one historian at least (De Blécourt) has described the public role of the woman healer in this period as a myth.[33] In addition, the college evidence provides images of interrelationships: not just those of the practitioners themselves, but those between patients, patrons, servants, relatives, spouses, strangers and acquaintances. It is possible to gain, at least for London, some idea of whether or not the world of women's illness and health care was a 'separate sphere' from that of men, in the way that midwifery was still almost exclusively a female concern. A major issue which intersects with the issue of gender in this period, and one already suggested by the college's letter to Fleetwood, is the extent to which the problem of women practitioners was primarily a problem of poverty.

Of the total number of irregulars pursued by the college over the ninety-year period, 110 were women (15.4 per cent). Given that medicine was increasingly being structured in male terms, if not practised in male terms, this is a very substantial proportion. Some, like Mrs Paine, were highly visible, and others, like Mother Flat Cap, were hardly visible at all, which led to marked differences in the extent of confrontation with the college. Nevertheless, the proportion of women among the irregulars, and the proportion of college attention devoted to them, did not vary greatly from year to year. That is, the numbers summoned after 1583 do not seem to bear any relation to sudden scares about the influence of women in particular. It seems obvious that the college's group could not be representative, let alone comprehensive, with respect to the numbers of women likely to be practising in London at the time. In 1560, the surgeon Thomas Gale, on a cross-sectional or snapshot basis, estimated that there might be sixty female practitioners active in London at that time, that is, about twice as many as there were college fellows half a century later. Finlay estimates the population of London in 1550 to have been seventy thousand; this gives a ratio of female practitioner to population of more than 1:1,200.[34] Easier to compare with the college figures are longitudinal figures for England's second city, Norwich, which suggest a minimum of twenty-six female practitioners over the period 1550–1640 for a population not exceeding seventeen thousand, less than a tenth of the size of London in mid-period (some two hundred thousand).[35] The ratio of female practitioner to population in Norwich suggested by this is 1:650. Supposing that Norwich and London had the same proportion of female practitioners to population (even though London appears, on our limited evidence, to have had a greater proportion of female to male practitioners), we can roughly estimate that there may have been about three hundred women practising in London in the ninety-year period (1:650 of 200,000), of whom the college failed to notice about two-thirds.

    The college had, in fact, no comprehensive source of information about practitioners, male or female; like other areas of the early modern state, it was heavily dependent upon informers, although it seems rarely to have used the semi-professional variety. Some women it knew about by hearsay; some, as already indicated, were reported by aggrieved patients or patients' friends, as instanced by the complaint of the 'wife of Edward Bate' against 'a certain old widow called Austen'. Austen confessed to years of practice in London and to having given purges to 'a hundred or more men'.[36] Some women were detected because they put up bills or advertisements on their houses. For example, Hester Langham of Fenchurch Street 'had fixed a bill on her door in which she offered a certain powder for sale against chlorosis, together with a certain type of diet'. Langham claimed that this was done not by her but by her husband as part of his regular practice, and that he had been practising in this way since before their marriage.[37] The college also pressured irregulars who were already under scrutiny to inform on other irregulars, and some women did this; it would be one way of suppressing the local competition, but on at least some occasions it seems

to have been offered as a defence – that is, that what the accused woman had
done was also done by a great many others, even in the immediate
neighbourhood.[38] Members of the college, especially those who were not full
members, were constantly exhorted to report on irregulars, and new members
seem to have improved their welcome by performing this role. The numbers of
women are too small for any obvious pattern to emerge, although some instances
are suggestive: the famous surgeon John Woodall, for example, seems to have
informed upon a female practitioner who was a near neighbour and probably
therefore a nuisance to him.[39]

The college could, of course, only concern itself with areas of practice which
might be defined as physic; however, this could be seen as more likely to include
than to exclude women, since physic, or internal medicine, included the vast grey
area of overlap between medicines and food, in which women had an established
role. One example of this is the college's campaign against the selling of diet
drinks and purging ales.[40] Whether or not the offering of a purgative substance
constituted the practice of physic could be very much in the eye of the beholder.
The college gained some moral advantage in its campaign of interference
because of the connection between drastic purgation and abortion. Similarly,
women could colourably be accused of inspecting urine, another of the
physician's definitive functions, because of the use of this technique in detecting
pregnancy, even though pictorially this role tended to be ascribed to men. One
irregular who was assertive about inspecting urine to detect pregnancy, Mrs
Woodhouse, made the interesting claim that she was wrong only four in a
hundred times.[41]

With respect to the women irregulars as individuals, the college was better at
describing them than at identifying them. The women's names have rather less of
the tendency to Shakespearean stereotype than is characteristic of the college's
account of the male irregulars, nor do they sound particularly exotic. Among the
most striking are Elizabeth Arden, Christiana, Maria Dolebery, Mother Flat Cap,
Mrs Joan Gabitus, Mrs Susanna Gloriana, Alice Leevers, Mrs Jane Phoenix, Mrs
Pock, Mrs Thomasina Scarlet, Mrs Scissor, Mrs Sweting, Goody Wake. By
contrast with other legal proceedings of the time, the college did not record ages,
even approximately, except in the case of some accounts of patients. It did,
however, describe at least 10 of the 110 female irregulars as old. No such age-
related descriptions are given for other age groups, though women were also
described as poor, little, ignorant, bold, blind and stubborn. Very occasionally, a
stronger face-to-face impression was given: one was 'aged, with a long face', and
another was a 'demented old wife'. These descriptions can be deceptive in social
terms: it may be noted in passing that the demented old wife, Alice Leevers, also
described as utterly ignorant of medicine, had to be treated with leniency because
she was protected by Lord Hunsdon.[42] With respect to the normal employments
of these women, one might not expect the college to be particularly informative,

Gabriel Metsu's *The Patient and the Doctor* (*c.* 1665).

since women were not legally and politically defined by their occupation in the way that men were.[43] One of the reasons why the information in the 'Annals' on actual practice by women is so valuable is that in most records women are described in terms of their marital status, with minimal reference to their occupations.[44]

Not surprisingly, the college described a number of the female irregulars simply as 'empirics', since this was the case it was trying to make, but it also identified four more as midwives, one as an alewife, another as the ex-servant of a glover, and others as a nurse (likely to be a children's nurse), a 'keeper' (the equivalent of a sick-nurse-*cum*-landlady), a matron of St Bartholomew's, and a superintendent of boys in a hospital.[45] One might have expected the college to be more informative about the women's husbands, if any, since this was the accustomed means of personal definition. In London, as historians have reasons to know, a name – even a name and a parish – was not enough for certain identification: the man's occupation was often necessary as well, even within one parish. Moreover, a husband was, in theory, legally responsible for his wife's actions, although possibly not if he was unaware of what she was doing.[46] Thus one husband, a grocer, excused himself to the college by claiming that his wife was selling pills without his knowledge.[47] Male relatives and even neighbours could be made liable for the woman's response to summonses, or for bonds for her good behaviour. In spite of these factors, the college recorded little about women practitioners' male relatives. One husband was a joiner, another a tailor, another a broker; further up the social scale, one was a minister, and another a king's musician. A few more husbands were surgeons and apothecaries. This lack of information points above all to the college's isolation from the civic organization of London, and to the limits of its contact with city life. More speculatively, it might also point to an unconscious tendency on the part of the college to see women as figures in their own right. It might be supposed, on the basis of stereotypes, that most of the women would be widows; interestingly, the college was not much more assiduous in recording marital status than it was in identifying husbands. More women were described as poor than as widows. A high proportion were given no marital status at all.[48]

At this point two examples can be given to illustrate the range of types of female practitioner. Note, however, that neither is typical: both were under observation by the college for long periods. Mrs Paine was first brought to the college's notice in 1607, by the Beadle of the Barber-Surgeons' Company. The beadle had somehow obtained a letter from Mrs Paine to a gentlewoman of Westminster, Judith Conert, agreeing to cure her son (aged thirteen) for 20 marks – a very considerable sum of money, well over £10 in contemporary terms. Mrs Paine had given the boy strong purges and vomits as preparatory medicine, anointed him nearly all over with a mercuric compound for three days, and sweated him for nine days on hot tiles to produce salivation. The boy had later died. His treatment suggests that he was thought to have syphilis, or a condition approximating to it. The mother alleged that Mrs Paine professed medicine and had many patients.[49] She apparently had an assistant called Rolfe, and claimed a business arrangement whereby she acted under the instructions of a well-known physician, Thomas Bonham.[50] She was not the only female practitioner to claim to work under the aegis of a physician: one even claimed to have learnt her medicine from a fellow of the college.[51] The case of Mrs Paine dragged on for several years. On one occasion the college recorded that she had sent two 'absurd' letters excusing herself. In 1615 someone told the college that the Archbishop of Canterbury had said that a Mrs Weinman had derived more good from Mrs Paine's treatment 'then from all the physitians'. The college felt obliged to take this up with the archbishop.[52] Its sensitivity to this piece of hearsay evidence is partly a measure of the college's sense of vulnerability, especially to disparagement among the elite, but also reflects contemporary convictions as to the power of speech, convictions which were important for attitudes to women. The last entry relating to Mrs Paine comes in 1623, sixteen years after the first. An apothecary was accused of making physic for her: he 'scorned' this, not denying that it happened but saying that it was not he but his neighbour who did it.[53] Mrs Paine clearly had good connections in London, socially as well as medically, and was probably literate.

Mrs Thomasina Scarlet, on the other hand, who first came before the college in 1588, admitted that she could not read, although she still managed to obtain a letter from 'some people of rank', requesting the college to release her from prison. She claimed to have given medical advice to at least a hundred people. Even though the college was able to order her imprisonment, Mrs Scarlet still refused either to abstain from practice, or to give any bond to that effect. She confessed to treating patients, even children, with mercury ointment and another poisonous heavy metal, antimony. Her husband, meanwhile, told the college of a Mrs Sharde, who had given purgatives to induce abortion. In 1610, twenty-two years after her first encounter with the college, Mrs Scarlet (by then described as extremely old) promised to give up practice. Nonetheless, she was summoned again a few months later, after which there is no further record.[54]

Mrs Scarlet, for whatever reason, was clearly dedicated to her own form of medical practice. Her husband's action suggests that she drew a distinction between herself and those whose practice she saw as indefensible. It is not clear what her husband did, or whether they were poor. In the case of other women, it is evident that they practised medicine by way of supporting their households, which could include a husband. One of these, defended by Queen Elizabeth through the agency of her minister Walsingham, was Margaret Kennix, an 'ignorant foreign woman' living in Seacoal Lane. Walsingham described her as a poor woman, with an 'espetiall knowlege' of simples which God had given her 'to the benefit of the poorer sort, and cheefly for the better maintenaunce of her impotent husband and charge of family, who wholy depend of the exercise . . . of her small Talent and Craft'.[55] This was probably a calculated defence, drawing upon a range of social, religious and occupational references, possibly including the so-called 'Quacks' Charter' of 1542–3.[56] Another practitioner, Alice Stanford, unusually noted as aged eighty, said that 'she had no other means of supporting herself and her family and that she had practised medicine throughout her whole life and was even now still practising'. The college was lenient 'because of her poverty and particularly her age'. Four years later this 'old woman of a stubborn nature' was still practising, even though first her son and then her son-in-law had entered into bonds on her behalf.[57]

None of these female practitioners, even Margaret Kennix, quite fits the stereotype of the wandering, isolated old crone, gathering her medicines from the hedgerows, excluded from the cash economy, and indeed cut off from society except for her dubious practice. Instead, these female irregulars should rather be seen in the context of evidence from poor populations in other urban settings, which suggests that older women were more likely to be working than older men; more likely than is the case now to have young dependants in their households; and somewhat more likely than younger women to have a recognizable occupation. These older, bread-winning women provide a contrast with the largely home-based figure of the wife's mother who makes herself available to the younger working-class generation, co-resident or otherwise, which is familiar from twentieth-century sociology and also from the work of Anderson for nineteenth-century industrial towns.[58] Many of the male irregulars, especially the better educated, practised in London on a piece-meal basis by way of supporting themselves while they were in the capital on business. It seems likely that the female irregulars, by contrast, were more likely to be resident in London, so that female practice, although less visible, was possibly more stable. Both Roper and Marland have also noted instances of women healers and midwives laying claim to decades of practice; this could be seen as a self-justifying tactic, or as a lack of numeracy, or both, but it has some right also to be taken literally.[59] As against the idea of stable residence, it should be noted that even the elderly poor migrated from place to place if they had to, and that the constant inflow of immigrants to London must have included subsistence migrants in the older age groups.[60]

As for the hedgerows, it is interesting, though hardly conclusive, that there is no evidence that any female practitioner was also one of the herbwomen who supplied the capital.[61] Rather, the evidence suggests that the female irregulars in London were just as likely to buy their medicines, or at least the ingredients, from apothecaries, and that they were fully involved in applying the drastic, novel remedies based on metals which were being used against unpleasant new diseases, in particular venereal disease. This was reflected in a plea by the college to the crown in 1632 for an edict banning grocers, apothecaries, druggists or chemists from selling poisonous substances to 'any poor woman or the meaner sort of people . . . but only to those who are willing to give their names and publicly reply regarding the item purchased'. The context was a poisoning case in which the practitioners, the accused and the patient/victim were in fact all male, with the exception of a female shopkeeper, Mrs Bacon, from whom the accused allegedly bought mercury sublimate, saying that it was for engraving knives.[62] The stereotype of women as poisoners overlapped in this period with a similar stereotype about doctors.[63]

Much of the practice of the female irregulars resembled that of the London barber-surgeons, including their encroachment into physic and, to some extent, their treatment of women and children. Given that London represented a highly diversified economy with a well-developed service sector, including medicine, it might be expected that female practitioners would have been limited to specialized areas to do with the disorders specifically of women and infants. There are examples which do give this impression, involving female practitioners, mothers, maidservants and young children: one is Joan Thumwood, who sought to excuse herself to the college on the basis of only treating children and infants. Interestingly, however, members of the Barber-Surgeons' Company joined her husband in pleading her cause.[64] The 'women's realm' effect was to some extent reinforced by the college's own attitudes: the request of James Blackbourne, for example, for a licence to practise in diseases of women was considered 'most unsuitable and impudent'. Blackbourne claimed to have practised for ten years, including administering 'a powder to ease childbirth', and, later, to have a licence to treat women's diseases from the Barber-Surgeons' Company. The college also disapproved of bachelors treating women's complaints.[65] In general, women in London did not practise only among women or children. Many women practitioners did make relatively modest claims to specialized forms of practice, which, they felt, in no way justified the hostility of the college. That is, they dealt with only one kind of ailment or gave only one kind of treatment and did not pretend to anything else. However, this was also true of many male irregulars and may have been an attempt to invoke a common law right to freedom of occupation. Many of the female irregulars appear to have practised in a manner reflecting the new problems and new opportunities of what was to become by 1750 Europe's largest city. Clearly, they learnt by informal methods; but it cannot be assumed from this that they were necessarily more ignorant than the bulk of the male practitioners who were active in the capital, since most of these also learnt by informal methods, if among these one includes apprenticeship.[66]

What happened to practice by women in London in the course of the seventeenth century is by no means clear. Historians continue to debate Alice Clark's thesis, first put forward as early as 1919, that there was a major decline in opportunities for women during the seventeenth century with the rise of capitalized industry and the decline of the domestic system of production. It is interesting to note, as Clark's later editors have observed, that she made

One version of Jan Steen's *The Physician's Visit* (*c*. 1665).

approving references to the position of women in the Netherlands, in spite of her general critique of the early modern acceleration towards capitalism.[67] Like many middle-class commentators from Adam Smith onwards, Clark saw the 'rise of the professions' as a semi-autonomous development, for which the seventeenth century was also a watershed. She felt that women lost ground as the formal knowledge base of occupations increased, because they were excluded from most types of formal education. This particularly applied to experimental science, and areas in medicine such as anatomy. Later historians have modified Clark's view primarily in the direction of denying that there ever was a 'golden age' for women in which their work was seen as of equal value to that of men, even in the domestic context.[68] Instead of Clark's single irreversible shift – or the opposing view, that industrialization transformed life for women – historians now point to the tendency of women to move in and out of the economy according to the vulnerability of established economic structures and the need for cheap labour or services. They also point to continuities of difference between men's work and women's work, such as the tendency for women's work to be locally based, general and flexible, while men's work is specialized and structured, with the likelihood of a wider geographic network. Medicine is a particularly complex and interesting test case for these arguments, for a number of reasons. On the one hand, more is claimed for the knowledge base in medicine than in most other occupations, and this was a strategy fully embraced by the London college from the time of its foundation. It is also a strategy which was eventually extremely successful, although medicine's acquisition of status came much later than was the case with the other professions, and its achievement of an effective knowledge base later still. On the other hand, the college's Galenic system of belief was under challenge from soon after the college's foundation. Moreover, medicine can be seen as inextricably tied to the domestic context and, at least to some extent, as a natural extension of the roles constantly attributed to women. This helps to account for the fact that medicine took so much longer to establish itself as a profession than either the law or the Church.

What, then, of the college's attitudes to old women? We have seen that some women practised all their lives, that few were noticeably itinerant and that fewer than one in ten of the female irregulars were described by the college at any time as old. It can be assumed that if the college was biased in its search at all, then it would be looking for old women in particular. Wrigley and Schofield estimate that, over the period in question, between 7.6 per cent and 8.3 per cent of the population was aged sixty and over – that is, about half the proportion of elderly people that was found in this country in the 1950s. Wrigley and Schofield's estimates are based primarily on rural populations. In poor populations, especially in towns, the proportion of elderly, and particularly of elderly women, could be rather higher.[69] Allowing for the fact that medicine was a means of support for poor women and their families, it appears that the proportion of elderly women among the female irregulars diverged little from the proportion in the population as a whole.

In terms of contemporary attitudes, however, things might have looked very different. The proportion of women to men in towns was apparently increasing from the later fourteenth century onwards, only to decline again, at least in London, by the later sixteenth century, as population structure shifted and economic opportunities for women became increasingly restricted.[70] Even so, in the mid-seventeenth century one of the alleged fallacies which the pioneering demographer John Graunt set out to disprove was that women outnumbered men in London by three to one.[71] One possible reason for this 'urban myth' was that women without men, especially older women, tended to be seen as a major part of the burden of dependency which was measured, from the late sixteenth century onwards, by the compulsory poor rate. This is a point which has been made by Thomas, among others, in respect of witchcraft allegations, primarily with reference to rural areas.[72] As it seems to have been very rare for even an old man to live on his own (and there were fewer of them), older women living alone were probably more obtrusive than might be supposed.[73] The Dutch artists were possibly, in part, responding to this conspicuousness. The notion of old women as peculiarly dependent does seem to be part of the ambivalence in the college's actual treatment of elderly female irregulars. The college certainly had some imprisoned, like Thomasina Scarlet, but if the old woman was submissive (as Mrs Scarlet was not), she could be leniently treated on the grounds of her being poor, little and old, and her practice could be (to some extent) winked at, just as old men who followed other occupations illegally were tolerated by the guilds and companies because their trade was small and essential for their support. However, in such cases dependency represented a way out for male authority, rather than something to be resented. In terms of the college's view of itself, the poor little old woman, however burdensome, was doubtless easier to stomach than the activities of the women, old or otherwise, who were protected by powerful patrons.[74]

It could also be argued, perhaps, that it was rather too soon for the provisions of the Poor Law to have induced a particular prejudice as to the dependency of old women, even though the Poor Laws of 1598 and 1601 were a codification of earlier practice. Generally, it could be concluded that female independence was at least as worrying to early modern authorities as was dependence. The specific timing of the college's first expressed concern about old women – the 1580s – suggests a more specific explanation, which also points to the ambivalence of contemporary attitudes.

In general, the college's level of activity against irregulars can be shown to be closely tied to the rise and fall of plague epidemics in London. College fellows left London during plague periods as a matter of course, but they were well aware that by doing so they damaged their reputations and lost ground to the

Another version of Jan Steen's *The Physician's Visit* (*c.* 1665).

apothecaries, the surgeons and the (other) irregular practitioners who stayed behind. Consequently the college tended to increase its pressure on irregulars at the first sign of an epidemic, and then to make even greater efforts against them when plague had died down, to cancel out the inroads made while the college had been away. Female irregulars were included in this, but the college may have seen a further threat in the role given to – or, to some extent at least, forced upon – older women in measures taken against plague at the parish level. This was first put in place in the late 1570s and early 1580s. The searchers of bodies – those responsible for identifying cases of plague – were women, but so also were many of those appointed to locate or look after the sick. These women may indeed have been selected partly because they were poor and expendable, but stress was also laid upon their maturity and experience. They were to be 'honest and discreet matrons', or 'sober ancient women'. This ambivalence was shared by the college, which may have been trying partly to counterbalance the tendency of plague to create new or more active practitioners, and partly to convey to the authorities that old women, although useful in certain circumstances, were not without their dangers.[75]

What, finally, can be said about these women in relation to the proposed 'crisis of misogyny' in the late sixteenth and seventeenth centuries? Although some have argued that the witchcraft trials were too sporadic to have had any sustained effect, and that in any case the English experience was atypical, the experience of older women has received attention largely in this context.[76] Similarly, women healers have become hostages in a debate between feminist historians and their critics. Hence, in part, the continued stress on hedgerow medicine, and on healing (or cursing) by words or charms. The lonely old witch on the edge of village life is taken to represent misogyny in the countryside; in towns, the role of victim is assigned to the young woman found guilty of infanticide.[77] The lesser-known example of plague nursing certainly shows that older women in towns could be used as scapegoats, or seen as behaving in a predatory (and independent) manner contrary to the self-sacrificial role assigned to them. Generally, however, the older women prosecuted by the college do not fit the witchcraft stereotypes very well. Some practised what might be called women's medicine, or folk medicine: many others did not. The case records certainly show a special alertness on the part of the authorities to the use of charms, an emphasis arising from a concern with religious deviance, but also consonant with contemporary belief in the power of words and in women's tendency to abuse them. However, the London evidence shows that urban women were as likely to be using purging ales or heavy metals as charms or herbs.[78] Their patients were drawn from a broad range of social classes.

As a group, these women are of particular interest not only for their own sakes, but also because they are being constructed for us through the spectacles of the humanist male intellectual, just as the Dutch women in genre paintings were being seen by male artists of largely burgher status. Using mainly continental evidence, Horsley suggested that the peasantry were quite capable of distinguishing between those who could cause, and those who could cure, illness, and that it was the intellectuals and bureaucrats who either could not draw this distinction or sought to blur it. Horsley's interpretation, as well as the related views of Monter, Estes and Joan Kelly, suggests a defensive aggression on the part of the humanist-inspired intellectual class, and it is certainly difficult sometimes to resist the impression that the still-Italianate college represented, or rather represented itself as, nascent middle-class rationalism at odds with the subjective world view shared by the highest and lowest classes.[79] However, although the college spent an inordinate amount of energy in pursuing irregulars, its proceedings against old women show little of the sporadic witch-hunting fervour that one might expect, even in England. Far from being the best illustration of witchcraft prosecution as an attempt to suppress the social roles of women, medicine in this case shows that the role of older women in society was complex and ambivalent, both in terms of lived reality and in terms of attitudes.

This does not mean, however, that the college was not distinctly queasy on the subject of gender, or that it was exempt from the contemporary climate of misogynistic feeling. As I have tried to show elsewhere, the college found itself in a set of difficulties arising from status and gender disadvantages, which were often only increased by its attempts to compensate for them.[80] These difficulties arose directly from the adverse stereotypes of women and women's work encouraged by early modern urban society. The college was either structurally isolated from sources of male authority or in a highly subservient role in relation to such sources. In addition the work, behaviour, associations and perceived functions of collegiate physicians necessarily overlapped with the world of women. Elsewhere I have taken this further to suggest that such ambivalence was reflected even in the structure of the families of origin of physicians and of the families they subsequently created, or rather failed to create, themselves. Collegiate physicians were, to put it baldly, close to women whether they liked it or not, and to some extent shared their disadvantages.[81] They were also gerontocratic themselves, and stereotypically attracted to rich older widows. I am not suggesting, of course, that older men were generally likely to identify with older women. However, there is some evidence that the post-menopausal woman was not seen in the early modern period as the totally useless, physiologically disabled being that she apparently became in the course of the eighteenth century.[82] The cold and insatiable lustfulness attributed to witches, as to the devil himself, has been seen largely as society's revenge on women who made sexual demands but who were no longer fertile. However, it can also be seen as an approximation in the older woman to the condition of men.[83]

Galenic physicians were best placed to view the post-menopausal woman as leaner, warmer, dryer, stronger and altogether healthier than her younger self, especially if she was or had been married. Having reached this state, she was, as they knew, likely to live longer than a man, and in addition she could be both experienced and knowledgeable. These 'manly-hearted' stereotypes are made explicit in the prescriptions for the ideal midwife laid down in town regulations on the continent.[84] One such strong-minded midwife facing the college was Mrs Elizabeth Hales, who contradicted a physician's directive, pronouncing firmly that 'none of her women weare ever lett blood, thoughe they weare in feavers'.[85] One could, finally, speculate that it is the practice of medicine by *younger* women which the college was least willing to recognize. Older women, in contemporary terms, could be easy targets; they could be made to look poor and pitiful; they could be opinionated and need controlling: but, on the other hand, they were at least more like men, and perhaps also were, in the minds of the physicians, a reminder of their own formative experiences.

Notes

1 This chapter is based on a paper first given in Oxford in June 1990. Later versions were given at Gresham College in October 1995, and at All Souls College, Oxford, in February 1996. I should like to thank those present for their comments, particularly Emma Smith. I should also like to acknowledge the assistance of Frances White in the preparation of this chapter.

2 M. Pelling (1996a), pp. 101–33; Pelling (1996b), pp. 221–51; Pelling, 'Older Women: Household, Caring and Other Occupations in the Late Sixteenth-Century Town', in my, *Poverty, Medicine and Urban Society in England 1500–1700* (forthcoming c).

3 S. Schama (1988), chap. 6, esp. pp. 430–3.

4 This is reproduced in Pelling (1996b), plate 10.11. It is one of several studies by Rembrandt of this theme.

5 Reproduced, with two similar versions by Ostade showing women of middling years, in P. Sutton (ed.) (1990), pp. 222–3. Warner (1995), esp. chap. 2.

6 This is reproduced in *John G. Johnson Collection: Catalogue of Flemish and Dutch Paintings* (Philadelphia, 1972), catalogue no. 529, p. 318. On Ostade and Dusart, see Sutton (1984), catalogues 89–94, 41.

7 This is reproduced in *John G. Johnson Collection. Catalogue of Flemish and Dutch Painting* (Philadelphia, 1972), catalogue no. 487, p. 231. On Lievens, see S. Slive (1995), pp. 100–2 *et passim*.

8 Cf., however, the study by Gerrit Dou, the pupil of Rembrandt, of an old woman in furs reading an illustrated Bible: Slive (1995), p. 103.

9 See Pelling (1997) in Loudon (ed.) (1997).

10 For access to some of the writing on Steen, see Sutton (1984), catalogues 102–10; L. S. Dixon (1995).

11 This is reproduced as 'Het keisnijden' in J. A. van Dongen (1967), Afb. 185.

12 For further discussion with reference to Brouwer and Teniers, see Pelling (1996b).

13 Dixon (1995), esp. Chapt. 2.

14 This is reproduced in Dixon (1995), plate 2. On Metsu, see Sutton (1984), catalogues 70–2.

15 Reproduced in Dixon (1995), fig. 66.

16 In other versions by Steen, the doctor is also a complicit figure in terms of sexual suggestion. In one, the doctor leans and leers while the old woman holds (and seems more concerned about) the flask of urine: Pelling (1996a), pp. 111–13, plate 5.1. For similar examples see Dixon (1995), plates 1, 5, figs 38, 65.

17 For Dixon (and others) this figure lacks interest. That the older woman is intended to be the mother of the sick girl seems likely only in occasional cases, such as a version by Ochtervelt: cf. Dixon (1995), pp. 1, 143, 147, 151, 166, fig. 76. For the stock figure of Juliet's nurse, see Everett (1972), pp. 129–39.

18 I would dissent from Dixon's view that such themes as pregnancy outside marriage were thought too scandalous to be likely subjects of Dutch genre: Dixon (1995), pp. 6–7, 145.

19 This is reproduced in Van Dongen (1967), Afb. 34. On Van Brekelenkam, see Sutton (1984), catalogues 17–19.

20 For the Dusart, see Pelling (1996b), p. 242.

21 I would agree with Dixon that these practitioners are not usually intended to be quacks, even where they appear uncomprehending, or lewd; however, I cannot agree that they are treated with the serious respect required by her argument, except in a few cases which tend also to be exceptions to her case (for example, one of Godfried Schalcken's versions of the 'Visit to the doctor': see Sutton (1984), plate 120; Dixon (1995), figs 13, 63, pp. 144–5). For further comment on Dixon's argument, see reviews by Helen King, *Medical History*, 40 (1996), p. 505, and Ian Maclean, *Isis*, 87 (1996), p. 352.

22 London, Royal College of Physicians, 'Annals', 28 January 1583, p. 18. I am grateful to the President and Fellows of the college for permission to quote from the 'Annals'. Page references are to the typescript translation and transcription.

23 On Fleetwood, see Tawney and Power (eds) (1953), vol. ii, pp. 335–9; Archer (1991), pp. 228–9 *et passim*. See in general Beier (1985); Salgado (1977). The last is unfortunately devoid of both references and index.

24 'Annals', 28 January 1583, p. 19.

25 Thomas (1976), pp. 12ff. See most recently Griffiths (1996).

26 For the college's attempts to control practice after 1640, see Cook (1986).

27 Unless otherwise stated, information on the college and irregular practitioners in this chapter derives from and is more fully discussed in a monograph under preparation, *The Strength of the Opposition: the College of Physicians and Irregular Medical Practice in Early Modern London* (Pelling forthcoming d).

28 The fellowship (as at 30 September) was at its smallest (17) in 1580, and its largest (39) in 1634. Candidates averaged 3 over the period, and Licentiates averaged 8.

29 The literature on women's work in the early modern period is now extensive. For an overview sensitive to women's working conditions, see Hufton (1995). For still-relevant detail and interpretation based on sources for England, see Clark (1982).

30 This is exemplified in a number of cases before the college, across a wide social range, in which it is presented as an excuse. Whether true or not in any individual case, it reflects contemporary expectations.

31 Clark (1982), pp. 254–7; Nagy (1988), chap. 5; Pollock (1993).

32 This is not to suggest that 'professionalization' as currently understood is applicable to the early modern period. For discussion, see Pelling (1987), pp. 90–128.

33 De Blécourt (1992), pp. 43–4.

34 Pelling and Webster (1979), p. 183; Finlay (1981), p. 51.

35 Pelling (1982), p. 163. Note that this figure of twenty-six includes midwives. Female practitioners comprised just under 9 per cent of the total number of practitioners located for Norwich.

36 'Annals', 7 June and 5 July 1594, p. 88.

37 'Annals', 30 January 1606, p. 181. For a similar claim or excuse, this time made by a surgeon against his wife, see *ibid.*, 8 January 1606, p. 180.

38 This apparent lack of solidarity can also be seen as an effect of patriarchal dominance, like that suggested by Larner in respect of witchcraft accusations: Ingram (1994), p. 66. Cf. Sharpe (1996), pp. 174 ff: in arguing for an empirical approach, Sharpe interprets witchcraft accusations as an expression of tensions between women. This latter interpretation is dealt with perceptively by Purkiss (1995). See also C. Holmes (1993).

39 'Annals', 3 December 1613, p. 51. Woodall appears as 'Udall'.

40 Diet drinks were a recurring problem; for a particular campaign against purging ales, see 'Annals', April–June 1631. For a literary reference, see Jonson: 'a good old woman— /Yes, faith, she dwells in Seacoal Lane, – did cure me,/ With sodden ale, and pellitory o' the wall – / Cost me but twopence' (*The Alchemist*, III. iv. 119–21).

41 'Annals', 3 July 1596, p. 101. Mrs Woodhouse also claimed to have restored to health patients bewitched by the stars or by sorcery: *ibid.* For a woman who claimed that her reputation had been ruined by a false urine test carried out by an old woman, and who looked to the college to back her story, see *ibid.*, 6 August 1605, p. 173.

42 'Annals', 15 March 1587, p. 40. This was probably Henry Carey, 1st Lord Hunsdon, soldier and governor of Berwick under Elizabeth and cousin to the Queen. Interestingly, Hunsdon, although lacking literary culture, was described by Gerard as taking a deep interest in botany. Carey was also the dedicatee of William Bullein's *Bulwark of Defence against all Sickness* (1562): see *DNB*, and Jeffers (1967), p. 12.

43 For a revealing discussion of these differences see Roberts (1985), pp. 122–80.

44 An example of this is Alice Glavin, a practitioner paid by the city of Norwich in the 1570s to perform substantial cures. Although she was also the wife and mother of surgeons, there was no clue to medical activity in her will: Pelling (1982), pp. 166–7.

45 The hospital is likely to have been an orphanage for poor children, like Christ's, rather than a sick-hospital. On sick-nurses, see Pelling, 'Nurses and Nursekeepers: Problems of Identification in the Early Modern Period', in Pelling (forthcoming c).

46 Houlbrooke (1988), p. 181.

47 'Annals', 28 December 1569, p. 42.

48 Of the total of 110 female irregulars, only 5 were actually described as widows, and 25 as wives or as 'Goody' or 'Goodwife'. Ten more emerged in the proceedings as having husbands. One woman, Avis Murrey, the wife of a surgeon, falsely claimed to be widowed: 'Annals', 7 April 1626, p. 203.

49 On her first appearance in the 'Annals' Mrs Paine is described in the margin as 'Mistress Payne, physician'.

50 'Annals', 6 November 1607, pp. 202–3; 27 November 1607, pp. 204–5; 22 December 1607, p. 206. For Bonham's own confrontation with the college, see Cook (1985), pp. 301–22, esp. pp. 310, 312.

51 This was Mary Butler of Mark Lane, who claimed a number of other sources of male authority for her practice, which included cupping, and other forms of bloodletting by a surgeon under her direction: 'Annals', 7 July 1637, p. 449.

52 *Ibid.*, 11 December 1609, p. 17; 26 June 1615, p. 73.

53 Pelling (1996a), p. 111; 'Annals', 16 May 1623, p. 167.

54 'Annals', 6 December 1588, p. 54; 6 and 12 February 1595, p. 92; 4 August 1598, p. 115; 7 September 1610, p. 24; 11 January 1611, p. 27

55 *Ibid.*, 19 December 1581, p. 5A; 22 December 1581, p. 6.

56 This Act condemned London surgeons in particular for venality and for harassing cunning men and women, especially those who (unlike Kennix) treated the poor for nothing: Pelling (1986), pp. 96–7.

57 'Annals', 5 April 1605, p. 170; 3 November 1609, p. 16.

58 This is discussed in more detail in Pelling (forthcoming a). See also Stearns (1980), p. 45.

59 Roper (1989), p. 47; Marland in Marland and Pelling (1996), pp. 287ff.

60 On migration among the elderly, see Pelling (1991), esp. pp. 80–2.

61 See also the apparent absence of herbwomen among the Norwich poor: Pelling, (forthcoming a). On eighteenth-century herbwomen see Burnby (1983), pp. 5–6.

62 'Annals', 30 May 1632, pp. 342–3; 28 May 1632, p. 336. Mid-century medical reformers, such as Nicholas Culpeper, deplored both the expertise of old women compared with Galenic physicians, and the over-dependence of the poor on apothecaries: Webster (1975), pp. 254, 271.

63 See Pelling (1996a), p. 105.

64 'Annals', 22 December 1581, p. 6; 7 January 1582, p. 8.

65 *Ibid.*, 7 February 1605, p. 181; 6 February 1604, p. 169; 12 February 1619, p. 120; 4 November 1614, p. 63.

66 For more on this issue, see Pelling (1995a), pp. 250–79.

67 Clark (1982), pp. xxviii, 261.

68 See, for example, Bennett (1992), pp. 147–75; Bennett (1991), pp. 166–88; Vickery (1993), pp. 383–414.

69 Wrigley and Schofield (1981), App. 3, p. 528, App. 1 (list of parishes); Pelling (1991), pp. 77, 87.

70 Goldberg (1992), pp. 297–300, 343.

71 Graunt, 'Natural and Political Observations . . . on the Bills of Mortality' (5th edn, 1676), in Petty, Hull (ed.) (1963), vol. ii, pp. 385–6. Graunt's own calculation was that there were in fact 14 men for every 13 women.

72 Horsley (1979), pp 714–15.

73 Pelling (1991), pp. 87–90. I hope to give more attention to widowers in a contribution to a volume on widowhood to be edited by Sandra Cavallo and Lyndan Warner.

74 The college also saw itself as the defender of poor little (old) women against the abuses of the irregulars: see for example 'Annals', 5 May 1598, p. 112. For a related tone, see *ibid.*, 2 February 1603, p. 156, when Edward Cocker denied practice, 'laying aside all sense of shame, and threw all the blame on an old woman now dead called Margery'.

75 F.P. Wilson (1927), p. 65. It is perhaps worth noting a concern in the early 1580s about 'old witches' in connection with a Catholic conspiracy against Elizabeth: Sharpe (1996), p. 46.

76 For Horsley, for example, English witches were more often diviners than healers: (1979), pp. 700ff. Particularly to be noted in the present context is MacDonald (ed.) (1991), which concerns a famous case involving one of the elderly female irregulars, Elizabeth Jackson, and the conflicting interpretations of the condition of her alleged victim, Mary Glover, offered by fellows of the college.

77 Monter (1987), p. 212. On witchcraft and healing in the English countryside, see Sawyer (1988–9). For a detailed case study of one English 'urban' witch who was elderly (though not poor) and a healer, see Gregory (1991). For Rye, a town of *c.* 2,000 inhabitants, Gregory stresses socio-economic factors.

78 Cf. De Blécourt (1992), pp. 52–4, who ascribes the continuing survival of cunning women in cities to their use of words, suggesting that the use of material means would have been rigorously suppressed. Note that the prescription of purging ales was not confined to women; for the surgeon, oculist and practitioner of physic Richard Banister, his own recipe was a valued part of his practice: Banister (1621). Estes also singles out women's powers of speech, though for the different purpose of suggesting that those women who used material means were less likely to be accused of witchcraft: Estes (1983), esp. p. 278.

79 Horsley (1979), pp. 705ff; Estes (1983) p. 212; Kelly-Gadol (1987), pp. 177, 188, 190. Cf. Monter (1969a), pp. 55–71. G. Zilboorg (1935), discusses exceptional medical figures from the psychiatric point of view. Holmes (1993) sees the influence of male officials as a chief factor in the shift in seventeenth-century English witchcraft crimes away from property and toward illness and death (hence the increased proportion of female witnesses).

80 Pelling (1996a).

81 Pelling (1995b), pp. 383–401.

82 Thomas (1976), pp. 33–4; Pelling (1991), p. 84; cf. Stearns (1980), pp. 45ff.

83 Pelling (1996a), p. 113.

84 Marland (1996), pp. 273–87.

85 'Annals', 3 June 1631, p. 312.

4

WOMEN AND DOMESTIC MEDICINE: LADY EXPERIMENTERS, 1570–1620

Lynette Hunter

There is a curious gap that confronts anyone interested in the history of women in England in the early modern period. Although there had been a thriving market growing from the 1550s for books addressed to women on household science, medicine and pharmacy, from 1617 to 1653 with one exception there are no new books published on the topic and even reprints of earlier texts are rare. My research tries to understand that gap by looking at what happened up to 1617, what happened after 1652,[1] and what was going on in the interim years.

One of the startling aspects of publishing in the 1650s is the sudden appearance of a group of books of scientific, pharmaceutical and medicinal texts by women. Traditionally these had been published alongside diet, cookery and household 'secrets', but by men. In the 1650s most are still published with cookery, and with household technology and fashion.[2] The first three books of the genre which are attributed to women are Elizabeth Grey's *A Choice Manual of Rare and Select Secrets* (1653),[3] Queen Henrietta Maria's *The Queen's Closet Opened* (1655)[4] and Alethea Talbot's *Natura Exenterata* (1655).[5] The first two, along with that one exceptional book published in 1639 'Lord' Ruthven's *The Ladies Cabinet Opened*,[6] follow explicitly a three-part pattern of medicine, household science and fashion, and food preparation and cookery, that had only been implicit in earlier texts. Yet it is the medicinal and pharmaceutical content that is directly attributed to their aristocratic writers, and Talbot's *Natura Exenterata* is almost entirely of this kind.

These works are the first printed books of technical and scientific material in England to be attributed to women, and this may underlie the scepticism about the direct involvement of these women in the production of the texts, and the resulting lack of discussion about them.[7] The late 1970s to 1990s have seen a substantial reinvestigation of the Renaissance, Commonwealth and Restoration periods, to find texts that were written by women and men, in groups of labouring workers and the new towndwellers as well as in circles of the new gentry and aristocracy.[8] The search has uncovered a large body of work, much of which does not fit canonical traditions of literature, such as ballads, tales, sermons, and some of which does. For example, we now know that women were writing and sometimes had printed plays, poetry, romances, devotional texts, political tracts and essays: but there is a silence on science and technology.[9] Hence it becomes significant if we find that these women were indeed involved in these published texts. It tells us different things about their lives, their education, the social world they inhabited, about the attitudes to science and more generally to knowledge, and it yields new perspectives on the interrelationships between men and women.

Two substantial questions form the basis for this chapter. First, what was so special about the 1650s, after such a long period of silence from 1617 to 1652, that led to these texts being published thirty to fifty years after they had been written? And, secondly, the specific focus, if it were plausible that these women had written, edited or compiled these texts, who were they and what was their context? How did they acquire the necessary skills and knowledge? I will argue that they turned a traditional pursuit of women in many communities into a leisure pursuit, and that in doing so they contributed to the movement into science as natural philosophy; yet I shall also argue that they did so while maintaining the basis of the pursuit as a social activity within the communities in which they participated.

WHO WERE THEY?

Elizabeth Grey and Alethea Talbot were sisters. They had both been close to Queen Anne, the wife of James I, being among her ladies of the bedchamber. Both subsequently became close friends of Henrietta Maria, wife to Charles I, Elizabeth going with her into exile in the Netherlands in 1642. With their sister Mary, they were the three surviving granddaughters of Elizabeth Barlow, Bess of Hardwick Hall, by her daughter Mary Cavendish. Bess, who had studiously 'married up' the social scale to reach the status of Countess of Shrewsbury on her fourth marriage, was closely involved in marrying off these young women, as she had already married off her daughters: Elizabeth to Charles Stuart (their unlucky offspring Arbella being second in line to the throne after James I and beheaded for it); and Mary to her step-son Gilbert Talbot, so that Mary became the next Countess of Shrewsbury. Alethea was married to Philip Howard, Earl of Surrey and Arundel; her sister Mary to William Herbert, Earl of Pembroke; and Elizabeth to Henry Grey de Ruthin, to become Earl of Kent.

Yet none of these was a 'safe' marriage: the Arundels were recovering from the beheading of the previous earl for treason, and the loss of their Norfolk title; William Herbert was only a few months out of the Tower where he had been put by Elizabeth for refusing to marry one of her ladies-in-waiting after making her pregnant; and Henry Grey was the son of a third son, with only a remote chance of inheriting a title if both his uncles died childless – which they did.[10] In each case, the luck of these men turned around and with it the fortunes of their wives. As William Herbert became influential at court, acting as Lord Chamberlain under James I, becoming Chancellor of Oxford, and a patron of the arts, so he also developed a long-term relationship with the writer Mary Wroth,[11] and Mary Talbot vanishes to the family home where she seems to have looked after the resulting children and at least one ward while having none of her own. Anne Clifford, who had married William's brother Philip, writes in her diary of visiting Mary 'with all her children', soon after she herself became the next Countess of Pembroke on William's death in 1631. Anne Clifford's diary also tells us of going to the masque in London in 1617 with Elizabeth Grey and Alethea Talbot, all of them in the box of Lady Ruthven,[12] Barbara Ruthven being another lady of the bedchamber to Queen Anne, whose daughter Mary married the Van Dyck, the painter of Alethea's portrait referred to below.[13]

Alethea Talbot's husband Philip Howard became one of the first wholesale British exploiters of foreign parts, sending back from his continental travels and especially Italy much sculpture and art; many items of his collection are now held in the Ashmolean Museum.[14] He was also immensely influential at court, being the First Knight of the Realm for a substantial part of Charles' reign,[15] and entrusted with taking Henrietta Maria into exile.[16] Henry Grey, Elizabeth's husband, appears consistently to have held court positions but assumed no particular public face; Elizabeth herself developed a long-term liaison with John Selden whom she married on the death of Henry.[17] Selden was the steward on Grey's Bedfordshire estate, but is known now for his historical and legal writings, as well as for his work on the attributions and translations of many of the classical antiquities Philip Howard was sending to England.[18] Elizabeth herself was recognized as a learned woman: John Florio dedicated the third volume of his translations of Montaigne's *Essays* to her in 1603;[19] John Aubrey attests to her reputation as a physician and apothecary, saying also that she daily fed and cared for more than seventy poor people in her community, marking this as exceptional;[20] certainly her receipts, particularly for the 'Countess of Kent's Powder', are scattered through books by others for the rest of the century, and the great cook Robert May cites her as a source throughout his *Accomplisht Cook* of 1660. Alethea is less notorious but is noted for her participation in the queen's masques,[21] and as I hope to demonstrate for her medicinal and pharmaceutical work.

Both sisters were clearly also politically powerful – again Anne Clifford's diaries tell how, when she seemed to be prevented from pursuing her claim to her inheritance, she put the case to Elizabeth and Alethea, who put it to Queen Anne, who persuaded James to allow Clifford to make her claim. It took many years to complete, but without the lobbying on her behalf would never have occurred. It is a small but telling incident that indicates the kind of backroom, bedchamber politics in which the sisters engaged. Their mother Mary was more direct; she is reported as debating the reconciliation of Bess of Hardwick and George, Earl of Shrewsbury directly with Elizabeth I, and of remonstrating

Portrait of Lady Elizabeth Grey, Countess of Kent by Paul van Somer (*c.* 1619).

loudly with James I himself over the incarceration of Arbella, her niece.[22] Outside England, Alethea behaved in a similarly direct manner when a plot was hatched to sully the Howard name in the Venetian Senate. As the official representative of her husband she called the bluff of the English ambassador Henry Wotton, insisted on speaking with the Doge who disclaimed any knowledge of the alleged treason of the Howards, and then demanded an apology from the Senate.[23]

I offer this anecdotal detail of their lives partly because so little has been written about them, yet they were clearly rather extraordinary people with active interests in the arts, in politics, in their communities, as well as in medicine, pharmacy and chemical science. Their aristocratic position was, I will argue, as important to their scientific activity as their intellectual environment. The association they formed with Henrietta Maria from the 1620s to the 1640s, threw them together with a group of men with similar intellectual interests, but largely without aristocratic position.[24] Once we begin to look at their circle of friends and correspondents, it is possible to recognize them for respected participants in what we would now call the cross-disciplinary or pre-disciplinary culture of the Renaissance. Henrietta Maria's chamberlain was Sir Kenelm Digby, a highly respected scholar and practiser of chemistry who was known throughout Europe as someone exploring the new experimental science. Theodore de Mayerne, who had been brought from France to act as court physician to James, was her doctor. Mayerne was responsible for compiling the first London *Pharmacopoeia*,[25] published in 1617 by the College of Physicians in an attempt to control the prescriptions that members of the newly inaugurated Society of Apothecaries were licensed to make. John Pell, the mathematician, was part of her entourage, as was John Evelyn – a man known to us now mainly through his diary, but also a noted botanist and naturalist who was interested in the physiological effects of foodstuffs, writing discourses on bread, on herbs and on raw vegetables (see Frances Harris's chapter in this volume). Henrietta Maria herself is a historically evanescent character, known largely from her impact on Charles I. Although one must be cautious about the claim, the title page of the work attributed to her household, *Queen's Closet Opened*, states that many of the receipts 'were honoured with her own practice, when she pleased to descend to these more private Recreations'. The existence of this circle of intellectuals, among others in her entourage, indicates someone willing to patronize and support scientific pursuits still subject to considerable scepticism;[26] furthermore, she clearly had a mind of her own, for at the same time as she is being attended by Mayerne, a leading member of the College of Physicians, she is also supporting the gardener and herbalist John Parkinson, whose *Paradisi in sole* dedicated to her in 1629 was being suppressed by that college. Even more interesting and raising a number of other questions, the publication was underwritten by Mayerne.

Alethea Talbot, Elizabeth Grey and Henrietta Maria were part of a group of people investigating the new experimental science and interested in new

The title page from *The Queens Closet Opened* (1655).

approaches to knowledge. These women appear, possibly because of their aristocratic status among men on the whole their social inferiors, to have sustained intellectual parity with them and indeed to have been recognized as providing intellectual leadership. There is a handsome portrait of Alethea and her husband Philip, painted in the 1620s by Anthony Van Dyck,[27] that shows the couple: she is seated beside a large globe of the world, and he seated partly behind it holding up a stick in his left hand and pointing, arm across the globe, at the island of Madagascar, as if to say 'Here next'. Yet the two are placed in substantially equal relationship,[28] he occupying a slightly higher position and looking directly at the viewer, she in the foreground, much more substantial as a figure, gazing past the globe, and holding in each hand the instruments of navigation. If Philip is of today, the source of power and mastery, Alethea is thinking elsewhere, presumably the uncharted future, and is the source of wisdom and knowledge. But what kind of knowledge did her pursuit of science, and that of her sister and friend, offer?

In retrospect it is odd to find so few references to these two sisters, Elizabeth Grey and Alethea Talbot, yet it is perhaps because conventional historical investigation focuses on public records and formal institutions. There has been a failure to assess other social structures, and in terms of science and medicine, the non-formal practices. There is also a profound inability to value domestic work, or work within the household, presumably because it is taken to be the most private activity, the furthest from the public domain. The contexts for their work, discussed below, are multiple and various and the scope too great to offer a comprehensive picture here. But without ignoring the formal and institutional history, I shall focus on the domestic and household structures in particular, and the individuals involved in them.

CONTEXTS: BOOKS

The three-part structure of medicine, household and food receipts common to the books by Elizabeth Grey, Henrietta Maria and the earlier 1639 *Ladies Cabinet Opened*, is unusual. The printed books of the period 1570–1620, during the latter part of which Elizabeth and Alethea were probably writing, offer combinations of medicine and cookery, or cookery and household science, or medicine and household science. Five of the most popular writers of works addressed to women in this period, Thomas Tusser, John Partridge, Thomas Dawson, Hugh Plat and Gervase Markham, emphasize one or two of the three areas, but do not equally weight all three as do the later publications. Yet the way the readers read these earlier books indicates that there was an avid audience for all these topics. For example Hugh Platt's *Delightes for Ladies* (1605) contains household and cookery recipes, and another book possibly by him, *A Closet for Ladies and Gentlewomen* (1602), contains household receipts and medicine, yet these books are frequently bound together indicating a need for each of the areas.[29]

The structure can tell us quite a bit about how women ran their lives during these years. The household receipts which derive from a tradition of books of 'secrets' for men,[30] largely consist of household preparations relevant to women's work within the house. While in the twentieth century an open kitchen cupboard may well contain window cleaner, bleach, washing soda, perhaps polish and varnish; or desktops hold ink, pencils, glue and so on; or the bathroom cabinet house soap, toothpaste, lotions and various beauty aids, in the sixteenth century people could not just go out and buy these items. There were no shops as we would recognize them, although a grocer could supply someone wealthy enough if they lived close enough to make delivery feasible. Otherwise people made them for themselves. One case in point is ink. I know of no receipt book or manuscript without its receipt for ink. Without ink, of course, neither the book nor the manuscript would exist, yet it is not an easy thing to get that balance of dense blackness with the essential quality of quick drying.

Another traditional genre of published books for men, that of husbandry and estate management, provided a structure for books on household management for women. These works covered at the least brewing, distillation, wine preparation, bread making, dairy-work – which was one of the only activities outside the house that was specifically undertaken by women – and the entire area of conservation and preservation.[31] This last area was of vital importance to the health and the economic soundness of the household, since without it harvested food and slaughtered animals would be wasted; yet without refrigeration or tins or vacuum-packing, the techniques relied on skilful expertise with drying, storing, pickling, brining, and the increasing use of sugar to conserve. Today, when in Europe most of this kind of work is done by large companies, we tend to take the skills for granted, only recognizing them in those jars of a friend's pickle or jam that are sometimes still received at specific times in the year.

The third primary genre of writing influencing the books addressed to women during the second half of the sixteenth century are those on food and diet which up until the middle of the century had been largely medicinal. Because Galenic medicine, which involved an understanding and care of the whole body, dominated sixteenth-century practice, recipes for food preparation and herbal remedy were indistinguishable as cookery or as 'regimen'. The focus on preventive medicine is underlined by a considerable influx of dietaries and regimens for health in the vernacular English that followed Andrew Boorde's *Dietary of Helthe* (1542). When printed as the sole topic for a book they were normally addressed to men, often as a vocational guidance;[32] but they are frequently combined with other topics such as the order of service, or other household receipts, and addressed to women. Food and diet were inextricably part of a woman's responsibility in maintaining the health of the household which was itself often an extended family that was part of a larger community.

However, it is in this area of food and diet that the greatest change takes place in the household work of the early modern world. During the sixteenth century, Paracelsian experimental science, with its associated medical remedies for curing disease or at least relieving the symptoms, begins to find its way into England.[33] It brought with it the ethos of treating the disease retrospectively, rather than preventing its occurrence; and it moved toward general remedies that could cure all people of one particular illness. With it, and with other associated factors of course, the published books begin to show evidence of a distinct split between food as cookery and food as medicine, and between herbal preparations as medicine and chemical preparations as medicine. By 1617 and the incorporation

A page from the Duchess of Norfolk's *Household Book*.

of the Society of Apothecaries, the world of print takes food, herbs and cookery to be women's work, while medicine belongs to men.[34]

The areas of household secrets, household management and food, diet and medicine, all overlap not only in the way they fit into daily life but also in their techniques, skills and the knowledge they require.[35] Even today issues of public health policy frequently take in household conditions. Foodstuffs such as sugar were used as medicines, as food, and held a substantial place in household receipts not only for conserving but also as indicators of wealth and status.[36] More directly, each area of practice would have drawn on similar skills in grinding, weighing, distilling, drying, purifying, heating, cooling and so on. With electric mixers, food processors and regulo gas ovens, it is easy to forget that these techniques required considerable expertise to achieve accuracy at a time when for many the open fireplace and the pestle and mortar were their only resource. While the kitchens and distillation rooms appear simple, they have their own technology and require craft to carry out the work.[37]

The works by Elizabeth Grey and Henrietta Maria closely render these different areas of a woman's life and although, as I shall suggest, probably trying to do something a little different, Alethea Talbot's book still implicitly offers advice on the three parts of women's work. Yet how significant is it that the parts of the books directly attributed to these women writers are those on medicinal and household science, and not those parts on household management and food? These texts, along with many other similar manuscripts by women, were not published when they were written, even though there were books on these topics by men addressed directly to women being printed from the 1550s through to 1617. This is the more curious because the books that were printed were very popular. Indeed, among those with the most frequent editions are books explicitly claiming to be from women's manuscripts or oral advice such as Partridge's *The Widdowes Treasure* (1585), Dawson's *The Good Housewives Treasurie* (1588) and Markham's *The English Huswife* (1615). Yet this publication is not indiscriminate. The books are aimed at the urban reader and the upwardly mobile gentlewoman: the large books on country-house management being precisely for this aspiring group. Many of the smaller books are vocational or training books for people going into service and we know that crowds of young people flooded into London in the latter decades of the sixteenth century, many of the women to become domestic servants, and many women and men to set up as apothecaries and doctors.

CONTEXTS: POPULAR AND FAMILIAL MEDICINE

Recent research by writers such as Margaret Pelling has initiated ground-breaking work in the field of popular and community medicine. Pelling's studies outline the wide spectrum of health care available, from members of the immediate family through to the professional physician. Within this spectrum she emphasizes, as has other research, the role of women. Despite some contemporary criticism of their involvement, William Harrison's *Description of England* (1587) clearly notes women's responsibility to have the surgical and pharmaceutical knowledge to maintain the family's health.[38] There has been much work on the earlier history: the treatment of women by the medical guilds and the grocers, including their expulsion from these guilds in fifteenth-century London; the need for their continued practice in many communities; their interaction with the incorporated institutions of physicians and surgeons throughout the sixteenth century; the frequent attempts to stop their practice, especially when it seemed to be commercially profitable.[39] Yet these controls were targeted not only against women, but also against many working men, especially as the physicians began to combine their practice with formal university training. There is continual tension from the early 1500s to 1617 between the College of Physicians, which wanted to control bad practice as well as exercise a monopoly, and the rest of the health-carers or providers in the community.[40] The tension culminates in 1617 in the incorporation of the Society of Apothecaries which was closely overseen by the physicians who, as I have mentioned, produced the London *Pharmacopoeia* to regulate prescriptions. Markham's 1616 translation of a book on country-house management contains a warning to women not to overstep their mark when using the receipts.

The invective against women goes hand in hand with invective against tradesmen, for example:

common Artificers, as smiths, weavers, and women boldly and accustomably take upon them great cures, and things of great difficulty (*An Act for the Appointing of Physicians and Surgeons*, 1512)

the rabble of these rude Empirics . . . be no chirurgeons: but mankillers, murderers, and robbers of the people: such are some hosers, tailors, fletchers, minstrels, couters, horseleeches, jugglers, witches, sorcerers, bawds, and a rabble of that sect . . . (*Certain Works of Chirugerie*)

Cutlers, Carters, Cobblers, Coopers, Coriars of Leather, Carpenters, and a great rabble of women . . . foresake their handicrafts, and for filthy lucre abuse physick and Chirurgerie. (*A Most Excellent and learned Work of Chirugery*)

all sorts of vile people . . . make gainefull traffique by botching in physicke . . . not only of Taylors, Shoemakers, Weavers, Midwives, Cookes, and Priests, but Witches, Conjurers, Juglers, and Fortune-tellers. (*A Short Discoverie of the Unobserved Dangers*)[41]

What holds this random group together is their practice of chemical technology. These quacks, empirics, women, shoemakers, tanners and so on, are the people buying the books of household and alchemical secrets, and turning them to commercial uses. An interesting feature of many of these books is the idea of the 'public good', of a 'common wealth' of knowledge to which everyone has a right of access, a need acknowledged in the statute of 1534:

> every person being the King's subject, having knowledge and experience of the nature of Herbs, Roots and Waters, or of the operation of the same, by speculation or practice within any part of the Realm of England, or within any other the King's dominions, to practise, use and minister in and to any outward sore . . . wound, apostemations, outward swelling or disease, any herb or herbs, ointments, baths, poultices and plasters, according to their cunning, experience and knowledge in any of the diseases, sores and maladies beforesaid, and all other like to the same, or drinks for the stone and stangury, or agues, without suit, berations, trouble, penalty or loss of their goods.[42]

With the change in population movements in the sixteenth century, the changes in available foodstuffs and materials brought about by increasing trade and exploration, the changes in lifestyle such as the increase in reading and writing without recourse to an optician; and with the recurrent plagues, these people, who were often cut off from their health-care community at home,[43] needed guidance and free advice and quick cures so they could get back to work.[44]

Perhaps these aristocratic women didn't publish their books because ladies of their status didn't need the receipts: they could afford to buy in the services of physicians, surgeons and apothecaries; they had servants to prepare household goods.[45] However, there is considerable evidence to the contrary. Aristocratic ladies were often highly involved in medicine and household science: one factor may simply be the traditional activities that women carried out in these areas; another may be the practical one that many aristocratic houses were far from the cities in which professional men lived; yet another may be a social factor deriving from the responsibility for the community that devolved on the old and new aristocracy and gentry after the dissolution and reallocation of monastic lands – after all, the abbeys and monasteries had been a primary source of hospital care for many people for centuries.

Among the many aristocratic women noted for their medical expertise is Lady Lisle, cited as having great skill with planting and herbs in the 1530s,[46] yet probably picked out simply because she was the mother of the Earl of Warwick and Northumberland who was highly influential at court from 1540 until he was beheaded for trying to put his daughter-in-law Jane Grey on the throne. From the 1560s and '70s there is Ann Dacre, Lady Arundel and mother-in-law to Alethea Talbot, noted for her personal participation in the preparation of remedies and receipts on the Arundel estates;[47] she also, as we will discover, was a gardener and herbalist. From the early 1600s, there is Margaret Hoby whose diary tells in detail of her consulting the herbal, preparing medicines, attempting surgery and continually helping the sick in her community.[48]

While there is an on-going history of this health-care work by wealthy aristocratic women engaging with their communities and treating their work frequently as a devotional exercise or social responsibility, the history is largely within the context of the country estate or semi-rural living. With the aristocracy increasingly focused on court life in London from the 1570s, the function of these practices, if women of the court continued these activities, must have changed. A clue may come from Mary Sidney, mother-in-law to Alethea and Elizabeth's sister Mary, who had facilities for scientific preparation that were used by her brother Philip and son William, as well as herself. As Margaret Hannay elaborates, John Aubrey calls her a practitioner of chemistry and says that she was the patron of at least two medical scientists, Adrian Gilbert and Thomas Mouffet.[49] The latter is an unusual choice because Mouffet was responsible for a substantial work on Paracelsian science, *Nosomantica Hippocratea*, published in Germany in 1588, but apparently not well received or translated into English until the 1650s. Mary Sidney's support for such a scientist indicates an unusual commitment to a new scientific approach, and underlines her intellectual rather than social or religious engagement.

CONTEXTS: EDUCATION AND LEISURE

Mary Sidney's intellectual engagement with matters of medical and household science begs the question of how aristocratic women were educated, and considerable background is provided by studies of these women in the name of literature. Recent research has suggested that in the latter part of Henry VIII's reign, possibly with the example of Thomas More's daughters in mind, some members of the court began educating their daughters in the classics to improve their chances of a good marriage. The Cooke sisters, whose father was a reader to Edward VI, were renowned for their learning and whether or not this improved their chances, they did marry well.[50] Norfolk had his three granddaughters highly educated, as did the Seymours and the Somersets.[51]

However, this education in classical humanism appears to have lost its impetus by the 1590s, with one scholar noting that of all the women at court only Arbella Stuart and Lady Oxford spoke Latin.[52] However, while this would appear a considerable underestimation, what is clear is that many of the new aristocracy and upwardly mobile gentry were educating their daughters in vernacular literature and languages instead. During the 1580s and '90s and well into the seventeenth century, there was a considerable production of writing in English by women such as Mary Sidney or Mary Wroth or Emilia Lanyer.[53] The taste for intellectual enjoyment and craft was still there but transferred into English, and there is evidence that many of these women formed reading circles to exchange and discuss their own writing as a social pastime.[54]

Alethea and Elizabeth Talbot were both educated during this later period of vernacular humanism, and just as they seem to have been trained in the literary skills of poetry and rhetoric, they both also received an education in basic chemical technology: the odd mixture of herbalism, alchemy and early Paracelsian chemistry that seems to have been prevalent. Probably this is not recorded because it was not formally taught.[55] Even boys at grammar school received largely a curriculum in the classics with some arithmetic and possibly some history and geography, but no science or technology.[56] Furthermore, this education in chemical technology and medical preparations was acquired by observation, by many while in service or apprenticeship, and by aristocratic women while in their houses observing their mothers, their own apothecaries, their friends. The vast amount of tacit knowledge upon which the sparse receipts rely underlines this mode of learning, which in common with other domestic knowledge we do not yet have an adequate means of valuing. It also seems reasonable to assume that the women may have formed circles exchanging receipts and experiences, possibly the same as their reading circles. There is evidence that leisure time was a difficult issue, that wealthy women had to work on their increasing isolation and the sense of ineffectualness it brought. For example, tucked away at the back of a copy of Tasso's serious and lengthy work on gastronomy, there is a rare pamphlet entitled *A Dairie Book for Good Housewives* written by one Bartholomewe Dawe in 1588. It is written in dialogue form to the gentlewomen of South Hampshire and advises them on how to make dairy-meats: cheeses, butters, creams, etc. Dawe publishes it, he says in his address to the reader, because women are not only peculiarly associated with dairy-work but also because they need physical activity to prevent them getting 'downe in the dumpes'. The short work also includes a poem by his wife Katharine on the virtues of getting up early. Certainly, circles for discussing anything with intelligent and interested friends would have helped to pass the time, and the practice of naming sources for their remedies even if they were merely from friends rather than well-known authorities, which is initiated in manuscripts by women from this period, seems to indicate that they were discussing possibilities with companions in one way or another.

Aristocratic ladies would have had, therefore, a number of reasons to practise, to write down and discuss receipts and remedies. It passed the time and was a social medium for exchange, a leisure activity. Medicinal and household science is still necessary in terms of country life, both for the women themselves and the community on their estates. Possibly, the responsibility of aristocratic ladies of the sixteenth century for these practices led to emulation of them by the new courtiers and gentry. For some, the responsibilities were part of a devotional exercise in serving the community. In any event, such work allowed women to function in public in the restricted sense of going out to perform a public service; and in doing so offered them a rare opportunity to leave the private sphere of the house.

At the same time, on the continent in Italy at least two universities trained women in medicine,[57] in other words, through training in medical practice they were most unusually permitted into a public institution. This recognition of women's intellectual capability would undoubtedly have been known in court circles in England, given the extensive travel by the English aristocracy and gentry to Italy at the time.[58] While women were not permitted into the universities in England, vernacular work on medicine, herbal treatment and household secrets, such as John Gerard's *Herbal*, credits women as the source for receipts and remedies.[59] It appears to have been a field where women's conventional domestic work and a growing commercial domain for men came together. There were common areas of knowledge, and hence interchange and some parity of knowledge and experience. Henrietta Maria's intellectual circle was made up of aristocratic ladies and more ordinary gentlemen, with common interests in medical science.

The books attributed to Henrietta Maria and Elizabeth Grey reflect aspects of all these areas of motivation. Both are also small books, octavo in format, and while Grey's is written with some style, neither has pretensions; they are practical products. Alethea Talbot's book is a rather different handsome quarto, and in conclusion it is worth considering its structure and asking again what kind of knowledge it offers. *Natura Exenterata* comes in part from a substantial manuscript[60] that shows its sources to be broadly the same as for many contemporary household manuscripts; indeed several receipts, such as the one for sugared and baked turnip to cure a cough, are the same as Elizabeth Grey's, indicating a common family practice. But the printed book rearranges material and adds rather different sections. It begins with Alethea's receipts and those of her circle, roughly in order of preparation technique: ointments, oils, etc. This is followed by some experimental receipts of the new chemistry, accompanied by chemical symbols. Then come Ann Dacre's receipts from the 1570s to 1580s, thirty to forty years earlier than Alethea's initial writing and a good eighty years before the publication, which include herbal preparations, planting and techniques for distillation. Accompanying the earlier work by Ann Dacre are medical receipts by her contemporaries, including letters of advice on specific ailments that give fascinating insight into doctor–patient relationships *c.* 1570. The printed book concludes with sections on horse-breeding, knitting, sugar cookery, and household science: partly a token gesture to household work but in fact a carefully selected set of instructions on topics relatively new to England in the seventeenth century.

The title page from *Natura Exenterata: or Nature Unbowelled* (1655).

The work is highly significant because it documents the movement from a herbal-based Galenic medicine to a balance of herbal and chemical. In the index the chemical receipts are not listed in a different section, as are the receipts for sugar cookery, but are added separately to the end of each alphabetical letter-listing of herbal remedy. While it is different in presentation from the books by Elizabeth Grey and Henrietta Maria, it is also different from most of the contemporary books by men which are either herbal or chemical in context. *Natura Exenterata* is making claims not only on skill and technology, but also on a new area of knowledge and the process of intellectual enquiry. Its frontispiece, engraved after the manner of the Van Dyck double portrait of the Howards, shows Alethea alone with the instruments of navigation replaced by the pearls of medicine. The knowledge and wisdom she is offering are in anticipation of the new experimental science, yet also rooted in the health care of her community which gives a practical and immediate cast to her use of chemistry and her pursuit of natural philosophy.

Notes

1 The year 1653 marks the advent of published texts in English by women on these matters, but it should be noted that the silence was broken by Nicolas Culpeper's translation of the London *Pharmacopoeia* in 1649.

2 For an account of the generic development of these books, see the section contributed by L. Hunter on 'Household Books' in the third edition of the *Cambridge Bibliography of English Literature, 1500–1700* (forthcoming).

3 Published by a W. I. and usually bound with *A True Gentlewomans Delight*, with which it was published in 1687.

4 Published by W. M. in three parts called *The Queen's Closet Opened: or the pearl of practise*, this being the medical section, along with *A Queen's Delight* and *The Compleat Cook*, in 1655.

5 *Natura Exenterata* (1655).

6 For a consideration of the authorship of this text see, A. Davidson and M. Bell, *The Ladies Cabinet enlarged and opened* (London: Prospect Books, 1985) which is a reprint of the enlarged 1654 edition. As this chapter suggests, the proximity of Lady Ruthven to the other women writing identically structured texts points to her having some involvement in the construction of the book.

7 Although Elizabeth David made Grey's book one of her first contributions to the periodical *Petits propos culinaires*, which focuses on issues of food history, technology, geography and literature; see David (1979a).

8 See, for example, G. Ziegler and S. Steen, 'Recent Studies in the English Renaissance', *English Literary Renaissance* (1993), pp. 229–74.

9 With the exception of the work by Elizabeth Tebeaux who, in addition to her contribution to this volume, has a forthcoming book on English Renaissance technical writing.

10 J. Burke, *Complete Peerage* (London, 1910).

11 Waller (1993).

12 Clifford (1990), p. 44

13 J. Burke, *Landed Gentry* (London, 1959), p. 2098.

14 For a compelling account see Howard (1969), with printings of many of the letters from this period.

15 Burke, *Complete Peerage* (1910), pp. 256–7.

16 See Howarth (1985).

17 Aubrey (1949/75), p. 271.

18 See Berkowitz (1988).

19 Lewalski (1993), p. 362.

20 See David (1979a).

21 See the account in Lewalski (1993).

22 See Durant (1977).

23 See the Howard letters in Howard (1969), for an account of this incident.

24 Status and power related to gender and status find interesting parallels in Ann Clifford's position on becoming Countess of Pembroke and a landowner; see Hodgkin (1985), p. 157. Furthermore there are parallels with the relationships built up between the clergy and aristocratic women; see Willen (1992).

25 Isler (1968).

26 She also agreed to act as patron to Mary Ward's schools for girls in 1625, probably on religious grounds, but Ward's schools were radical in their plan for the intellectual education of girls; see F. Fraser (1987).

27 This painting is held in Arundel Castle.

28 The letters published in Howard (1969) strengthen this impression of an equable relationship.

29 See L. Hunter (1991) for an extended discussion of the generic development.

30 A helpful bibliography of these books, not only in and for the English, is Eamon (1994).

31 For introductions to the history of conservation and preservation see C.A. Wilson (ed.) (1991b).

32 See Slack (1979).

33 For a broader account of this influence, see MacLean (1972).

34 Isler (1968) p. 7.

35 Underwriting this opinion find Cook (1986) quoting from Clark (1919).

36 Brears (1991).

37 On the importance of the stillroom see Nagy (1988) and the references in that work to Christina Hole, *The English Housewife in the Seventeenth Century* (1953).

38 Quoted in 'The Ladies of Elizabeth's Court', Furnivall (ed.) (1868), p. xc.

39 See, in particular, the work by Hogrefe (1975,1977), Beier (1987), Pelling (1987), Rawcliffe (1995), Warnicke (1983).

40 Cook (1986), p. 46.

41 Beier (1987) and Nagy (1988) cite several of these references.

42 Quoted from Rawcliffe (1995).

43 For an excellent overview of research on relevant conditions see Cook (1986).

44 Further evidence provided for this need may be found in Pelling (1994).

45 Mary Cavendish had her own apothecary, see Aubrey (1949/75), pp. 138–9.

46 Noted in Rawcliffe (1995).

47 See Hanlon (1965).

48 Hoby (1930), pp. 137,167–8; for an account of Hoby's work see Beier (1987), pp. 218ff.

49 Webster (1979).

50 Although it is less often noted that they practised science in their homes: Thomas Bright refers to the '*domus Caeciliana*' of Elizabeth Cooke (Cecil) as a 'university' (in Hoby (1930), p. 255) and she is the dedicatee of Markham's *English Huswife* (1615), possibly even the compiler; this book and Henry Buttes' *Dyets Dry Dinner* (1599) which is dedicated to her sister Anne Cooke Bacon (mother of Francis Bacon the scientist), are the two of the three in this genre directly connected with aristocratic women in the pre-1617 period. The third is really a sub-section of another, Thomas Tusser's *One hundreth Points of Good Husbandry* (1563), and forms *One hundreth Points of Good Huswifry* which was dedicated to Elizabeth Paget in 1570.

51 See Warnicke (1983) for an extended argument of this suggestion.

52 *Ibid.*, p. 130.

53 Lewalski (1993).

54 Schleiner (1994) pp. 3–4.

55 Warnicke (1983) speaks of this as a general reason for lack of recorded education for girls.

56 Grafton and Jardine (1986).

57 Beier (1987).

58 Pelling (1979).

59 Gerard (1597). Jeffers (1967) provides a helpful breakdown of contributors to Gerard's *Herbal*.

60 Held in the Worthing county museum: I thank the curator Dr Sally White for permission to study this manuscript (No. 3574). The Wellcome Institute manuscript (No. 213 Ac 39881) provides an interesting link since it is the housekeeper's book of the Arundel family under Alethea's mother-in-law Ann Dacre. A comparison of the contents of the two manuscript books indicates that the housekeeper was largely responsible for food and cookery, not the scientific and medicinal.

5

'How I These Studies Prize': The Countess of Pembroke and Elizabethan Science

Margaret P. Hannay

Mary Sidney Herbert, Countess of Pembroke (1561–1621), the first woman to achieve a literary reputation in England, was also interested in investigations of the natural world: chemistry, particularly in its practical medical applications; embryology; and New World exploration. Although the many dedications to her are more likely to praise more conventional qualities, such as her beauty and virtue or her skill in music and needlework, they often do mention her learning. William Gager, for example, combines ritual praise of her beauty and bright eyes with praise of her learning and Abraham Fraunce similarly characterizes her as 'pious, beautiful and erudite'.[1] Most dedications connect her with her famous brother Sir Philip Sidney; Aemilia Lanyer even lauds her as her brother's superior in 'virtue, wisedome, learning, dignity'.[2] When she was celebrated for her learning, that usually meant her knowledge of languages and her skill in rhetoric, as when Michael Drayton equates learning and poetry by praising her as 'learnings famous Queene', one who wears 'the Lawrell crowne'.[3] That limited definition of learning is equally evident when Nathaniel Baxter acclaims her 'wisedome' and 'learning' and her 'skill, in mightie Poesie' as demonstrated by 'her learned Poems, and her Layes'.[4] The term 'learning' is used for her religious devotion as well as her knowledge of languages and literature, as in Walter Sweeper's praise of her 'learning humane and divine'.[5] Her learning is also connected to her patronage of both poets and clergy by those whose sought her favour, as Nicholas Breton's address to her as 'the Right Honourable, discreete, and vertuous Lady, the Nourisher of the Learned and favorer of the Godly'.[6]

The Countess of Pembroke achieved a literary reputation by her patronage and by her own writings and translations, which circulated fairly widely. Two of her translations from French were printed in 1592: *A Discourse of Life and Death* by Philip de Mornay and *Antonius*, a tragedy by Robert Garnier. Two original works were also printed in her lifetime: 'The Dolefull Lay of Clorinda' in Edmund Spenser's *Astrophel* (1595) and a 'Dialogue . . . in praise of Astrea' in Francis Davison's *A Poetical Rapsody* (1602).[7] She also translated from the Italian at least one part of Petrarch's *Trionfi*, 'The Triumph of Death', which had limited manuscript circulation, as did her original dedicatory poems to Queen Elizabeth I and Philip Sidney. She was primarily celebrated for her completion of the metric Psalms paraphrases begun by her brother Philip. Based on the 1560 Geneva Bible and the Psalms in the Book of Common Prayer, supplemented by study of virtually every translation and commentary available to her in English, French, Latin and quite possibly Hebrew, her *Psalmes* evidence both biblical scholarship and mastery of a wide variety of English metric and quantitative verse forms. Restricted to manuscript circulation in the aristocratic fashion, they were praised and imitated by other poets, including John Donne, Aemilia Lanyer and George Herbert. Her *Psalmes* were most famously praised by Samuel Daniel, who said they would keep her 'fresh in fame' even after '*Wilton* lyes low levell'd with the ground', forming a 'Monument that cannot be over-throwne'.[8] Her reputation for scholarship was thus based on her contribution to languages and literature – learning in the humanist definition of the term.

An interest in chemistry and medicine was not usually considered 'learning' in the poets' sense. For example, John Aubrey says that her son Philip Herbert, later Earl of Montgomery and 4th Earl of Pembroke, 'espoused not Learning'. Then he declares that 'His chiefest Diversion was Chymistrie, which his Lordship did understand very well and he made Medicines, that did great Cures'.[9] Philip Herbert's interest in chemistry and in making medicines was evidently shared by his mother. Mary Sidney may well have had an active role in providing medical help to the household and surrounding community. Certainly some knowledge of chemistry, particularly that branch dealing with practical medicine, would have been the norm for an educated woman during the seventeenth century (see Lynette Hunter's chapter above). Gervase Markham's *The English Housewife* (1615), for example, assumes that every woman will have some medical knowledge. His first chapter gives instruction on 'her general knowledges both in physic and surgery, with plain approved medicines for health of the household, also the extraction of excellent oils fit for those purposes'. Markham explains 'that sith the preservation and care of the family touching their health and soundness of body consisteth most in her diligence, it is meet that she have a physical kind of knowledge; how to administer many wholesome receipts or medicines'. Although he maintains that the 'depth and secrets' of medicine are restricted to 'learned professors', he assumes that she will undertake the primary care of her family.[10] That obligation could extend to the larger household of servants and local villagers, as is evident from the diaries of Margaret Hoby and Grace Sherrington Mildmay.

Margaret Dakins Devereux Sidney Hoby was related to the Countess of Pembroke, for her beloved second husband was Mary Sidney's youngest brother Thomas; widowed for a second time at age twenty-five, Margaret was then married to Thomas Posthumous Hoby. Her diary, begun as a spiritual exercise, also gives many practical details of her life at Hackness, including her medical work (Hoby, 1930). In her entry for 30 January 1599, for example, she writes, 'After I had praied privatly I dressed apoore boies legge that Came to me, and then brake my fast with Mr Hoby: after, I dressed the hand of one of our servants that was verie sore Cutt . . . after to supper, then to the lector: after that I dressed one of the mens handes that was hurt, lastly praied, and so to bed'.[11] On 31 January she 'dressed :2: that was hurte', on 2 February she 'dressed the sores that Cam to me' and after dinner 'I rede of the arball [herbal]', on 4 February 'at 5 a cloke I dressed my patientes', and so on. Dressing injuries such as 'Hilares finger' (ibid., p. 186) was a routine task, noted in many entries, as was her administering of medicines, her distribution of herbs from her garden and her attendance during childbirth. She also made medicines, recording that she was busy 'makinge of oile and in my Clositt tell towardes diner time' (p. 134) and that she distilled 'Aqua: Vitae' (p. 180). Most astonishing is her bold, if unsuccessful, attempt to operate on an infant: 'this day, in the afternone, I had had a child brought to me that was borne at Silpho, one Talliour sonne, who had no fundement, and had no passage for excrementes but att the Mouth: I was ernestly intreated to Cutt the place to se if any passage Could be made, but although I Cutte deepe and seearched, there was none to be found' (p. 184). Such an entreaty would indicate that the local people had confidence, perhaps excessive confidence, in her surgical skills.

Similarly, Grace Mildmay records that her mother had 'good knowledge in phisick and surgerie', and that the gentlewoman who educated her 'let me read in Dr. Turner's Herball and Bartholomew Vigoe', identified by Rachel Weigall as William Turner's *New Herball* (1551) and *The most excellent workes of chirurgerye made and set forth by maister J. Vigon* (1543).[12] Later in her life Lady Mildmay recorded that she spent part of each day studying 'in the Herball and books of phisick, and in ministering to one or other by the directions of the best phisitions of myne acquaintance; and ever God gave a blessing thereunto'.[13] In addition to her diary and her household account books, she left several manuscript books of receipts, copied after her death by her daughter Mary.[14] As was customary, the receipts were clearly identified by their authors: 'A medecine for the Falling sickness taught by Mrs. Stacey', 'To take awaie a corne of the toe, taught by Mr Clarke', 'A very good receipt against the Jaunders [jaundice], taught by olde Mistress Bash'.[15]

Other educated women undertook similar medical responsibilities, which seem to have been considered routine. All three of Thomas More's daughters were educated in medicine as well as religion and the classics, for example, as were the learned Cooke sisters.[16] Margaret Clifford also had medical knowledge, as her daughter Anne records: 'She was a lover of the Study and practice of Alchimy, by which she found out excellent Medicines, that did much good to many; she delighted in the Distilling of waters, and other Chymical extractions, for she had some knowlege in most kind of Minerals, herbs, flowers and plants'.[17] Margaret

Clifford evidently passed down that knowledge to her daughter, for in the Clifford 'Great Picture' Anne is shown with a library which includes not only religious works, the classics and contemporary literature, but also works such as John Gerard's *The Herball or Generall Historie of Plantes*, Henry Cornelius Agrippa's *Vanity of Sciences*, and Loys le Roy's *Variety of Things*, as well as Abraham Ortelius' *Theatrum orbis terrarum*.[18] The women of the family took care of each other. When Margaret and Anne Clifford were exposed to the 1603 plague, Lady Warwick, Margaret Clifford's sister, sent them medicines. When her mother was very ill in 1616 and nearly died, Anne Clifford sent her cordials to speed her recovery.[19] Other seventeenth-century diaries, letters and memoirs document aristocratic women's medical skill. For example, Alice Thornton and her mother also nursed each other, as well as others in the household; Lady Anne Howard, Countess of Arundel, was renowned for her medical skill; and during the Civil War women such as Lady Ann Halkett undertook the care of wounded soldiers.[20] Bathsua Makin, the scholarly tutor of Princess Elizabeth Stuart, was also reputed to be 'a good Chymist' with considerable medical knowledge.[21] In using the famous description of a virtuous woman from Proverbs 31 to justify education for women, Makin argues that 'She could not look well to the wayes of the Houshold, except she understood Physick and Chirurgery'.[22] That is, caring for her household not only justifies but requires scientific knowledge for a woman, a factual statement, but also a clever rhetorical ploy. Makin herself had a keen interest in astronomy, demonstrated by her request that her brother John send her information on 'the new comet'.[23]

Mary Sidney may well have undertaken similar responsibilities for primary medical care, but lacking a diary like those of Hoby and Mildmay, or a child's reminiscence as we have for Margaret Clifford and for Grace Mildmay's mother, there is no direct evidence that she did so. What is certain is that the Pembrokes were wealthy enough to retain the services of a physician in residence in the household, whether they were at their primary estate of Wilton, or their other estates at Ramsbury, Ivychurch, or their London home Baynards Castle, or at one of the official residences of the Lord President of the Marches of Wales, such as Ludlow Castle.

Any attempt to recover Mary Sidney's scientific work is frustrated by reliance on John Aubrey, who asserts that 'Her Honour's genius lay as much towards chymistrie as poetrie'.[24] Although his biographical notes are almost as much gossip as fact, Aubrey seems more likely to make up references to sex than to chemistry.[25] When he says that 'She was a great Chemist, and spent yearly a great deale in that study', he appears to base his assertion of her interest in chemistry on her own chemical work and her association with scientists: Adrian Gilbert, one 'Mr. Boston', Thomas Moffet and Matthew Lister.[26] Fortunately, there is some material evidence to substantiate her chemical work and her association with these scientists.

Aubrey says that 'She kept for her Laborator in the house Adrian Gilbert (vulgarly called Dr. Gilbert) halfe-brother to Sir Walter Raleigh, who was a great Chymist in those dayes'.[27] Aubrey says elsewhere of Gilbert, 'He was a man of great parts, but the greatest buffoon in England; cared not what he said to man or woman of what quality soever. Some curious ladies of our country have rare receipts of his.'[28] The Countess of Pembroke was one of those ladies, as can be verified by virtually identical receipts. 'Adrian Gilbert's Cordiall water' is made of roses, cinnamon, gillyflowers, scallions, cloves, peaches and other spices and herbs, as well as a somewhat rarer ingredient, a unicorn's horn. The water was to be distilled, combined with civet, musk and ambergris in a linen bag, and then thoroughly aired before additional distilling. It was said to be beneficial for a wide variety of diseases, including consumption, digestive problems, measles, pox, fever, and also 'delivereth women and maketh to goe out theire time'. The receipt says that a large spoonful is 'good in all diseases and hurtfull to none'; in extreme cases the dose may be increased to two spoonfuls.[29] Another receipt called the '*tragea Comitisse Pembrokiae*' is nearly identical, but omits the unicorn's horn. The similarity of these receipts probably does indicate, as Mary Lamb suggests, that 'Gilbert worked with his patron in her laboratory to produce medicines'.[30] While these household manuscripts were usually compiled over several generations, and receipts may have been entered by other countesses, this particular receipt does provide material evidence both for Mary Sidney's involvement in such household medicine and for her association with Gilbert.[31]

Adrian Gilbert was the brother of the explorer Sir Humphrey Gilbert and of William Gilbert, one of the most able physicians and scientists of the age. He was also half-brother to the Herberts' kinsman and ally Sir Walter Ralegh, who was himself interested in chemistry and medicine, as well as New World exploration. Furthermore, Adrian Gilbert worked closely with the chemist and astrologer John Dee, whom Philip Sidney had visited on occasion, as had the queen and many members of the court.[32] Dee's *Mysteriorum Libri V. His conference with angels*, a holograph manuscript written between 22 December 1581 and 30 May 1583, asks, 'Adrian Gilbert how far, or in what points is he to be made privie of our practice, seeing it . . .was sayd, "That none shall enter into the knowledge of these mysteries with me, but onely thir worker". Truely the man is very comfortable to our society.' The answer is given, 'He may be made prive to some things: such as shall be necessrie.'[33]

Philip Sidney evidently studied chemistry with Dee. Thomas Moffet records that he could 'never be so far misled as to taste' astrology 'even with the tip of his tongue' because of his religious devotion. But 'led by God, with Dee as teacher, and with Dyer as companion, he learned chemistry, that starry science, rival to nature'. He was not, as Moffet admits that he himself was, deterred by 'the variety of opinions, the tricks of the teachers, the high costs, the uncertainty of results', but pressed ahead in his search for knowledge. Moffet claims that Sidney 'made corrections upon various authors of scientific works [such as Aristotle, Plato, Plotinus], and by his methods led sundry to writing more correctly – or at least to observing more correctly'.[34] So whatever Mary Sidney's active involvement in scientific enquiry, she certainly lived in a household where science, particularly chemistry, was valued.

The next scientist Aubrey mentions is 'one Mr. Boston'. Boston, a resident of Salisbury, remains a shadowy figure. Aubrey called him 'a good Chymist' who did 'great cures with his art'. Like many scientists of the day, his work was on the border between chemistry and alchemy, and his life reads like a morality tale. 'The lady Mary, Countesse of Pembroke, did much esteeme him for his skill, and would have had him to have been her operator, and live with her, but he would not accept of her Ladyship's kind offer. But after long search after the philosopher's stone, he died at Wilton, having spent his estate. After his death they found in his laboratory two or three baskets of egge shelles, which I remember Geber saieth is a principall ingredient of that stone.'[35] Or, as Dick renders the passage, he 'did undoe himselfe by studying the Philosophers-stone, and she would have kept him, but he would have all the golde to himselfe, and so dyed, I thinke, in a Gaole'.[36] If this unsubstantiated statement were at all accurate, then Mary Sidney might have been interested in the philosopher's stone as well as in practical medical cures, but her association with Thomas Moffet suggests a more rigorous approach to chemistry.

Thomas Moffet was the family physician as well as an entomologist, of whom Aubrey says, 'the learned Dr. Mouffet, that wrote of Insects and of Meates, had a pension hence'.[37] Moffet not only wrote the learned *Insectorum sive minimorum anamalium theatrum*, but also a more playful volume, *The Silkewormes and Their Flies*, dedicated to Mary Sidney. That lively account in mock heroic verse gives fanciful mythological explanations for every aspect of the silkeworm's life; it also gives precise scientific information on their culture. No doubt the countess, like some other aristocratic women, did raise silkworms for cloth production, a natural supplement to the wool production for which Wilton is famous. If she were directly involved in raising silkworms, it would have been helpful to know to incubate the eggs by laying them in a box lined with white paper, and to feed the worms only mulberry leaves, preferably those from black mulberries. Moffet tells the ladies to put each worm in a separate 'paper/coffin fine' when it begins to spin its cocoon. Once the worms complete their metamorphosis into flies, the ladies should harvest the empty cocoons for silk and mate the flies to produce new offspring.[38]

Aubrey's claim that Mary Sidney gave Moffet a generous annual pension is quite plausible, for he was part of the Pembroke household. He wrote *Nobilis* celebrating Sir Philip Sidney as a model for her eldest son, William Herbert, later 3rd Earl of Pembroke. Moffet drops into his account of Sidney's life praise of Mary Sidney, no doubt meant for her eyes. She was 'a sister', Moffet says, 'as no

Englishman, for aught I know, had ever possessed before . . . too great for any praise or for any speech of mine.'[39] *Nobilis* includes intimate details about the family, like Philip Sidney's resolution when his first child was a daughter, and his distress over the illness of his sister Mary. Moffet not only lived at Wilton, but also travelled with the household. In his practical medical volume *Health's Improvement*, for example, he describes Ludlow as the ideal location: 'the best situation of a house or city, is upon the slaunt of a southwest hill (like to this of Ludlow, wherein we sojourne for a time)'. He also celebrated Christmas there with the family, for he mentions the 'Wild Calves' of Wales, 'whence one was brought this last Christmas to Ludlow Castle, where I did eat of it rosted and bak'd'.[40]

After Moffet's death in 1604, his place was taken by the 'handsome and learned' doctor Matthew Lister, some ten years younger than the recently widowed countess. This noted doctor was evidently more than her physician. Aubrey repeats a rumour of her marriage to Lister, adding 'Jack Markham saies they were not maried'.[41] They were not married, for she retained the property that she would have lost under the terms of her husband's will, which stipulated that she must be 'solo and unmaryed'.[42] Her flirtation with Lister is well documented. John Chamberlain also reported the rumour of this marriage: 'Here is a suspicion that the old Countesse of Pembroke is maried to Doctor Lister that was with her at the Spa' where she had gone to take the waters in 1614 to 1616.[43] Lister's relationship with the countess is dramatized in *Loves Victory*, a pastoral play by Mary Sidney's niece Lady Wroth. Lister appears as the 'Lissius' loved by 'Simeana' (Mary Sidney); after a tempestuous relationship, they become 'the couple Cupid best doth love'.[44] Lister apparently cared for Mary Sidney's daughter Anne, who died unmarried after a long illness in the early Stuart years, and he was part of her household at Houghton House in Bedfordshire. Aubrey says that he built Houghton House for her, and that 'He was her surveyour, and managed her estate'.[45] Lister's exact duties remain unclear, but John Chamberlain gossiped after her death in 1621 that she had left him a legacy of 'sixe or sevenscore pound a yeare', adding 'which is well worne in her service, for they say he lookes old'.[46] Lister, not too seriously worn, lived until 1656, subsequently serving as physician to Robert Cecil, Earl of Salisbury, to Queen Anne, and then to Charles I, who knighted him in 1636.

So what can we know for certain about Mary Sidney's interest in chemistry and medicine? She is said to have enjoyed the company of physicians and scientists, to have worked in her own laboratory with professional chemists, to have developed medicines, to have raised silkworms, to have been interested in the philosopher's stone and, more scandalously, to have supervised the breeding of Wilton's famous racehorses.[47] We also know that she supported New World exploration, a topic that fascinated her brother Philip and was enthusiastically supported by her sons. She herself subscribed £28 to Frobisher's journey, presumably from her own resources, for her husband pledged more than £172.[48]

Portrait of the Countess of Pembroke by Simeon van de Passe (1618).

Unfortunately, they were not prompt in making their payment. The countess later did support Fenton's voyage and was a stockholder in the Virginia Company.

We see confirmation of these scientific interests in her paraphrases of the Psalms. Much of her own experience is reflected in these poems, including her interest in New World exploration and in embryology, both included in Psalm 139. This Psalm, entitled in the Geneva version 'Nothing secret to God', begins 'O Lord, thou hast tryed me and knowne me'.[49] The psalmist develops this idea by explaining that wherever he may travel, God will be with him; indeed, God has been with him even from his mother's womb. Even if he could travel to the heavens or to hell, God would be there, nor could he escape God if he would 'take the wings of the morning, and dwell in the uttermost parts of the sea' (v. 9). In rendering this passage Mary Sidney obviously interprets the biblical phrase, 'the uttermost parts of the sea' as the west, or the New World, the furthest reaches of the globe from her perspective. Here she echoes Théodore de Bèze (v. 9), 'the formost part of the west', but she is also expressing an interest in New World exploration.[50]

> O sunn, whome light nor flight can match,
> suppose thy lightfull flightfull wings
> thou lend to me;
> and I could flee
> as farr as thee the ev'ning brings;
> ev'n ledd to West he would me catch,
> nor should I lurk with western things. (Ps. 139, ll. 29–35)[51]

God is present even in the uttermost west, a concept that no doubt reassured explorers. For example, Sir Humphrey Gilbert, just before his ship was swallowed by waves on his way home from Newfoundland, was said to have shouted 'We are as near to Heaven by sea as by land'.[52] Elsewhere she draws on New World accounts of bestial savages when she describes the ungodly who devour God's people as 'Wolvish Canibals' (Variant Ps. 53, l. 15), an expansion of her brother Philip's reference to 'Caniballs, who, as if they were bread,/ Gods people do devower' in his rendition of Psalm 14, ll. 14, 15.

Although Mary Sidney was obviously well aware of Copernican astronomy and of the circular earth, she, like other poets such as John Donne and John Milton, continues to use the Ptolemaic cosmos for poetic purposes. In Psalm 139, l. 24, for example, she refers to the 'starry Spheare', and she also speaks of the distance of 'the Sphere of farthest starre' from 'earthly Center' in Psalm 103, ll. 42, 43.

Her expansion of biblical references to pregnancy and childbirth has been studied primarily as reflections of her own experience.[53] These references, however personal, also demonstrate a real interest in embryology. When she

writes of the fear that came upon the ungodly 'as upon a woman in travaile'
(Ps. 48: 6), she obviously speaks from her own experience as a woman who has
borne children and who has assisted in the childbirth of friends and family, as
was her duty. She expands the reference to intensify the pain: 'as the wife, whose
wofull care/the panges of child-bed findes' (Ps. 48, ll. 17–18). Yet she also records
a detailed observation of a miscarriage or still birth. Whereas the Geneva Bible
reads, 'Let him consume like a snaile that melteth, and like the untimelie frute of
a woman, that hathe not sene the sunne' (Ps. 58, l. 8), she gives a more detailed
description of the miscarriage:

> so make them melt as the dishowsed snaile
> or as the Embrio, whose vitall band
> breakes er it holdes, and formlesse eyes doe faile
> to see the sunn, though brought to lightfull land. (Ps. 58, ll. 21–4)

She has clearly seen a foetus with its unformed eyes, either her own child
(perhaps the tragedy alluded to in her letter to Barbara Gamage), or that of a
woman whose labour she attended.[54]
   More detailed is her treatment of Psalm 139, ll. 13–16, a description of God's
care for the psalmist even from the womb. The biblical passage reads as follows:

> For thou hast possessed my reines: thou hast covered me in my mothers wombe.
> I wil praise thee, for I am fearfully and wonderously made: marvelous are thy
> workes. . . .
> My bones are not hid from thee, thogh I was made in a secret place, and
> facioned beneth in the earth [explained in a note as 'in my mothers wombe'].
> Thine eyes did se me, when I was without forme: for in thy boke were all things
> writen, which in continuance were facioned, when there was none of them before.

The intent of the passage is explained in a note: 'Seeing that thou didst knowe
me before I was composed of ether flesh or bone, much more now must thou
knowe me when thou hast facioned me.' In Pembroke's rendition more attention
is paid to the process of fashioning the child itself, to the process by which we all
are ' wonderously made'.

> Each inmost peece in me is thine:
> while yet I in my mother dwelt,
> all that me cladd
> from thee I hadd.
> thou in my frame hast strangly delt;
> needes in my praise thy workes must shine
> so inly them my thoughts have felt. (Ps. 139, ll. 43–9)

Here her emphasis is on the process by which our 'frame' is 'cladd', that is, the process by which the embryo develops into a child. As she so frequently does, she turns to the commentaries of de Bèze and Calvin to render this Psalm. In the next stanza she develops metaphors of 'raftring', or building, and of embroidery, both present in John Calvin's commentary on this Psalm.[55] The 'frame', the skeleton, is described both as the architectural framework of a building and the frame on which embroidery is stretched for working. De Bèze conjoins the embroidery metaphor with the dark cave or secret place of the womb: 'when I was . . . fashioned in the darke cave, as it were with needleworke' (v. 15). As John Rathmell has observed, Calvin draws a tighter connection between the images by comparing the womb to the 'dark denne' of the tailor's workroom.[56] Pembroke amplifies these metaphors to discuss God's creation of the human body:

> Thou, how my back was beam-wise laid,
> and raftring of my ribbs dost know:
> know'st ev'ry point
> of bone and joynt,
> how to this whole these partes did grow,
> in brave embrodry faire araid,
> though wrought in shopp both dark and low. (Ps. 139, ll. 50–6)

Whereas the psalmist says that God saw him 'when I was without forme', Pembroke develops de Bèze's phrase, that he was an 'unfashioned lumpe without shape' (v. 16):

> Nay fashonles, ere forme I toke,
> thy all and more beholding ey
> my shaplesse shape
> could not escape. (Ps. 139, ll. 57–60)

That is, God alone could foresee the form, the shape of the child when it was yet unformed and shapeless. The Geneva version explains that God could foresee the end of the project 'for in thy boke were all things writen, which in continuance were facioned, when there was none of them before' (v.16). Both Calvin and de Bèze discuss the complex process necessary for forming the child, but de Bèze makes clearer the image of the craftsman's book detailing the project: 'my fashioning, and also the verie time appointed thereunto was set downe in thy booke, before any part of that workmanship was made' (v. 16). Once again Mary Sidney expands the metaphor, depicting God laying out the project in his work book, with a schedule for completing each stage:

all these, with tymes appointed by,
ere one had beeing, in the booke
of thy foresight, enrol'd did ly. (Ps. 139, ll. 61–3)

This idea of the child as shapeless at first and then gradually assuming a form
fits the embryology of the period. Considered mysterious because it was difficult
to observe, the process was believed to begin with the male and female seed
'curled together in a mass'; membranes then enclosed the mass and fibres formed
within it, before three specks formed which were to become the brain, liver and
heart. The foetus was 'a milky blob for six days, then a blood-mass, then flesh'
and then a tiny human being by eighteen days after conception.[57] Pembroke's
metaphor precisely matches this process of the formless taking form under God's
watchful eye. She expresses delight in embryology, for she exclaims,

My god, how I these studies prize,
that doe thy hidden workings show! (Ps. 139, ll. 64–5)

Like her contemporary Francis Bacon, she sees science as revealing the
'hidden workings' of God in nature. Her religious convictions thus encouraged
her scholarship, both her study of the scriptures and her study of science. As
Bathsua Makin uses the book of Proverbs to justify scientific education for
women, so the Countess of Pembroke uses the Psalms to express her joy in her
study of the natural world: 'how I these studies prize'.

Notes

1 Gager (1592); the dedication appears in the Huntington Library copy, without signature number.
Fraunce (1592), sig. A2.

2 Lanyer (1993), p. 28.

3 Drayton (1931), 1: 74, 76.

4 Nathaniel Baxter, *Ournia*, sig. A2, B1, B4[v], N2[v].

5 Sweeper (1622), sig. A2[v].

6 Breton (1966), 1.j.3.

7 Her authorship of 'The Dolefull Lay' is disputed. See Hannay (1990), pp. 63–7 and Sidney, ed.
Hannay, Kinnamon and Brennan (forthcoming).

8 Daniel (1594), sig. H6[v].

9 Aubrey (1949), p. 139. Editions of Aubrey's scattered biographical notes differ considerably. I
have consulted the expurgated version edited by Andrew Clark (1898) and the modernized version
edited by Richard Barber (1982), but, unless otherwise indicated, I quote from Dick's edition as the
most complete.

10 Markham (1986), p. 8.

11 Hoby (1930), p. 100.

12 Weigall (1911), pp. 120–1.

13 *Ibid.*, p. 125. See also Warnicke (1989).

14 On Mildmay's receipts in relation to Galenic, Paracelsian and alchemical medicine, see Pollock (1993).

15 Weigall, p. 131.

16 Hurd-Mead (1979), p. 343.

17 Anne Clifford, BL MS Harl. 6177, cited from Hoby (1930), pp. 57–8. See also Lewalski (1993), p. 134.

18 See Lewalski (1993), p. 137 and a photograph of the 'Great Picture', *ibid.*, p. 124. See also Holmes (1975), p. 138; and Lamb (1992).

19 *Diary*, 12, 26.

20 For women as 'Popular Practitioners' of medicine in the seventeenth century, see Nagy (1988), pp. 54–78. Nagy observes that the lives of the aristocracy are better documented than the lives of those from lower classes, but their duties were not necessarily much different.

21 'Bathsua Makin' in Blain, Grundy and Clements (1990), p. 704.

22 Bathsua Makin, 'An Essay to Revive the Antient Education of Gentlewomen', in Wilson and Warnke (1989), p. 300; see also Teague (1992).

23 Teague, in Wilson and Warnke (1989), p. 292. 'The comet was either the Great Comet of 1680 or Halley's Comet of 1682.'

24 Aubrey (1969), p. 89.

25 Aubrey, writing more than fifty years after her death, famously asserts that Mary Sidney was promiscuous and incestuous; his unreliability on such matters is readily demonstrated by his opening statement that William Herbert, 1st Earl of Pembroke, warned his son to keep young Mary at home lest he be cuckolded, but William Herbert had died in 1570, seven years before the marriage. At the time of William Herbert's death, Henry Herbert was still married to Catherine Talbot and Mary Sidney was a small child.

26 Aubrey (1949), p. 139.

27 *Ibid.*

28 Aubrey (1969), p. 90 and (1982), p. 139n. Sir Walter Ralegh, who was closely connected to the Herbert family, was himself known for his interest in medicine.

29 Bodleian Library MS Ashmole 1499 V, f. 209 and MS Ashmole 1385, f. 145.

30 BL Sloane MS 1988, f. 138; Lamb (1976), p. 107.

31 Another receipt is entitled 'My Lady of Pembrookes Vomett', which if drunk while 'fasting it will make you vomytt', MS Ashmole 1481 V, f. 13. Nagy (1988) notes that the practice of keeping such receipt books 'must have been widespread', for the Bedfordshire Record Office contains at least ten such books and other examples can be found in the British Library. 'One receipt book is known to have been passed down through six successive generations of females in a matriarchally linked family.' For almost a hundred and twenty years each generation added to the book 'as it was passed from mother to daughter' (*ibid.*, p. 67).

32 Dee (1842).

33 BL Sloane MS 3188, f. 103.

34 Moffet (1940), p. 75.

35 Aubrey (1969), 2: 90.

36 Aubrey (1949), p. 139.

37 Aubrey (1969), 2: 89.

38 Moffet (1599), sig. H4v–K1.

39 Moffet (1940), pp. 85–6.

40 Moffet (1655), pp.18, 72.

41 Aubrey (1949), p. 139.

42 Will of Henry Herbert, 2nd Earl of Pembroke, f. 2.

43 John Chamberlain to Sir Dudley Carleton, 5 April 1617, in Chamberlain (1979), 2: 69.

44 Wroth (1988), p. 162. The identification of Lissius with Lister was first made by Josephine Roberts (1983).

45 Aubrey (1898), 2:35.

46 Chamberlain (1979), 2:400.

47 Aubrey says that she was salacious in viewing the mating through a 'vidette', or peeping hole, built near her house (Aubrey (1949), p. 138).

48 *Acts of the Privy Council of England* (London: HMSO, 1906), 10:414–15. See also Hannay (1990), p. 42.

49 All biblical references are to the Geneva version (Geneva, 1560. Facsimile. Madison: University of Wisconsin Press, 1969).

50 De Bèze (1581).

51 *Psalmes* quotations are taken from Noel J. Kinnamon's transcriptions for our forthcoming *Collected Works of Mary Sidney Herbert, Countess of Pembroke*. The Penshurst *Psalmes* MS is quoted with the kind permission of the Viscount de L'Isle, from his collection at Penshurst Place.

52 Hoffmann (1977), p. 192. Humphrey Gilbert drowned in 1583, more than a decade before Pembroke completed her *Psalmes*.

53 Fisken (1985), pp. 166–83; Hannay (1994), pp. 20–35. For other passages on conception and childbirth, see her paraphrases of Psalms 51, 71, 104, 113 and 127.

54 Mary Sidney Herbert, Countess of Pembroke, to Barbara Gamage, Lady Sidney, dated from 'Willton this 9 of September 1591', corrected to 1590. Bound in British Library Additional MS 15232.

55 Calvin (1571).

56 Sidney and Sidney (1963), p. xx.

57 Eccles (1982), p. 43. See also such recent studies as Fraser (1984), pp. 440–63; Hobby (1988), pp. 177–89; Otten (1992); Keller (1985).

6

LUCY HUTCHINSON, ATOMISM AND THE ATHEIST DOG

Reid Barbour

Sometime between 1645 and 1658, Lucy Hutchinson took on and completed the enormous task of translating the ancient scientific epic of the Latin poet considered by her contemporaries to rank among the most obscure, dangerous, yet valuable – the *De rerum natura* of Lucretius.[1] For Hutchinson and her contemporaries, Lucretius' danger and value were closely associated. Committed to the transmission of Epicurean physics and ethics, the Roman poet maintained that the world had been created by the fortuitous collision and combination of atoms in an infinite void; that all worlds and everything in the world, including mortal human souls, are made of atoms and void; that matter is eternal or uncreated; that human happiness depends on the imitation of gods whose bliss derives from their detachment from the world, not their governance of it; that tranquillity follows from the analysis of all phenomena in atomic terms, which leads in turn to the expulsion of human fears about death, the afterlife and the gods. As manuscripts of her work continue to emerge, scholars are further demonstrating what her famous writings suggest, namely, that Hutchinson (just as many so-called 'Puritans') was a person of considerable learning with rich cultural interests. Yet in so far as these Epicurean principles are seriously at odds with her deep commitment to providence as the driving force in public and private history, the choice of Lucretius for translation has struck Hutchinson's modern readers as something of a conundrum.[2]

At least by 1675, when she dedicated the only surviving manuscript of the translation to the Earl of Anglesey, Lucy Hutchinson herself had come to view the work as a 'wanton dalliance' with atheism. Although she undertook her translation of Lucretius with her children all around her, she now worries in the years after the Restoration that his degenerate and loathsome philosophy will debauch those unfortunate novices who come upon it. Rejecting almost wholesale (like Milton's Jesus in *Paradise Regained*) the errors and evils of paganism, Hutchinson's scorn for Lucretius is especially intense, assuming the shape of a conversion narrative '[a]s one, that, walking in the darke, had miraculously scapd a horrible precipice, by day light coming back & discovering his late danger, startles and reviews it wth affright' (Lucretius MS, f. 4v). But given her care for the preparation of the manuscript, it remains unclear how much value Hutchinson believes to reside in the poem: on the one hand the self-evident ills of atomism are themselves offered as a 'seamarke, to warne incautious travellers' about the sweet poison of human learning, but on the other her indictment of the 1670s as 'this drolling degenerate age' is directed against the new, court-sponsored rejection and misappropriation of 'all sober & serious studies', including her Lucretius. In her dedication to Anglesey, that is, Hutchinson's refutation of Epicurean doctrine as a prominent strain of pagan learning is closely and ironically tied to her alienation from a culture that in its trivialization of paganism evinces little regard for grace, virtue and liberty.

Even in the dedication, then, a conundrum remains: is the translator angry most of all at the transformation of Lucretius into a droll, or does she find it monstrous that anyone could ever find value in the atomism of a hedonistic atheist? Hutchinson allows that the Roman's atomism was directed against those superstitious ceremonies that she herself abhors, and her marginalia alongside the verses are more often than not designed for the clear exposition of Epicurean physics. All the same, both her dedication and marginalia express the translator's horror that she ever wantonly dallied with Lucretius and atomism. Whatever uses she may have derived from her work on Lucretius are largely cancelled after the Restoration. But her gift to Anglesey of the translation suggests that in her view the problems of the war are still with them and that a wise, pious and beleaguered reader might still gain something from Lucretius.

For some understanding of Hutchinson's motives for labouring over the *De rerum natura*, we must return from 1675 to 1645 and just after. We must consider, that is, the newly intense and complex mid-century relations between Epicurean atomism and Christian theology but also between a wartime ethics of tranquillity and the perceived irenicism of scientific method. Read selectively as most Renaissance pedagogues would urge, Lucretius addressed so many concerns of English intellectuals in the 1640s and '50s that Hutchinson's translation was as typical of her social circles and intellectual milieu as it was exceptional for a seventeenth-century woman operating within the culturally bounded masculine jurisdiction of both amateur science and classicism.

I

No one knew better than Lucy Hutchinson herself that her translation of Lucretius' ancient atomism into English couplets was an exceptional and audacious feat for a seventeenth-century woman, especially one with such clear commitments to Christian notions of providence and hierarchy. Some writers thought it an impossible feat for a female wit. In a poem encouraging Alexander Brome to translate *De rerum natura*, Aston Cockayne disparages the efforts of a certain lady who has vainly taken on the task. According to Cockayne, the lady will never finish her rendering because the Latin of Lucretius is too manly.[3] In a preface to his own selected translations, Dryden agrees that Lucretius lends himself only to masculine wits, for 'from this sublime and daring Genius of his, it must of necessity come to pass, that his thoughts must be Masculine, full of Argumentation, and that sufficiently warm'.[4] More than this, Dryden's image of Lucretius as a tyrannical schoolmaster not only locates the translation of *De rerum natura* in the masculinist tradition of humanist learning but also links the dogmatic authority of its author to the modern and 'perpetual Dictatorship' of Hobbes.

Whatever the disagreement among scholars about the extent of Latin learning among Elizabethan and Stuart women, Walter J. Ong is surely right to argue that in general, 'the rites [associated with Latin study] . . . are for boys alone'. Ong continues: 'in helping to maintain the closed male environment the psychological role of Latin should not be underestimated. It was the language of those on the "inside", and thus learning Latin at even an university level was the first step toward initiation into the closed world.'[5] There were, of course, exceptional women who profited from the presence of a brother's tutor, from the beneficence of a charitable parent, from the leisure allowed by royal or noble status, or from an industry charged with making the most out of a little spare time. But whatever the degree of Latin obtained by these women, the Jonsonian tendency to privilege a poetry informed by the 'consent of the learned' in terms of masculine wit is pervasive in Stuart culture. Although William Wotton can look back on a 'very modish' tendency in the Elizabethan age for women 'to believe that *Greek* and *Latin* added to their Charms', he insists that the age was exceptional in this regard, the underlying implication being that, as Thomas Overbury put it, 'Books are a part of Man's Prerogative'.[6]

For Lucy Hutchinson, then, Lucretius' *De rerum natura* was not just a scientific and an ethical treatise but a Latin epic placed prominently (if not squarely) among the monuments of Roman culture – in short, a poem that even Vergil strove to imitate. It might be argued that the very instability of Lucretius' place in the humanist tradition, together with the infamous presence of women in the Epicurean garden, offered ambiguous warrant for Stuart women to study the *De rerum natura*.[7] Such a claim is supported by the special, conflictive interest taken by Margaret Cavendish and Aphra Behn in atomism, natural philosophy and Lucretius as these matters pertain to their own imagination and education. But it is also lent credence by Hutchinson's own mixed and aggressive responses to Lucretius' treatment of women in Books 4 and 5. Omitting much of the passage describing sexual acts, she includes the one claiming that according to the laws of nature, the desires of women are just as valuable as the desires of men. But by contrast, having translated the Roman's satire on the variety of defective women, she transforms his section on fertility into a character of the good wife who should learn to please her husband.[8]

Given the rest of her work, it is clear that no issue caused Lucy Hutchinson more conflict than the status and authority of educated women. Nothing repelled her more than uxorious men or insubordinate women; but male authority is hardly uniformly good for Hutchinson, and there is ample evidence in her memoirs that she celebrated the classical and scientific education of women. Throughout the pages of her memoirs, Hutchinson applauds the education of women. There is her husband's mother, Margaret Biron, who was 'embellisht with the best education those dayes afforded'. Mr Hutchinson himself 'spar'd not any cost for the education of both his sons and daughters in languages, sciences, musick, dancing, and all other quallities befitting their father's house'. Then there is the extraordinary digression concerning the maternal grandmother of John Hutchinson, a woman whose attainment of 'a greate degree of learning and languages' is 'therefore more glorious because more rare in the female sex'. Even when this woman is stricken with madness, she is (we are told) 'not frantick, but had such a pretty deliration that her ravings were more delightfull than other woemen's most rationall conversations'.[9]

But it is Lucy Hutchinson's own extensive knowledge of Latin that elicits from her the most telling apologies. In an early scene in her narrative of the war, she confronts and implicitly criticizes the male monopoly of Latin when she tells the story of how her husband fell in love with her: as she recreates the scene, the women in their social circles pressed John Hutchinson to consider Lucy's scholarship as an unattractive eccentricity, but he came into her room, saw her Latin books before he ever saw her, and fell madly in love. In the fragment of her autobiography, Lucy lingers over her own zeal for learning in general but also over the mastery of Latin that gave her access to authors such as Lucretius and his legacy of atomism. This mastery was gained, she points out, despite a number of impediments including the distractions of such customary 'female' occupations as needlework, her mother's prohibition of excess in study, the poverty of wit in her Latin instructor and her own negative associations of the pursuit of learning with pleasure, pride, secrecy and thievery. What N. H. Keeble has said of her authority to write history might also be said of her authority to translate Lucretius: given her insistence 'on the propriety of women's subordination to men', her work 'is a gross impropriety'.[10]

When it comes to defending her translation of *De rerum natura*, she admits to the Earl of Anglesey that it extended beyond the normal sphere of women's activities ('things out of my owne Sphaere'). 'Had it bene a worke', she apologizes, 'that had merited glory, or could my sex, (whose more becoming vertue is silence,) deriue honor from writing, my aspiring Muse would not haue sought any other Patrone then your Lordship' (Lucretius MS, f. 2r). This is a strange defence, given the fact that her 'aspiring Muse' is indeed seeking the patronage that here she only hypothesizes. But clearly she takes little pride in her deviation from gender norms, even as she ridicules the 'masculine witt' – Evelyn – who wears the laurels on his title page for having published his translation of only one book of the poem. In fact, Lucy Hutchinson recommends only one alternative

translator to herself, not a man but a midwife. Omitting the notoriously racy
passage on human sexuality in Book 4, the translator gives her reason in the
gloss: 'The cause & effects of Loue which he makes a kind of dreame but much
here was left out for a midwife to translate whose obsceane art it would better
become then a nicer pen' (Lucretuis MS f. 97r). In this condescending note,
Hutchinson has in mind such contemporary authors as Jane Sharp, whose
Midwives Book (1671) deals explicitly with anatomy and sex. But for all the disdain
with which she severs nice literature from obscenity, Hutchinson's connection
between the art of the midwife and the nitty-gritty details of the body ironically
secures a further bond between women and the scientific epic of Lucretius. That
is, one strategy for discouraging seventeenth-century women from the classics
involved some concession to these women that the mundane practicalities of such
domestic sciences as herbal medicine were more appropriate for them.

More than the uneasy fit of the *De rerum natura* in the classical tradition, the
poem's authority in scientific circles offered Stuart women a point of entry in so far
as science was sometimes viewed as an appropriate hobby for women to have.
According to Patricia Phillips, 'scientific ladies' were considered less threatening
and insolent than those bluestockings who invaded the male jurisdiction of classical
learning. Put simply, the practice of science could be considered more like kitchen
work than the study of Ovid and Horace.[11] In fact, we know from Lucy
Hutchinson that her mother patronized the scientific experiments of Walter Ralegh
in the Tower of London, and that Lucy herself was required to have medical skills
during the war. 'Sir Walter Rawleigh and Mr. Ruthin being prisoners in the
Tower', she writes in her autobiography, 'and addicting themselves to chimistrie,
[Lucy's mother] suffer'd them to make their rare experiments at her cost, partly to
comfort and divert the poore prisoners, and partly to gaine the knowledge of their
experiments, and the medicines to helpe such poore people as were not able to
seeke to phisitians'.[12] If 'chimistrie' is a legacy that her mother left to her,
Hutchinson's practice of aiming her own literary activities at the edification of her
children suggests that in some measure her work on atomism was carried out to
afford them a useful knowledge later made repugnant to her family with the
royalist appropriation of science as well as Epicureanism after the Restoration.[13]
Whatever her eventual disclaimers, then, and given the bold deviation from gender
norms that her classicism and study of cosmic theories involved, Hutchinson was
sufficiently convinced of the relevance and value of atomism in the interregnum to
exert enormous effort on its transmission.

II

In her dedication to the Earl of Anglesey, Hutchinson explains that she undertook
the work in order 'to understand things I heard so much discourse of at second
hand' (Lucretius MS, f. 2v). These 'things' are, first and foremost, the widely and

fervently debated theories of atomism, a philosophy that fascinated physical theorists, empiricists, theologians, and moral essayists alike. Although the remark about 'so much discourse' makes plain the prominence of Epicureanism in Hutchinson's social circles, we cannot be sure whether her second-hand access to atomism was mainly textual or oral. In her narrative of the years leading up to the war, she places a high premium on refined conversation, so much so that she admits to dreading her family's removal to the north from the London area and 'from the friends and places she had so long convert in'.[14] In the 1640s, however, with the dreaded move to Nottinghamshire, she lived nearby the estate of the Cavendish family, which, as is well known, was active in importing atomistic ideas from the continent to England and in patronizing those persons most interested in what Robert Hugh Kargon has called a 'wide spectrum of "atomism"' in letters and publications.[15] Although Hutchinson grew more and more scornful of William Cavendish, in her narrative of the war she allows that around the time of her move north, he was 'a Lord so much once beloved in his Country . . . that no man was a greater prince than he in all that Northerne quarter, till a foolish ambition of glorious slavery carried him to Court, where he ran himselfe much in to debt, to purchase neglect of the King and Queene and scornes of the proud Courtiers'.[16] If Hutchinson's social and family circles intersected with those of the Cavendish family, then in turn her work on Lucretius would have gained the attention of such a widely connected poet as Aston Cockayne. Indeed, Hutchinson herself tells the Earl of Anglesey that the translation earned her a 'little glory among some few of my intimate friends', but also that a manuscript of the translation escaped the boundaries of this 'intimate' coterie.[17]

Whatever the specific channels of conversation through which Lucy Hutchinson heard about and contributed to the study of atomism, the more easily definable mode of transmission is of course the ready availability of texts. Even if we omit sixteenth- and seventeenth-century revisionary efforts stretching from the discovery of the manuscript of Lucretius in the fifteenth century to the serious attention paid to atomism by Francis Bacon and Thomas Harriot among others, Hutchinson had a wealth of relevant contemporary and famous works at her disposal – by, among others, Descartes, Digby and Sennert.[18] But the leading advocate of Epicureanism in the 1640s and '50s was Pierre Gassendi. This, the most famous, reviver of the ancient school began his work years before his major texts emerged between the late 1640s and late 1650s. How much Gassendi's work was known in England before Walter Charleton began to popularize it in the 1650s is hard to determine.[19] But Gassendi's intimacy with the Newcastle circle was secure throughout the 1640s; as Kargon puts it, '[d]uring the 1640s, Gassendi was in close contact with the Newcastle circle, the members of which eagerly received his published works. It was to a very large extent, through the members of this group, and especially Hobbes (Gassendi's good friend), that certain circles in England became aware of Gassendi's physics'.[20]

Gassendi is significant for any study of Hutchinson's Lucretius because he mounted such Herculean efforts to baptize Epicureanism in the name of the Christian God. The marriage of Epicurus and Christ was always bound to be what one scholar has called an 'unstable compound'.[21] Especially for such scholars as John Wilkins who were deeply committed to the ties that bind natural philosophy and the faith, the new physics was often better if shed of its Epicurean baggage because the Epicureans brought with them the spectre of atheism. This atheism often amounted to the idea that even if there are gods, they play no formative, sustaining or salvific role in the world. Indeed, this denial of divine creation and providence is the centrepiece of *De rerum natura* and, as such, had to be confronted by the scholars who took great pains to rework the scientific epic in the 1640s and '50s. Even more than Hutchinson, who denounces the 'dog' Lucretius in her dedication and in a handful of marginalia, the glossator of Creech's translation is elaborate in demonstrating the impious theology of the Epicurean. Another translator of Lucretius, John Evelyn, is firmly cautioned about the project in his correspondence with Jeremy Taylor, while John Worthington, in his preface to the reader of John Smith's *Select Discourses*, rightly stresses that one of Smith's most pressing concerns is the refutation of the newly revived atheism of the Epicureans. 'The Author', we are advised, 'pursues his discourse [on immortality and atheism] with a particular reflexion on the *Dogmata* and Notions of *Epicurus* and his followers, especially that great admirer of him, *Lucretius*, whose Principles are here particularly examined and refuted'. The reader is especially warned about 'the more wary and considerate modern *Epicureans*', who are all the more seductive for their careful revision of Epicurean 'principles' – in the sense of 'atoms' as well as 'tenets'.[22]

Despite and in answer to the commonplace rejection of Epicurean atheism, some notable mid-century philosophers and poets strive to baptize atomism and its corollary of countless inhabited worlds in an infinite space. There are the smaller efforts of such writers as Henry More, whose *'Democritus Platonissans'* follows Bruno, Burton and others in lauding the 'very noble Patronage for the cause [of infinite worlds] among the ancients, Epicurus, Democritus, Lucretius, &c.'.[23] But closer in spirit to Hutchinson herself is the attempt made by Jan Comenius to reconcile atomism with Scripture. In *Naturall Philosophie Reformed by Divine Light or a Synopsis of Physics* (trs. 1651), the influential reformer holds atomism up to the light of the Bible, reason and sense, and finds that the physical theory has merit. In discussing first principles as they are presented in Genesis, Comenius believes that the formlessness of God's first created matter is best explained as 'a Chaos of dispersed Atoms, cohering in no part thereof'. Atoms, he continues, are a perfect gloss for the Bible's motif of a world made from, and returned to, the particles of dust. 'Therefore', Comenius concludes, '*Democritus* erred not altogether, in making Atomes the matter of the world'. Even so, the ancient sage was mistaken in his theory that the atoms were eternal, autonomous and fortuitous, 'by reason that he was ignorant of that which the Wisdom of God hath revealed unto us, that the Atomes were conglutinated into a mass, by the infusion of the Spirit of life, and began to be distinguished into formes, by the comming in of the light'. Like so many mid-century students of the atom, Comenius is prepared to marry particle physics with Christianity, provided that the former is properly dressed. So it is that in Comenius' reformation of physics, atomism is shorn of its association with a vacuum.[24]

Around the time of Hutchinson's translation, the Englishman most responsible for baptizing atomism was Walter Charleton, who from text to text grapples at length with the array of arguments offered by Lucretius against divine creation and providence. Beginning in 1652 with *The Darknes of Atheism Dispelled by the Light of Nature, A Physico-Theological Treatise*, the royal physician follows in the line of Gassendi when he boldly defends the philosophical and experimental strengths of atomism in the course of exploding what is unchristian about Epicureanism.[25] For Charleton, as for Gassendi, such a refutation is part of the complicated and fitful process of culling what is acceptable about atomism as a form of scientific explanation in a Christian framework. According to Gassendi and Charleton, atomism can be embraced as the most feasible theory for explaining natural phenomena provided that it be added that God created, animated and disposed the atoms in the first place, and that a physical commitment to atomism does not compromise the rational as well as the devotional belief in the immortal soul. The impact of Gassendi on Charleton is more full and obvious in the *Physiologia Epicuro-Gassendo-Charltoniana* (1654), but even in the apparently anti-Epicurean defence of providence in the earlier text, Charleton anatomizes Book 5 of *De rerum natura* with Gassendi's authority already in evidence alongside Plato and Lactantius. With these forces, Charleton confronts the various arguments against providence, including these: that the gods could derive no benefit from creation; that human beings would have been happy without existence; that most of the earth is barren, and even a good harvest can be ruined by bad weather; that human beings are weak, and life calamitous.

Although it was essential for Charleton to find a place for atomism in his defence of providence, an even more extraordinary claim was made by a number of mid-century writers regarding the marriage of Epicurean physics and Christian theology. It was argued from time to time, and by some argued obsessively, that atomism is a more suitable physics for Christian theology than the other view of four elements. Several reasons were offered in support of this paradoxical claim, including these two: that it is all the more likely that atoms would require divine aid in forming an orderly and beautiful world than it is that four elements would require that aid; and that the microscopic study of the mechanical workings of nature did nothing but reveal a supremely wise creator. After all, Lucretius might emphasize that worlds are created by chance, but his view of nature is nothing if not ordered and predictable. For Bacon, Charleton and Boyle, however, even the fortuity of the atoms lent itself to a providential view; as Kargon explains, '[a]n atomistic world could not be the result of a Godless evolution; *God* was required to supply the exact proportions'.[26] Lest the divine creation of the world out of atomic chaos entail that the creator is only a clockmaker who constructs the clock and sets it in motion, advocates of a new Epicureanism maintained that the Epicurean definition of the divine nature errs on the side of elevating that nature above any compromising involvement with the corruptions of the world. In defence of St Jerome, whose views on God threaten to trip the reader with an Epicurean scandal, Charleton insists that Jerome's 'diminution of the universality of Providence, may seem the pardonable effect of immoderate devotion, and but a high strained description of the glory of that essence, which in strict truth, can be concerned in nothing but it self'.[27] As Charleton put the point in 1656, Christians should worship God for the sake of two things: for the perfection of the divine nature itself and for the benefits that God gives us; it is more honorable, he concludes, to err on the first side with the Epicureans than on the second, presumably with the stoical puritans.

If Charleton (like Thomas Browne) found specifically anti-puritan theological uses for atomism, radical sectarians such as John Webster embraced it in repudiating the traditional curriculum that in their view had supported the powers of oppression in state and Church. This stance implies an analogy between the return to natural principles (atoms) and the return to spiritual purity and political liberty.[28] Other translators and transmitters of Lucretius concentrated on what John Dury calls the 'choice parcels' of natural philosophy as a way of avoiding controversy altogether: for instance, Sir Edward Sherburne translated several hundred lines of the poem's treatment of atomic principles (Book 1, ll. 162–710), skipping over the invocation to Venus, the eulogy for Epicurus and the attacks on religion and divine creation.[29] Just so, Charleton's recognition that the Epicurean ethical ideal has more to do with virtuous pacificism than with sensory gratification is translated into a way of understanding why science was thriving in the interregnum. As a pastoral alternative to the religious and political turmoil of the day, natural philosophy is said to have prospered not just in spite of the Civil War but also because of it. 'Give me leave, a little to wonder', begins an interlocuter in Charleton's *The Immortality of the Human Soul* (1657), 'how it comes about, that *Apollo*, who seldom plants his Laurel in a Land yet wet and reaking with blood, and delights to reside only where Peace and Plenty have long had their habitations; should thus take up his mansion in a Nation so lately opprest by the Tyranny of *Mars*, and scarce free from the distractions of a horrid Civil War'.[30] In appealing to the spirit of the age ('its peculiar Genius'), Athanasius finds a providence in the 'vicissitude of things': 'our late Warrs and Schisms, having almost wholly discouraged men from the study of Theologie; and brought the Civil Law into contempt: The major part of young Schollers in our Universities addict themselves to Physick; and how much that conduceth to real and solid Knowledge, and what singular advantages it hath aboue other studies, in making men true Philosophers; I need not intimate to you, who have so long tasted of that benefit'.[31] Although the personal losses of the war still cast their shadow over the discussion, the interlocutors take comfort in the catalogue of achievements given as evidence that Englishmen have been forced out of theology or law into the more 'neutral' study of nature. Indeed, like Charleton, who imagines scientific debate taking place in a garden, another translator of Lucretius, Evelyn, describes the text of Lucretius as a variegated garden.[32]

As a number of twentieth-century scholars have argued, the Epicurean pastoralism of interregnum science had its greatest effect on the conception of method. These scholars maintain that the revival of Epicureanism and the promotion of natural philosophy were abetted by the widespread desire for latitude, toleration and mitigated scepticism.[33] In Charleton's *Immortality of the Human Soul*, it is the figure of Lucretius who longs, 'after so many troubles, dangers, and changes of Fortune' from the Civil War, to proceed 'freely and calmly in some Argument or other in Philosophy'.[34] What had gone wrong with English society, many believed, was that tyranny and idolatry had abounded on all sides, on the side of a Romish, self-idolizing king who was unwilling to budge, and on the side of radicals who claimed too much authority for what were fundamentally private visions. Despite their sometime reputation for dogmatism, the Epicureans were considered pre-eminent examples of a careful and irenic method for a wide range of English moderates in the aftermath of the war. On this score, if for no other reason, a Lucy Hutchinson and a Walter Charleton might approach one another, despite their clear and profound political and religious differences.

But one would not want to over-emphasize this imaginary meeting. The atomism of Lucretius was no doubt attractive to Lucy Hutchinson as a way of neutralizing and even articulating the horrors of a war driven by faction and ambition; indeed, *De rerum natura* indicts the same wartime desires and corruptions exploded in her narrative of the English Civil War. But atomism also lent itself to Hutchinson's polemical opposition to royalist war-mongering and superstition. That is, if atomism offered her a pastoral exit from the havoc of war, it also offered her a theoretical entrance.

III

In the wartime and interregnum years in which she undertook her translation, Lucy Hutchinson found much to admire – or at least to use – in the elaboration of atomism and its ethical corollaries in *De rerum natura*. As her marginalia reflect, first there was the matter of separating atomic principles from theological impieties. To this end, the translator guides the reader of her manuscript with

marginal glosses, many of which are aimed simply at helping the reader master
the physical principles set forth in the poem while a few resist or denounce the
egregiously blasphemous passages. Thus in the margins one reads for example
that 'nothing springs of it selfe without principles'(f. 8v); that 'there are vnseene
bodies'; that 'Bodies & Vacuitie comprehend all things in nature'(f. 13v); that 'the
first bodies are sollid'; that 'the Principles are Eternall' and that they 'cannot
admitt of change'(f. 16r–v); that 'the same principles variously disposd produce
various things'; and that 'the vast Vniverse hath no bound'(f. 21r, 23v). At times
Hutchinson allows seemingly impious notions to stand with such a bare marginal
comment as 'That the world was made by the casuall conjuncture not the
designe of Principles'(f. 25r). Similarly, several pages of Lucretius' demonstration
of the mortality and atomic constituents of the soul pass by – each with
Hutchinson's straightforward pointers in the margins – until the translator finally
exclaims in a gloss that Lucretius is a 'poore deluded bewitcht mad wretch'
(f. 70v). Another marginal comment mocks Lucretius' madness from a 'Philtrum
his wife gaue him', yet still allows that the poet wrote his scientific epic during
lucid intervals (f. 26v). Some comments suggest – without elaborating – a religious
response on the translator's part, for example the one pointing out that Lucretius'
account of the atomic swerve is 'Against Destiny' (f. 32v). If such a removal of
destiny – *contra* Stoicism – can make way for God's providence, so too might such
comments as the gloss 'That there is a certeine order in the coniuncture of seed'
(f. 41v). Indeed, a few comments appear to presuppose a creator prior to the
atoms, for instance, 'That Principles are not indued with sence though of them
sensible creatures are made' (f. 44v). But when it comes to Hutchinson's gloss 'Of
the vndisturbed quiet of the Gods and the free actings of nature', she is compelled
to add her outrage that the passage is 'Horribly impious' (f. 49v).

   In the time of war and political turmoil, however, the fortuity of atomism is as
much a test for Hutchinson's commitment to providence as it is a removable
impediment. Lucretius himself emphasizes the metaphorical links between civil
war and atomism in the *De rerum natura*: as his seventeenth-century readers were
well aware, in a number of passages the properties and motions of atoms are
likened to the horrors of the civil wars and political instability that the Latin poet
experienced and from which he sought quiet consolation in natural philosophy.

   Just as English students of Lucretius in the 1640s and '50s often discuss his life
and his account of civilization in terms loaded with contemporary relevance, so
they also follow his lead in constructing analogies between civil havoc and the
collision of particles.[35] In 1645, Clarendon launches his narrative of the period by
describing the causes of the war as just so many atoms colliding against one
another: 'The pride of this man, and the popularity of that; the levity of one, and
the morosity of another; the excess of the court in the greatest want, and the
parsimony and retention of the country in the greatest plenty; the spirit of craft
and subtlety in some, and the rude and unpolished integrity of others, too much

despising craft or art; like so many atoms contributing to this mass of confusion now before us.'[36] Conversely, in 1653, Charleton describes the chance jostling of atoms as an on-going 'civil war', while Margaret Cavendish writes of the driving force of the war as 'Fortune' and 'Chance'.[37] Hutchinson herself begins her autobiography by remarking that she is unfolding her life story as a way of remembering that fortuity cannot be the world's governing principle. Many mortals forget, she writes, that providence 'conducts the lives of men from the cradle to the tomb' and that 'the most wonderfull operations of the greate God' are scarcely just 'the common accidents of humane life'.[38] But she herself has been 'in some kind guilty of this generall neglect', reason enough to 'remember . . . the generall and particular providences exercis'd to [her]'. In essence, the comparisons between civil war and atomic fortuity are so habitual during these years that a struggle with one often implies a struggle with the other: for Hutchinson, a narrative of the war and a translation of Lucretius involve the same difficulty of staring in the face of powerful arguments against providence, and then of heroically emerging from the battle with a stronger faith.

If the wartime uses of atomism were pastoral, irenic and devotional, they were also hotly polemical and, as such, directed against Roundheads and Cavaliers alike. For instance, Cavendish and Waller linked what they found to be the chaos of democracy to the physical model of random collisions between equal particles. The more careful Charleton compares the Epicurean universe to a republic, only to insist that the atomic republic is more orderly and predictable than the 'unstable and irregular judgments' of its human analogue. Similarly, Thomas Browne resists the splintering of faith into 'Atoms in Divinity'.[39]

The polemical interest of atomism for Hutchinson is more complex and analytical than these caricatures of puritanism and republicanism – and more so than the puritan caricatures of Cavaliers as vicious Epicures or of Arminians as godless proponents of a free will that Lucretius links to the atomic swerve. For Hutchinson, the atomism of Lucretius affords the social critic a powerful weapon against the anxious and ritualistic superstition, the myopic tyranny and delusional hypocrisy that yield the wartime sacrifice of children, the martyrdom of aristocratic saints and the bloody spectacle of limbs writhing on the ground. Indeed, her gloss on one key passage connects Lucretius' 'Apologie for his doctrines' to the poet's demonstration of 'the mischiefe superstition hath brought forth'(f. 7v).

One can readily imagine that when Hutchinson translated Lucretius' famous condemnation of 'religio' ('tantum religio potuit suadere malorum' [I, l. 101]) in terms of 'superstition', she had in mind the court and Church of the benighted Charles I. Whatever his refinement of court manners, this uxorious tyrant (she believed) had prostituted England to the rituals of popery. Not surprisingly, one finds a Lucretian frame of reference in Hutchinson's other work on superstition. Her translation of John Owen's analysis of Christian theology in its relationship to fallen knowledge includes a substantial portion on the ills of pagan superstition.[40] It is not surprising that 'Lucretius the Epicurean' is cited as an especially corrupt authority 'in making the eternall iudgment, and the divers lotts of men after death, a ridiculous mockery'.[41] But given the horrific and famous scene from Book 1 of *De rerum natura* in which King Agamemnon sacrifices his daughter so that he might go off and win the Trojan War, Lucretius is also quoted as an incisive critic of the practice of obscuring the real causes of natural phenomena in myths. When it comes to the sacrifice of children as a way of settling 'the fluctuating anxious minds of men, agitated with the guilt and horror of their sins', there is no specific mention of Lucretius, only that 'the stories of Meneceus and Iphigenia are knowne instances'.[42] Whatever she thought about classical atomism, then, it is clear that Lucy Hutchinson agreed with its explosion of the violent 'mischiefe superstition hath brought forth', especially given the very real danger that her own children would become sacrifices to the religion of state and its anxious superintendents.

But with the fracture of her own party and the ascendancy of Cromwell, the ethical corollaries of Lucretian atomism are just as condemnatory of the puritan and republican objects of Lucy Hutchinson's wrath as they are of the party of Charles and Laud. After the war, when she and her husband were in retirement, Hutchinson wrote a poem in praise of the tranquil life in which ambition, politics and war have no place. In a number of phrases, the poem evokes the major ethical tenets of *De rerum natura*, which celebrates the happiness that comes from the tranquil study of nature made possible by detachment from the contests, rivalries and vanities of the world.[43] Similarly, in her narrative of the war, Hutchinson emphasizes in bitter terms that despite the parliamentary victory, her husband and she have been betrayed time and again by the treachery of ambitious politicos on their own side, from minor figures such as the 'factious, ambitious, vaineglorious, envious, and mallitious' Charles White to Cromwell himself. As N.H. Keeble has remarked, Lucy Hutchinson's disgust at the hypocrisy and corruption running rampant among the victors resembles Milton's, not least in her on-going attempt to justify the ways of God's providence. But her prose description of the years of retreat at the Hutchinson country estate is as much Lucretian as it is Miltonic, elaborating the 'innocent recreations during Oliver's mutable reign' as Lucy and John are said to dwell in their 'absolute private condition' beyond the reach of ambition's 'epidemicall disease'.[44]

Just so, in his second, third and fifth books Lucretius powerfully condemns ambition and recommends the study of natural phenomena and their principles as a retreat from the 'engag'd armies in the field'. For Lucretius, the painful and anxious 'maze of error' afflicts the rich and lofty most of all, but also 'all times & persons'. In response, the Epicurean philosopher-hero finds safety and tranquillity at a distance from the warring, 'wandring troopes' pursuing 'vain endeavors' through the wide world. Rather than allow themselves to be tossed like so many atoms, the Epicureans pursue an understanding of nature that keeps a 'body free from payne, a mind / Full of content, exempt from feare or care' (Lucretius MS, f. 28r). As Hutchinson's poetry and prose of retreat tend to clarify, that is, the atomist is right in at least one respect: in a world driven by vain desire, the best option is the life of repose in a garden with family or friends. It is a retreat that Charleton and Evelyn recommended for the natural philosopher.

IV

To summarize: the atomic physics of Lucretius afforded Lucy Hutchinson and her contemporaries a range of responses to and conceptions of the cultural, religious and political cataclysm of the 1640s and '50s. Epicurean atomism laid the groundwork for a pastoral retreat from the war as well as a method and course of study in conflict with war's havoc. For some, atomism proved a comfort in the storm precisely because, as Lucretius stresses, atoms cannot be divided or broken: although atoms represent the utter dispersion of state and Church under the rule of chance, readers of Lucretius in the 1650s would also find a physical theory that limited dispersion and ensured an orderly, predictable state of affairs in nature. Atoms guarantee order, the argument runs, because they certify that human beings can dismantle their world only so far. Or, for those who still managed to glimpse natural order through the cloud of human warfare, the anti-Epicurean argument for providence gained strength from the old paradox that if elements can sort out themselves, only a careful God can sort out atoms.

In the poetry of Lucretius, moreover, Epicurean science indicted the abuses leading to the war, especially tyranny, ambition and superstition, and it constructed a fortress against the fears that result from war, above all the fear of death. Atomism provided theories for explaining the sinful motives of the war, but also metaphors and images evocative of its physical horrors. In a range of texts, the philosophy served partisan politics but it also assaulted partisan politics in the name of toleration and peace. Epicurean physics and ethics emerged together, then: Robert Boyle wrote treatises on atoms and on classical ethics concurrently. But for Hutchinson as for her contemporaries, the reception of Epicurean physics was never wholesale or freewheeling: the manuscript of her translation makes it clear that her reading of Lucretius is selective and defensive. One whole section of Book 4 is omitted altogether while a portion of Book 3 is celebrated in inverted commas. As proof that Lucretius was at long last a believer against his will, that God is omnipotent and the atheist a fool, Hutchinson on one occasion even slants the Roman poet's words towards a belief in immortality and providence. When Lucretius stresses the shameful error of those fictions invented by men who almost unconsciously posit their survival after death, Hutchinson turns the passage into a moment of unsought spiritual insight for the atheist dog who, imposed on by divinely given reason, is forced to admit his inkling 'That something beyond humane life extends, / And part of them the mortall bound transcends' (f. 70v). 'How much,' the margin gloats, 'this poore deluded wretch striues to put out the dimme light of nature which while he contends against he acknowledges.' For Hutchinson and her contemporaries, there can be no greater argument for providence than this cross-bias played by God against the would-be atheist. Yet in leaving the translation for posterity, Hutchinson admits the possibility that the atomist has cross-biased her.

Notes

1 The manuscript is British Library Add. MS 19333, cited hereafter as Lucretius MS. Evidence for its date comes from Hutchinson's dedication to the Earl of Anglesey and from Sir Aston Cockayne, 'To my ingenious Friend Mr. Alexander Brome on his Essay to translate Lucretius', in *Small Poems of Divers Sorts* (1658), p. 204. I am in agreement with Samuel Weiss (1955), p. 109, who argues that the translation should be dated to 'the latter part of the 1640's or even the 1650's'.

2 For providence in history, see Hutchinson (1973). Further references will be given in the text from this edition. Responses to the translation include Mayo (1934), Kroll (1991), Warburg (1937); Harrison (1934); Real (1970); Munro (1858); Jones (1989); de Quehen (1996). Also Hutchinson, ed. Quehen (1996).

3 In the poem cited in note 1, Cockayne writes that 'I know a Lady that hath been about / The same designe, but she must needes give out: / Your poet strikes too boldly home sometimes, / In geniall things, t'appear in womens rhimes. / The task is masculine, and he that can, / Translate *Lucretius*, is an able man'.

4 Dryden (1958), I, p. 395.

5 Ong (1971), pp. 113–41; for the quotations see pp. 117, 121.

6 Reynolds (1920), p. 22.

7 Renaissance views of the uneven relations between Lucretius and the epic tradition are exemplified in Torquato Tasso (1973), pp. 8, 30, 97 and 111. For a modern summary, see Fleischmann, II, pp. 349–65. For Cicero's famous response to women in Epicurus' garden, see *De Natura Deorum*, trs. H. Rackham, pp. 90–1.

8 Hutchinson's treatment of these sections is noted in Greer *et al.* (1988), pp. 218–20.

9 Hutchinson (1973), pp. 17, 18, 19, 207.

10 Keeble (1990); the quotation can be found on p. 235.

11 Phillips (1990). See also Dennis Meyer (1955).

12 Hutchinson (1973), pp. 286–7.

13 Hutchinson's historical and theological writings were directed mainly towards the audience of her children, and she executed her translation of Lucretius 'in a roome where my children practizd the severall quallities they were taught', though the point of this remark is that she 'did not employ any serious studie' in the work (Lucretius MS, f. 2v).

14 Hutchinson (1973), p. 34.

15 Jacquot (1952); and Kargon (1966).

16 Hutchinson (1973), p. 61.

17 Found in her dedication to Anglesey, this protest is of course commonplace.

18 For the early Stuart revival, see Barbour (1993). Descartes' major works began to appear in

1637 with a second flourish in 1641 and 1644. In 1644, with the Cavendish family in exile, Sir Kenelm Digby published his treatises on the body and soul. Although the *Two Treatises* were underwritten by Aristotelian assumptions about substance and qualities, Digby nonetheless incorporated facets of the mechanical and atomic philosophies. The work of such continental atomists as Daniel Sennert was imported into England in the 1630s and after.

19 See Kargon (1966), pp. 65–8.

20 *Ibid.*, p. 67.

21 The phrase is found in Jacob (1977), p. 72.

22 John Smith (1979), p. xxi, cf. John Wilkins (1649). For important accounts of these issues in Wilkins, Boyle and others, see Shapiro (1969); Osler (1991); Kroll *et el.* (1992).

23 More (1878), p. 90. For More on God and space, see Grant (1981), pp. 221–8.

24 Comenius (1651), pp. 28–9, 38.

25 On Charleton, see Sharp (1973), and Kargon (1966).

26 Kargon (1966), p. 86.

27 Charleton (1652), p. 96.

28 On John Webster's approval of Gassendi's Epicureanism, see Greaves (1990), p. 104; and Debus (1970).

29 Sherburne (1961), p. 177.

30 I cite the facsimile edition (1985), p. 49.

31 *Ibid.*, p. 50.

32 See 'The Interpreter to Him that Reads', in Evelyn's *An Essay on the First Book of T. Lucretius Carus De Rerum Natura* (London, 1656). Cf. John Aubrey's belief that 'the searching into Naturall knowledge began but since or about the death of King Charles the first', quoted in Michael Hunter (1975), p. 42.

33 See Kroll (1991); Shapiro (1969); McAdoo (1965); and Henry (1992), pp. 178–209. For 'mitigated skepticism', see Popkin (1979); and Van Leeuwen (1963).

34 Charleton (1657), p. 3.

35 For contemporary accounts of the life of Lucretius, see Evelyn (1656), pp. 100–1; and *T. Lucretius Carus, of the Nature of Things*, trs. Thomas Creech (London, 1714), I.A3v. For examples of the Civil War–atom analogy in Hutchinson's translation, see 108r and 134r.

36 Hyde (1888), I, p. 4.

37 For Charleton's usage, see (Charleton (1652), p. 43. For Cavendish and 'Fortune', see Cavendish (1872).

38 Hutchinson (1973), p. 278.

39 Waller links atomism to democracy in his commendatory poem to Evelyn's *Essay*. For Cavendish on the democracy of atomism, see Sarasohn (1984). For the Browne quotation, see Browne (1977), p. 88. For Charleton, see Charleton (1652), p. 100.

40 Hutchinson's theological papers were edited by Julius Hutchinson (1817). The source of *On Theology* was identified by Narveson (1989).

41 Hutchinson (1817), p. 255.

42 *Ibid.*, pp. 275, 276.

43 The text of the poem can be found in Greer *et al.* (1988), pp. 220–1.

44 For Hutchinson on ambition, see Hutchinson (1973), pp. 69, 94, 107, 112, 146, 179–80, 191–3, 205, and 207–12. For Keeble's remarks, see Keeble (1990).

7

A Memorial of Eleanor Willughby, a Seventeenth-Century Midwife

Adrian Wilson

The biographeme suspends narrative time and the *telos* that only such time can insure. Its ethos has affinities with . . . memory. Those who have lost their nearest and dearest do not recall their departed in the manner of the monumental biographer, but through discrete images, a love of cats and flowers, a liking for particular cakes, watery eyes like Ignatius of Loyola.

Sean Burke[1]

1 Introduction

Through the pages of Percival Willughby's *Observations in Midwifery*[2] – the classic source on childbirth in seventeenth-century England – there flits intermittently a daughter of Willughby's who practised as a midwife, both in tandem with her father and in her own right. She is unnamed in the treatise, but can be identified with the aid of further documentation as Eleanor Willughby, later Eleanor Hurt.[3] I shall suggest: (a) that the contours of Eleanor's practice are recoverable, even though her work is accessible only through her father's writings; (b) that while her connection with her father made her very different from most midwives, her practice helps to illuminate the activities of other midwives; (c) that the style of her midwifery practice reciprocally sheds light on that of her father; and (d) that Eleanor's presence in the *Observations* is wider and deeper than at first appears. We shall be attempting, then, to recover the agency of a woman from the writings of a man. The attendant hermeneutic problem is by no means confined to the case of Eleanor Willughby; for, ironically enough, the very fact that seventeenth-century childbirth was a collective female event is known to us chiefly from male documentary sources.[4] As we proceed, therefore, it will be appropriate to attend to the premises of our exercise – so far as we can identify those premises, for we may presume that no reading can in fact attain that transparency which (so it would seem) every reading tends to claim or to seek.[5]

Our enterprise raises a further issue, which is registered in the epigraph I have taken from Sean Burke, namely the tension between memory and biography. If a 'memorial' is to succeed in its aim, if it is to create a memory, it should offer what Roland Barthes called 'biographemes': that is (so Burke explains) flashing glimpses, detached images, linked with each other not through the medium of time but on the contrary in rigorously atemporal juxtapositions.[6] As I take it, this is precisely how the 'biographeme' mimics memory – establishing as it does a connection between its subject and ourselves whose very form defies the flow and the ravages of time. A memorial to Eleanor Willughby, then, ought rightly to present such biographemes. Yet we are constrained to proceed towards this *telos* in a starkly contrasting way, that is, in something like the ponderous 'manner of the monumental biographer', which Burke rightly depicts as the very antithesis of memory. For although we are already supplied with discrete glimpses and images of Eleanor, each and every one of these images was constructed by her father – which means that in order to build up our own biographemes of Eleanor, we have first to examine and to dismantle the images which her father constructed. Indeed, it may be doubted whether it is actually possible to free Eleanor from the circle of her father's representations; whether, in a case such as this, it is meaningful to posit a *hors-texte*; in short, whether our intended memorial can be made at all. But rather than debating the possibility in abstract terms, I shall proceed on the wager that this can be done. It will be up to the reader to decide whether that wager has been justified.

Having made this apology, I shall begin with a brief overview of what we know and can surmise of Eleanor's life – seen, inevitably, in reciprocal connection with that of her father. It will then be necessary to consider the form and content of her father's *Observations in Midwifery*; and his text will also serve as a lens through which to examine the world of practice from which it emanated, namely the contrasting roles of midwife and male practitioner in the management of seventeenth-century childbirth. In due course, as we turn to Eleanor herself, it will emerge that it was precisely this contrast which structured her practice as a midwife – in so far as we can reconstruct that practice from those surviving fragments which we will be taking as evidence.

The developing professional relationship between father and daughter can be divided, schematically, into three phases. Firstly, in about 1654, at the tender age of fifteen or sixteen, Eleanor embarked on the practice of midwifery – probably at her father's behest, and perhaps to augment the family's income in the wake of their recent move from Derby to Stafford. Working in cooperation with him, she practised as a midwife for five or six years, first in Stafford and then in London; and she helped her father with at least one delivery after the family's return to Derby in late 1659. Soon after this time, her father began to write his *Observations* – a midwifery treatise, designed chiefly for 'young country midwives', illustrated with 'observations' (that is, case histories) from his past and present practice. Secondly, by the time of her marriage to Thomas Hurt in 1662 Eleanor had stopped practising midwifery; and she now embarked on her own childbearing career. During the next ten years or so, while Eleanor Hurt was giving birth to the first six of her nine children, her father was working intermittently on his book – particularly after the death of his wife, Eleanor's mother, in February 1667. He added more and more illustrative case histories from his continuing practice 'in the midwife's bed'; in 1668, he produced a finished version of the work and tried to get this published (though without success), and eventually in 1671–2 he wrote a complementary 'little work' or *Opusculum*. During these years Eleanor's life was entwined with her father's in a new way; for she called on his help in at least two of her own pregnancies and lyings-in, and she may even have used him in place of a midwife for all her deliveries. Thirdly, in 1672, Percival asked someone – we do not know whom – to edit his now unwieldy manuscripts for publication; and he duly entrusted to this intended editor the 'Opusculum' and his master copy of the 'Observations'. So far as we know, this unidentified individual did not succeed in the task of editing the texts, but she or he produced at least two verbatim transcripts of these works. And there are grounds for suspecting that this copyist was none other than Eleanor Hurt. If this surmise is correct, then Willughby's writings were chiefly delivered to posterity by his daughter's hand.

2 THE FORM AND CONTENT OF THE RECORD

We must first of all consider Willughby's *Observations* and the midwifery practices to which that work attests. Since no summary can do justice to a complex text of some ninety thousand words (for such was the length that the book had attained by 1672), let us instead start as Willughby himself often did: that is, from a particular case history. This will serve to exemplify the form of his 'observations' and, no less so, the complexities entailed in our own attempts to interpret such a story. For this was precisely a story, a story with an autobiographical element:

> Grace Beechcraft, the wife of Joseph, in St Peter's parish in Derby, being in labour several days, and having suffered much sorrow, desired my help. The child came with the head first, but it was great. Her midwife, with herself, desired my assistance, for that she could not deliver her. For her condition Divines were consulted, and in their opinions they were divided. Several women frowned upon some of these Divines, and upon the women's dislikes, they turned their coats and changed their opinions. I would not use the crotchet, for fear the child should be alive, but turned the head and brought it forth by the feet, after the way afore mentioned. The child was dead, but the woman's life was saved, and she recovered very well after this delivery.[7]

Willughby indicated the date of this particular case only obliquely (he was writing it down from recall), but we can locate the delivery at the end of September 1655.[8] His highly compressed account reveals that Grace Beechcraft's delivery was a complex drama, which involved at least five different agents or parties – mother, midwife, several women, divines, Willughby himself. Further, the divines were certainly of different minds, at least initially, and the women were probably divided as well;[9] so the number of distinct view points involved in the management of the case was at least six and very likely seven. What is more, reference to the other extant version of the 'Observations'[10] would add another one or two such view points – for Willughby there framed and told the story in a slightly different way. This underlines a point which is obvious enough, but deserves to be mentioned explicitly: Willughby's 'record' of the case was highly partial, in the double sense of being told very much from his own point of view and of being, like any narrative, incomplete. For instance, Willughby was living in Stafford at the time of this delivery, and so must have been called all the way from Stafford to Derby to deliver Grace Beechcraft; yet this circumstance, which he recorded for another Derby delivery around this time, was not included in his account of this particular case.[11]

In some respects this case description or 'observation' is typical of those in the *Observations* – utterly so in the fact that 'several women' were involved, in addition to the mother and her midwife, and very largely so in the fact that Grace had been in labour for some days by the time Willughby was called. Yet certain aspects of the case, or of Willughby's account of it, were atypical: for instance, his call to the delivery seldom came from the midwife, for midwives often resented his intrusion, and only occasionally did he report that 'Divines were consulted'. And some features of the story were unique: in no other case did he mention divisions of opinion among such ministers of religion, nor the pressure which women exerted upon them in Grace Beechcraft's case. If we partition the story along these lines, we arrive at the schema shown in Table 7.1, where the progress of the delivery is represented downwards line by line.

Table 7.1 Willughby's report of Grace Beechcraft's delivery, broken down into typical/untypical elements

Typical	Semi-typical	Unusual	Unique
several women present			
	birth by the head[a]		
	in labour several days[b]		
	only one midwife present[c]		
		called by mother+midwife[d]	
	child dead[e]		
		diagnosis uncertain[f]	
		Divines consulted[g]	
			Divines divided
			women frowned
			Divines turned
	delivered by the feet[h]		

Notes:

[a] In about half of Willughby's reported deliveries the child presented by the head.

[b] This was typical of 'emergency' calls (Willughby's primary practice), as distinct from 'advance calls' and 'onset calls' (Willughby's secondary practice); these distinctions are explained below.

[c] In about one-third of Willughby's emergency calls two or more midwives were present before he was called (see further below).

[d] The 'calling agents' were specified in about half the cases; mothers, fathers, midwives and the mother's attending friends all participated in this process, in various combinations. Calls by mother and midwife combined were unusual (as were calls by the midwife alone).

[e] In the great majority of emergency calls, though not in all, the child was dead before Willughby was called.

[f] Usually Willughby was confident in his judgement as to whether or not the child was alive, though there were a few other cases where the diagnosis was uncertain.

[g] Such consultations were reported in only a handful of cases.

[h] Willughby usually delivered obstructed head presentations by craniotomy with the sharp hook or crotchet; but sometimes, as in this case, he turned the child to the feet instead.

It so happens that the more or less typical themes appear in the early stages of this particular 'observation'. Other cases reveal a different pattern in this regard, as we shall see;[12] but the fact that the case history offers an admixture of the typical and the atypical was itself the norm. Indeed, the typical and the atypical in Willughby's case descriptions were mutually enfolded in complex ways. For instance, although the 'frowning' of the women was attested in this case alone, we can be confident that Willughby was always operating in a political field of force within which women were the dominant agents: for it was women who ran childbirth, and who were responsible for summoning him to the delivery.[13] Hence the fact that fathers-to-be are largely absent from his 'observations' – though, as will emerge in due course, this rule also had its exceptions.[14]

The case history we are considering reported both bodily events ('the child came with the head first') and social events ('her midwife, with herself, desired my assistance'); and the same was true of Willughby's 'observations' in general, including his descriptions of his daughter's cases. This interweaving of the bodily and the social was not merely a rhetorical device: on the contrary, it reflected the concrete experience of Willughby himself and (as we shall see) of Eleanor as well. Thus, in order to understand Willughby's practical choices in this case ('I would not use the crotchet . . . but turned the head, and brought it forth by the feet'), we must consider first the bodily processes of childbirth and then the various paths by which different practitioners were called to deliveries.

Largely following Willughby's categories[15] (though also drawing selectively on later obstetric knowledge), and leaving aside various rarities and complexities,[16] we may classify births into three broad types according to the way that the child presented.[17] By far the commonest occurrence was for the birth to present by the head; less often the child could present by the breech; and on rare occasions, perhaps one birth in 250, the child came by the shoulder or arm. Between these three categories, happily enough, difficulty corresponded to rarity. At one extreme, almost all births by the head delivered spontaneously, though a tiny minority of these became obstructed. At the opposite extreme, virtually every case of arm presentation was obstructed. And births by the breech, which were of intermediate frequency, were also intermediate in difficulty: most of them delivered spontaneously, though often with more trouble than births by the head, but a few of them became obstructed, and the incidence of such obstruction was greater than for births by the head. To some extent, this association between rarity and difficulty also obtained at the finer level which we are suppressing from consideration here: thus among breech births, one unusual variety was presentation by the feet or knees, and there is reason to suspect that these were more difficult than other forms of breech presentation.[18] Overall, about 1.5 per cent of births were obstructed. In addition, a small number of births – perhaps 0.4 per cent – were associated with serious difficulty due to other causes, notably 'flooding' (haemorrhage, in today's categories) and 'convulsion fits' (nowadays called eclampsia).

All births were managed by a well-developed and consistent popular ritual which was run by women collectively. But one woman in particular – the midwife – presided over both the social arrangements and the bodily management of birth: indeed, the midwife's authority was one of the central features of the ritual itself.[19] If difficulty arose, and if the midwife could not deliver the mother, there were two possible recourses. On the one hand a male practitioner could be called, as Willughby was in Grace Beechcraft's case. On the other hand, a second midwife might be summoned, and indeed sometimes a third or even a fourth midwife, as is shown by a number of cases where none of these midwives could deliver the mother, so that Willughby's services were finally required. (The practice of sending for a second midwife in such difficult births was required in some versions of the oath which midwives had to swear before receiving a licence from the Church; in this respect, as in some others, the oath probably reflected popular custom.)[20] Thus midwives were called to births not only in a *primary* capacity but also as *secondary* attendants, specifically for difficult births. Yet even if we make a generous allowance for this practice,[21] it is clear that the midwife's experience was overwhelmingly concentrated upon normal births. This point is illustrated in Table 7.2, which offers an educated guess as to the profile of a typical midwife's experiences over a ten-year period. Here it is assumed that the typical midwife's primary case load was twenty births per year; this figure, though derived from independent evidence, is consistent with the plausible expectation that most midwives practised over a small territory of one or two villages. The notion of such a typical midwife is of course a hypothetical abstraction, for some midwives – particularly those living in the larger towns –

tore it hee cannot be turned otherwife with the hand conveyed in, the labouring-woman is to be brought to her bed, where, if fhe fhall be faint and feeble, fhe muft be refrefhed and comforted with convenient meats, and now fhee muft procced in the manner often fpoken of before, untill the forme of a more convenient birth fhall come.

CAHP. X.

Of the tenth forme and cure of it.

IT cómeth fometime to paffe that the birth appeareth with the necke turned awry, the fhoulders bending forward to the birth, but the head turned backeward, and the feete with the hands lifted upward. In that cafe, the Midwife fhall remove the fhoulders of the childe backward, that

A page from Jacob Rüff's *The Expert Midwife*, translated in 1637.

practised at much higher rates and were of more than local repute.[22] Nevertheless, Table 7.2 probably presents a reasonably reliable picture of the norm around which midwives' practical experiences revolved. Indeed, 'rural' case loads (of the order of twenty births per year) could be found at this time even in towns, up to and including London.[23]

Table 7.2 Estimate of a typical midwife's experience in 10 years

| | Numbers of births (rounded to nearest whole numbers) presenting by: | | | |
	Head	Breech	Arm	Total
Primary attendance:				
normal births	190	6	–	196
difficult births	3	–	1	4
total deliveries	193	6	1	200
Secondary attendance:				
normal births	–	–	–	–
difficult births	5	–	2	7
total deliveries	5	–	2	7
Total attendance:				
normal births	190	6	–	196
difficult births	8	–	3	11
total deliveries	198	6	3	207

Assumptions: (a) The typical midwife attended 20 births per year in a primary capacity. (b) The incidence of different presentations, and their associated rates of obstruction, were as follows: births by the head 966 per 1,000, of which 1 per cent were obstructed; breech births 30 per 1,000, of which 2 per cent were obstructed; arm presentations 4 per 1,000, all of which were obstructed. (c) An additional 4 births per 1,000 involved serious complications ('flooding', i.e. haemorrhage, or convulsions, corresponding to the modern eclampsia); the incidence of such complications was independent of presentation type (which means in practice that the few such cases all presented by the head). (d) All difficult births (i.e. cases of obstruction or serious complications) were attended by two additional midwives before a male practitioner such as Willughby was called. (e) Such secondary attendances were evenly shared among all midwives. (The latter two assumptions are generous: see note 21 to the text.)

Although the numbers suggested here are only approximations, we can be confident that some 95 per cent of the midwife's cases consisted of normal births – even including those where her attendance was in a secondary capacity. Correspondingly, midwives probably accumulated very little experience of difficult deliveries. To take the case of arm presentations, our case load estimate of twenty births per year implies that the typical midwife saw such a birth only once in ten years in her primary practice, and another twice during that time in a secondary capacity. In all, therefore, she would encounter such a case about once every three years or so – indeed, more likely only once every four years.[24] And while our estimate of the average case load is only a guess, much the same implications would follow even if we doubled this to an implausibly high forty births per year. We may therefore venture the preliminary assessment that most midwives were unable to deliver these unusual and difficult cases.[25]

Percival Willughby's experiences 'in the midwife's bed' – very different from those of the midwife – were structured by the specific ways he was called to deliveries. Simplifying somewhat, we may distinguish in his practice three main 'paths to childbirth', which I term advance calls, onset calls and emergency calls. In an advance call he was summoned to reside in the mother's house in advance of the delivery; onset calls required him to attend from the onset of labour; and emergency calls, like that to deliver Grace Beechcraft, were occasioned by difficulty during the birth.[26] His advance and onset calls (which came only from wealthy mothers) resembled the primary practice of the midwife – but with this major difference, that he usually attended only as an adjunct to the midwife; his emergency calls (which took him to deliveries of all social ranks) corresponded to the midwife's secondary practice. Willughby's *Observations* supply various indications of his case loads in both primary and secondary midwifery; using these clues and some guesswork, we can estimate the profile of his practice over ten years as shown in Table 7.3. Here the key point is that emergency calls (Willughby's form of secondary attendance) comprised his chief form of practice.

This picture of Willughby's practice confirms our preliminary inference that most midwives were unable to deliver obstructed births and cases involving serious complications. For it was precisely these births that comprised the principal niche of practice for Willughby himself; and in view of the size of his catchment area and the incidence of difficult births, he would scarcely have had an emergency midwifery practice at all if midwives had been able to manage such cases.[27] Indeed, we can be more specific: Willughby's usual task was to deliver a dead child, in an obstructed birth by the head, in order to save the mother's life. Among his reported cases, over half the births which he actually delivered – as distinct from those he merely attended as an adjunct to the midwife – were of this kind; and as Table 7.3 implies, the proportion was probably higher still in his practice as a whole.

Schematic though they are, the numbers in Tables 7.2 and 7.3 probably offer a fair guide to the experiences of a midwife on the one hand and of Willughby on the other. As it happened, Willughby's overall case load was probably very similar to that of the typical midwife, at around twenty births per year; but the profile of his practical experience was very different indeed from hers. We can identify four

Table 7.3 Estimate of Willughby's experience in 10 years (based on his cases from the 1660s)

| | Numbers of births presenting by: | | | |
	Head	Breech	Arm	Total
Primary attendance:				
normal births	57	2	–	59
difficult births	1	–	–	1
total deliveries	58	2	–	60
Secondary attendance:				
normal births	–	–	–	–
difficult births	117	6	40	163
total deliveries	117	6	40	163
Total attendance:				
normal births	57	2	–	59
difficult births	118	6	40	164
total deliveries	175	8	40	223

Assumptions: (a) Willughby's primary practice (i.e. 'advance' and 'onset' calls) amounted to 6 cases per year. (b) The catchment area for Willughby's secondary (emergency) practice comprised 1,000 births per year. (c) Within this catchment area, Willughby was called to all obstructed births by the arm and breech, to 2/3 of obstructed births by the head, and to ½ of the births involving serious complications. (NB Excluded are cases of retained placenta.)

main contrasts. In the first place, the midwife's deliveries were concentrated on normal births, whereas Willughby's work centred on difficult deliveries. Indeed, this contrast was even more marked than our tables suggest; for in his primary practice, Willughby left the delivery to the midwife if the birth proved normal, as of course it almost always did. Thus difficult births made up not just 73 per cent of his total experience (the proportion suggested by the balance between his primary and secondary forms of practice), but probably well over 90 per cent; and this was the precise inverse of the midwife's experience. Secondly, and correspondingly, their expected roles were precisely complementary. The task of the midwife was to deliver a *living* baby – whence the fact that midwives were adept at reviving a weakly child[28] – and also to supervise the social arrangements for the birth. In contrast, what was chiefly expected of Willughby was to deliver a *dead* child, and he had little if any influence over the childbirth ritual.[29] Thirdly, Willughby saw a very different balance of presentation types from that which a midwife encountered – particularly with regard to malpresentations. In the midwife's experience, births by the breech far outnumbered births by the arm, particularly in her primary practice; but in Willughby's practice, 'the birth by the arm' was much more common than what he called 'the birth by the buttocks'. Finally, the midwife and Willughby had sharply differing experiences of one particular type of delivery, namely 'the birth by the buttocks'. In a ten-year period, they saw similar numbers of such births; but whereas all of the midwife's breech cases delivered spontaneously,[30] most of those which Willughby encountered were obstructed. This was, of course, an artefact of Willughby's particular 'paths to childbirth'. Much the same was true of births by the head – but in these cases Willughby had the countervailing experience arising from his primary practice, thanks to which he was well aware that births by the head could deliver by the natural powers. With respect to breech births, in contrast, his experience only rarely offered this practical lesson. As we shall see, Willughby's proclaimed views on the management of such births are intelligible in this light.

We are now in a position to appreciate the practical methods which Willughby mentioned as possible choices in Grace Beechcraft's delivery: the 'crotchet' on the one hand, turning to the feet on the other.[31] The crotchet or sharp hook was used to deliver a dead child in an obstructed birth by the head: it enabled the operator to exert traction, and was very effective for this purpose, but it could of course not be used on a living child. Devices of this kind, which took various forms, represented a standard part of the surgeon's armamentarium – which is one of the reasons for believing that Willughby's practice in midwifery was typical of its day. The crotchet was Willughby's preferred instrument for this purpose, and was also favoured by most other English male practitioners of the seventeenth century. The practice of turning to the feet[32] could be used on either a living child or a dead one; the point of the manoeuvre was that it enabled the surgeon or midwife to exert traction. This was the master-method advocated throughout Willughby's 'Observations' and 'Opusculum'. Although the technique had been introduced in the sixteenth century by Ambroise Paré, it was only slowly adopted in midwifery treatises; in endorsing turning, Willughby was out of line with most of the published advice of his time, and more in tune with the subsequent writings of Mauriceau and Deventer, who were to be the chief practical obstetric authorities of the early eighteenth century. Willughby had picked up this method in about 1646, that is to say after more than fifteen years of practice.[33] Once he had mastered the technique, he applied it in a variety of circumstances: for malpresentations such as the breech or arm;[34] for cases of 'flooding'; and sometimes for obstructed births by the head – particularly if the child was still alive, or was thought by some parties present to be alive. Hence the decision which Willughby took in Grace Beechcraft's case: 'I would not use the crotchet, for fear the child should be alive, but turned the head, and brought it forth by the feet.'

Indeed, it was one of the central messages of the *Observations* that turning to the

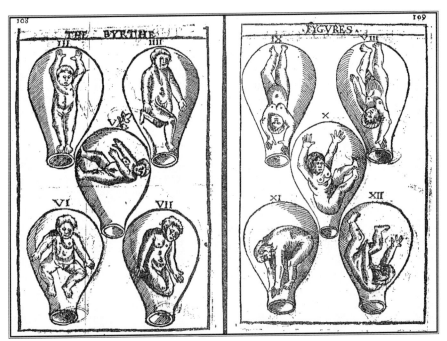

From Eucharius Rösselin, *The Byrth of Mankynde* translated by Richard Jonas (1626, first published, 1540).

feet was the master-method for delivering 'all difficult and unnatural cross births'.[35] Yet there was also another message: that if the birth was natural, no interference was required; on the contrary, the birth was best left to 'Dame Nature, Eve's midwife'. The critical question, then, was whether any given birth was to be regarded as difficult or natural – a question to which 'Nature' herself did not always offer a clear answer. In practice, Willughby's encounter with nature was of course mediated by the social paths which brought him to childbirth; and it was this conjuncture of the bodily and the social which governed his practical choices. And the 'birth by the buttocks', discussed above, nicely illustrates this issue and the way Willughby resolved it.[36] On the one hand, as will emerge below,[37] Willughby was well aware that breech births, unlike certain other malpresentations such as births by the shoulder or arm, could deliver spontaneously. On the other hand, as we saw in Table 7.3, most of the (few) breech births which he encountered were obstructed. And this predisposed him to treat such births as 'unnatural', and accordingly to deliver them by turning the child and drawing by the feet. Indeed, it so happened that his very first recorded use of turning to the feet, or at least his first recorded success in attempting the manoeuvre (on 14 January 1646/7), had been with a breech birth in an emergency call.[38] Hence Willughby's proclaimed advice: breech births were not to be left to nature, but were to be classed as 'unnatural' and delivered by turning. In this and other respects, the lessons of 'friendly Nature'[39] which Willughby imbibed so eagerly and retailed so lavishly were in fact refracted through culture – that is, through the social arrangements for the management of childbirth.

3 WRITINGS STILLBORN

Percival Willughby spent his long working life, which extended from before 1630 to at least the early 1670s, delivering stillborn babies. Thus it was perhaps a fitting irony that all of his writings on midwifery were stillborn. Between 1661 and 1672 he produced at least two and probably three versions of the 'Observations': the first, very likely an initial version, completed in 1662; the second certainly a finished version of 1668, which he sent to medical colleagues in London; and also a third, less polished but more complete version, comprising his master copy as this stood in early 1672. And as we have seen, he also wrote in 1671–2 a supplementary work, *The Country Midwife's Opusculum, or Vade-Mecum*, which was designed to accompany and to complement the 'Observations'. But despite Willughby's hopes, none of this literary output found its way into print: during this time, then, he produced two stillborn books, one of them at least twice and probably three times over. In contrast, his daughter Eleanor, the former midwife, was meanwhile giving birth to six living children (and also, as we shall see, to one stillborn child). The counterpoint between the activities of father and daughter was here at its sharpest.

Yet although they remained unpublished during his lifetime, most of Willughby's writings were preserved in manuscript after his own death in 1685. Of the (probable) initial version of the 'Observations' no copy is known to survive; its very existence is conjectural.[40] But we do have copies of the version of 1668 (this first surviving recension we may call the 'London version'), and also of the text of 1672 (which I term the 'Derby version'), the latter accompanied by the 'Opusculum'.[41] In fact the survival of these manuscripts was to occasion a further irony. For Willughby's hopes of publication were eventually realized – but not until long after his death, when most of his advice was out of date, and for very different audiences from the 'country midwives' for whom he had been writing. The 'London version' of the 'Observations' was published in 1754, some eighty-six years after it had been written – in a Dutch translation, intended for male obstetric surgeons, and merely as an appendix to a book on the newly publicized midwifery vectis (an instrument of which Willughby had been unaware). And after another nine decades (that is, in 1863) the 'Derby version', together with the accompanying 'Opusculum', was printed in English, in a limited edition produced by Henry Blenkinsop of Warwick. By this time, of course, the interest of these works was purely historical, and in any case Blenkinsop failed to sell out the 100 copies of his edition. A century later, in 1972, the two books again saw the light of day, in a facsimile reprint of Blenkinsop's edition. Once again their publication was not much of a success, for the facsimile edition was remaindered within a few years. Still, this edition has at long last supplied Willughby with an attentive audience – in the form of late twentieth-century historians of medicine.

Indeed, such ironies extend back to Willughby's own purposes and didactic methods. Willughby wanted to argue that practical experience was the only effective teacher; yet his medium contradicted his message, for he was using the written word. He sought to advise midwives on the delivery of normal births; yet his own experience was almost entirely restricted to difficult deliveries. He repeatedly criticized 'young midwives' and extolled the benefits of long experience; yet at the same time he vaunted the abilities of his daughter, who was less than seventeen years old when she embarked upon practice. He argued that all difficult births could be managed by a single method, namely turning to the feet; yet he also asserted that every case was different, and indeed the very cases which he used to illustrate his message also exemplify this bewildering variety, thereby distracting attention from Willughby's main argument. But perhaps the supreme paradox pertains to the use which Willughby made of William Harvey's essay 'De Partu', the concluding section of Harvey's *De Generatione* (which had been published in 1651, and translated into English in 1653). As it happened, Willughby had been personally acquainted with Harvey: indeed, in 1642, on the eve of the battle of Edgehill, Harvey, who was then attending Charles I, rode across to Derby to visit Willughby. Their conversation at this time concerned 'several infirmities incident to the womb'; Willughby's account gives no hint that they also discussed methods of delivery.[42] Nevertheless it came about that their subsequently recorded views on delivery showed certain similarities – and Willughby vastly exaggerated these resemblances. More precisely, when writing on midwifery in the 1660s he presented himself as following in the footsteps of Harvey (who had died in 1657); and since he also depicted his daughter's practice in the same light, our own purposes require us to notice this rhetorical framing on Willughby's part.

Harvey's discussion of birth was chiefly theoretical in intent; yet it had certain practical implications.[43] His argument was that birth was due to the joint efforts of (a) the foetus and (b) the entire body of the mother – not just of her uterus.[44] Both 'the woman in travail' and 'the foetus that is to be born' had to be 'ready for the business'; otherwise, 'the birth will scarcely ever follow with success, for it must occur at the hour that fits their joint maturity'. It followed, Harvey explained, that midwives should not attempt to 'accelerate and facilitate' the delivery by such practices as 'distending the parts' and 'offering medicinal draughts', for such efforts 'rather retard and prevent the delivery'. Harvey's argument neatly accounted for the fact that a normal birth proceeds head first: 'the foetus itself, *with its head turned downwards*, approaches the gates of the womb and opens them by its own strength and struggles out into the light'. But Harvey went on to explain that different considerations prevailed in difficult births:

> Nevertheless in an abortion and where the foetus is dead, or where otherwise the delivery would be difficult and hands would have to be used in the business, the more convenient way of coming forth is feet first, for by that means the narrows of the womb are opened more easily as if by driving in a wedge. Wherefore when the chief hope of giving birth lies in the *foetus* as being strong and lively, *there must be a striving to produce it head first*, but if the business depend chiefly on the *uterus*, then *its arrival feet first must be procured*.[45]

The point of turning the child to the feet was that its feet served as a wedge; what drove the wedge and thereby opened the 'narrows of the womb' was the action of the uterus.[46] In a normal birth, the foetus opened the 'narrows of the womb' with its head; turning to the feet, by producing a 'wedge', enabled the action of the uterus to substitute for the action of the child.

Willughby took this passage as a talisman, despite the vast gulf which separated Harvey's philosophical interest in birth from his own practical obstetric concerns. As he portrayed the matter, Harvey had produced a practical account of the methods of delivery, an account which precisely accorded with his own approach. Normal births were to be left to nature; difficult births were to be delivered by the feet. As Willughby put it (but with emphases added):

> Dr Harvey's learned observations about the birth ought be esteemed for their worth and goodness. The *oft reading* of them, with a due observation of his method, will be sufficient to make a midwife to understand her calling.

So much for the need for practical experience! Willughby went on:

> He showeth, in the first place, what to observe and how to deliver a woman labouring in a natural birth. And in difficult births, and abortive births, and where the foetus is dead, he maketh mention how to perform the work by the child's feet. In his works, he wishes midwives not to be too busy at the first approaching of labour, by striving to hasten or promote a sudden or quick birth; but willeth them patiently to wait on nature, to observe her ways, and not to disquiet her, for that it is the sole and only work of nature.[47]

Here Willughby, in characteristic fashion, inserted a case history – one which we shall have occasion to consider in due course.[48] Having completed the story, he returned to its practical moral:

I know none but Dr Harvey's directions and method, the which I wish all midwives to observe and follow, and oft to read over and over again; and in so doing, they will better observe, understand and remember the sayings and doings of that most worthy, good and learned Dr., whose memory ought to be had for ever in great esteem with midwives and child-bearing women.

Elsewhere Willughby stressed that midwifery was not to be learnt from books;[49] yet when it came to Harvey, he insisted on precisely the opposite message. But this was only one of the contradictions surrounding his claim to have followed 'Dr Harvey's directions and method'. For although Willughby's expectant approach to the management of normal births was precisely in line with Harvey's proclaimed views, his approach to *difficult* births was far removed from Harvey's – and this in several respects.

In the first place, we have seen Harvey advising that 'when the chief hope of giving birth lies in the foetus as being strong and lively, there must be a striving to produce it head first'; yet Willughby repeatedly argued against this technique.[50] Secondly, the whole burden of Harvey's account was that the child should be delivered by the feet 'if the business depend chiefly on the uterus'; yet Willughby stressed, on the contrary, that by turning the child to the feet, 'the woman may be laid without throes', that is, without any action on the part of the uterus. To put this another way, Harvey simply did not consider the case where neither the foetus nor the uterus could accomplish the birth, that is, when the foetus was dead and the powers of the uterus were extinct – yet this was precisely what Willughby encountered in his routine practice. Thirdly, and correspondingly, Harvey depicted manual delivery by the feet as purely passive in intent – whereas Willughby turned the child to the feet *in order to exert traction*.[51] Finally, Willughby's own case histories demonstrated, as we shall see in due course,[52] that births which presented by the feet were even more difficult

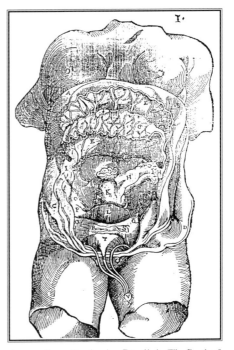

A page from Eucharius Rösslin's *The Byrth of Mankynde*, translated by Richard Jonas (1626, first published, 1540).

than the 'birth by the buttocks': thus if, as Willughby believed, the unaided powers of the uterus could not be relied upon to deliver breech births, still less so could the uterus bring about a delivery which presented by the feet. Hence the efficacy of turning to the feet depended not on substituting for the action of the foetus, as Harvey claimed, but on the contrary on augmenting or replacing the powers of the uterus. In short, although Willughby was doubtless sincere in asserting that 'I know none but Dr Harvey's directions and method', that remark is not to be taken at face value. On the contrary, his use of Harvey was strictly rhetorical: it represented a rather strained attempt to give textual and learned support to his own argument in favour of delivering difficult births by the feet.

If the ironies associated with the *Observations* 'extend back', as I have been suggesting, to Willughby's very purposes, they also stretch forward to our own enterprise. For the very act of using Willughby's *Observations* as a historical source is inescapably fraught with contradictions. The book was a condensation of Willughby's experience; we want to reconstruct (as far as we can) the wider field of action from which he condensed it; thus to use the book as a source entails a necessary violation of Willughby's purposes; and yet this also requires us to attend to those very purposes. In particular, we are hoping to disentangle Eleanor Willughby and her practice from her father's presentation of her; yet as we shall now see, her very identity as a midwife was intimately bound up with her father's practice and indeed with his rhetoric.

4 ELEANOR WILLUGHBY'S PRACTICE IN STAFFORD

Of the 190-odd case histories described in the *Observations*, Eleanor is mentioned in just eight – but this small number becomes more impressive when we notice that it includes seven of the thirty-one cases from the five years or so when she and her father were living in Stafford (for no more than two years, between 1654 and 1656) and London (from May 1656 until late 1659). Let us now examine these cases one by one, beginning with the four Stafford cases. One of these was an emergency summons of Percival himself, but Eleanor accompanied him:

> I was sent for from Stafford, to come to a lady beyond Congerton [i.e. Congleton, Cheshire]. Her midwife had kept her several days in labour. I took my daughter with me. We travelled all night, and we were wetted with much rain to skins. We came, by break of day, to the place. But this Lady was dead, undelivered, before our coming. I much desired to see her corpse, but the midwife would not permit it. I knew this midwife not to be very judicious in her profession, and I believe that she was ashamed that her work should be seen Anno 1655. This midwife was gentle in habit of clothes, but ignorant in the ways of practice of midwifery.[53]

This case is chiefly of interest for the fact that Willughby took Eleanor with him. Although this is the only such instance mentioned in the *Observations*, we may surely presume that he was training her in midwifery – perhaps to augment the family income, for Willughby's own practice must have been disrupted by his move to Stafford. Other aspects of the case display the same mixture of the typical and the untypical that we encountered in Grace Beechcraft's case from the same year, 1655.[54] The very late call ('several days in labour') is characteristic of Willughby's emergency cases; so, too, is Willughby's claim that the midwife was 'ignorant'. The long journey was semi-typical: such calls came from a wide catchment area, with a radius of 10 miles or so, but seldom from the distance of over 20 miles which separated Congleton from Stafford. But the fact that the mother died undelivered before Willughby could arrive was unusual, and the description of the midwife as 'gentle in habit of clothes' is unique. Notice, finally, the authority of the midwife: she was in a position to prohibit Willughby from seeing the body of the deceased mother. Although this particular prohibition is unique, the authority which it reflects was probably typical, as we have seen.[55]

Eleanor's other three documented Stafford cases were births which she herself delivered; there is no hint that her father was present at these occasions, or indeed that he was involved in any way at all. Strikingly, all three were examples of 'the birth by the buttocks', and Willughby presented them together. In the light of our earlier guesses as to the structure of his practice (Table 7.3), it is not difficult to see why he resorted to Eleanor's practice for this purpose: in all probability, he had relatively few experiences of his own to draw upon when it came to breech births, in contrast with births by the head or by the arm. His argument in this passage – largely embedded in the case histories themselves – was that although breech births sometimes delivered spontaneously, prompt turning to the feet was the best method to adopt in such cases. And the first of these three case histories made it clear that this was Eleanor's own preferred practice, as will be seen from the phrase I have emphasized:

An inn-keeper's wife in Stafford desired my daughter's assistance for her delivery. Her labour was quick. The child followed the flowing of the waters, sitting in the birth with the buttocks. The birth was so speedy, that it would afford *no time to turn the child*. The mother, with the child, lived, and did very well after this birth.[56]

Willughby immediately commented, referring also to another similar case,[57] perhaps of his own: 'But one swallow, or two, doth not make a summer.' That is, these particular lessons from his alleged teacher, 'friendly Nature',[58] were *not* to be heeded: instead, breech births were to be treated as difficult deliveries from the outset, and were therefore to be delivered by the feet. It was just this argument which Eleanor's remaining two cases were meant to convey. The next

case was clearly a secondary attendance, for Eleanor was the fourth midwife
called to the birth:

> In Staffordshire, nigh to Newcastle, Anno 1656, my daughter quickly laid this
> birth, according to the foresaid way, by the feet, where, otherwise, three old
> midwives had let the woman perish, taking the buttocks for the head. They
> knew not how to help her, until she showed them the way of delivery of this
> birth by the child's feet.[59]

The remaining case was described only briefly, with no explicit indication as to
whether it involved a primary or a secondary attendance:

> She laid a barber's wife in Stafford of the same birth, after the same way. She,
> and her child, be living.

Observe that this little case history adds nothing new; it is merely another
example. The impression this conveys is that Willughby has now recounted *all* of
his daughter's breech deliveries from her time in Stafford; we may take this as
our preliminary, working assumption.

Despite their brevity, these case descriptions bring several different themes into
play. In addition to the mother herself – who she was (for instance, a barber's
wife), how she fared after the delivery – Willughby mentioned the place, the
course of the birth and how his daughter managed it; and we can also infer the
timing of the call. As it turns out, these features of the three cases were
interconnected, as emerges in Table 7.4.

Table 7.4 Structure of Eleanor Willughby's three Stafford cases

Place	Mode of attendance	Course of the birth	How E.W. delivered
1 Stafford	primary	delivered naturally	no time to turn to feet
2 near Newcastle-under-Lyme	secondary	obstructed	by the feet
3 Stafford	?	?	by the feet

The first two cases were of complementary kinds. Case 1 was a primary
attendance, and it was typical of such cases in that the birth delivered
spontaneously. In contrast, Case 2 was secondary in type; correspondingly, this
was an obstructed breech which, if Willughby is to be believed, would not have

been delivered without Eleanor's help. This is precisely in accordance with the different locations of these two cases. Eleanor's primary attendance (Case 1) took place in the town where she lived – which is as we should expect, for the midwife had to be on hand as soon as the mother fell into labour, and indeed this very case illustrates how quickly a spontaneous birth could proceed, even if it presented by the breech. But Eleanor's secondary attendance (Case 2) was located perhaps 14 miles away, and this is intelligible enough. In Stafford itself, we would not expect any obstructed breech births to have taken place during Eleanor's short stay;[60] but in the larger pool of births from the surrounding area such a case could plausibly have arisen even in this brief span of time.[61] And these considerations help us to interpret Case 3: it becomes well-nigh certain that this was a primary attendance (like Case 1), rather than a secondary one (like Case 2). In Case 3 there was evidently time to turn the child to the feet, suggesting that the labour proceeded more slowly (as indeed we would expect with a breech presentation); but otherwise this delivery resembled Case 1, for it took place in Stafford itself and no other midwives were present.

Within a period of some two years, then, Eleanor attended at least two breech births in a primary capacity, both of them in the town of Stafford. If we refer back to Table 7.2, it becomes apparent that she probably practised at something like the same rate as the typical midwife, perhaps indeed at a slightly higher rate. And this implies that the three breech cases which her father later included in his 'Observations' represented just a small sample of her total practice at this time. Thus, *in all probability, Eleanor delivered many other births in Stafford during her brief stay in the town* – though none of these was reported in her father's 'Observations'. Just how many births she managed in a primary capacity we can only guess, but we can be confident that she delivered more than ten mothers in this time,[62] and our best guess would be some sixty or so deliveries[63] – that is, about half of all the births in Stafford during the short time that she was there.[64] It would appear, then, that Eleanor Willughby was one of those urban midwives whose case load was rather higher than the twenty or so births per year of the typical midwife. For a girl of fifteen to sixteen years, newly arrived in the town, this was a remarkable achievement; and we may observe that in this short time she probably acquired more experience of normal births than her father accumulated in a lifetime's practice. Furthermore, her expertise was by no means confined to the management of normal birth. Perhaps the most impressive feature of her secondary attendance (Case 2) is the distance from which the call came: her reputation had extended – rightly, as it turned out – over 10 miles afield. To put this another way, we may observe that a typical midwife would be called in this way to an obstructed breech birth no more than once in twenty years or more,[65] and yet Eleanor received such a call within her first two years of practice. This in turn is consistent with our inference that her practice in Stafford itself was more extensive than that of most midwives. Notice in addition that our earlier working assumption was probably correct: it appears that all Eleanor's breech cases from her time in Stafford were indeed included in her father's 'Observations'.[66] For during the two years (or less) which she spent there, probably only about three or four normal breech births took place in the town itself,[67] and just a single obstructed breech in the surrounding hinterland.

Even if her rate of primary practice was similar to that of midwives in general (which is difficult to assess), Eleanor Willughby was in other respects a most unusual midwife. Not only was she single, whereas most midwives were married or widowed;[68] she was also extraordinarily young when she embarked on practice. Further, she had been taught by a male practitioner, namely her father, whereas few if any other midwives embarked on practice in this way;[69] and correspondingly, she delivered breech births by turning the child to the feet, a method which most midwives probably did not use. It is also noteworthy that she applied this technique for breech births not only if these became obstructed but also, if there was time, in the early stages of labour – in effect, as a prophylactic method.

5 ELEANOR AND HER FATHER IN LONDON

In May 1656, Eleanor Willughby's practice in Stafford was cut short – for her father moved to London, 'there to live', as he later explained in his *Observations*, 'for the better education of my children'. With the help of 'an apothecary that formerly had lived in Stafford', he 'quickly had some practice in midwifery, among the meaner sort of women'.[70] What about Eleanor's practice in London? Again we have just three case descriptions to go on; as we shall see, their import is very different from that of the Stafford cases.

The first of Eleanor's three recorded London cases was another 'birth of the buttocks' – specifically, a secondary attendance. Although Willughby left this 'observation' undated, we can infer that the birth took place some substantial time after he moved to London; for by the time of this delivery, he had established there not only a reputation in midwifery, but also a circle of friends. His account of this case immediately followed Cases 2 and 3 from Stafford:

> She laid the same birth of the buttocks by the feet in Shoe lane, at London, where an ancient midwife knew not how to do it. I was send for to this woman, and, finding the birth to come by the buttocks, I sent for my daughter, and willed her to go to the woman, and to give me an account of the birth, sitting all the while with Mrs Joanna Mullins.

> She came from the travailing woman to us, and said that the birth came by the buttocks, the which the old midwife took for the head. Before Mrs Mullins the wife of old Mr. Edward Mullins the chirurgion, I asked her what hopes she had of laying this woman. She answered that she doubted not but that,

through God's assistance, she could quickly deliver her. So with the former old midwife's permission, the work was soon performed by the feet.[71]

Thus it was not only for the edification of his readers that Willughby invoked his daughter as the expert in breech births; he had also done so in actual practice, for he referred this particular birth to his daughter *because* it 'came by the buttocks'. Once again Eleanor succeeded in the task: although she reported the condition of the birth to her father, she delivered the child – as usual, by turning to the feet – without his help.

In two respects this case differed markedly from Eleanor's Stafford cases. In the first place, Eleanor gained access to this birth by way of her father – whereas in Stafford she had been practising independently of him. Secondly, when it came to the delivery itself, she secured 'the old midwife's permission' before delivering the child by the feet – whereas such 'permission' was not mentioned in her comparable case from near Newcastle-under-Lyme.[72] We shall return to these points a little later, when reviewing Eleanor's London practice as a whole.

The next case we must consider took place in 1657, and concerned one Mrs Wolaston. We have already encountered the rhetorical context of this story; for this was the very 'observation' which Willughby used to illustrate his encomium to William Harvey.[73] Thus the moral of Mrs Wolaston's delivery – or, rather, two deliveries – would be Willughby's endorsement of what he depicted as 'Dr Harvey's directions and method'. Like the unnamed mother in Shoe Lane, Mrs Wolaston first sought Willughby's services in an emergency:

My assistance was desired by Mrs Wolaston, a watchmaker's wife, of Threadneedle Street near the Old Exchange. When the midwife perceived that I was sent for, she resolved to hasten her work. She caused several women perforce to hold her by the middle, whilst that she, with others, pulled the child by the limbs one way, and the women [pulled] her body the other way. Thus, at the last, the child, by violence, was drawn from her, and made at the separation (as she told me) a report as though a pistol had been discharged.

A little while after this tugging and struggling usage I came, and found this woman faint and weak, but through God's mercy, with cordials she was restored. Her midwife's enforcements had made such deep remembrance in her senses, that she resolved to forsake her; at which time she pitched her affections on me, making a request unto me, if that she should have any more children, that I would be pleased to deliver her.[74]

This was a truly remarkable request, for very few women ever asked Willughby, or any other male practitioner, to act in lieu of a midwife.[75] Willughby declined – for he believed that normal birth was the province of the midwife, not of the male practitioner[76] – and made a different suggestion:

I desired her to spare me, and rather to engage my daughter, the which thing she was contented to do, so that in her extremity, I would not be far from her.

Thus *father and daughter were practising as a team*. Eleanor would deliver the mother; if difficulty arose, Percival 'would not be far'. This intended arrangement echoed what we have seen in the Shoe Lane case, where Eleanor, while taking responsibility for the delivery, reported the state of the case to her father before proceeding.

In due course Mrs Wolaston acted on this suggestion: that is, for her next delivery she engaged Eleanor as her midwife. For as Willughby went on to explain:

Being with child afterward, and my daughter with her, when the time of her delivery was come, and that the waters issued, a sharp throw accompanied the birth, and the child speedily followed the waters.

Then she began to grieve and complain (not imagining that the child was born), and to say, now I shall fall into my old pains and sufferings, and [I] perceive that it will be no better with me. My daughter, smiling, asked her what she meant, and whether she had two children, for one was born. She scarcely believed it, until that she heard the child to cry. The after-birth being fetched, and she laid in bed, she took my daughter by the hand and said to her, Surely you have art in these fingers, otherwise so quickly and happily I should not have been delivered.[77]

Doubtless the birth came by the head, though Willughby's account does not explicitly say so. This is the only such case of Eleanor's given in the *Observations*: all the others were breech births. Mrs Wolaston's two deliveries perfectly fitted the rhetorical setting in which Willughby placed her story, that is, the picture of normal birth which Harvey had sketched in his *De Generatione*. In the previous birth, the midwife's interference had inflicted unnecessary pain and suffering on the mother – bearing out Harvey's criticisms of 'officious' midwives. But in Eleanor's hands the birth proceeded naturally and easily, doubtless because Eleanor had waited for 'the time of her delivery', that is, for the moment when both mother and foetus were (as Harvey had put it) 'ready for the business'. As we have seen, Willughby immediately observed: 'I know none but Dr Harvey's directions and method'.[78] And in the London version of the 'Observations' he added: 'the which she always observed'.[79] That is, as Willughby depicted the matter, his daughter had been following Harvey's 'directions and method'.

Notice again the contrast with Eleanor's Stafford practice: she had gained access to Mrs Wolaston, just as she had to the mother in Shoe Lane, only by way of her father. Notice, too, that in each of these two London cases, Willughby was on hand should difficulty arise, though his services were not required in either case. This teamwork between daughter and father was also evident, albeit in a slightly different way, in Eleanor's remaining London delivery.

This final case of Eleanor's illustrates once again the complex intertwining of the typical and the atypical in Willughby's cases. In the first place, the delivery was typical of Eleanor's recorded cases in being yet another breech birth. Secondly, however, this was in other respects a remarkable delivery, and Willughby's description of the case has several unique features. Yet, thirdly, even the unusual aspects of the case (if not of Willughby's account of it) turn out to exemplify themes which were characteristic of his practice and indeed of seventeenth-century midwifery in general.

The delivery took place in 1658; Willughby located it not in London but in 'Middlesex' – that is, doubtless in the country house of the family in question. Willughby identified the mother cryptically (in the Derby version only) as 'Sir Tennebs Evanks lady': this was a code for someone with the surname Bennet – the key being 'Evank', i.e. 'Knave' reversed, which indicates what Willughby thought of the father.[80] It is almost certain that 'Sir Tennebs Evank' was Gervase Bennet – an irascible Puritan, who was (as Willughby described him in the London version) 'one of Oliver's creatures', that is, a client of Cromwell's, and who was active both in London (where he had a minor government post) and in Derby (where he served for a time as an alderman).[81] Bennet's first wife had died in 1655; this must have been either the first or the second delivery of his second wife. Willughby's account gives no indication of how Eleanor was chosen as midwife; but it is safe to assume that the choice had been made by Mrs Bennet herself (not by her husband), and it seems likely that she knew of Eleanor and/or of Percival not through London contacts but rather via some Midlands connection. Willughby's account of the birth began as follows:

In Middlesex anno 1658 my daughter, with my assistance, delivered Sir Tennebs Evanks lady of a living daughter.

All the morning my daughter was much troubled, and told me that she feared that the birth would come by the buttocks, and that she foresaw the same by the falling down of her belly.

About seven a clock that night labour approached. At my daughter's request, unknown to the Lady, I crept into the chamber upon my hands and knees, and returned, and it was not perceived by the Lady. My daughter followed me, and I – being deceived through haste to go away – said that it was the head. But she affirmed the contrary, however, if it should prove the buttocks, that she knew how to deliver her.

Her husband's greatness and oliverian power, with some rash expressions that he uttered flowing too unhandsomely from his mouth, dismayed my daughter.[82]

From the other recension of the *Observations* we learn what these 'rash expressions' were: 'Her husband, standing by us, said, what luck had he to be deluded by children and fools.' The word 'children', of course, referred to Eleanor's tender age (she was now nineteen or twenty years old); 'fools', to her father's ungainly crawling in and out of the lying-in chamber. We may picture Bennet as the anxious father outside the door – perhaps all the more anxious because he had lost his previous wife three years earlier, and forced to wait outside for the simple reason that husbands were always excluded from childbirth at this time. Indeed, the fact that the father is mentioned at all is one of the many unusual aspects of this particular 'observation'.[83] Willughby's account proceeded:

> She could not be quieted, until I crept privately again the second time into the chamber, and then I found her words true.
>
> I willed her to bring down a foot, the which she soon did. But being much disquieted with fear of ensuing danger, she prayed me to carry on the rest of the work.
>
> The Lady was safely laid of a living daughter by the feet. The child cried strongly and loudly, and was spriteful and very lively.
>
> Had this birth come by the head, I believe that it would have proved difficult, and more troublesome to the Lady, not without some disgraceful reflection upon me and my daughter.
>
> For the child's head, with the breast, was great. It would have slid very difficultly through the bones, and so the midwife could not have helped more than by anointing the body, and, with patience, waiting and expecting when that nature's force with the throes would have driven forth the child.
>
> But, when the birth cometh by the feet, the woman may be laid without throes – as hath formerly been said, and showed by several examples.[84]

There is much of interest in this remarkable story. In the first place, we see that Eleanor was better able than her father to diagnose the presentation; indeed, she correctly predicted, even before 'labour approached', that the birth would come 'by the buttocks'. This suggests that she had acquired significant experience not only of breech-births but also, for comparison, of births by the head – in line with our earlier inference as to her practice in Stafford. Secondly, and conversely, her father's misdiagnosis, which he explained as the result of his 'haste to go away' (that is, his concern to remain undetected by the mother), is also intelligible in the light of his limited experience of such cases, particularly in their early stages. Indeed, this may well have been the first time he had ever encountered a breech birth so early in the labour. Thirdly, it will be observed that Willughby's concluding remark – 'the woman may be laid without throes' – puts paid to Harvey's interpretation of the efficacy of delivery by the feet. The point of the manoeuvre was not, as Harvey had claimed, to assist the efforts of the uterus but,

on the contrary, to replace those efforts.[85] Had Eleanor and her father literally
been following 'Dr. Harvey's directions and method' when turning the birth to
the feet, they would thereupon have left the delivery to the powers of the uterus;
in fact, of course, they did the very opposite, for they turned the child to the feet
in order to exert traction. This confirms that, as was observed earlier, Willughby's
use of Harvey was rhetorical rather than literal.

Finally, the most striking aspect of the case is the fact that Willughby crept in
and out of the lying-in room on his hands and knees – something unique among
his case histories. The point of this deception, surely, was simple enough. The
arrival of the male practitioner signalled that the birth was difficult; thus
Willughby concealed his presence so as to avoid disquieting the mother. And
what made this possible was the fact that the midwife was his own daughter; for
the deception absolutely required the midwife's collusion, and there was no other
midwife with whom Willughby enjoyed the necessary relation of mutual trust. In
its very uniqueness, then, this feature of the story reflected entirely typical
themes: the association of the male practitioner with difficulty and danger, and
the fact that Willughby's relations with midwives were fraught with tension.

Equally significant is the sequel to the delivery – for this probably explains why
Willughby included the case in his 'Observations'. Reverting again to the London
version of the text, we find the following account:

> He sent me home; I came several days after, but was scarce made to drink . . .
> [and was] never thanked for the care that I had of his wife.[86] [Here 'never
> thanked' means never paid.] About the 3rd or 4th day I asked him whether he
> had a nurse; he replied me, No, and said that he scorned that his child should
> suck any pocky whore. The child was fed with unfitting slip-slop nourishment;
> about the 7th day a nurse was procured, that would have given it the breast,
> but the infant had forgotten how to suck. Presently after the red-gum
> appeared, and for want of help, the child died.[87]

Now came the point:

> Within a few days after, he endeavoured to blacken my daughter's practice,
> saying that she had made a hollowness in his child's head. Had his little
> worship known that all children have loose disjointed bones, with hollowness
> in the head, when they are born, his poor judgment would have been silent –
> seeing that every woman can assure him that without this hollowness and
> loose bones, a child will not be born. Had he had a nurse in fitting time,
> doubtless the child might have lived.

Bennet's vindictive efforts did not stop at his attempt to 'blacken' Eleanor's
reputation in and about London, for as we shall see in a moment, he also put

about in Derby a story against Eleanor's father. We may guess that Bennet had not omitted to tell the hands-and-knees story, for Willughby could thus be ridiculed.

There can be little doubt that Willughby's account of the case was written in riposte to the rumours which Gervase Bennet was putting about. This becomes still more clear from a postscript which he added to the text a few years later, that is, after Bennet's death in 1670. With regard to Bennet's remark that 'he scorned that his child should suck any pocky nurse in or about London',[88] Willughby now commented: 'He well knew many unworthy women in that, and other places' – and posed a rhetorical question: 'And was he free from the lues venerea when he died?' Thereupon Willughby went on to assert that

> He loved variety of places, and several pastures. He reported about Derby, to disgrace me, that I would not come near to help his wife before that he had given me a hundred pieces [100 sovereigns – a very large sum]. He was never so worthy as to give or offer me the worth of a penny. And *if ever it be found out what his true name was*, and where he lived and died, let this postscript affirm, that he would not let me come near his wife after her delivery. And although I came several times, yet he did not afford me so much civility as to offer me a cup of ale or beer, or that ever he did give me the worth of a brass farthing for my oft visiting her afore her delivery; or for my being with her in her labour, and helping of her; or for my several visits after her delivery [emphasis mine].[89]

Plainly Willughby intended that his readers should be able to identify 'Sir Tennebs Evank' – but since this version of the 'Observations' languished in manuscript, this hope went unrealized.

Taken as a group, Eleanor's London cases suggest a very different profile of practice from that which she had enjoyed in Stafford. If, as is plausible, Willughby included all of her breech cases in his 'Observations', it is suspicious that although she spent nearly twice as long in London as she had in Stafford, we find only one instance of her acting in a primary capacity at a breech birth from London (namely the case of 'Sir Tennebs Evanks lady'), as against two from Stafford. This might, of course, be a random effect, yet *prima facie* it suggests a much lower rate of practice;[90] and other considerations point in the same direction. We have seen that Eleanor gained access to two of her three recorded London cases – the primary delivery of Mrs Wolaston and her secondary attendance on the mother in Shoe Lane – through her father. And her remaining recorded London case, namely the delivery of 'Sir Tennebs Evanks lady', had a Midlands connection: thus there is every possibility that 'Sir Tennebs Evanks lady' was aware of Eleanor through some Staffordshire link, rather than from any

London reputation of Eleanor's. What is more, this case, too, may have come Eleanor's way thanks to her father – for it will be observed that Percival himself had (if his postscript is to be believed) been attending the mother before the delivery. In short, there is strong reason to suspect that Eleanor was unable to achieve in London the success she had attained in Stafford in recruiting a clientele. In Stafford she had arrived as an unknown girl, yet had rapidly secured a remarkable reputation; but in London this eluded her, despite the experience she had by now acquired. Yet, meanwhile, her father's experience had been quite different, for as we have seen, on moving to London he had 'quickly had some practice in midwifery, among the meaner sort of women', thanks to 'an apothecary that formerly had lived in Stafford'. This double contrast with her own Stafford practice and with her father's achievements in London underlines the puzzle that has now arisen: why did Eleanor experience such difficulty in establishing herself as a midwife in London?

The explanation is probably to be sought in a set of arrangements which Willughby himself attested in a separate context, and which are also known from various other sources.[91] 'The young midwives in London', Willughby wrote, 'be trained seven years first under the old midwives, before they be allowed to practice for themselves.'[92] That is, in London – uniquely – a midwife was expected to begin practice as a deputy to an already established midwife: this custom was well established long before this date, for it was attested in the midwife's oath for the diocese of London as early as 1588.[93] This arrangement, which was evidently created by the midwives themselves, effectively constructed a guild system; yet it managed to achieve this without the institutional apparatus of enforcement usually associated with guilds. Notably, the deputy system *antedated* the various seventeenth-century attempts to create a London incorporation or college of midwives;[94] and whereas all these initiatives came to naught, the deputy system lasted for a century or more. Just how this system interacted with ecclesiastical licensing is unclear, and is indeed a matter of contention among historians.[95] But when the Willughby family was in London, that is, in the late 1650s, the deputy system certainly did not depend on church licensing – for that licensing had been a dead letter for fifteen years or more, with the suspension of the church courts after 1641. According to the later testimony of Mrs Elizabeth Cellier, London midwives were subject at this very time to licensing by the Company of Barbers and Surgeons;[96] thus if Mrs Cellier's picture is to be trusted, there was perhaps a form of institutional backing for the deputy system in the 1640s and '50s. But Mrs Cellier was a highly interested party (in 1687, when she recounted this story, she was trying to create a 'college of midwives' with herself at its head) and an unreliable witness, and there is no other evidence to indicate that any such arrangement in fact obtained.[97] In short, it appears that the deputy system was constructed and maintained by the midwives themselves, without the help of any institutional sanctions at all.

The various fragments of evidence which attest to the existence of the deputy system do not make clear how effective the system was in practice. But Eleanor Willughby's experience offers us an indication of this – for in view of her limited practice in London, it is plausible to infer that the system was highly successful. That is to say, *Eleanor was largely excluded from primary practice in London because she had not been trained as a deputy there.* Correspondingly, in the London secondary case which she obtained thanks to her father, she required 'the old midwife's permission' before delivering a child by the feet,[98] whereas no such permission was mentioned in her secondary case from Staffordshire. This authority of the older midwife, which was specific to London, becomes intelligible in the light of the deputy system, and again indicates that the system was functioning effectively at this time. Furthermore, Willughby's 'Observations' supply yet another reason for believing that the deputy system actually worked. For that system should have raised the standards of practice, by enabling midwives to pool their experience across the generations; and sure enough, we find that Willughby held a much higher opinion of London midwives than he did of their Midlands counterparts.[99] In short, there is every reason to believe that the London deputy system was thriving in the 1650s, and doubtless long before that time.

The very existence of the deputy system represented a remarkable achievement on the part of the London midwives. That achievement becomes truly astonishing if the system actually succeeded along the lines I have been suggesting. Yet there seems to be no other way of accounting for the remarkable disparity between Eleanor Willughby's meagre practice in London and the substantial practice she had sustained in Stafford.

6 ELEANOR AND HER FATHER IN DERBY

Towards the end of 1659 the Willughby family moved yet again, this time back to their starting-point in Derby. This move, which probably reflected a change in the political climate in Derby, seems to have curtailed Eleanor's midwifery practice, for no further cases of hers are recorded in the *Observations*. Nevertheless, we find her assisting her father in one case, and an important one at that: a delivery of Mrs Jane Molyneux of Woodcoats, Nottinghamshire. This was a case which Willughby recorded in immense and almost unparalleled detail, and with good reason. The mother's previous obstetric history supported his own views on the ignorance of midwives; her delivery gave him direct access to a birth from the onset of labour; the outcome was a happy one; and last but not least, the case occurred while he was beginning to write his 'Observations'.

Mrs Molyneux sought Willughby out for her delivery, and came to stay in his house for the last month of her pregnancy. She had been driven to this highly unusual course of action – using Willughby in lieu of a midwife – by losing no less than four children, under four different midwives, all in footling births.[100] (We may presume that she had some particular predisposition, for footling presentations were very rare.) When she fell into labour the birth came yet again 'by the knees doubled'; Willughby delivered her with the combined help of his daughter and one of the attending women – a 'threefold united force' – and Mrs Molyneux gave birth to a living child, a girl baptized Mary. Not surprisingly, this won her confidence for the future: she subsequently came to Derby again for three further deliveries, two of them after her remarriage in 1666 to Mr Thomas Wildbore.[101] These cases, too, Willughby wrote up in his 'Observations', one of them in lavish detail. But what we must notice is that when first helping Mrs Molyneux, Willughby involved his daughter as his equal in the procedure of the delivery even though it was to him not to Eleanor that Mrs Molyneux had come in the first place.[102] For this there was a simple but telling reason, which was mentioned in passing when we considered the case of Mrs Wolaston.[103] Just as very few mothers asked him to play the role of midwife, so too Willughby himself – for all his criticisms of practising midwives – believed that the female midwife, not a male practitioner such as himself, was the proper person to manage childbirth.[104] This ingrained assumption on Willughby's part reflected the conceptual horizon imposed by the fact that the male practitioner's task was to deliver a dead child, not a living baby.[105]

By this time, as we have seen, Eleanor Willughby seems to have stopped practising midwifery; perhaps she was now caught up in her impending marriage to Thomas Hurt, which took place in 1662, and which took her away from Derby (I have not ascertained precisely where the Hurts lived, but this was at some distance).[106] Notably, her father did not involve her in the subsequent deliveries of Mrs Molyneux/Wildbore in 1665, 1667 and 1669: indeed in the delivery of 1669 he was forced to entrust Mrs Wildbore to a Derby midwife, since he himself was already engaged elsewhere, and yet Eleanor did not play this role. This is hardly surprising, for at this time (November 1669) Eleanor had three young children of her own and was six months pregnant.[107] But meanwhile she had acquired a new connection with her father in the sphere of midwifery – for she called on his help in the management of at least two of her deliveries and lyings-in, and Willughby included these two cases in his 'Observations'. Although her father identified her in the text only as 'a young gentlewoman', not mentioning her in this context as his daughter, his marginalia and index name the patient as 'El. Hurt',[108] and it is well-nigh certain that 'El. Hurt' was indeed his daughter Eleanor.[109] Indeed, we shall see that Eleanor may even have taken the remarkable step of using her father in lieu of a midwife for all her deliveries, though this is a matter of conjecture.

After one of her first three deliveries (that is, in 1663, 1665 or 1666),[110] Eleanor was bleeding with clots for some seven weeks. Accordingly, she called on her father's help: after trying two prescriptions without success, he administered 'the powder of an unripe gall', which 'in thrice taking . . . quite stopped the flux'.

A few years later, during her seventh pregnancy (in late 1671), she experienced a different problem: the baby had ceased to move in the womb. She asked her father 'to come and stay with her'; after ten days, she fell into labour and he delivered her of a dead child, which came naturally and did not need to be turned to the feet.[111] Early in the 'Observations', Willughby stated: 'I have delivered, through God's gracious permission, a gentlewoman of several children'[112] – implying that this particular mother had used him in lieu of a midwife, for a whole sequence of deliveries, and apparently without any precipitating reason of the kind which had driven Mrs Molyneux to call on his services.[113] And it does indeed seem that he had acted as a midwife for this mother, for he had had something of a say in the social arrangements for these births: 'I . . . desired her, in the time of her travail, not to have her chamber thronged with much company.' This form of involvement was unique in the cases described in the 'Observations' precisely because even in Willughby's 'advance calls' it was not he but the midwife who presided over the social arrangements, just as it was the midwife who managed the birth as a bodily event. Thus this particular mother reposed a special trust in him, using him as she did in the role of a midwife. Who might this have been? There is no way of knowing, for Willughby completely concealed this gentlewoman's identity; but conceivably this too was Eleanor Hurt. If so, it would appear that she chose her father, in place of a midwife, from the outset of her childbearing career.

By early 1672, Percival Willughby's still-unpublished writings on midwifery had attained a paradoxical form, arising from the inevitable tension between systematic advice and its empirical exemplification, and from his changing handling of this problem. Originally, that is to say in the early 1660s, his 'Observations' had fused these two elements, using only a few selected case histories and subordinating these to a larger didactic frame. But since that time he had interpolated dozens of new cases into the text; and this additional illustrative material had come to obscure the structure of the work. Thus when three new popular books on midwifery were published in 1671,[114] he was spurred to re-state his argument in a new text, systematic in form and devoid of case histories. Accordingly he swiftly penned a new treatise, which he called 'The Country Midwife's Opusculum, or Vade-Mecum' – emphasizing by its very title that this was, in contrast with the now unwieldy 'Observations', a 'little work'. Yet he still wanted to support his claims with empirical proofs – 'de facto, what I have really performed'[115] – and he now recruited the 'Observations' for this purpose. His plan, then, was to publish the two works together so that they complemented each other: the 'Opusculum' would set out his advice systematically, while the 'Observations' would supply the illustrative case histories. Accordingly the 'Opusculum' referred explicitly to the 'Observations',[116] and Willughby also supplied some less explicit cross-references in the other direction.[117]

of Children. 115

caufe him to fucke a Goate ; which I haue caufed
fome to doe.

A Treacle water for the little child.

℞. *Theriac. veter. ℥ i. Cons. Rofar. anthos. Borag.* *Aqua Theria-*
Buglos. an. ℥ ij. Rafur. interior. lign. Indi. ℥ i. *calin.*
Rad. farfæ par Chinæan.℥fs. Rad. fcorzoner. ℥
vi. flor. Cordial. Calendul. Genift. an. m. ij.
Aquar Cardui Benedict. Scabios. Borag. Buglos.
Meliffæ an. lib. 3. ponantur omnia in Alembico
vitreo, poftcà macerentur fpatio xxiij. horar.
deinde fiat deftillatio, vt artis eft.

Let the child take a fpoonfull of this water, three
times a day, in the morning, at noone and at night,   *The vfe.*
adding thereto a little fuger Candy or firup of Li-
mons. The nurfes may alfo take two ounces of it in
the morning.

And becaufe the true Antidote againft this dif-
eafe, is Quickfiluer, therefore will it be very fit to
annoint the childs puftules with fome fuch Ointment, not bringing him to a fluxe of the mouth.

℞. *Vng. Rofat. Mes.℥iiij. Hydrargiri cum fucco li-*   *The Oint-*
monum extincti ℥ s. mifce, fiat vng. pro litu.   *ment.*

If the child bee elder, let him bee purged twice
with a little *Sene*; and firup of Cichory, with *Ru-*
barb, neither will it be amiffe (if hee be bigger and
ftronger) to open a veine, and take away a faucer
full of bloud: He may alfo vfe the forefaid decoction, and Opiate fome eight or ten daies: onely dimi-
nifhing the dofes of the Ingredients.

Bbb   *Of*

A page from Jacques Guillemeau's *Child Birth or the Happy Deliverie of Women*, translated in 1612.

Had the 'Observations' consisted solely of case histories, Willughby would thus
have arrived at precisely the literary form that was to be adopted a little later by
François Mauriceau and again in the eighteenth century by William Smellie: that
is, the textual separation of obstetric system on the one hand and its concrete
exemplification on the other. But Willughby's pair of texts represented only an
imperfect approximation to this solution, for the 'Observations', which were
meant to supply the empirical component, still contained systematic advice as
well. Further, the two works were structured in different ways, making it no easy
matter for the reader to move between them as Willughby's new plan required.
   Well aware of such problems, Willughby now placed the two texts in the hands
of someone who was to act as editor; and he inserted some marginal instructions
which recognized the unwieldy nature of the 'Observations' and gave this
intended editor a free hand to revise the text as she or he saw fit.[118] In all
probability, it was this individual who produced the two copies of the
'Observations' and 'Opusculum' which have come down to posterity. We do not
know who this individual was; but there are grounds for suspecting that this was
none other than Willughby's daughter Eleanor Hurt, the former midwife.
Certainly the copyist was someone close to Willughby and indeed devoted to
him. She or he copied out the whole text a second time for the sole purpose of
incorporating 'The Index of the Auctor' (that is, Willughby's index of personal
names). Further, this copyist also compiled 'An Additional Table' – to wit, a
detailed subject-index, something which Willughby himself had not supplied.[119]
With its 284 headings and 460 page-entries this table was remarkably complete,
including as it did such headings as 'This book contains chiefly the Auctor's own
ways in midwifery'; 'How a London midw: made' (referring to the deputy
system); and 'When the Auctor left Stafford'.[120] Yet, strikingly, this copyist made
no reference in the index to the 'Auctor's' daughter and her practice. The
'Additional Table' *did* cite Eleanor's cases – but merely under the headings 'Belly,
back, buttocks'[121] and 'Dr. Harvey commended'.[122] It would appear, then, that
this copyist deliberately refrained from including in the index the fact that the
'Auctor's' daughter was a midwife. And I suggest that the most plausible
explanation of this omission is that the copyist was Eleanor herself.
   This is, of course, only a conjecture; I have not been able to test it, for nothing
has so far come to light which is known to have been written in the hand of
Eleanor Hurt neé Willughby. But the conjecture is attractive – for it would mean
that the *Observations*, in the physical form of their larger extant version, are
themselves a memorial to Eleanor Willughby.

Notes
1 Sean Burke, *The Death and Return of the Author* (1992), p. 39.
2 Percival Willughby, *Observations in Midwifery. As also the country midwife's opusculum or vade mecum*
(1863; facsimile reprint 1972); cited hereafter as *Observations*. This printing is based on the manuscript

as it stood in 1672, and includes the accompanying 'Opusculum', discussed below. An earlier recension, produced by Willughby in 1668, is BL, Sloane MS 529, ff. 1–19; this has never been published in English, though the Dutch printing of 1754 was based on essentially the same text. I refer to this 1668 recension as the 'London version' of the 'Observations' (cf. below, at note 41); a transcript is given in Appendix B of Adrian Wilson, 'Childbirth in Seventeenth- and Eighteenth-Century England' (D. Phil. thesis, University of Sussex, 1982). On the various MSS and editions, see Ch. 8 of the latter thesis, and also John L. Thornton's introduction to the 1972 reprint.

3 Percival Willughby and his wife Elizabeth (née Coke), who were married in 1631, had two daughters: Eleanor, baptized as Hellena on 10 February 1638/9, and Dorothy, baptized on 15 June 1642 (both at St Peter's, Derby). The midwife-daughter was practising in 1655; this surely rules out Dorothy, since she was only thirteen years old at this time. See further Wilson (1982) 'Childbirth', Appendix E.

4 Thus we learn more about the routine management of childbirth from Ralph Josselin's diary and from Willughby's *Observations* than we do from Alice Thornton's retrospective account of her deliveries. See Thornton (1873), pp. 84–98, 123–7, 139–51, 164–7; Josselin (1976), pp. 37–50, 101–11, 145–65, 231–57, 313–25, 399–415, 453–65, 496–502; *Observations, passim*.

5 Cf. Paul de Man (1983), particularly the essay 'The rhetoric of blindness: Jacques Derrida's Reading of Rousseau' (pp. 102–41).

6 Burke (1992), pp. 38–9.

7 *Observations*, p. 125; this case will be discussed in detail in my *A Safe Deliverance: childbirth in sevententh-century England* (London, UCL Press, forthcoming). In this and most other extended quotations I have modified Willughby's punctuation.

8 Willughby's account suggested that the delivery took place a 'few years' before Grace Beechcraft was buried (after another difficult birth) on 24 September 1657. In fact the case he delivered occurred only two years before her burial, for the stillbirth he delivered can certainly be identified with a (double) entry in the register of St Peter's, Derby, referring to the burial of an 'infant filia Joseph Beechcraft' on 1 October and 30 September 1655: see Wilson (1982), 'Childbirth', Appendix C (p. 4).

9 Had the women been united in this respect, Willughby would probably have written that 'the women' frowned upon some of these divines; but in fact he wrote only that '*several women*' did so.

10 'Observations', London version, p. 22. On the extant versions, cf. below, at note 41.

11 *Observations*, p. 94 (the case of Clare Pearson). Similarly, it is quite possible that he took his daughter to Grace Beechcraft's delivery (as he did in another case around this time: below, at note 53), even though this is not mentioned in his account of the case.

12 Above, at pp. 161 and 166–7 (Mrs Bennett, Mrs Molyneux).

13 See my essays 'The ceremony of childbirth and its interpretation', in Fildes (1990) and 'William Hunter and the varieties of man-midwifery', in Bynum and Porter (1985).

14 Above, p. 162.

15 In the case of births by the head, what is nowadays regarded as most important is the *orientation* of the foetal head. But Willughby never reported this; in his eyes, what counted was the *size* of the child's head. In fact these aspects were probably related: cf. A. Wilson (1995).

16 Particularly compound presentation (hand and foot). These can probably be regarded as a

variant of arm-presentation; including these would make little difference to the picture presented below.

17 Cf. A. Wilson (1995), pp. 11–15.

18 Incidence: Galabin (1904). Difficulty: below, at note 100.

19 See 'The ceremony of childbirth and its interpretation', Fildes (1990).

20 See for instance Hitchcock (1967); the origins of the various clauses of the oath will be considered in A. Wilson (forthcoming).

21 This allowance is achieved by assumptions (d) and (e) in Table 7.2, each of which probably overstates the case. As to assumption (d), only in about a third of Willughby's emergency cases was more than one midwife present (though, admittedly, the number was sometimes as high as four, or 'several'). As to assumption (e), certain individual midwives were probably favoured in calls of this kind, and these particular midwives must have received a disproportionate share of the total. For some justification of the first three assumptions, see A. Wilson (forthcoming), chs 2 and 3.

22 Thus Willughby referred to one midwife 'that was accounted the prime midwife of Staffordshire': 'Observations', London version, p. 33.

23 Thus in Derby, where Willughby was based for most of his working life, there were three midwives in a single parish in the 1680s. See further A. Wilson (1995), pp. 33–5, and Wilson (1982), Table 5.3.1.

24 The incidence of arm presentations has been inflated by rounding. The estimate of 1 such primary case in ten years has been rounded up from 0.8; the estimate of 2 such 'secondary' cases in ten years has been rounded up from 1.6. A more accurate estimate of the total number would thus be 2.4 in ten years, i.e. about one such case every four years.

25 As Bernice and Jeffrey Boss have correctly observed, systematic training could have conferred the requisite experience, even with low prevailing case loads: Boss and Boss (1983). But there was no such system of training in seventeenth-century England – with the important exception of London (p. 165, above).

26 For further details and illustrative cases, see my 'William Hunter and the varieties of man-midwifery' in Bynum and Porter (1985).

27 As presented here, this reasoning appears to be circular, since Table 7.3 has assumed (for convenience) that Willughby was called to most of the difficult births in his catchment area. But, in fact, this assumption is itself derived from an analysis of his recorded cases, to be presented in A. Wilson (forthcoming).

28 Revival of the child: *Observations*, pp. 40, 66, 82 (but contrast p. 186); A. Wilson (1995), p. 36.

29 But if he was called to act in lieu of a midwife, he did take an interest in such matters: cf. below, after note 108.

30 In Table 7.2 this is an artefact of rounding; the estimated incidence of such cases, according to the assumptions used in constructing the table, was in fact 0.37 obstructed breech births in ten years (0.12 in a midwife's 'primary' practice, plus 0.25 in her 'secondary' practice). That is, in a ten-year period about one in every three midwives would encounter a case of breech obstruction. Further, most midwives probably saw no obstructed breech births at all in their 'primary' practices – since even in thirty years of practice (a generous assessment of the typical midwife's working life), the expected number of such cases was only 0.36.

31 For a fuller discussion of what follows see A. Wilson (1995), pp. 19–22.

32 In later technical jargon: internal podalic version with traction.

33 This relative lateness of his arriving at the method was well concealed in the *Observations* – for good reasons, which will be discussed in A. Wilson (forthcoming). Cf. notes 38, 50, 57 below.

34 'Let midwives therefore be persuaded, that as oft as they perceive the child to be coming forth in an evil posture, either with his belly or back forward, or as it were doubled, in a crooked posture, or with his hands and feet together, or with his head forward and one of his hands stretched over his head, or with the buttocks, that they ought to turn the birth, and to draw it out by the feet' (*Observations*, p. 56).

35 'Observations', London version, p. 35. In practice Willughby was remarkably equivocal about using turning for obstructed births by the head: see A. Wilson (1982), pp. 282–9, and A. Wilson (forthcoming). For 'Dame Nature' (below) see *Observations*, pp. 10, 234.

36 Precisely the same tension was manifested by twin births, by the management of the placenta, and in births by the head where the child was still alive. On the placenta and twins see A. Wilson (1995), pp. 162–3; a more detailed discussion of Willughby's experiences will be included in A. Wilson (forthcoming).

37 'I have known some children coming by the buttocks, and so born' (*Observations*, p. 56); below, at note 57.

38 *Observations*, pp. 132–3 (John Plimer's wife). Note that in the case of 'Tab's wife', from 1632 (p. 130), Willughby had *not* turned the child to the feet, but instead had 'alter[ed] the posture' in some unspecified way. He left unclear in the 'Observations' just what this earlier technique was – because he no longer followed the method. Cf. notes 33 above, 50 and 57 below.

39 *Observations*, p. 6.

40 On the postulated initial version of 1662, cf. A. Wilson (1982), pp. 171–3 and Appendix D.

41 On these MSS, and also on the printed editions discussed below, see John L. Thornton, 'Introduction' to *Observations*, and A. Wilson (1982), Ch. 8.

42 *Observations*, p. 257.

43 William Harvey, *Disputations*, tr. Gweneth Whitteridge (1981), pp. 393–419, quoted from pp. 403–4; my emphases in the following quotations.

44 Yet cf. note 46 below.

45 Harvey (1981), pp. 405–6.

46 At this point Harvey was curiously eliding his own argument that it is not just the uterus but the whole of the mother's body which accomplishes the delivery.

47 *Observations*, p. 118.

48 Above, p. 159.

49 *Observations*, pp. 12, 151, 191; cf. also pp. 73, 156, 158, 206, 310, 324 and 342, where Willughby asserted the need for practical experience.

50 *Ibid.*, *passim*, esp. pp. 324, 326 (this passage is part of the 'Opusculum'). In fact, Willughby had followed this method in his early practice, as we discover fortuitously from a case of 1633 which he 'inserted' for other reasons: see *Observations*, pp. 97–8 (Goodwife Osborn). Cf. notes 33, 38 above, 57 below.

51 Cf. above, p. 149.

52 See above, p. 166; also *Observations*, p. 126 (case of Mrs Okeover).

53 *Ibid.*, p. 158.

54 Above, at Table 7.1.

55 Above, p. 145. On the midwife's authority, cf. above, pp. 159, 165.

56 *Observations*, p. 130.

57 *Ibid.*, 'One Mrs Staynes, a chirurgion's wife in Derby, was delivered of a child in such a posture, in the year 1630, the child coming double, sitting with his buttocks in the womb. She did very well after her delivery, and her child lived.' Willughby left it unclear whether he had actually carried out this delivery, doubtless because he now wanted to distance himself from this expectant approach. Cf. notes 33, 38, 50 above.

58 *Observations*, p. 6; cf. above, p. 150.

59 *Ibid.*, pp. 134–5.

60 No more than 75 births were taking place each year in Stafford at this time, and probably fewer: see note 64 below. If there were 75 births per year, an obstructed breech birth would take place there only once in twenty years, on the assumptions of Table 7.2.

61 If the catchment area accounted for 1,000 births per year, we find (again applying the assumptions of Table 7.2) that one such case would take place every twenty months, which is just enough to account for this one such case of Eleanor's.

62 If the incidence of breech births was 1 in 30, and Eleanor saw 2 breech births from the onset of labour, then the odds are more than 20 to 1 against her rate of practice being as low as 10 cases per year. This result is reached by binomial probability, for which see Spiegel (1975), p. 108.

63 This from the fact that breech births were about 1 in 30 of all births (1 in 33 on the assumptions of Table 7.2). Precision is impossible because the occurrence of rare events (in this case, breech births) is subject to massive random variation. Even a very low case load cannot be ruled out absolutely (cf. the previous note); conversely, a high case load is also possible (for instance, if Eleanor attended as many as 100 deliveries, there would still be a better than 1 in 3 chance that she saw as *few* as two breech cases or less).

64 The population of Stafford at this time was probably somewhere between 1,400 and 1,800. Assuming that the birth rate was in the range 30 to 40 per 1,000, the annual numbers of births fell somewhere between 42 and 72. A best guess might be a population of 1,600, a birth rate of 35 per 1,000, and thus some 56 births per year. See *Victoria County History Staffordshire*, vol. 6 (1979), p. 186; Whiteman and Clapinson (1986), pp. 438, 454; Wrigley and Schofield (1981). In view of the figures from the town survey of 1622 and from the 1666 Hearth Tax returns (*VCH Staffs*, vol. 6), it would appear that the Compton census return for 'Stafford' included the whole town (as Whiteman assumes at p. 438), rather than the parish of St Mary alone (as Whiteman suggests at p. 454, note 219).

65 Even if each obstructed breech birth drew in as many as four midwives in a 'secondary' capacity, a typical midwife would have been called to just one such case every twenty years (on the assumptions of Table 7.2). If such cases drew in three 'secondary' midwives (as obtained in Eleanor's Case 2), this becomes almost twenty-eight years; if they drew in just two 'secondary' midwives, it would take over forty years for the typical midwife to receive such a call.

66 Above, p. 156, after note 59.

67 Even if as many as 75 births took place each year in Stafford, this would only yield 4.5 breech

births in two years; the more plausible estimate of 60 births per year implies 3.6 breech births in two years (cf. note 64 above).

68 Harley (1993).

69 I have come across no examples of this in some dozens of Norwich testimonials for ecclesiastical licences *c.* 1700: Norfolk and Norwich Record Office, Norwich diocesan records, TES/8, file i.

70 *Observations*, p. 238.

71 *Ibid.*, p. 135.

72 Cf. above, at note 55, and see further below, at note 98.

73 Above, p. 153.

74 *Observations*, pp. 118–19.

75 When Alice Thornton was disappointed by her midwife, she found another midwife rather than securing the services of a male practitioner. Again, when the wife of an eminent apothecary in Newark (Notts) 'resolved never more to make use of the midwife's assistance', she did not resort to a male practitioner but instead gave birth unassisted, alone in her bedroom. Further, Willughby's cases include only a few mothers who used his services in lieu of a midwife, and in such cases special circumstances prevailed. See Thornton (1873), pp. 123–7; *Observations*, pp. 40–2, 240–1; note 113 below.

76 Cf. p. 167.

77 *Observations*, p. 119.

78 Above, p. 153.

79 'Observations', London version, p. 10.

80 Willughby also used 'evank' for 'knave' to refer to two other individuals: *Observations*, pp. 31, 249.

81 I owe this identification to Gerald Aylmer; detailed supporting reasons and further biographical details are given in A. Wilson (1982), Ch. 9, notes 76 and 77.

82 *Observations*, pp. 135–7.

83 Cf. above, p. 142.

84 *Observations*, p.136.

85 Cf. above, p. 153.

86 I have modified the wording here; in the MS this reads as follows: 'I came several days after, but was scarce made to drink; however never thanked for the care that I had of his wife.'

87 *Observations*, p. 21.

88 Notice that in this, the Derby version, Willughby slightly reworded the quotation from Bennet: e.g. 'pocky nurse' for 'pocky whore'.

89 *Observations*, p. 137

90 It will be recalled that in Stafford, her case load was probably well over 10 births a year (cf. note 62 above). In London, by contrast, a best guess would be less than 10 births a year, for she had one breech case which she had attended from the onset of labour, suggesting a total practice of 30 cases in a period of three and a half years.

91 Cf. Aveling (1882), p. 37, and other references cited below.

92 *Observations*, p. 73.

93 Hitchcock (1967).

94 Two such attempts were made by members of the Chamberlen family in 1617 and 1634: see Aveling (1882). A final such initiative came from Mrs Elizabeth Cellier in 1687; see King (1993), pp. 115–30, and cf. below.

95 Doreen Evenden suggests that ecclesiastical licensing worked to support the deputy system; I have argued that the efforts of the Church worked in the long run to undermine the deputy system. See Evenden (1993), pp. 9–26; A. Wilson (1995), p. 33.

96 Elizabeth Celleor (*sic*) (1688), p. 6, quoted in Aveling (1872), p. 89.

97 Cf. King, 'The politick midwife', p. 122. For Mrs Cellier, including her earlier stormy political career, see also *DNB*; Donnison (1977), pp. 18–20; Aveling (1872), pp. 63–85; Fraser (1984; 1985), pp. 513–22.

98 Above, p. 159.

99 *Observations*, pp. 45, 239, 240 (though cf. also pp. 22–4, and of course the cases of Mrs Wolaston and the Shoe Lane mother, pp. 118–19, 135, discussed above).

100 *Ibid.*, pp. 138–40.

101 *Ibid.*, pp. 140–6; see also pp. 22, 330.

102 As it happened, Willughby was to act as midwife to another mother (Lady Byron) just a few months later, in August 1661 (*ibid.*, pp. 40–2). Surprisingly, Eleanor was not involved on this occasion; perhaps this was because this particular engagement involved Willughby's staying in the mother's house.

103 Above, pp. 158–9.

104 Hence the fact that several of his uses of the word 'man-midwife' were scornful and associated with what he saw as malpractice: *Observations*, pp. 22, 88, 248 (though for neutral references see pp. 17, 340).

105 Cf. A. Wilson (1995), Ch. 4.

106 The marriage took place on 23 October 1662 (the year is given as '1663' in A. Wilson (1982), Appendix E, p. (1), but this is a typographical error). Although the family lived at some distance (as we know from the case discussed above, p. 168), Eleanor's children were all baptized in Derby (see note 107 below).

107 Dates of her children's baptisms (and burials), from the bishop's transcripts for St Peter's, Derby (Lichfield Joint Record Office): 6.8.63; 9.6.65 [bur. 4.12.67]; 25.9.66; 8.10.67 [bur. 18.1.71/2]; 21.12.68 [bur. 20.2.68/9]; 15.2.69/70; 11.2.72/3; 1.9.74; 23.12.80.

108 Marginalia: 'El. Hu.' (*Observations*, p. 179), 'El. Hurt' (*ibid.*, p. 254). Index: 'El. H. El. H.' (*sic*, p. 281, citing both the former entries).

109 The date of her stillbirth (6 December 1671) falls within a three-year gap in the sequence of recorded baptisms for Eleanor Hurt's children (i.e. between 15 February 1669/70 and 11 February 1672/3): cf. note 107 above and see A. Wilson (1982), Appendix E, p. 4.

110 The fact that this case was included in the London version dates it to before April 1668, thus restricting it to Eleanor's first four deliveries; the fact that the case was undated probably rules out her fourth delivery, since at this time (October 1667) Willughby was giving exact dates to all the cases he included in the 'Observations'. (Cases which occurred during the years 1663–6 were mostly written down later, from recall, and were thus left undated, as in this instance, or were dated only approximately: A. Wilson (1982), Appendix C.) *Observations*, p. 179; London version, p. 32.

111 Willughby inserted the case as an illustration of a technical point from Harvey: that when the foetus has died yet the delivery proceeds naturally, 'the water is the cause of the delivery . . . in that by its corruption and acrimony, it doth extimulate the uterus to relieve itself', *Observations*, pp. 254–5.

112 *Ibid.*, p. 38.

113 The few other women who resorted to Willughby in lieu of a midwife did so either because they had previously had difficult births (Mrs Wolaston in London, Mrs Molyneux in the Midlands) or through 'great fears' of giving birth (Lady Byron: *Observations*, pp. 40–2). In contrast, Willughby's account of the deliveries of this unnamed 'gentlewoman' include no mention of any expected difficulty in the birth.

114 Sermon (1671), Sharp (1671), Wolveridge (1671).

115 *Observations*, p. 210. This remark is not from the 'Opusculum' itself; but for words to similar effect from the latter, cf. *Observations*, pp. 311–12.

116 *Ibid.*, pp. 304, 315, 318 (margin), 324, 326.

117 *Ibid.*, pp. 101, 164, 166 ('See the schemes', etc.).

118 See *ibid.*, pp. 93, 99 (marginalia).

119 It appears that the copyist first proceeded without attending to pagination; that on encountering Willughby's index, she or he realized that this created a problem of collation; and that she or he accordingly produced a second copy which followed Willughby's pagination. See A. Wilson (1982), Appendix D.9.

120 *Observations*, pp. 296, 296, 298 respectively.

121 *Ibid.*, p. 277, referring to pp. 91, 120, 129, 130 'etc.', i.e. 130ff.

122 *Ibid.*, p. 294, referring to pp. 118–19.

8

SISTERS OF THE ROYAL SOCIETY: THE CIRCLE OF KATHERINE JONES, LADY RANELAGH

Lynette Hunter

The first books to be printed in English on medical science and applied chemistry, and attributed to women, were published in the 1650s. Elizabeth Grey's *A Choice Manual of Rare Conceits* (1653), Queen Henrietta Maria's *The Queen's Closet Opened* (1655) and Alethea Talbot's *Natura Exenterata* (1655), emerged after a thirty-year moratorium on any new books of pharmacy, household science and medicine for women, and possibly up to fifty years, in some parts, after being written. My earlier chapter in this collection, 'Women and Domestic Medicine'(see above, pp. 89–107), investigated some of the contexts for the manuscripts: the social and personal history of the writers, household work for women during the period, the participation of women in medical science in particular, and aspects of their education and aristocratic status. I was concerned to ask what kind of science they were engaged in, and how and whether it fitted into our understanding of formal training at the time. The second part of this study will focus on the circle of Katherine Jones, Lady Ranelagh in the 1640–60 period, and add the following questions: how were people at the time *doing* science, where were they doing it, why did they do it, and how were the women practitioners in particular perceived by those around them.

In 'Women and Domestic Medicine' I argued that the compilers or writers of the three texts under study were moving science into an intellectual leisure pursuit, at the same time as deriving their experience of it from the social work they adopted and carried out in their communities. Two of the three books address medicinal, household and food receipts in distinctly different parts of equal weight. Yet the parts on medical and some household chemistry, which were those attributed directly to the women, only went into further editions for a few years, while the parts on general household work and on food were republished well into the eighteenth century. Alethea Talbot's *Natura Exenterata*, which emphasized medical and household science, has only one edition. Hence it would seem that the parts on medical science and applied chemistry were not nearly as popular as the others, and not worth republishing after the early 1660s: so why did printers and publishers take a chance on them in the first place?

If the manuscript texts were written for a small circle of friends with common intellectual pursuits, they were printed and published for rather different reasons. First, it is likely that the printers thought they would make money out of them, possibly believing that in the growing atmosphere of unease at the beheading of Charles I they might capitalize on books attributed to women closely associated with him – and who closer than the exiled queen? A second factor was that Nicolas Culpeper's translation of the London *Pharmacopoeia*, which outlined the legal prescriptions to be prepared by the Society of Apothecaries, had appeared in 1649. This was the first substantial work on pharmacy in the vernacular English to have been published since the society's incorporation in 1617. Although much corroborative research remains to be done, this publication seems to have opened the door for many others that would not have appeared had there not been a need for the receipts among the general public.

A third factor concerns those who were associated with the publications, either listed as contributors or sources within the texts themselves: by and large these people were men involved in the new experimental science, and these publications may be a recognition of a field of learning that was coming into being. Henrietta Maria's court, both in England and then in exile, brought herself, the sisters Elizabeth Grey and Alethea Talbot, together with a notable circle of men interested in Paracelsian and Baconian science. In addition, Alethea had travelled with her husband to Italy on a number of occasions, probably visiting the de Medici laboratories with him,[1] and offering among her receipts some from continental scientists. Part of the story about these texts involves gentlemen acquiring status for their activities by analogy with the aristocratic status of the women – two of the three writers were at the top of the aristocratic hierarchy of the time. And as I hope to demonstrate, part of the story is also allied to a shift from 'Kitchin-Physick' to 'Ladies Chemistry' that becomes clearer in the 1640–60 period.

The intellectual circle around Katherine Jones in London in the years 1640 to 1660 is closely associated with the correspondents to the scriptorium run by Samuel Hartlib[2] with which Katherine was considerably involved. Contributors to the scriptorium refer to Elizabeth Grey's receipts[3] and to her book and to *The Queen's Closet Opened*;[4] and they were with a quite different level of energy looking forward to the publication of *Natura Exenterata*.[5] Very little is known directly about Katherine Jones, given the place that she held in scholarly, political and religious circles. Nearly all her letters are gone from the Hartlib collection, and are rare elsewhere. However, one book of her medical receipts is with the British Library, and one book of more general remedies is held in the Wellcome Institute Library. She was close to her brother Robert, and they lived together for the last thirty years of their lives, dying within a few months of each other in 1692. I would like to introduce her by quoting from the sermon read at her brother's funeral:

She lived the longest on the publickest Scene, she made the greatest Figure in all the Revolutions of these Kingdoms for above fifty Years, of any Woman of our Age. She imployed it all for doing good to others, in which she laid out her Time, her Interest, and her Estate, with the greatest Zeal and the most Success that I have ever known. She was indefatigable as well as dextrous in it: and as her great Understanding, and the vast Esteem she was in, made all Persons in their several turns of Greatness, desire and value her Friendship: so she gave her self a clear Title to imploy her Interest with them for the Service of others, by this that she never made any use of it to any End or Design of her own. She was contented with what she had: and though she was twice stript of it, she never moved on her own account, but was the general Intercessor for all Persons of Merit, or in want: This had in her the better Grace, and was both more Christian and more effectual, because it was not limited within any narrow Compass of Parties or Relations.

She had with a vast Reach both of Knowledg and Apprehensions, an universal Affability and Easiness of Access, a Humility that descended to the meanest Persons and Concerns, an obliging Kindness and Readiness to advise those who had no occasion for any further Assistance from her; and with all these and many more excellent Qualities, she had the deepest Sense of Religion, and the most constant turning of her Thoughts and Discourses that way, that has been perhaps in our Age.[6]

Katherine Jones came to London from Ireland in 1642, and may have been introduced to Samuel Hartlib by her aunt Dorothy Moore. At the time Hartlib was a good twelve years advanced into a rather extraordinary project to disseminate knowledge. Hartlib undertook to receive letters from people in England, Ireland and Scotland, on religious, educational, scientific and other matters, and copy them to continental writers. The continental writers in return would send him information in letters, essays, sermons and so on, which he had copied for his home audience.[7] By the 1640s Kenelm Digby, John Pell, John Evelyn and Theodore de Mayerne, who were all part of Henrietta Maria's circle, were closely involved, as were John Dury, the scientist Benjamin Worsley, poet John Milton and continental writers such as René Descartes. There is a significant increase in correspondence about natural philosophy and science in the late 1640s and through the 1650s. It has been suggested that this reflected a conscious decision to avoid discussion of the political and religious conflict of the time.[8] But in any event many of the people involved in the scientific discussions of the 1650s at Gresham College and at Wadham College in Oxford that led to the founding of the Royal Society were also contributors to the agency and corresponded with Katherine Jones, whose house on Queen Street was often used as an address by Hartlib himself.[9]

Gresham College, London, 1834.

The correspondence yielded a very considerable exchange of letters initially on religion and then increasingly on education, language and natural philosophy. Unusually for the period, the contributors included a number of women[10]: among others were in the 1630s Lady Barrington, from 1640 Dorothy Moore and from 1643 Katherine Jones. Dorothy Moore was an exceptional woman who was in the Netherlands arguing the case for a woman's ministry with Protestant Reform Church theologians. She and Katherine Jones seem to have had a plan for the education of young women in the early 1640s which was not realized but about which we are given some clues from a letter she wrote several years later outlining the need for an education in reason and intellect rather than dancing and 'curious inventions'.[11] It is also noteworthy that Henrietta Maria herself showed an unusual interest in education for women when she agreed to become the patron for Mary Ward's schools as early as 1625.[12] John Dury, who became Dorothy Moore's husband in 1645, was a key contributor on religious and educational issues, and was close friends with the scientists Benjamin Worsley and William Petty.[13] During the 1650s the Durys became attached to Henry Oldenburg, secretary to the Royal Society from 1662 and editor of its *Transactions* for many years.[14] The Durys' daughter, Dora Catherina, was left to his care after their deaths, and Oldenburg eventually married her, their own children Sophia and Robert becoming wards of Katherine Jones and Robert Boyle when the Oldenburgs died.

This detail about Dorothy Moore is offered partly because she was Katherine Jones's closest associate but also to indicate the way intellectual and familial ties often overlapped, the intellectual community providing a kind of extended family. Not that Katherine Jones needed one: as a daughter of the immensely wealthy colonialist Richard Boyle, Earl of Cork, she had many family connections: Royalist, Parliamentarian, Roman Catholic, Protestant and Puritan.[15] At Queen Street in the 1640s her house was a meeting place for people of quite different politics and religious persuasions. Later, in Pall Mall, her house became a centre for visiting scientists as well.[16] All her brothers and sisters, with the single exception of Robert, were placed in a variety of aristocratic positions. While their husbands were fighting on opposite sides during the Civil War, two of her well-married sisters continued to develop their interests in sugar-cookery and in medicine. Lettice Goring's recipes occur in a number of manuscripts and books of the period,[17] while Mary Rich, later Countess of Warwick, became well known for her skill as a physician and apothecary in the community in which she lived.[18]

Katherine herself kept those two books of receipts. One is a general book of household science and specialized food cookery receipts, a combination that came to be known as 'Kitchin-Physick'.[19] It also included the receipt for Spirit of Roses 'My brother Robert's way' which is appended at the end of this chapter to indicate the kind of skills and technological expertise that were expected in day-to-day household work. The other notebook is a more detailed and focused account of herbal preparations and chemistry,[20] akin to Alethea Talbot's *Natura Exenterata*. The manuscript contains technical receipts with a guide to chemical symbols at the back which are referred to as 'our' symbols – possibly Katherine's and Robert's. The symbols are derived from commonly known alchemical symbols, and while there are many more of them, they are identical to those in Alethea's book. The measurements are accurate and the descriptions precise, in tune with the new chemical or 'spagyricall' methodology. Yet the receipts are for the same medical complaints as those in many contemporary manuscripts, and use largely similar ingredients.

Where did Katherine Jones practise this science? Just as Mary Sidney, Lady Pembroke allowed her brother Philip and son William to use her 'facilities' in the 1590s, so Katherine seems to have had facilities that both she and her brother used.[21] The histories of laboratory work are rather coy about what these facilities were. There are suggestions that experimental equipment was brought in via the continent, or adapted from alchemical technology, and both suggestions are highly probable. But it is also clear that virtually everything that they might have needed was readily available in the kitchen or still room of any substantial estate,

Alembics used in the distilling process, from *The Practise of New and Old Physicke* (1599).

which may provide a reason for the absence of a specific word to denote an area for scientific practice until much later in the seventeenth century.[22] Access to water, to heating and cooling methods, to weights, to preparation tools for chopping, grinding, sifting, straining and so on, had been necessary to both the alchemist, the cook and the housekeeper, and was also necessary to early scientific work in chemistry and medicinal experiment. In addition, all used the equipment of the distillation room with its alembics, collecting vessels and furnaces.

Illustrations from 1707 of the Golden Phoenix laboratories, a construction thought to have been akin to that built by Robert Boyle on to the back of Katherine's house in Pall Mall,[23] show a variety of tools identical to those in a well-stocked *batterie de cuisine*, ranging from instruments to deal with the heating of various items, to knives, long-handled forks, trivets, straining ladles and tongs, to sieves, jelly-bags, cutting blocks and pestles and mortars. The illustrations also show the importance of a variety of regulated sources of heat[24] that is mirrored in the variety of cooking and cooling sources in the kitchen. There are open fires, closed fires of various kinds to heat air, furnaces controlling heat by controlling the temperature of water in a *bain marie*, charcoal braziers, and three-legged heating pots for on-the-floor fires. While

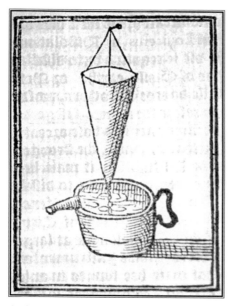

A piece of equipment used in distilling, from
The Practise of New and Old Physicke (1599).

most kitchens would have had an
open fire and possibly on-the-floor
bake-stone fires, more substantial
houses would have had bread ovens,
as well as rows of braziers
maintained at different temperatures
for stewing and simmering; the
distillation rooms contained furnaces
and tubs of water with pipes running
through them for cooling down
distilled liquors, as well as
conserving equipment such as large
charcoal-fed braziers for preparing
comfits and sugar preserves; the
brew houses often had screw presses.
The most heavily used piece of
equipment is the alembic or
distillation vessel, many of which are
illustrated in the 1707 laboratory,
and which provided the essential
technology of the commercial
distillation houses of the 1590s,[25] of
earlier alchemical distillations and,
of course, of the distillation rooms of houses on estates.

The technology upon which the 1707 laboratory depended was long-lived. It
had been in place for many years and would continue with roughly the same
structure until the end of the nineteenth century. A listing of the contents of
Kenelm Digby's laboratory at Gresham College in 1648 indicates the consistency
implied in the similarity between the illustrations from the 1590s' book on
distillation and the 1707 Golden Phoenix:

In Sir Kenelm Digby his Laboratory
at Gresham College
In the first Room
A Great Glass Case with several great Glasses
An Anatomy Board with drawers

In the Next Room
A Driving Oven
An oven with Iron retorts
A deliquium stone & Cellar
A Closet and little lodging Room, A Table and forms

In the great Room
A Reverberating Calcining Oven
A [Balneum] Mariæ
3 Sand Retort furnaces
A furnace for Retorts in open fire
An Ashanon a digest Furnace
20 Limbeck bodies of several sizes
2 Glass basins
6 Glass Funnels and some Galley Glasses
A pair of Tongs 2 supporters for Recipients
13 Iron Trevells
Several pieces of earthen vessels
A water Cistern Cock and Sink
Several old materials
A Large Table, dresser board, shelves & drawers
& small Iron Grate
A chopping plank
Several Glass bottles of several Sizes
2 Grinding stones of speckled marble

In the other Room
A great screw Press
A stone mortar and wooden Pestle
2 Grinding stones
A search
A Great Balneum Mariæ
3 Vaporatories
2 Vesicæ cum Refrigaratoris
2 sand furnaces
A Balneum Roris: or for Land
4 stools to set Recipients
Pieces of lead for the Balneum Mariæ
A Great Iron Plate[26]

There is little in the list that would not also have been found in the domestic setting of a wealthy household except possibly the cooling vessels, although there were ice houses and cooling equipment in continental households from at least the sixteenth century.[27]

It seems likely that Katherine Jones practised her general and her experimental chemistry in her kitchen and distillation room, but how was that practice perceived? While there is a great deal of evidence that many women practised 'Kitchin-Physick', with several examples up to 1600, there are many more during the seventeenth century including Lady Mildmay whose epitaph from the 1620s refers to her skills in these areas,[28] Lady Barrington who was corresponding with Hartlib on religious matters in the 1630s and sending him receipts,[29] and the already mentioned Mary Rich, Katherine's sister, who was working in her community during the 1660s and '70s. In 1993, in the 1680s Lady Masham complained to John Locke that she had so many responsibilities in this area that she scarcely had the time to read a book (Hutton, 1993) – and there were many others. As to Katherine Jones herself, throughout the 1640s and '50s she was in continual contact with Samuel Hartlib and his correspondents. The authors of many letters addressed to him ask to be reminded to Katherine Jones and Dorothy Moore, and while there are few of her own letters in the archive there is a constant flow of letters to her. It was a rich intellectual community that included several women, increasingly non-aristocratic women, up to the end of the 1650s.

Many of the correspondents were also part of the Oxford circle concerned with matters of natural philosophy; it was made up of Robert Boyle, Thomas Willis and John Wilkins[30] and Katherine Jones visited it once. It was said of this circle, possibly rather caustically, that 'The Lords are the Lords and the Ladies are the commons',[31] a comment which combines an implicit devaluing of the women with an indication of their unpredictability, even their unruliness and, given the historical context, their willingness to debate. Thomas Willis was the writer who updated Mayerne's *Pharmacopoeia* into a text of chemical experiments in the 1660s; he was also a renowned physician and one of the first to work on a vocabulary for physiology. He seems to have worked alongside Katherine Jones; certainly he completed her medical receipt book and some of her receipts ended up in his *Pharmacopoeia Rationalis*. Given that later in life he employed the apothecaries Hazelwood and Guthrie to make up his receipts, Katherine may have acted in this capacity during their work together. It may be significant that Willis was fairly ordinary by birth, and was apprenticed to a tutor whose wife was a well-respected doctor.[32]

Willis recognized Katherine Jones's skill in using her receipts, just as Hartlib's *Ephemerides* or commonplace book records dozens of receipts and remedies which he is receiving from ladies and gentlemen throughout the 1640s and '50s; Robert Boyle notes the usefulness of women's receipts in many of his manuscripts;[33] Kenelm Digby's 'Closet Opened' of 1657 attributes many receipts to women and John Evelyn's diary describes working alongside his wife at experimentation.[34] The practice of chemistry, general or experimental, was clearly seen as appropriate to the aristocratic lady, possibly even peculiar to her class in the 1640s.[35] There are, after all, no manuscripts from the pre-1617 period written by aristocratic men that are published in the 1650s. It may be that the kind of experimentation these women were doing, which was new and subject to great scepticism, was in common with the work of a number of non-aristocratic men, who saw the status of these ladies as legitimating their work.

A page from Nicholas Bonnefons' *Le Jardinier Français* (1661).

At the same time it may be that there were growing numbers of aristocratic men who, like the ladies, had time on their hands, and while practising this kind of science felt it inappropriate to publish. So just as women in this period did act on behalf of men in politics – both Dorothy Moore[36] and Lady Verney represented the cases of specific men directly to Parliament[37] when those men were prevented from entering England – equally these women could be seen as acting on behalf of their male counterparts, testing the water so to speak. The fact that the experimental science was for them a leisure activity appears to have been decisive. Women lower down the social scale were being educated as usual in cookery, sugar work and household chemistry as domestic skills, but increasingly also as vocational skills with commercial value.[38] Yet Dorothy Moore was severely criticized for wanting to earn money by selling chemicals in 1649;[39] she was just too close to the aristocracy for this to be acceptable. Indeed, it has been suggested that Boyle's 'Invisible college' of the 1640s never materialized in public precisely because it may have been a scheme to make money from the new science.[40]

But then something odd occurs. Amid this general recognition, respect and even reliance on chemical practices by aristocratic women, John Beale, who had been corresponding with Katherine Jones and other women for a number of years through Hartlib's agency,[41] exchanging receipts with them quite happily, suddenly turns around in 1658 and disparages the triviality of these women who practise 'Ladies' Chemistry'.[42] His phrase is significant for a number of reasons. First of all it indicates that chemical practices were definitely perceived as a realm for 'Ladies' to engage with; secondly, it indicates a new and unexpected undermining of such activity, echoing the view that 'the ladies are the commons'. However, Beale partly retracted the criticism in a series of letters in 1659, including one praising 'illustrious Lady-Physicians', possibly Katherine Jones who was an important patron, although he continues to insist that lady chemists should emulate their husbands rather than pursue their own whims.[43]

Beale's critique raises several issues, and I would like to put one hypothesis in this way: as medicine and chemistry become an activity for aristocratic men during the 1650s, those men needed a way of differentiating their work from that of their female counterparts, partly to avoid being trivialized, partly to enter the public realm, and partly because of a growing differentiation between gendered activities. In addition, as Steven Shapin has recently argued, these men needed a way of legitimating the activity for upper-class gentlemen, preferably of the aristocracy.[44] The Royal Society was markedly aristocratic in make-up, and there were even complaints about the number of ordinary gentlemen proposed for membership partly because of this concern for legitimation.

The shift from kitchen to laboratory is minimal in terms of technology and expertise, except that the kitchen is the woman's preserve and the laboratory the man's. In practical terms the development of the laboratory must have been

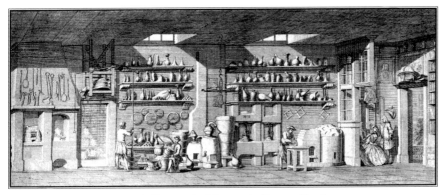

Ambrose Godfrey [Hanckwitz]'s chemical factory in Covent Garden.

useful because of the increasing use of specialized equipment upon which many early members of the Royal Society focused. Yet that equipment could have its application in the kitchen just as well as in the laboratory, as did Denis Papin's 'Digester' or pressure cooker.[45] Furthermore, as gentlemen wanted to spend more time doing chemistry it would be impractical to stay in a busy kitchen or still room. But the development is also part of a seventeenth-century trend to separate gender-distinguished work that resulted in the use of different rooms for activities that were predominantly male or female, such as the work of the butler and that of the housekeeper, and eventually in the separate wings of houses on eighteenth-century estates.[46] This is an element that becomes acutely obvious when the Royal Society institutes its demonstrations: the society would be a place where people could demonstrate proven and repeatable experiments,[47] repetition being a central element in the methodology of proof needed by the new science.[48] In effect this meant that experiments had to be tried out, tested and perfected elsewhere – if the practitioners were wealthy enough and committed enough, possibly in a purpose-built laboratory, but more likely in their kitchen. After which testing and perfecting, they would go up to London to demonstrate.[49] The experimental work would be carried out in the proximity if not company of servants, wives, daughters and others, while by contrast the demonstration displayed the lone man as the scientific individual.[50]

The notion of the individual scientist runs counter to the circles of intellectual exchange that operated around Henrietta Maria, Elizabeth Grey and Alethea Talbot; and counter to the circles of commonly discussed knowledge in the world of Katherine Jones, Dorothy Moore, Benjamin Worsley, Robert Boyle and Thomas Willis. Just as the three published books in question follow manuscript practice and acknowledge their sources, so one of the earliest publications by

Robert Boyle in 1655[51] was a call for a sharing of knowledge and acknowledgement of its source. Interestingly, several years after the inauguration of the Royal Society, that unintentional encourager of the myth of original genius, Boyle's agenda runs counter to this as he expresses concern in a letter to Henry Oldenburg[52] about people putting their names to experiments he attributes solely to himself.[53] The earlier impulse was communal but also born from there being no financial need to insist on ownership, the later both an understandable concern with private ownership but also a product of the institutional science they were creating.

The problem for these aristocratic gentlemen, unlike for their female counterparts, was legitimation of the usefulness or value, often in religious and social terms,[54] of this science. Especially in the field of medicine and pharmacy[55] the work being carried out by the Hartlib group, the Oxford Circle, the men of Gresham College and then the members of the Royal Society,[56] was an investigation of the difference between Galenic medicine and chemical remedy.[57] The signal aspect of Galenic medicine was the doctor's advice, dependent upon knowledge of the patient's whole body, life and community, knowledge firmly tied to the diet and specific conditions of the individual.[58] One of the reasons for the continued success of women in medicine and their continued employment as nurses and sources of remedies must have been their often domestic position within the community which allowed them to observe these aspects in minute detail.[59] Their remedies, which are found in many manuscripts in the seventeenth century, are only implicitly generic. They rarely claim to be able to cure specific diseases or disorders, often providing fifteen to twenty receipts for one illness. Instead, they offer guides to possibilities open to the patient and physician. Yet their scripts are heavily reliant on tacit knowledge, and are as devoid of generalized commentary on the patient as physicians' texts were of receipts.

The aristocratic gentlemen taking over this science were not taking over the variety of social roles that went along with them in the lives of women, even in the lives of aristocratic women. Neither were they after making money, nor after the esoteric knowledge of the pedantic scholar, but nor were they after direct application to medical or technological practice. Earlier researchers (including myself in the early 1980s), tended to put their investigations firmly down to the privileging of rational analysis and empirical experiment, but recently many commentaries, including this one, want to emphasize the fuzzy area occupied by the mixture of hypothesis, experiment and application/explication that began to emerge and the difficulty that it posed for its practitioners.[60] Robert Boyle's second published work was *Some Considerations touching the Usefulnesse of Naturall Philosophy*, as if the elaboration of natural philosophy could offer a legitimation and use for experimental science.[61] In effect, we can also see this as part of a development in the traditions of printed texts for men, parallel to those for women: books of husbandry, secrets and herbs. As this tradition developed into writing by men such as John Harrington and John Evelyn, far more discussion and explication is added.[62] Kenelm Digby comments in the preface to a translation he makes in the 1650s of a sixteenth-century book of secrets[63] that the earlier writer had paid too much attention to substance and not enough to the form, had focused exclusively on the receipts rather than describing method or offering explanation. Again, much research has been carried out on the rhetorical and literary basis for this change, usually with reference to the work of Francis Bacon. Yet we need also to consider that it was possibly just because these gentlemen were not drawing on shared tacit knowledge that they needed to develop explication; they needed a language or discourse to legitimate their otherwise hypothetical, fictional, almost fantastical work.[64]

The manuscript tradition of women's texts on medicine and household chemistry finally achieves publication in the 1650s, at precisely the time that it was taken over. It is a much more complex story than I have told here, of course: issues of economics, religion and the perception of print and its public audience would tell other parts of the story. On the positive side, after publication of the books by Henrietta Maria, Elizabeth Grey and Alethea Talbot many more women began openly to print works of cookery, domestic technology, kitchen physick and related daily work. But few seem to have moved along the lines of 'Ladies' Chemistry' after 1660.[65] Some women did continue to develop elements of natural philosophy, women such as Anne Conway and Margaret Cavendish about whom Sarah Hutton has written for this collection (see pp. 218–34). They even acquire a vocabulary for extensive commentary, although as Sarah Hutton discusses, given the disparaging remarks made about Cavendish's style one wonders how seriously it was taken.

One more example, I hope, of many more yet-to-be-found texts, is a brief notebook by a Sarah Horsington,[66] which is constructed as a commonplace book as were so many scientific notebooks of her male counterparts. It consists of quotations, detailed descriptions of experiments (frequently from Boyle's *Usefulness of Naturall Philosophy*), commentaries on method, observations on the effects of her own and her husband's remedies, and some pages of hypothesis on the physiology of women. The effect is patterned on Boyle's style and Willis's commentaries, yet is hard at work hammering out a distinctive vocabulary and syntax for discussion. However, for the most part women did not become published writers of experimental methodology or scientific and medical hypothesis from experiment, for centuries: Katherine Jones' receipts were published under the name of Thomas Willis and Robert Boyle,[67] and no doubt of many others – unquestionably with her support. Why this became so after the brief flurry of publication in the 1650s is clearly a topic for further research.

Appendix A

SARAH HORSINGTON HER MANUSCRIPT. 1666

Arcana
or
Mysteries, in the Theory of Physiology and Chymistry,
Being Authentick Rules for Preparing Spagyricall Medicaments, for my owne
observation and satisfaction.
Also
Manyfold Rare Private Receipts, and Remedies, Prescriptions of T: H: M: D:
Collected by the Industry of the Transcriber of this Manuscript uxorisejus S:
H:

making Salis Armoniack according to Robert Boyle

Sal: Armoniack XXX Brick and unslakt lime and loij, pound them all severally, and
grossly in an Iron Morter mix them not, till you are just ready to put them into the
retort because of a subtl fetid urinous steame which will xhale from the Misture,
Lute on a Glasse Body as a receiver, close the Joynt round the Neck well with Past &
wet double Browne Paper, increase the fire Gradually at the first, as is requisite in all
Distillations, but this preparation requires a very strong fire, (which Regiment of heat
hereafter I shall vie the Appellative Ignis Rota) to draw it off. The next morning
when you take it up, somtimes you will find the flowers sublim'd into the neck of the
retort of a yellowish colour, which to preseve must be kept in some warmth.
 2 other wayes according to Mr Boyle, the 1st is, by mixing 2 parts of S:
Armoniack with 3: or 4 of quicklime, whose vertur has not bin impayred by
being exposed to the Aire. Ths way, as that worthy Person Mentions, afforded
some dry sublimate in the Neck of the Retort, a little volatile salt in the
Receiver, & a very strong and yellowish sp: so exceeding penetrant, and
stinking, that 'twas not easie to hold ones nose, to the open mouth of the viall
wherein t'was kept without danger of being struck down, or for a while disabled
to take breath, by the plenty and violence of the exhaling spirits but the liquor
forced over by this method, though exeeding vigorous, was inconsiderable as to
its quantity, therefore to vary this way a little, we proceed to the second

Let the Quicklime ly abroad in the open Aire, but protected from all other moisture
except that of the ayre for divers dayes, in which time the imbib'd humidity of the
Ambient ayre, would in some degrees slake it, and make it somwhat brittler, then it
was before, and the lime thus prepar'd, being mingled with S: Armoniack & distilld
in all circumstances after the former manner afforded a liquor so copious, & yet so
strong that we hitherto acquiesce in this way of distilling this wild salt.

The sp: Sal: Armoniack may serve for a succadaneum to the spiritis of Hartshorne urine, & Blood &:

The salt is much of the same nature with that of urine & soot, whereof sal: Armoniack consists being a factitous preparation consisting or urine, soot and sea-salt.

The vertues, use, and dose,

is it singular good to smel to for giddyness of the head & in violent Headaches, & in epileptick fits. but by reason of its Diuretick qualitie, being given 0, 10, 20, or 30 gr: in a cup of beere or any convenient vehicle first, & last, it provokes urine.

In a Human body, great alterations may be made by very subtil effluvia, appeares evidently as, many are purg'd by the bare odour of Potions & a greater proofe of the power of steams upon the body may be taken from the Propagation of Infectious Diseases, which being convey'd by insensible Effluvia, from a sick into a healthy body, are able to disorder the whole oeconomy of it, & act those sad tragedies, which Physitians do so often unsuccessfull indeavor to hinder, but you will cease to doubt the corpuscles, though so small, as to be below the sense, should be able to performe great matters upon Humane Bodies; if you consider what alternations may be produc'd therein by the bare Actions of the parts upon one another. This may appear by the effects of several passions of the mind, which are often excited by the bare, if attentive, thoughts of absent things in obstinate griefe & Melancholy, there is that alteration made in the disposition of the heart, & perhaps some other parts by which the blood is to circulate that the lively motion of that liquor is thereby disturb'd and obstructions and other no easily remov'd distempers are occassion'd. The bare remembrance of a loathsome potion does oftentimes produce in me a Horror atended with a very sensible comotion of divers parts of my body, especially with a kind of a convulsive motion, in, or about the stomach & I doubt not, but the like though may have the like operation in many others.

read next what is written in the last leaf of all. . . .

Really, it seemes to me not only Highly dishonorable for a Reasonable soule to live in so Divinely built a Mansion, as the Body she resides in, altogether unacquainted with the exquisite structure of it; but I am confident, it is a great obstacle to our rendring God the Praises due to Him, for His having so excellently lodg'd us, that wee are so Ignorant of the Curious workmanship of the Mansions our Soules live in; for not only the Psalmist, from the Consideration of the Divine Art display'd by God, in the moulding and fashioning his body in the wombe, takes a just occasion to celebrate his Maker, Psalm: 139 verse 14, 15, 16, I will praise Thee (Sayes he) because I am fearfully & wondrfully make; marvellous are thye works, and that my soul noweth right well: my substance was not hid from thee, when I was made in secret, and curiously wrought (with as much curiosity as Tapestry or Embroder, as the Hebrew Rukkamti seemes to import). In the lowest parts of the Earth, thine eyes did see my substance, yet being imperfect; and in Thy Book all my Members were written, which in Continuance were fashion'd, when as yet there were none of them. But even from Gallen himself Anatomical Reflections have bin able to Extort Expressions of Devotion, & from the consideration of so dispicable a part as the skin of the sole of the foot He takes occasion to Magnify, the wisdom of God & sayes rearely well, though some creatures seem made of much courser stuff then others yet, even in the vilest the Makers Art shines through the despicableness of the matter, for idiots admire in things the Beauty of their material, but Artists that of the workmanship: to which after a great deale of Phylosophical discourse, Gallen, he adds, Nor is th foot worse contriv'd then the Brain or eye, provided each part be duly dispos'd for performance of the actions to which it was design'd: Since the Braine could not conveniently want the foot nor the foot the braine, for I conceive that one stands in need of a support for local motion, and the other of a source from whence to derive the faculties of feeling

Natura desidera preservare te ipsam

what power the passions have to alter and determine the course of the blood, may appear more manifestly in modest & bashful persons, especially women, when meerly upon the remembrance or though of an unchast, or undecent thing, mention'd before them, the motion of the blood will be so determin'd as to passe suddently and plentifuly enough into the cheeeks (& somtimes other parts) to made them immediately weare that livery of vertue (as an old Philosopher styl'd it) which we call a Blush and Passions, may not only alter the motion of the Juyces of the body, but likewise make some separation & evaluation of them, may appear in greife, which is wont especially in women to make all the Passions commotions requisite to weeping: whereby oftentimes a considerable quantity of Briny liquor, is excluded at the eyes, under the forme of teare, by which divers (especially Hystericall) persons are wont to find themselves much refreshed, though with some it fares otherwise in teeming women. also that vehement desire we call longing, may well be supposed to produce great alterations in the body of the Mother, which leaves such strange and lasting impressions upon that of the infant; since tis the mother only, and not at all the infant that conceives those importunate desires.

William Andrews Clark Memorial Library MS

Appendix B

FROM KATHERINE JONES'S GENERAL RECEIPT BOOK (PUNCTUATION ADDED)

To make Sprts of Roses my brother Robert Boyls way

Take of damask Roses both leaves and seeds, for the seeds yield the most oyle, what quantity you please; and so many leaves as you can possibly grasp with your hand put as much salt as you can cover with your hand; and in a stone mortar beat them very well. Then take this mass out of the mortar and put in the like proportion of salt and roses and beat fine as the others, and so do till you have the quantity you please. Then take them all and put them into some well glazed earthen pott and to every Bushell of Roses you have salted pour a quarte of beare wherin the quantity of a walnut of leaven hath bine first desolved. This may be stilled in Aug: or Septr in a limbick, and will yeald odoriferous watter with a spirit swimming at the tope of it of a snow white culler, which must not be take off with anything of iron . . . but with some ivory or some other inodorous matter.

Lozenges for the Cough, Dr Coks

Take of the purple of marshmallow roots extracted by decoction in the distilled water of Scabious and Hyssop, an ounce of the finest powder of Spanish Liquorice, 3 drames of white gumme of Brinian, 3 scruples of the whitest hard sugar, a quarter of a pound of sugar candy, mingle all these very well in fine powder and with as much of the clammy juice of marshmallows as will suffice make it into paste adding a bout a quarter of an ounce of the purest wheat flower. Of this past you must make Lozenges to be hild under the tongue which will melt and so by degrees to be swallowed dowen.

Wellcome Institute MS
Boyle Family Western MS 1340

Notes

1 Thomas Howard visited the Medici estate and its still-room facility during 1613 (see Brennan 1991), and Alethea was travelling with him on this journey (Howarth 1985).

2 Since the Hartlib Project at the University of Sheffield produced these letters as an electronic database (1989–94) much has been written about the scriptorium; for earlier helpful studies see also Turnbull (1947) and C. Webster (1970).

3 For example Hartlib letter 28/1/32B.

4 Hartlib letter 62/25/1A.

5 Hartlib letter 26/72A

6 The quotation is taken from Maddison (1969), p. 183.

7 For some sense of the extent of this influence see the early work of C. Webster (1970).

8 For this suggestion see Maddison (1969).

9 Several letters in the Hartlib archive from the 1650s indicate this.

10 Although Smith (1982) has noted that the Commonwealth period opened up many opportunities for women, which it undoubtedly did, few institutions for what we would now think of as higher education recognized women

11 This later letter is quoted in full in Hunter (1997).

12 See Fraser (1987), who also notes several other educational plans for women including a more conventional boarding school for girls in Hackney run by a Mrs Winch in the 1630s as well as Lettice Falkland's plan for the education of young gentlewomen in 1649.

13 My thanks here to Frances Harris of the Manuscripts Room at the British Library who alerted me to the Petty papers.

14 See Porter (1989) for a sense of the way in which the *Transactions* are almost a continuation of the Hartlib letters.

15 For an account of some of this background, see Kaplan (1993).

16 Maddison's (1969) biography of Robert Boyle offers a reconstruction of the use of Katherine's home.

17 For example *The Ladies Companion* (1653).

18 Among other accounts, see Mendelson (1987), p. 99.

19 Wellcome MS 1340.

20 British Library, Sloane MS 1367.

21 Maddison suggests this to have been the case (1969), p. 129.

22 James (1989).

23 Illustrations of the Golden Phoenix may be found in the Wellcome Institute for the History of Medicine, London.

24 In an often quoted letter of 1646, Robert Boyle complains to Katherine of yet another furnace that he has purchased at great expense failing to arrive in one piece at his home in Stalybridge; see Maddison (1969), pp. 70–1.

25 For detailed examples, see Baker (1599).

26 Hartlib letter 16/1/6A–B.

27 For some background to English and contintental use of refrigeration techniques see David (1979b) and Stallings (1979).

28 See Beier (1987), p. 239.

29 See Nagy (1988) not only for an outline of work by Lady Barrington, but also for a broad discussion of the participation of women in this field.

30 Many of the Oxford circle were also the correspondents of Samuel Hartlib.

31 Hartlib letter 15/17A.

32 For some of the fascinating background to Willis' life, see Isler (1968).

33 See Sargent (1995).

34 Thanks to Frances Harris of the British Library for pointing this area out, and offering invaluable help in finding the manuscripts.

35 That the women were practising may have been as much of an incentive for men to marry them as was the possibility that these women could also provide funding for their husband's activities (see Webster 1975, p. 85); and it may be significant that the celibate professors of Gresham College were not pursuing the natural sciences, but geometry, astrology, rhetoric, divinity, law, mathematics, music and physic, while associated scientists, such as Digby, who were married, were doing so.

36 Throughout 1644 Dorothy Moore was continually writing on behalf of Dury to various people in England, and she journeyed to London on at least two occasions to speak on his behalf.

37 George (1988, p. 38) quotes William Denton on this event, which is recorded in Verney (1970, vol. 2, p. 240).

38 A prime example of this trend would be Hannah Woolley, whose *Gentlewoman's Companion* (1664) stresses the need for ingenious ladies to learn such trades.

39 Hartlib letter 26/33/1.

40 Maddison suggests that this is why we know so little about the 'Invisible college', that it may have had as one of its aims the garnering of profit (1969), p. 69.

41 See for example Hartlib letters 55/21/3A-4.

42 Hartlib letter 51/147.

43 Hartlib letter 19/3/59.

44 See Shapin (1991).

45 Papin (1687).

46 For a detailed account of the shift from late sixteenth century to the early nineteenth century, see Brears (1996).

47 Dear (1991), p. 153.

48 Cantor (1989), p. 162.

49 Golinski (1992), p. 3.

50 Shapin (1988), p. 375.

51 Boyle (1655), published in Hartlib (1655) it may have been written in 1647 and 'Philaretus to Empiricus', see Kaplan (1993).

52 Oldenburg (1965–86).

53 But see Porter (1989) for a rereading of the idea of attribution.

54 Shapiro (1991).

55 F. Holmes (1991), p. 165.

56 Hoppen (1970) notes the very large number of members of the Royal Society drawn from the Society of Physicians.

57 Webster (1982).

58 Rawcliffe (1995), p. 112; Wear (1989), p. 294; and on Boyle's concern with holistic medicine see Kaplan (1993), p. 4.

59 Both Cook (1986) and Pelling (1994) discuss the employment of women in medicine during the seventeenth century.

60 Shapiro (1983), p. 53.

61 For an extended discussion see Kaplan (1993).

62 Porter (1989), p. 278.

63 Digby (1654), p. A4v.

64 Wear (1989) outlines the dilemma at length.

65 Evidence for things that do not happen is scarce: but see Crawford (1984) for the lack of commercial ventures into medicine by women in the late seventeenth century.

66 In the William Andrews Clark Memorial Library, Los Angeles; extract above.

67 In Willis (1684) and Boyle (1692).

9

Living in the Neighbourhood of Science: Mary Evelyn, Margaret Cavendish and the Greshamites

Frances Harris

When Margaret Cavendish, Duchess of Newcastle paid her ceremonial
visit to London in the spring of 1667 most of those who witnessed it
were prepared to enjoy the show. Courtiers flocked to see her as if she
had been the eccentric Queen Christina of Sweden. Pepys joined the crowds
which pursued her cavalcade about the streets. John Evelyn, foremost of the
English virtuosi, was so 'much pleased with the extraordinary fanciful habit,
garb, and discourse of the Duchess' that he wrote a ballad to celebrate them.[1]
Only Mary Evelyn, normally more tolerant of aristocratic vagaries than her
husband, remained coldly disapproving.

Between 1653 and 1666 the duchess had published, in handsome folios and at
her own expense, a variety of works ranging from plays and verse to *Philosophical
and Physical Opinions* and *Observations upon Experimental Philosophy*. These she
presented to the libraries of Oxford and Cambridge, as the nearest approach to
realizing her ambition of expounding her theories publicly in the schools. In
return she was thanked, dutifully or fulsomely, according to the sympathies and
expectations of the recipients.[2] In London in 1667 she was invited (at her own
solicitation) to attend the Royal Society, and was herself much visited, by some
men of learning among the sight-seers. The Evelyns, who had known her for
many years, took their turn, and it was after one such visit that Mary Evelyn
wrote to her son's tutor Ralph Bohun at Oxford:

> I am concerned you should be absent when you might confirm the suffrages of
> your fellow collegiats, and see the mistress both universities court; a person
> who has not her equal possibly in the world, so extraordinary a woman she is
> in all things. I acknowledge, though I remember her some years since and
> have not been a stranger to her fame, I was surprised to find so much
> extravagancy and vanity in any person not confined within four walls. Her
> habit particular, fantastical, not unbecoming a good shape, which she may
> certainly boast of. Her face discovers the facility of the sex, in being yet
> persuaded it deserves the esteem years forbid, by the infinite care she takes to
> place her curls and patches. Her mien surpasses the imagination of poets, or

the descriptions of the romance heroine's greatness; her gracious bows, seasonable nods, courteous stretching out of her hands, twinkling of her eyes, and various gestures of approbation, show what may be expected from her discourse, which is as airy, empty, whimsical, and rambling as her books, aiming at science, difficulties, high notions, terminating commonly in nonsense, oaths, and obscenity . . . I found Dr Charlton with her, complimenting her wit and learning in a high manner; which she took to be so much her due that she swore if the schools did not banish Aristotle and read Margaret, Duchess of Newcastle, they did her wrong and deserved to be utterly abolished. My part was not to speak, but to admire; especially hearing her go on admiring her own generous actions, stately buildings, noble fortune, her lord's prodigious losses in the war, his power, valour, wit, learning and industry – what did she not mention to his or her own advantage? Sometimes, to give her breath, came in a fresh admirer; then she took occasion to justify her faith, to give an account of her religion, as new and unintelligible as her philosophy, to cite her own pieces line and page in such a book, and to tell the adventures of some of her nymphs. At last I grew weary and concluded that the creature called a chimera, which I had heard speak of, was now to be seen, and that it was time to retire for fear of infection; yet I hope, as she is an original, she may never have a copy. Never did I see a woman so full of herself, so amazingly vain and ambitious.[3]

Sometimes quoted in conjunction with this is an excerpt from another letter from Mary Evelyn to Bohun of some years later, concerning the proper sphere of women:

Women were not born to read authors, and censure the learned, to compare lives and judge of virtues, to give rules of morality, and sacrifice to the muses. We are willing to acknowledge all time borrowed from family duties is misspent; the care of children's education, observing a husband's commands, assisting the sick, relieving the poor, and being serviceable to our friends, are of sufficient weight to employ the most improved capacities amongst us.[4]

It seems the classic opposition: the conventional woman recoiling with disapproval before her eccentric contemporary, who had taken advantage of wealth, rank and an indulgent husband to flout every norm of accepted female behaviour in her unseemly pursuit of singularity and fame.

Yet Mary Evelyn was sympathetic to female learning and these letters of hers are carefully composed set pieces; so obviously so that it prompts one to ask in what context they came to be written. They form part of a small selection of her correspondence published as an appendix to a mid-nineteenth century edition of her husband's famous diary. Apart from them little information has been available, even in the diary itself, about a woman who lived a long and observant life, as she put it, 'under the roof of the learned and in the neighbourhood of science'.[5]

Mary Evelyn was the carefully nurtured only daughter of Sir Richard Browne, from 1641 Charles I's Resident in Paris, whose house and chapel in the Faubourg St Germain were a refuge for exiled Royalists and Anglican worship throughout the 1640s and 1650s.[6] In fact it was in this chapel that Margaret Lucas, a gauche maid of honour to the exiled Queen Henrietta Maria, married the middle-aged William Cavendish, then Marquess of Newcastle, in 1645. It should be said at the beginning that one reason for Mary Evelyn's lingering resentment of Margaret Cavendish was that an extravagant promise of money said to have been made to the Brownes for their part in facilitating the marriage was quickly forgotten. But the connection was sufficiently remembered for the duchess to refer fulsomely to Mary Evelyn in later years as 'daughter', and to disregard the difference in their rank so far as to escort her down to the courtyard of the Newcastle mansion at Clerkenwell when she left to write her letter to Bohun.[7]

Although Mary Browne was only a child in 1645, her own marriage, also to a man much older than herself, was not far off. When John Evelyn, a young Royalist travelling on the continent to avoid the disturbances in England, first encountered her in her father's house, he recalled: 'I could call her woman for nothing but her early steadiness, and that at the age of playing with babies, she would be at her book, her needle, drawing of pictures, casting accompts and understood to govern the house . . . she began to discourse not impertinently, was gay enough for my humour . . . I made this creature my wife and found a pearl'.[8] When they married in 1647 Mary was barely thirteen and he twice her age.

Brought up in France from the age of five, she had been well educated in the humanist tradition. Unlike the Duchess of Newcastle, who never learnt to speak French and whose handwriting and spelling were almost unreadably chaotic, she wrote a fine italic hand, understood Italian, was fluent in French and confident enough of her style in English, both written and spoken, to criticize the shoddy vernacular of some male classicists. She had also studied drawing and mathematics well beyond the level of conventional female accomplishment.[9] Both she and her parents were concerned that marriage so young should not prevent her continuing her education or put a stop to her life of the mind. When Evelyn made plans for them to move back to England and set up house for themselves in 1652, she went reluctantly: 'I should have bin very glad for some time to have practised those things I now begin to understand, fearing the care of house keeping will take up the greatest part of my time.'[10] It was the first mention in her correspondence of a long debate between intellectual life and domesticity.

She loved Paris, writing of it in later life 'with that affection persons in age remember the satisfaction of their youth, to which happiness was the nearest, at least in their opinion, and so past that there is no hopes of a return'.[11] In coming to England she exchanged the pleasant suburb of St Germain for Sayes Court, a small, dilapidated manor house set close to the wall of Deptford dockyard, then one of the largest industrial complexes in England. This, assisted by Evelyn's renovations, she made the best of: 'For the house itselfe I cannot think it like a Parisien palace, noe it is somthing inferior', she wrote to her father, 'yet really it will be very convenient . . . [and] my Cabinet, closet and coach are very fine'.[12] But she also exchanged Parisian society, where women such as Marie le Jars de Gourney, Madeleine de Scudéry and the *salonières* had given women an accepted public role in intellectual life, to encounter for the first time 'that ancient and formidable legacy of misogyny',[13] which lingered more stubbornly in England than elsewhere. According to this latter orthodoxy, female learning was suspect and women were admonished to be silent, subordinate and mind their houses.[14] Both influences left their mark on her. Though she never again travelled out of England, she appeared to her countrymen as one in whom 'English Gravity' was 'moderately allayed, sweetened and spirited, by the mettlesome Aire and education of France'.[15]

Evelyn was prepared to give priority at first to his wife's continuing education. His renovations to Sayes Court provided her with her own 'Closset of Collections' over the porch.[16] She continued to have a French drawing-master and under his tuition, her husband noted, 'improved to admiration; few painters in England being able to design more masterly'.[17] One should not make too much of her actual accomplishments, which were competent but unoriginal. The flower paintings which survived at Wotton earlier this century are described as well executed but stilted and conventional.[18] The frontispiece which she designed for her husband's translation of Lucretius' *De Rerum Natura* in 1656 had the distinction of being engraved by Hollar, but was derived in its design from that of a French translation of 1650 by Michel de Marolles: a central portrait medallion surrounded by representations of Venus and the four elements; though these have undergone a significant softening and feminization in the process, particularly the presiding many-breasted Venus and the figure of Earth, in the French version a grim reaper grasping her sickle, but here replaced by a serene figure with her lap full of fruits and produce.[19] One of Mary Evelyn's few other recorded works was a miniature copy after a Raphael Madonna, 'wrought with extraordinary pains and judgment' for presentation to the king at the Restoration.[20]

Evelyn himself was well fitted to continue her education in other matters, indeed most at ease in relationships in which he could take a didactic or parental role. By marrying so young she had in effect been transferred from one form of parental custody to another. His care of her education, she wrote in retrospect with a significant order of words, was 'such as might become a Father, a Lover, a Friend and Husband'.[21] But Evelyn's attitude to female learning was ambivalent. In compliment to the Duchess of Newcastle he could reel off lists of learned women of the classical and European past, from 'Hilpylas, the mother-in-law of

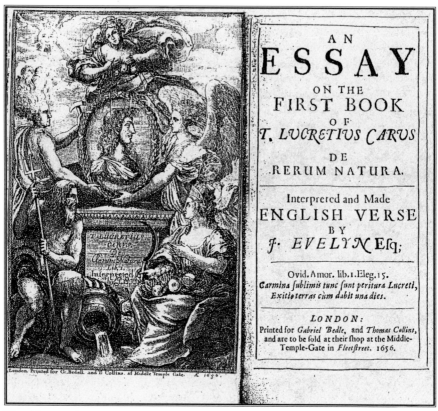

The title page from John Evelyn's *An Essay on the First Book of T. Lucretius Carus De Rerum Natura* (1656). Frontispiece designed by Mary Evelyn.

young Pliny' to their famous Dutch contemporary Anna Maria von Schurmann.[22] Drawing, an acceptable female accomplishment, could have his unqualified encouragement. In other matters he showed a conventional repressiveness, writing to his father-in-law that his wife had 'a very good faculty in translating & her modesty may be well trusted with more than the ordinary erudition of her sex, whome learning dos commonly corrupt'.[23]

He was also insistent that housekeeping should have priority over all other claims on her attention. On the authority of the Bible and of Aristotle it was prescribed as the natural role of women.[24] His mother had been renowned for her housewifery, and one of reasons he had chosen Mary Browne as his wife, as we have seen, was that she had been trained from a child 'to govern the house'.

His present to her on marriage was a calligraphically written treatise of his own composition on marital duties, entitled 'Instructions Oeconomiques', designed to make her 'such a wife as I may truly call Auxilium commodium or Help-meet for me'. A woman, it reminded her again, was designed 'principally to be a lover and keeper at home . . . [to] governe the house'.[25] Although he agreed that she should have assistance at first, this was only to be 'till you are a little entered in the misterye of that calling for which you were ordayned by nature'.[26]

Yet in the current intellectual climate this was not altogether to relegate her to a separate sphere. Having to postpone his ambitions for a role in public life while Cromwell's regime lasted, Evelyn made his house and garden central to his intellectual projects in the 1650s. Begun as an occupation and a means of bringing some amenity to the unpromising surroundings of Sayes Court, they developed into an enterprise which would promote both 'virtue and sanctitie' and natural philosophy.[27] His ground-plan of 1652 delineates in every detail not only the elaborate garden layout, which drew on the continental models seen on his travels, but also the domestic offices. These included the kitchen, buttery, still-room, pantry, larder, dairy, wash-house, brew-house, and beyond them the ornamental glass beehive, carp pond, hogsties, hen-house and cow-house. In addition to the ornamental gardens, there was a kitchen garden with thirty-eight beds and an orchard of 300 fruit trees 'of the best sorts mingled'.[28]

All of these meant produce in such quantities that a small kitchen and still-room industry was needed to process it, and again this had its place in Evelyn's intellectual scheme. In Paris he had begun to systematize all the knowledge he had acquired by reading and through conversation in a matching set of folio volumes. These included sermon notes, letterbooks, library catalogues and commonplace books covering the whole range of human learning and skill. Among the latter was a recipe book, divided into four parts: Receipts Medicinal, Receipts Chirurgical, Receipts for Preserves and Perfumes, and Receipts for Cookery.[29] Although in his 'Instructions Oeconomiques' to his wife he had recommended her to begin collecting such things, the receipt book was at first his own project; all the early entries are in his own hand or that of his professional scribe Richard Hoare. When he wrote to his sister in 1650 for recipes ranging from hog's pudding to syrup of violets and surfeit water, he added that he hoped 'to live to restore them in kind, for I am of late a great collector of such curiosities'.[30] 'Though they are indeed but trifles in comparison of more solid things', he wrote to a friend a few years later in a classic statement of the virtuoso's all-embracing enterprise,

yet if ever you should live a retired life hereafter, you will take more pleasure in these recreations than you can now imagine. And really gentlemen despising those vulgar things, deprive themselves of many advantages to improve their time and do service to the desiderants of philosophy, which is the only part of

learning best illustated by experiments, and after the study of religion certainly
the most noble and virtuous.[31]

In another of his commonplace books he set down the essentials for the still
room at Sayes Court in the minutest detail, from the retort, furnace, sublimatory,
bain-marie and refrigeratory, down to the spatula, tongs, fork, shovel, scissors,
corks, packthread, wax, wire, bladders, oil press and hour-glass.[32] As Lynette
Hunter has pointed out, the equipment of the still room was similar in many
respects to that of the experimental philosopher's laboratory.[33] For all his concern
to embrace still-room matters, however, Evelyn reserved himself a separate space
for his own chemical experiments. Opening on to the private garden at Sayes
Court was his own 'Elaboratorie' with a portico 20 feet long, an imposing
building well removed from the domestic offices.

Gradually Mary Evelyn's hand appears in the great receipt book, alternating
with that of her husband and his amanuensis, until about midway through each
section, probably at about the time of the Restoration (as comparison with the
handwriting of her letters suggests), when hers takes over entirely. By this time,
for all her earlier reluctance, she had not only assumed the supervision of every
aspect of the household,[34] but had become renowned for her skills in the kitchen
and still room. At the Restoration, having noted Evelyn's standing as a virtuoso,
Samuel Hartlib added that 'his wife is admirable in the way of preserving
conserving etc. and for all manner of sweetmeates most rare'.[35] Her brother-in-
law William Glanville sent her supplies: 'though gally potts and stone bottles are
no Rarityes, That which I desire you herewith to accept, may serve for foyles to
those excellent conserves and Wines with which Deptford is so constantly
stored'.[36]

But at one point in the late 1650s, for both public and private reasons, the
Evelyns contemplated a complete change in their mode of life. By this time they
had suffered the loss of all but one of the four sons born to them between 1652
and 1657. The second child, his mother's favourite, 'of a quiet & mild disposition
like her selfe', died at a few months old in 1654, and four years later the eldest
and the youngest of the remaining boys died within weeks of each other; the
latter, 'the most beautifull & lovelie child', at only a few weeks old, the former at
the age of five, already a prodigy and in his mother's words, 'the jewell, the joy of
our lives'. His death, she added, was so sudden and unexpected, 'that without
God's great mercy to me I must have sunk under its sorrow, all my constancy
being too weak to carry me through'. The health of their one remaining boy was
a constant cause for concern.[37]

Depression and anxiety were compounded by the sense of anarchy and
confusion in public affairs following the death of Cromwell, so much so that in
the autumn of 1659 Evelyn devised a plan for their retreat to a small community
of half a dozen separate cells, each with a study and a garden. This was to be

part religious foundation on a Carthusian model, part scientific college, where 'every person of the Society shall render some public account of his studies weekely . . . and especially shall be recommended the promotion of experimental knowledge as the principal end of the institution'. The unusual feature, as he explained to Robert Boyle, his proposed partner in the enterprise, was that he and his wife would both be members of this community, though living 'decently asunder' in separate cells. But even in this case he emphasized her house-keeping role; her presence would 'be no impediment to the Society, but a considerable advantage to the economic part'.[38]

With the Restoration the Royalists entered again into their kingdom and such schemes of retreat were put aside. Evelyn was drawn into public life and became a founder member of the Royal Society. Mary Evelyn for a time hoped for a place in the household of the new queen, until a further succession of pregnancies confined her again to Sayes Court.[39] But the scheme for a religious community of experimental philosophers, each in his (or her) separate cell, remained in her mind as an ideal. During one of her husband's absences shortly after the Restoration she wrote to him: 'Doe but imagine how we designed to live in our cells and you may judge of my life from the time I rise to my going to bed, as regularly and as pleasantly as I could propose it if I might add the contentment of visiting you in your solitude which is the only want I finde, my ambition being not soe great as it is beleeved'.[40]

By his middle years Evelyn was, on his own admission, transformed by his private griefs and public responsibilities: 'I grew so severe and stoical, as it had even twisted my very countenance, and given me a peruq of grey haires, before I was of Age to Countenance the Decays of Nature'.[41] The household remained an intellectual and a spiritual one and as such his wife was always a participant in it. Time was set aside for discourse with visitors, yet there is little sense of community in her description of their isolated winter fireside, 'circled with a philosopher, a woman, and a child, heaps of books our food and entertainment, silence our law so strictly observed that neither dog nor cat dares transgress it, the crackling of the ice and whistling winds are our music'.[42] The women whom Evelyn encountered at court, he noted wryly, thought his wife the unhappiest woman in the world,[43] and it was other male relations and friends who helped to disperse the monastic atmosphere of Sayes Court and provide her with intellectual communication and encouragement during these years.

The first of them, to whom her description of the fireside was written, was her cousin Sir Samuel Tuke, a Roman Catholic convert 'of very fine discourse', who had spent many years in France; an early member of the Royal Society and a successful playwright, of whom Mary Evelyn wrote, 'I believe it almost impossible to meet with a person so worthy in himself, and so disposed to esteem me again'.[44] Tuke shared the view that Evelyn exercised a repressive influence on his wife: 'you have layen soe long with a Philosopher, that you thinke us Lay-men no part of the Creation and despising your kindred by the flesh, you are alltogether for spiritual cognation. . . . I heartily wish I were that houre every day in the Wooden Parlour, which you allow for discourse.'[45] In her letters to him, of which she kept copies, she felt free to make mild mockery of her husband's growing fame, comparing his most popular works, *Sylva or a Discourse of Forest Trees* and its appendix the *Kalendarium Hortense*, the first works sponsored by the Royal Society, to an astrologer's almanac, 'foretelling the disasters of plants if not sett just in such a face and minute of the Moone, with rules and secrets how to governe plantation from the Tallest Tree to the meanest shrub'. Of his constant alterations to the garden at Sayes Court she observed that 'there is no end of improvement and that the various fancies of men have the reward of praise, when poore women are condemned for altering their dresse, or changing the patron [pattern] of a gorget, and for this esteemed vain creatures'.[46]

Another of her regular visitors and correspondents was her brother-in-law William Glanville, the same who sent her supplies for the still-room. But it is the correspondence with her son's tutor, Ralph Bohun, which survives in the most complete form on both sides.[47] He came into the Evelyns' household in 1665 as tutor to their one surviving son Jack, then ten years old, and remained for nearly six years, spending part of his time at Sayes Court and part at Oxford with his rather wayward pupil. In January 1671, 'having well & faithfully perform'd his Charge', as Evelyn noted in his diary, he parted company with the family, but the correspondence with Mary Evelyn continued for the rest of her life.

A fellow of New College, Bohun was also the nephew of Dr Ralph Bathurst, President of Trinity, and had been recommended to the Evelyns by him and by Dr John Wilkins, the Warden of Wadham, both of them founder members of the Royal Society.[48] He shared their interest in the theoretical as well as practical aspects of the new science. His letters to Evelyn include a long and thoughtful account of the relations between the Royal Society and the universities and between Aristotelian and experimental learning, and his one published work, written shortly after he left the Evelyn household, was *A Discourse concerning the Origine and Properties of Winds*.[49]

Like Mary Evelyn's husband and father, Bohun was a highly educated man. Unlike them he was not set in authority over her. On the contrary, he had a subordinate status in a household of which she was mistress. Yet he lived there informally and on equal terms with the family. In asking Wren to recommend a tutor Evelyn had assured him that 'he will find his condition with us easy . . . and the conversation not to be despised; this obliges me to wish he might not be a morose or severe person, but of an agreeable temper'. Bohun for his part accepted the post, though the Evelyns' powers of patronage were limited, because it would enable him 'to live in good company & see the world with lesse restraint than in a Bishop's family'.[50] He had a sense of humour – Mary Evelyn called him a 'droll' – and he was a good talker. Like Tuke, he relished the time spent with her in the 'wooden parlour', discussing books and authors. During his periods in Oxford they continued their conversations by letter. Of Sprat's *History of the Royal Society*, for example, Mary Evelyn wrote to him:

If I may with the same liberty and safety at this distance judge and censure Authors, as I have done sometimes within the bounds of the wooden rooms, I will own the reading of the History of the Royal Society, which though it needs not my suffrage to make it passe for an admirable piece both for witt and eloquence, force of Judgment and evennesse of style, yet suffer me to do my selfe the right to acknowledg I never liked any thing more; not only because it it is written in defence of worthy and learned men, or of a cause which promises so many future advantages, but that his notions are conveyed in so just easy and polite expressions, in knowne and yet not vulgar English.[51]

Their letters made little reference to Jack Evelyn's education. Bohun had set out his plans for this to the boy's father, among other matters dismissing the writings of the Stoic philosophers, which Mrs Evelyn admired, as consisting 'rather of sophistry, extravagant ideas of vertue, & a few Rhodomontades in morall philosophy than any methodicall & digested body of sentences', and therefore unsuitable as a basis for university teaching.[52] Instead the correspondence with Mary Evelyn took the form described by her husband elsewhere as 'that innocent, yet salt and pleasant diversion, which in France [is] called Raillarie . . . a witty, & a civil description of one anothers persons'.[53] The basic premise, adopted with much elaborate self-parody on both sides, was that Bohun brought companionship and stimulation to Mary Evelyn's secluded domesticity, while she exercised a much-needed civilizing influence over a personality formed by the pedantic and masculine collegiate life of the university. In this context the wooden parlour was less like the common-room of a group of monastic cells than a kind of miniature anglicized salon. 'Though I never breathed the soft aire of the continent', Bohun wrote,

yet since my admission into the good company of Says Court, I am almost grown civil by contact. . . . But I utterly despaire that any thing on this side the narrow seas should please you, whome I know of so exotique a Gusto, that I am confident you look upon your selfe as sent home by the malice of fortune, & banish'd into your native country by the Angry gods: yet I dare assert that the lady so much addicted to the Continent, so much a votary to the nobler clyme, is as much admird in the plegmatique Island as the magick of most excellent conversation can produce.

In the same spirit Mary Evelyn adopted the persona of one who would not have known of the Fire of London if she had not been taken to Southwark to see

the flames, or of the Dutch invasion of the Medway if she had not heard the guns
go off at Chatham; so, Bohun added, 'I hope you'l acknowledge my company
though with some grains of rudenes much better then the solitude either of the
Wooden Parlor & working closett'.[54] But at the same time he hinted persuasively
that by shutting herself away from the world in this way, she was concealing
abilities which would have brought her fame more deserved than the Duchess of
Newcastle's if they were more widely known:

> Certainly your witt is greater than anything but that modesty which regulates
> it; you are almost the only Lady living that can content your selfe with doing
> well & not dote upon prayse: you performe that in a silent closset which whole
> courts & Theaters would unanimously applaud.[55]

He praised her letters as well as her conversation, hinting that if he had not
seen her write them he would have suspected her husband's assistance. She
showed him the notebooks in which she kept copies, and he encouraged her to
regard them not just as private communications but as formal compositions
suitable for public display, a means of gaining a wider audience. When he
returned to Oxford with his pupil, he made it clear that he talked of her abilities
there. He was soon reporting that 'Dr Bathurst has importun'd me in the
company of Dr Wren to shew some of your admirable letters to confirm his
character of you'. Soon it became a matter of course and of Mrs Evelyn's full
knowledge that her letters to Bohun, and copies of her letters to others such as
Tuke, were shown around his Oxford circle (which also included Thomas Sprat
at Wadham).[56] There is no doubt that the long letter concerning the Duchess of
Newcastle, written shortly after this exchange, was intended as a rebuke to all
these men of science and learning for making any acknowledgement of her
pretensions.

   Another recurrent theme of their correspondence was Mary Evelyn's domestic
and especially her still-room activities. These increased during the time of
Bohun's residence at Sayes Court. Her first daughter was born in 1665, just as he
took up his appointment. Two more followed in 1667 and 1669; while his ideal,
fostered by collegiate life, remained a household 'where the kitchen & Nursery
[are] as remote as your pigeon house'. In his letters to Mary Evelyn these
domestic spaces symbolized the squandering of her finer abilities:

> is it not something odd to consider that a Lady who has been applauded in
> two great courts, prays'd and admir'd, and her friendship desir'd of all, that
> has been celebrated by the penns of so many fam'd Wits, & no less for the
> excellencie of her own . . . shoud now wholly be abandon'd to the conduct of
> her domestic affairs, And her most important concerns either to make laws in
> the nursery, or pyes and tarts in the kitchen, or serve under Mrs Turner in the

stilhouse. These are employments that degrade from her self, & render her mortal as other women. Thus Madam Evelyn is farr greatest in idea, & the way to maintaine her character to the best advantage is not to contemplate her in the stilhouse or nursery, but as she was hertofore in her agreeable conversation . . . so that those who are her ladyships greatest admirers ought to be carefull of visiting her at home least they loose her shining character in some wholesom methods of good husewifery & find the perfections she boasts of most at present to be confind in the parlour cupboard, lock't up with the spirit of mint & oranges, & a new receipt for plum cake. . . . [These are] but raileries and not so nice as Mrs Evelyn uses, but I really and in earnest condole within my self, to foresee that a Lady who might have been compared to Madam Scureman or Scudery for her refined and admirable parts must now in a few years degenerate into a good Queen Elizabeth Huswife.[57]

The opposition between domesticity and female learning was of course a well-established one in other respects than this. If housewifery was the prescribed role for women, satires on *femmes savantes* could readily conjure up a picture of their neglect of family and household duties.[58] Margaret Cavendish, while admitting that she had 'somewhat Err'd from good Huswifry, to write natures Philosophy', might suggest that women undertook more elaborate forms of cookery and still-room work only to fill up their idle time.[59] But not only was she a duchess with a large household of servants; she was also childless, probably a more important factor in her determination to achieve fame through expounding her philosophy than has always been acknowledged.[60] A more sympathetic male commentator could attribute women's failure to participate in the advancement of learning to their exacting household responsibilities, acknowledging that most had 'therein business enough'.[61] When Mary Evelyn (in a letter which does not survive) made this point to Bohun, he acknowledged the force of it. His allusion to Margaret Cavendish's latest publication, a description of a feminist utopia called *The Blazing World*, hinted at the ridicule which awaited her if she put aside these traditional responsibilities. Yet he still did not abandon his teasing position that domestic pursuits were trivial in comparison with the life of the mind, thus making her double bind quite clear:

we often rally what we admire & I could make much pleasnt'ner reflexions, should you neglect your family concerns only to appear a vertuosa, should the lady be counted a wit while the children look't like little blacks & the house in disorder, whilst she was composing poems & books of Blazing worlds. Mrs Evelyn has passed through severall degrees of applause always agreable to her circumstances & age, admired & courted when a child, since applauded for her wit and conduct, her agreeable humour and conversation, her discreet management of all her affairs, & now if she arrive at the perfection of the stilhouse, tis only deserving a new sort of prayse; & if it had prejudiced your conversation or style, & the spirit which was there be transferred into the stilhouse, its a judgment upon us, that we did [not] profit more under the dispensations of reason, that now we are condemned to the pleasurs of the tast instead of the mind, & if instead of select sentences, characters, & reflexions upon authors we have only extracts of Orange and Juniper, as those were most agreeable to your understanding, these are no lesse gratifying to the senses.[62]

In all this there was no hint of the links between the still-room and the experimental philosopher's laboratory. Yet Hartlib, as we have seen, had been willing to value household skills along with other trades and expertise, and if, as Thomas Sprat argued, only common sense and careful observation were necessary to make a contribution to the programme of the Royal Society, and technical skills were more important than a knowledge of the classics, there was in theory no reason why women should not participate in Baconian science. In fact it might be argued that they were particularly suited to do so.[63] Yet, as Mary Evelyn well knew, after the Restoration they were never welcomed at an institutional level. Sprat, in the *History of the Royal Society* which she had so attentively read, went out of his way to represent empirical science as a distinctively masculine activity, and while he encouraged the contributions which might come 'from the Shops of Mechanicks; from the Voyages of Merchants; from the Ploughs of Husbandmen; from the Sports, the Fishponds, the parks, the gardens of Gentlemen', he said nothing whatever of the kitchen and the still-room.[64] Apart from the formal invitation to the Duchess of Newcastle, which had been warmly debated and extended only out of respect to her rank, the Royal Society had no dealings at all with women.[65]

In her *Observations on Experimental Philosophy* in 1666 Margaret Cavendish did suggest that women might be employed as laboratory assistants, 'for the Woman was given to Man not onely to delight, but to help and assist him; and I am confident, Women would labour as much with Fire and Furnace as Men, for they'll make good Cordials and Spirits'. But this was said in deliberate mockery not just of 'our Moderns' and 'their Experimental or Mode-Philosophy' but also of all over-elaborate and time-consuming housewifery. Women, she continued, could 'inform the world how to make artifical Snow by their Creams and Possets beaten into froth, and Ice by their clear, candied or crusted quiddities or conserves of fruits; and Frost by their candied herbs and flowers', leaving men (and herself) free to devote themselves to the higher study of 'Contemplation-Philosophy and Reason'.[66]

Faced with the formidable display of experimental technique staged for her benefit by Boyle and Hooke, she retreated professing herself 'all admiration' and afterwards muted her criticism of the new science.[67] But the polemics which began to proliferate against the Royal Society in the early 1670s from both the advocates of scholastic learning and the court wits (including the king himself) also disparaged experimental science in much the same way as house-keeping and kitchen physic: for being trivial, unsystematic and lacking theoretical foundations.[68] Mary Evelyn was well aware of this controversy and it was only in ironic reference to it that she was prepared to imagine any role for herself in experimental philosophy. Thus in a letter of 1674 she wrote to Bohun:

> I find the slight cares of a family are great hindrances to the study of philosophy, and that one grows less and less capable of improvements by books, as one grows more acquainted with the world; yet amongst those fine experiments which fall in my way, could I meet with any one equally curious with those of the Greshamites, though as unuseful and trifling, I might hope in time to be in something famous; learning is become so easy of access by the late industry of some who have removed the bar language put to the illiterate.[69]

Yet she cannot be set down simply as a woman of intelligence and cultivation who had been repressed by the conventions of her society. She prided herself most not on her learning, but on being 'a great mistress of her passions', the quality in which women were traditionally held (by men) to be most deficient.[70] For her, as she explained to Bohun, the community of religious cells remained the site where such conflicts were resolved:

> It is for persons who are active by nature and have stations to furnish the occasions to shew their inclinations and power; they possibly may discover shining vertues. Without exercise what is goodnesse, or valor, or any thing! What had Alexander been had he wanted a world to conquer? Or any of the celebrated Heroes, but for noyse and tumult. A hermit may live long enough in his cell without being considered one [a hero], who fights only with himself whose Enimies are his passions, and whose greatest care is not to make an esclat here, who reserves his triumph for another world . . . you I am assured know which to chuse.[71]

The Duchess of Newcastle was unusual for a woman of her time in her lack of recourse to conventional piety; her religious theories, Mary Evelyn had sardonically commented to Bohun, were 'as new and unintelligible as her philosophy'. But it had been religion and the teachings of stoic philosophy, not the new science, which had enabled Mary Evelyn to survive the crippling bereavements of her early marriage. For a period of five or six years in the late 1660s and early 1670s, under Bohun's stimulus, an opportunity to converse with university and Royal Society men on terms which the duchess would have envied had opened to her. But by the mid-1670s the time had passed and the former

Portrait of Mary Evelyn, the wife of John Evelyn.

patterns of her life reasserted themselves. As her daughters grew beyond infancy they required most of her time. Bohun left Oxford to become a country clergyman, and styles of preaching became a more appropriate subject for their letters. In the Evelyn household also a renewed religious intensity prevailed, a concern with the values of 'primitive Christianity' which was probably the result of Evelyn's passionate friendship with Margaret (Blagge) Godolphin, his 'Seraphick' as Mrs Evelyn described her to Bohun: a friendship which came to extend almost equally to his wife and children.[72]

Like the Duchess of Newcastle, Mary Evelyn eventually retreated before the teasing, inhospitable and potentially hostile display of masculine learning and science, professing only 'admiration'. When she delayed in writing to Bohun, she explained in the most measured statement of her personal position, it was not because her domestic duties made it impossible:

> Should I confess the real cause, it is your expectation of extraordinary notions of things wholly out of my way. Women were not born to read authors, and censure the learned, to compare lives and judge of virtues, to give rules of morality, and sacrifice to the muses. We are willing to acknowledge all time borrowed from family duties is misspent; the care of children's education, observing a husband's commands, assisting the sick, relieving the poor, and being serviceable to our friends, are of sufficient weight to employ the most improved capacities amongst us; and if sometimes it happens by accident that one of a thousand aspires a little higher, her fate commonly exposes her to wonder, but adds little of esteem. . . . A heroine is a kind of prodigy; the influence of a blazing star is not more dangerous or more avoided. Though I have lived under the roof of the learned, and in the neighbourhood of science, it has had no other effect on such a temper as mine, but that of admiration, and that too but when it is reduced to practice. I confess I am infinitely delighted to meet in books with the achievements of the heroes, with the calmness of philosophers, and with the eloquence of orators; but what charms me irresistibly is to see perfect resignation in the minds of men, let whatever happen of adverse to them in their fortune: that is being truly knowing and truly wise; it confirms my belief of antiquity, and engages my persuasion of future perfection, without which it were vain to live. Hope not for volumes or treatises; raillery may make me go beyond my bounds, but when serious, I esteem myself capable of very little.[73]

And so the epistolary debate between them on this subject lapsed. But their correspondence continued and although they ceased to discuss the issue directly, she did not let Bohun's trivializing of her domestic skills go unchallenged. Instead, she continued to dwell unemphatically but meaningfully on their civilizing and socializing value, and despite his distance continued to include him

within their influence. After smallpox among the neighbouring families at
Deptford had kept them isolated from one another for weeks she described to
him how, when it was safe to do so, she invited them all to a dinner of venison
pasty: 'the Venison was sent me out of Lecestershire and was perfectly good, my
successe in the oven not so ill, so that we were very merry at the eating of it . . .
your company being only wanting'. And when Bohun, whose living was too poor
to support a family, became isolated and inclined to succumb to melancholy and
self-doubt, she rallied him with a trace of their old teasing manner:

> I beleeve Mr B a person of much wit, great knowledge, infinitly judicious,
> diserning, charitable, well natured, obliging in conversation, apt to forget and
> forgive injuries; eloquent in the pulpit, living according to knowne precepts,
> faithfull to his friend, generous to his Enemy and in every respect an
> accomplished person, this in our vulgar way is a desirable Character; but you
> will excuse if I judge unrefinedly who have the care of piggs, stilling, cakes,
> salves, sweetmeats, and such usefull things, the success of which sometimes
> tempts me to wish you a share of them.[74]

Mary Evelyn's life exemplifies the variety of practical and ideological difficulties
faced by a woman with conventional female responsibilities in negotiating a
significant position for herself 'in the neighbourhood of science', even when her
environment appeared to offer the possibility of it. Nevertheless, her long
correspondence with Bohun is an example of the networks by which women
excluded from more obvious forms of public participation in intellectual life were still
able to maintain their links with it. It is also in its way a contribution to the much
older debate about the ultimate function of learning; between the intellectual one of
increasing the stock of knowledge and the moral one of teaching one how to live.

Notes

1 Grant (1957), pp. 15–26.

2 Cavendish (1676), *passim*.

3 Evelyn (1859), IV, pp. 8–9: Mary Evelyn to Bohun [April 1667].

4 *Ibid.*, pp. 31–2: Mary Evelyn to Bohun, 4 January [1673/4].

5 See note 73 below.

6 Evelyn (1959), p. 326.

7 *Ibid.*, p. 508; Evelyn (1859), III, p. 246.

8 Hiscock (1955), p. 17.

9 BL, Evelyn Papers (unnumbered): calligraphic exercise book of Mary Evelyn, 1649; Helen
Evelyn (1915), pp. 98–9: Bohun's character of Mary Evelyn and her letter to him, 22 March 1668;
BL, Add. MS 15950, ff. 178–88: mathematical diagrams by Mary Evelyn, 1650, the first annotated
'*pour amour de mon Maistre Monsr Mallet philomat*'. I am grateful to Professor Douglas Chambers for
drawing my attention to the last reference, and for reading and commenting on this chapter in draft.

10 BL, Evelyn Papers, letter no. 709: Mary to John Evelyn, 30 March 1652.

11 Evelyn (1859), IV, p. 13: Mary Evelyn to William Glanville [1668–9].

12 BL, Evelyn Papers (unnumbered): Mary Evelyn to Sir Richard Browne, 28 September 1652.

13 Phillips (1990), p. 12.

14 *Ibid.*; Pollock (1989), pp. 242–4.

15 Dr William Rand, in the introduction to Gassendi (1657), sig. A6.

16 BL, Evelyn Papers: plan of Sayes Court, 1652. For Evelyn on the use of the closet of curiosities 'to Entertaine your wife and Virtuoso Ladys', see *Memoires for my Grandson*, ed. Geoffrey Keynes (Oxford, 1929), pp. 55–6.

17 Quoted in Hiscock (1955), p. 33.

18 H. Evelyn (1915), pp. 93–4.

19 M. Hunter (1995), p. 88, citing the reproduction of the Marolles frontispiece in C. A. Gordon, *A Bibliography of Lucretius* (1962), Plate 16, points out the similarities in Mary Evelyn's design, but not the differences.

20 Evelyn (1959), p. 423.

21 H. Evelyn (1915), p. 110: will of Mary Evelyn, 9 February 1709. Her closest friend Elizabeth Carey, afterwards Viscountess Mordaunt, also called him 'Master' or 'Governor' and the court women of the Restoration described him as a 'scole-master'; see BL, Evelyn Papers, correspondence, nos 1004–17: Elizabeth Carey to Evelyn, 1656; and MS 304: John Evelyn, 'The Legend of Philaretes and the Pearl', *c.* 1675.

22 Evelyn (1859), III, pp. 244–5: Evelyn to Duchess of Newcastle, 15 June '1674'; the letter is obviously misdated, as is the copy in Evelyn's letterbook from which it is taken; the duchess died in 1673.

23 BL, Evelyn Papers, correspondence, no. 1439: Evelyn to Sir Richard Browne, 29 November 1656.

24 Sommerville (1995), pp. 13–15.

25 BL, Evelyn Papers, MS 143; the manuscript is badly affected by damp and only partially legible.

26 BL, Evelyn Papers (unnumbered): Evelyn to Mary Evelyn, 22 February 1652.

27 Parry (1994).

28 BL, Evelyn Papers: plan of Sayes Court, 1652.

29 M. Hunter (1995), pp. 72–4; the receipt book is BL, Evelyn Papers, MS 51.

30 BL, Evelyn Papers, correspondence, no. 1416: Evelyn to Jane Glanville, 17 November 1650.

31 Quoted in Houghton (1942), p. 57.

32 BL, Evelyn Papers, MS 44: commonplace book concerning husbandry, p. 181.

33 L. Hunter (p. 182–9 above).

34 BL, Evelyn Papers (unnumbered): dairy accounts of Mary Evelyn, 1665–75. Her skill in all aspects of housekeeping is apparent in the instructions for setting up an urban household on a limited income which she wrote for Margaret Godolphin in 1676; see John Evelyn (1939), App. B, pp. 223–30.

35 Sheffield University Library, Hartlib Papers (UMI electronic edn, 1995), Ephemerides 1660, 29/8/10B.

36 BL, Evelyn Papers (unnumbered): Glanville to Mary Evelyn, 1 June 1664.

37 BL, Evelyn Papers, correspondence, nos 1434, 1445: Evelyn to Sir Richard Browne, 23 January 1654, 13 December 1657; Mary Evelyn's letterbook (unnumbered): to her aunt [Susan Hungerford? 1658]; Evelyn (1959), p. 398.

38 Evelyn (1859), III, pp. 116–20; Evelyn to Boyle, 3 September 1659; see also Parry (1994), pp. 132–3.

39 Evelyn (1959), p. 418; BL, Evelyn Papers, Mary to John Evelyn, 27 September 1661; Mary Evelyn's letterbook: to Lady Mordaunt [1661–2?].

40 BL, Evelyn Papers, correspondence, no. 714: Mary to John Evelyn, 27 April 1660. Many years later Evelyn could still describe his household as 'this Monastrie' (ibid., MS 39b, Letterbook II: to Mrs Boscawen, 1 October 1689).

41 BL, Evelyn Papers, MS 304: Evelyn, 'The Legend of Philaretes and the Pearl' [c. 1675].

42 BL, Evelyn Papers (unnumbered): Mary Evelyn to Sir Samuel Tuke [1660s].

43 BL, Evelyn Papers, MS 304: 'Legend of Philaretes and the Pearl' [c. 1675].

44 DNB; Evelyn (1859), IV, p. 24: Mary Evelyn to Bohun, 29 January [1674].

45 BL, Evelyn Papers, Tuke to Mary Evelyn, 22 May 1663.

46 BL, Evelyn Papers (unnumbered), fragment of a letterbook of Mary Evelyn, letter 27 [to Tuke, late 1663].

47 In some cases Mary Evelyn's letters survive in two or occasionally more versions: the originals preserved by Bohun, now part of the Evelyn archive because he died as rector of Wotton, the copies entered in her letterbooks and a few in loose draft or copy as well; I discuss these in my article, 'The letterbooks of Mary Evelyn' in English Manuscript Studies (forthcoming).

48 Evelyn (1959), p. 479.

49 M. Hunter (1981), pp. 145–7, 149.

50 Evelyn (1859), III, p. 154: to Wren, 4 April 1665; BL, Evelyn Papers, correspondence no. 306: Bohun to Evelyn, 22 April 1667.

51 BL, Evelyn Papers (unnumbered): Mary Evelyn to Bohun [3 February 1668].

52 BL, Evelyn Papers, correspondence no. 301: Bohun to Evelyn [1668]; ibid. (unnumbered): Bohun to Mary Evelyn, 12 April 1668.

53 A Character of England (1659), reprinted in Evelyn (1995), p. 87.

54 BL, Evelyn Papers (unnumbered): Bohun to Mary Evelyn, 13 February [1667–8]; Evelyn (1859), IV, pp. 14–15: Mary Evelyn to James Tyrrell, 10 February 1669.

55 BL, Evelyn Papers (unnumbered): Bohun to Mary Evelyn [March 1667?].

56 BL, Evelyn Papers (unnumbered): Bohun to Mary Evelyn [Jan.–March 1667].

57 Ibid., 26 Oct [1675?]. 'Scureman': i.e. Anna Maria von Schurman.

58 A classic statement is that of the husband, Chrysale, in Molière's Les Femmes Savantes (1672); see also Gagen (1954), pp. 49, 57.

59 Philosophical and Physical Opinions (1655), dedication, quoted in Schiebinger (1989), p. 58; Cavendish (1666), pp. 102–3.

60 Grant (1957), pp. 96–7, takes her claim that she was glad to be free of the trouble of children at face value; Mendelson (1987), pp. 25–6, 29, is more perceptive.

61 François Poullain de la Barre, De L'égalité des deux sexes, p. 25, quoted in Schiebinger (1989), p. 177.

62 BL, Evelyn Papers (unnumbered): Bohun to Mary Evelyn, 29 March [1668]. 'Vertuosa': i.e. feminine of 'Virtuoso'.

63 Phillips (1990), pp. 27–9.

64 Schiebinger (1989), p. 137; Sprat (1667), pp. 71–2.

65 M. Hunter (1981), p. 72.

66 Cavendish (1666a), pp. 102–3.

67 Grant (1957), pp. 24–6, 208–10; Mendelson (1987), pp. 46–7.

68 M. Hunter (1981), pp. 131, 148–53.

69 Evelyn (1859), IV, p. 34: to Bohun, January [1674].

70 BL, Evelyn Papers (unnumbered): William Glanville to Mary Evelyn, 25 May 1669; Sommerville (1995), p. 12.

71 BL, Evelyn Papers (unnumbered): Mary Evelyn to Bohun, 12 April [?early 1670s].

72 BL, Evelyn Papers (unnumbered), Mary Evelyn to Bohun, 19 November [1677]. Hiscock in two books (1951, 1955), argued that, spiritually at least, Evelyn was unfaithful to his wife in his friendship with Margaret Blagge; but the above letter and that written to Bohun on Margaret's death in September 1678, among a number of references in both women's correspondence, indicate that the friendship extended to Mary Evelyn as well.

73 Evelyn (1859), IV, pp. 31–2: to Bohun, 4 January [1674].

74 BL, Evelyn Papers (unnumbered): to Bohun, 20 September 1675; 23 November 1674.

10

ANNE CONWAY, MARGARET CAVENDISH AND SEVENTEENTH-CENTURY SCIENTIFIC THOUGHT

Sarah Hutton

The names of Anne Conway and Margaret Cavendish do not appear in the annals of the history of science. Nonetheless, they were both deeply engaged with the natural philosophy of their day. At a time when the nature and direction of developments in science were matters of intense investigation and debate, both made contributions to the seventeenth-century discussion of the nature and make-up of the physical world. Margaret Cavendish (*c.* 1623–73) set out her thoughts on natural philosophy in several folio volumes. These include her *Philosophical and Physical Opinions* (1655a), *Observations upon Experimental Philosophy* (1666) and her *Grounds of Natural Philosophy* (1668). Anne Conway (*c.* 1630–79) has one treatise to her name, her posthumously published *The Principles of the Most Ancient and Modern Philosophy* (1692).

Both Anne Conway and Margaret Cavendish were well aware of the new theories of their day: they were acquainted with the work of Descartes, of Hobbes and with the investigations sponsored by the Royal Society. They were also acquainted, as we are not, with some of the significant lesser figures on the seventeenth-century intellectual scene: with Walter Charleton the English promoter of the theories of Pierre Gassendi, with the great iatro-chemist, Jan Baptiste van Helmont and his son Francis Mercurius, with the Cambridge philosopher Henry More.[1] They both, apparently, performed experiments – Margaret Cavendish records making and testing 'Rupert's drops' with Christiaan Huygens. And there was evidently a laboratory at Anne Conway's home, Ragley Hall.[2] What is remarkable about these two women is that, in an age when learned discourse was very much the province of men, they each produced a body of theory. Moreover, they each *published* a body of theory about the workings of nature. Each was prepared to advance criticisms of the dominant theories of her day. And, when doing so, each came up with theories that were very much her own. Although they do not appear to have been acquainted with one another, there are some striking parallels in the theory of substance each advanced. But there are many contrasts. This pattern of contrast and parallels extends to their lives and the conditions under which they came to natural philosophy.

Margaret Cavendish and Anne Conway came from a similar social background: daughters of the gentry, they both married into the aristocracy. Margaret Cavendish was born Margaret Lucas, daughter of Sir Thomas Lucas of Colchester, a Royalist whose family suffered during the Civil War for their support of the king. Apparently at her own request, she became maid of honour to Charles I's queen, Henrietta Maria, whom she accompanied to exile in Paris. It was there, in 1645, that she met and married William Cavendish, 1st Duke of Newcastle, formerly a commander in the Royalist army and by then a widower refugee in France. Cavendish was closely involved with the exiled English court, having charge of the education of the Prince of Wales. He was some thirty years older than his second wife, but it was, in her account, a love-match. He also had hopes of fathering a male heir. But their marriage was childless.[3]

Anne Conway was born Anne Finch, the youngest member of a family who had made their name in politics and law. Her father, Sir Heneage Finch died before she was born. He had been Speaker of the House of Commons. Her half-brother, Heneage, rose under the restored monarchy to become Lord Chancellor and Earl of Nottingham. She married into a family which had served the Stuart kings for three generations, and been rewarded with estates in Ireland. Her husband, Edward, 3rd Viscount Conway, was an influential figure in Anglo-Irish politics, becoming, for a brief period after the death of his first wife, Secretary of State to Charles II. Anne Conway's only child, her son Heneage, died in early infancy. In spite of attempts to found a dynasty after her death, Lord Conway died *sans* issue.[4]

The parallel between the biographies of Anne Conway and Margaret Cavendish ends there. Their educational histories are strikingly different. Anne Conway was possibly the most highly educated woman of her generation, in so far as she was the lucky recipient of the equivalent of a university education. This in itself is a remarkable story. It came about through her brother John Finch, to whom she was very close. He put her into contact with his tutor at Cambridge, the Platonist philosopher Henry More, who was one of the first English proponents of Descartes. Since she, as a woman, could not attend the university, More agreed to give her instruction by letter. The result was the first recorded correspondence course in Cartesian philosophy. As their life-long correspondence shows, More remained a mentor and intellectual sparring partner throughout her life. Although, in her only published book, she rejected the Cartesianism of her philosophical education, the book, in its closely structured, at times almost scholastic, style of argument, carries the imprint of a mind disciplined by exercise in academic reasoning.[5]

Margaret Cavendish made no secret of the fact that she had received no systematic education. 'I had neither Learning nor Art to set forth these Conceptions,' she wrote in *Philosophical and Physical Opinions*, 'My Work goes out into the World like an Unpolish'd Stone'.[6] Her lack of academic training is everywhere apparent in her writing which is repetitive and does not lend itself to sustained argument. But she determined to make good her lack of education by setting herself to read the leading thinkers of her day, including Hobbes, Descartes and the works of the Flemish alchemist and physician Jan Baptiste van Helmont.[7] Through her marriage to William Cavendish she became part of a family distinguished by its interest in new ideas. The Cavendishes, like their cousins the Earls of Devonshire, were patrons of Thomas Hobbes. William's brother, Sir Charles, was a member of the Paris circle of Marin Mersenne, to which Descartes belonged.[8] Margaret Cavendish mentions that Hobbes and Descartes dined with her husband, but denied being party to their conversations. She does acknowledge contact with another member of the Cavendish circle, Walter Charleton. And, while on her travels in Holland with her husband, she met and conversed with the Dutch physicist Christiaan Huygens. To judge by the effusive prefaces and prefatory poems which her husband contributed to her books, he encouraged her in her intellectual pursuits. In her *Philosophical and Physical Opinions* she claimed that her teachers had been her family, 'my own brothers, my Lords brother, and my Lord'.[9] So, whether we accept her story or not about never talking to Descartes and Hobbes, it is probable that she inhabited a climate favourable to her interest in natural philosophy.

Cavendish was a prolific writer who wrote many books besides her several books on natural philosophy. These were all published in expensive folio volumes, proudly announcing their female authorship. Anne Conway wrote only one book which she did not publish. It was found, written in black lead pencil, among her personal effects when she died in 1679 and was published anonymously in Latin translation by her personal physician, Francis Mercury van Helmont in Amsterdam in 1690.[10] It subsequently appeared in English in 1692.

The publishing history of both women bespeaks their difference of style and project. Although she professed shyness, Cavendish cultivated a histrionic self-image. She was famous for the audacity of her dress; crowds used to flock to see her when she drove in Hyde Park. 'The whole story of this woman', wrote Samuel Pepys, 'is a romance, and all she doth is romantic' – 'her dress so antic and her deportment so unordinary'.[11] In the prefaces to her books she calls attention to the fact that women writing philosophy were considered an anomaly – 'men in petticoats'. And she seems deliberately to have made a virtue of the eccentricity that this implies in order to make a niche for her learned pursuits. So successful was she in her cult of eccentricity that she earned the nickname, 'mad Madge'. Samuel Pepys dismissed her as 'a mad, conceited, and ridiculous woman'. Her reputation for outlandishness has stuck to this day, so much so that there are even those among her admirers who take her 'madness' literally![12]

Anne Conway, by contrast, led a retired life, a situation forced on her by ill health. She suffered all her life from periodic fits of terrible pain, the most constant symptom of which was an incurable headache. This condition became

Here on this Figure Cast a Glance,
But so as if it were by Chance,
Your eyes not fixt, they must not stay,
Since this like Shadowes to the Day
It only represent's; for Still,
Her Beuty's found beyond the Skill
Of the best Paynter, to Imbrace,
Those louely Lines within her face,
View her Soul's Picture, Iudgment, witt,
Then read those Lines which Shee hath writt,
By Phancy's Pencill drawne alone
Which Peece but Shee, Can justly owne.

Portrait of Margaret Cavendish from *The World's Olio* (1655).

worse as she grew older, so much so that she spent the last ten years of her life as a virtual recluse at the Conway home, Ragley Hall in Warwickshire. However, her illness brought her into contact with the leading medical practitioners of her day in her search for a cure. William Harvey, Theodore de Mayerne and Thomas Willis were among the eminent doctors who attended her, as was Francis Mercury van Helmont through whom her work became known to Leibniz.[13] Anne Conway sought neither recognition nor notoriety. She enjoined her faithful correspondent, Henry More, to keep their learned correspondence private. And it is doubtful whether she intended that her book should be published. Nor was she comfortable with having a public reputation for learning: in 1652 Henry More dedicated his book, *An Antidote against Atheism*, to her. In response, she wrote to him,

> I am forced to tax you with one fault which I cannot forbear to doe; and that is, that in this booke, where you deliver nothing but serious truths, you have not made your dedicatory epistle shutable to the rest of the book, for, really, I could not read what you have published of me without blushing, which proceeded from my being conscious to my selfe of not deserving that commendatione you would seem to give me there, and in this Sir I cannot but thinke you have done yourselfe some injury (in regard I cannot make good what you mention of me). . . .[14]

In contrast, Margaret Cavendish courted a scholarly readership: she made sure to send presentation copies of her books to the learned men of Europe. Most recipients were duly grateful and said so in letters of unparalleled unctuousness and flattery. The hyperbole is a sure indication that few of them actually read what she sent them. Nonetheless, Margaret Cavendish collected together their replies and published them in 1670 as a public seal of approval in a collection entitled *Letters and Poems in Honour of the Incomparable Princess, Margaret Dutchess of Newcastle*. Cavendish was, moreover, quite outspoken about the lack of opportunities available to women and the negative attitudes encountered by those who tried to make opportunities for themselves. She complained in the letter of dedication to her *Philosophical and Physical Opinions* (addressed 'To the Two Most Famous Universities of England') of

> the carelesse neglects and despisements of the masculine sex to the effeminate, thinking it impossible we should have either learning or understanding, wit or judgement, as if we had not rational souls as well as men. And we out of custom of dejectednesse think so too, which makes us quit all industry towards profitable knowledge, being imployed only in looe and pettie imployments which takes away not only our abilities towards arts, but higher capacities in speculations, so we are become like worms that only live in the dull earth of

ignorance, winding ourselves sometimes out, by the help of some refreshing rain of good educations, which is seldom given us.[15]

Where Anne Conway's fame was confined to the small circle of friends surrounding More and van Helmont, Cavendish received recognition of a sort from the male scientific establishment of her day. On 30 May 1667 she paid a visit to the Royal Society at Arundel House where, as Pepys records in his diary, 'Several fine experiments were shown her of Colours, Loadstones, Microscope, and of liquors: among others, of one that did turn a piece of roasted mutton into pure blood'. Pepys notes that Cavendish was 'full of admiration' in her response.[16] If so, she must have concealed the fact that she was singularly unimpressed by the demonstrations of microscopy. For, in the previous year, in her *Observations upon Experimental Philosophy*, she had criticized it as a useless science, a view she did not revise in *The Grounds of Natural Philosophy*, which appeared the year after her visit.

MARGARET CAVENDISH'S NATURAL PHILOSOPHY

Margaret Cavendish called natural philosophy 'the most Difficult to be Expressed, so it is the most Difficult to be Understood, especially in Treating of Hidden Causes and Effects'.[17] It was perhaps the hypothetical character of much seventeenth-century science that attracted her:

> It gives room for the untired appetites of man to walk or run in, for so spatious it is, that it is beyond the compasse of time; besides, it gives pleasure in varieties, for infinite wayes are strawed with infinite varieties, neither doth it bind up man to those strickt rules as the other Sciences do [i.e. moral philosophy, theology, logic, rhetoric, mathematics], it [natural philosophy] gives them an honest liberty, and proves temperance is the greatest pleasure in nature.[18]

As this quotation implies, Margaret Cavendish was not a systematic thinker. Her writings on natural philosophy range from poetic 'fancies' as she called them, to prose essays in orderly sequence. In the course of time she made every effort to present her ideas in a more systematic way. For example, in her *Grounds of Natural Philosophy* she starts with a definition of matter: 'Matter is what we name body', then proceeds through general definitions (e.g. of matter, motion) to particular bodies (what she calls 'productions'), with particular focus on the human body (covering such topics as the mind, the 'vital parts', humours, excretion and digestion). She then deals with its ailments (the plague, smallpox, fevers) as well as cures. Throughout she refers to each topic in terms of the properties of body, and the order is from the general to the particular. This hardly amounts to a rigorously deductive sequence of argument from first principles, but it does

represent a concerted attempt to arrange her subject matter logically, starting
with general principles and working towards particular phenomena.

In content her various treatises overlap with one another, but she also changed
her opinions in certain important respects. Leaving these changes aside, for the
moment, I shall concentrate on some of the main features of her work. In general
Cavendish's writings sound a didactic note: she normally devotes her energies to
expounding her opinions rather than explaining how she arrived at them. She
seems to have derived immense satisfaction from deflating the theories of others.
Her Utopian fiction, *The Description of a New World, Called the Blazing World*, is a
fine example of her powers of ridicule in action.[19] This tale features an empress
who assembles an academy of philosophers and scientists at her court in order to
discuss natural philosophy. These *virtuosi* are representatives of the different
strands of natural philosophy of her day, but they are shown to be contradictory
and absurd in almost every particular, and the empress revels in one-up-manship
over her scientific experts, or *virtuosi*. The latter are all given generic animal
names: the chemists are denominated 'ape men', astronomers 'bird men',
experimental philosophers 'bear men', and so on. The heroine's chief method of
deflation is to demolish the theories of others by the 'sound bite' principle. That
is, she takes an opinion completely out of context and sets it against others.
Truncated and cited out of context, opinions on everything from the cause of
thunder to the motion of the sun sound patently absurd. And it is not difficult to
demonstrate an astonishing lack of consensus among the *virtuosi* by setting such
opinions alongside each other. The chief object of her ridicule is the 'bear men',
that is the microscopists and the experimenters. This critique of Royal Society
science is carried further in her *Observations on Experimental Philosophy*, published in
the same volume. Cavendish's criticism of the opinions and methods of other
investigators of nature was motivated in large part by her desire to distance
herself from them in order to be credited with originality. Her attack on
observational methods is more than a little disingenuous, since she herself
scrutinized her subjects in minute detail and brought her findings to bear in her
theoretical writing. A fine example of her acute powers of observation is her
description of a chrysalis in her *Observations upon Experimental Philosophy*:

. . . it was about the length of half an inch or less, the tail was short and
square, and seemed to be a Vegetable, for it was as green as a stalk, growing
out of the aforesaid piece of stone or wood; the part next the tail was like a
thick skin, wherein one might perceive a perfect pulsation, and was big in
proportion to the rest of the parts; The part next to that, was less in compass
and harder, but of such a substance as it was like Pewter or Tin: The last and
extreme part opposite to the first mentioned green tail or stalk, seemed like a
head, round, onely it had two little points or horns before, which head seem'd
to the eye and touch like a stone, so that this creature appeared partly

Vegetable, Animal or Mineral; but what is more it was in continual motion, for the whole body of it seemed to struggle as if it would get loose from that piece of wood or stone the tail was joined to, or out of which it grew.[20]

But as Margaret Cavendish pointed out in relation to Robert Hooke's *Micrographia*, closely observed details, howsoever acute, do not, by themselves, amount to science. So what of the theories that accompany such observations?

The first thing to mention is that Cavendish adopted the Baconian principle of the separation of theology from natural philosophy. She specifically declined to speculate about matters metaphysical, confining the scope of her enquiries to the physical world, or what she called 'Nature'. And, like Bacon, she placed emphasis on the utility of knowledge: in her *Philosophical and Physical Opinions* she notes the importance of natural philosophy for practicalities of life:

> without Natural Philosophy Men could not tell how to Live; for Natural Philosophy doth not onely Instruct Men to Know the course of the Planets and the Seasons of the Year, but it Instructs Men in Husbandry, Architecture, and Navigation, as also Combination and Association, but above all it instructs Men in the Rules and Arts of Physick.[21]

In keeping with her strictures about metaphysics, she postulated that there is no immaterial substance, but that everything in nature is corporeal, including the soul ('I conceive Nature to be an Infinite body, bulk, or magnitude').[22] Matter is, however, variegated. There are different degrees of matter, some more refined and rarified, some more compact. All matter has 'figure' (i.e. shape), 'parts' (i.e. is composite), and 'place'. The properties of individual bodies are explicable in terms of the shape, combination and location of the component parts: thus earth is constituted of circular particles, fire of fine, pointed, smooth particles. There is no vacuum, but body and place are different aspects of the same thing. Matter is in a continuous state of motion. But this is self-generated motion, not motion derived from external impact. Just as motion is continuous, without end, so the process of compounding parts of matter continues endlessly. Particular bodies or creatures are aggregations of matter. Such 'productions', as she calls them, involve change of components, change of external form, but not changes in substance. All natural changes, growth, transformation, death, involve a recombination of parts. Matter itself is imperishable.

> There can be no *annihilation* in *Nature*, because the *matter* remains that owes the *cause* of those Motions and Figures.[23]

Cavendish distinguishes three types of matter, animate, sensitive and inanimate, with the result that,

the several Parts of Nature are Living and Knowing . . . there is no Part that
has not Life and Knowledge, being all composed of rational and sensitive
matter, which is the life and soul of Nature.[24]

In her *Observations upon Experimental Philosophy* she summarizes her concept of
nature as

> a perpetually self-moving body, dividing, composing, changing forming and
> transforming her parts by self-corporeally figured motions. . . . she has infinite
> sense and reason, which is the cause that no part of her is ignorant but has
> some knowledge or other.[25]

From this very compressed account three things are apparent. First, Cavendish's
natural philosophy takes up many of the theories proposed in the new mechanical
philosophies of Hobbes and Descartes. Like them she tries to account for all
natural phenomena in terms of the properties of matter, that is in terms of the
shape, size, position and movement of bodies. She is closer to Hobbes in her
rejection of metaphysics, and in her denial of the existence of anything other than
body.[26] The second point to note is that these 'modern' views are combined with
more traditional doctrines, such as the Aristotelian doctrine of the four elements
(air, fire, earth and water) whose characteristic properties (cold, heat, dryness and
moisture) account, in their various permutations and combinations, for the basic
qualities of all things. Cavendish, while retaining this doctrine, accounts for the
differences between the elements in terms of the shape, size and movement of the
components parts. In so far as she grafts new ideas on to old ones, her natural
philosophy recalls that of another free spirit of her acquaintance, Sir Kenelm
Digby.[27] Thirdly, it is clear that while she took a modern stance in her materialism,
Cavendish was unconvinced by the claims of the new physics to account for all
phenomena in terms of the impact of moving bodies on one another. Life and
action could not be accounted for by the chance collision of moving bodies. Now,
Cavendish was not the only contemporary of Descartes and Hobbes to make this
objection. Others, such as the aforementioned Henry More, proposed a vitalist
alternative, namely that movement, life and thought were the business of
incorporeal forces, or spirit.[28] Cavendish, however, imputed life, motion and mental
powers to body itself. In her *Philosophical Letters* she expresses this view as follows:

> There is not any Creature or part of nature without this Life and Soul; and
> that not only animals but also Vegetables, Minerals and Elements; and what
> more there is in Nature are endued with Life and Soul, Sense and Reason.[29]

Cavendish's answer to scientific mechanism was therefore not just vitalistic, but a
monistic, materialistic solution.

ANNE CONWAY

This is the appropriate point to turn to Anne Conway. For she too was a monist: that is she postulated that there was only one substance in created nature, and that all things were composed of this single substance. She too was a vitalist, for she imputed life, motion, perception and thought to this substance. But in her case the substance in question was not body; rather it was a form of spirit. Nonetheless, as in the case of Margaret Cavendish, Anne Conway put forward her theory of substance in response to the inadequacy, as she saw it, of the mechanical hypothesis for explaining life and action.[30]

Superficially, the central postulates of the theories of substance Margaret Cavendish and Anne Conway adopt appear similar. Both proposed that all things are constituted from one single substance and that all phenomena of the physical world are to be explained in terms of the properties of that substance. Although, in each case, the properties of that substance include the properties attributed to matter by mechanical philosophy (shape, size and moveability), neither limits the properties of the basic substance to the classic mechanical ones. Both deny that this substance is passive. They both impute life, the power of thought and the ability to move to the single substance. The difference turns on how each conceives the elementary substance. Superficially, this difference seems to hang on the choice of one term: body or spirit. In fact, underlying this apparently small distinction in terminology is an entirely different structure of thought that reveals that the divergence between the two is of fundamental proportions. The common ground is the perception of a problem with the new physics, namely, that you cannot explain the life and other operations of nature in terms of the shape, size, configuration and movement of bodies. Conway's answer denies the existence of bodies, at least in the sense Cavendish and others conceive body. The difference in her solution is therefore not simply a difference of semantics, but a *systematic* difference.

At first sight, Anne Conway's treatise, *The Principles of the Most Ancient and Modern Philosophy*, appears to have little to do with science. It is a work of metaphysics, which deduces the nature of things from the nature of God. For Conway, theology has everything to do with natural philosophy and you cannot separate the two. Her argument is set out as an entirely internally consistent piece of *a priori* reasoning, that is, she starts from the idea of God as the most fully perfect being conceivable, and derives everything thence. In some respects this is a classic Cartesian way of proceeding. But, as will become apparent, there are other elements that come into play, among them a strain of Neoplatonism (which is not surprising, since her philosophy teacher had been one of the leading Cambridge Platonists). She proposes three orders of being: God, Christ and created things. It is with the last that I shall be concerned now. This third order of being is differentiated from the others because it is subject to change. If God is, as she conceives him, 'a spirit, light and life, infinitely wise, good, just, strong, all-knowing, all-present, all-powerful',[31] this must be reflected in what he creates. Accordingly everything must be living and the created world must be the best possible world, in keeping with his goodness. Created substance consists in particles or monads, infinite in number in imitation of his infinity. And this substance, like God, is a form of spirit. These monads of spirit are differentiated according to whether they are higher or lower in the scale of being. The lower they are, the more like body they are in the traditional sense of the term. But, according to Conway there is no such thing as body, at least not body conceived as inert matter. For that is dead, and God, being infinite life, produces nothing that is the antithesis of himself. Even apparently inanimate things such as stones are composed of configurations of monads endowed with life. All created things are composed of configurations of these spiritual particles, which contain within them the properties any Platonist would expect of spirit: life, perception and the principle of self-movement. Since created nature is subject to change, and since there is a built-in possibility of becoming more refined or less so, all things have the capacity to metamorphose and up-grade, so to speak, their condition of being. In theory, therefore, the particles which make up a horse can, by refinement during the life of the horse and recombination after death, become a man.

On this account, Anne Conway's system could be set aside as a philosopher's dream, which bears little or no relationship to the external world as we experience it. However, as becomes clear in the later chapters, underlying this metaphysical presentation of her ideas are issues of contemporary physics, chemistry and biology. Not only does she advance some theoretical objections to the mechanical philosophy, but experience of a sort underlies her points – I use the expression 'of a sort' advisedly, because the appeal to experience does not amount to a full-scale application of the principles of experimental philosophy. She does from time to time adduce examples of natural phenomena, but she also invokes, for example, the wisdom of alchemy. One can also detect the impact of other theories in natural philosophy, most notably the biological ideas associated with Helmontian medicine, according to which all things derived from the single primary element, water.[32]

To begin with her engagement with contemporary science at a theoretical level. In the last chapter of her book, she criticizes the mechanical philosophers for being unable to account for life and action solely in terms of the movement of bodies. In this chapter she acknowledges Descartes as pre-eminent in the new physics:

> Descartes taught many remarkable and ingenious things concerning the mechanical aspects of natural processes and about how all motions proceed according to regular mechanical laws, just as nature does herself.[33]

But, she goes on, Descartes' laws of motion do not account for all the operations of nature:

> For truly in nature there are many operations that are far more than merely mechanical. Nature is not simply an organic body like a clock, which has no vital principle of motion in it; but is a living body which has life and perception, which are much more exalted than a mere mechanism or a mechanical motion.[34]

The Cartesian account of body as extension differentiated only by the size, shape and motion of its parts, cannot account for life and perception. Instead, she advances a hypothesis of change that fits with her own monism of spirit: she proposes a theory of 'vital action' or 'internal motion', inherent in all things. This operates rather like a field of force, and achieves its effects by stimulating a response in other things:

> Vital motion or action occurs when one thing uses another as an instrument which serves to excite a vital action in the subject or percipient.[35]

In this respect, therefore, Anne Conway's natural philosophy is worked out in the light of the explanatory shortcomings of the new philosophy of her time, though always consistent with her deep-seated religiosity.

But she also appeals to experience in order to challenge the explanatory value of other systems. At bottom, this is just the application of common sense, or perhaps common experience. An example comes in her criticism of dualist theories, that is those which propose that in addition to matter there is mind or soul, distinct from matter. Such dualistic theories attribute life and perception to the soul or spirit. However, as Conway points out, such theories, having made an absolute separation of mind and body, fail to account for mind–body interaction. In her own monistic theory of substance no such difficulty arises. Against the dualists, Anne Conway adduces a range of logical difficulties about mind–body interaction. But she also appeals to experience, the experience of pain:

> why does the spirit or soul suffer so with bodily pain? For if, when united to the body it has no corporeality or bodily nature, why is it wounded or grieved when a body is wounded, whose nature is so different?[36]

In the light of what we know of the unrelievable physical pain from which Anne Conway suffered most of her life, this observation has a particular poignancy. It is quite understandable that she could not accept a dualistic separation of mind from body.

Detecting the experiential element that underlies Anne Conway's philosophy involves a certain amount of extrapolation, since she does not present her arguments inductively. Nor does she give an account of the observed phenomenon in question separately from her interpretation. An example of this is her observation of the freezing of alcoholic liquid, which she adduces in support of her contention that all things are merely modes of the same single substance, which, in its more congealed mode forms body, in its more tenuous state constitutes spirit. She further contends that even corporeal things (that is the most compacted forms of the single spiritual substance) retain an element of their original spirit state. This is how she puts it:

> We see this excess of subtler and stronger spirits in an alcoholic liquor change from grosser and harder parts into better and more tenuous ones. Such a liquor freezes when the stronger spirits (having left behind the harder parts which are especially exposed to the outside cold) withdraw to the middle of the body which remains tenuous, so that every single drop of that liquor (which does not freeze but always remains liquid in the innermost parts of that frozen body) has in itself the multiplied strength of all those parts which are frozen.[37]

We may not agree that Anne Conway's observation of the effect of freezing alcoholic liquid is to be explained according to her hypothesis. But the example surely has illustrative value as an example of a natural substance capable of becoming on the one hand more solid and, on the other, more vaporous – that is, in her terms, capable of forming body and spirit. Strictly, it is an argument by analogy rather than induction. But it does show that her metaphysical theories rest on the perceived need to explain certain natural phenomena.

Another example of her appeal to experience occurs in her discussion of change, in particular her hypothesis of the interchangeability of natural kinds, of the possibility for metamorphosis within the natural order. This time she adduces the commonplace instance of digestion, by which one thing, say a plant, is consumed by another, say an animal, and is thereby transformed into part of it. In Anne Conway's account this kind of experiential instance is usually accompanied by others which nowadays appear more dubious, but then carried credence: so, in support of her theory of change, she adduces, on the one hand, the alchemical theory of the transmutation of metals, and on the other the theory of spontaneous generation according to which (until the work of the microscopists, Swammerdam, Redi and Leeuwenhoek proved otherwise)[38] some creatures appeared to be produced by the very earth or out of decomposing matter. She also uses examples which she can only have known by report: for instance – in support of her theory that all things are constituted of the same single substance – she mentions two rivers in Hungary. The water of one has the capacity to dissolve stones, while the water of the other appears to produce stones. Anne Conway never travelled to Hungary. The example must be derived from her physician, Francis Mercury van Helmont, who uses it in one of his own treatises.[39] Nonetheless, most of these examples from experience are critical in respect of Cartesian science and other versions of philosophical mechanism, in the sense that they are phenomena which do not lend themselves readily to explanation in terms of those theories.

We can perhaps answer the question of *how* Anne Conway and Margaret Cavendish became involved in scientific investigations more cogently than we can answer the question of *why* of all possible pursuits they chose *natural philosophy*. In spite of everything Margaret Cavendish said about the educational and social disadvantages suffered by women – and most of her charges ring true – both she and Anne Conway were undoubtedly blessed by opportunities which very few of their contemporaries enjoyed. The attraction for them of the new natural philosophy – the science of their day – was perhaps the fact that it was new. By that I do not mean that it was a mere novelty, a fashionable curiosity. Rather, as a new field of enquiry, natural philosophy did not have a weight of book-learning to support it, and it existed outside the institutions of learning. For these reasons it was accessible to people who were not in possession of an academic education, and it was open to those excluded from the academies, including women. Descartes himself said that the only qualification needed for understanding his philosophy was common sense. This is, of course, particularly true of a system such as his worked out by *a priori* deduction. One of the portraits of Margaret Cavendish shows her sitting alone in contemplative mood. To underline her contention that her only debt was to her own native wit, the accompanying verse runs

> Studious she is, and all alone,
> Most visitants when she has none;
> Her library on which she looks,
> It is her head; her thoughts her books:
> Scorning dead ashes without fire,
> For her own flames do her inspire.[40]

But, before I conclude, I would like to advance one further suggestion. And it is this: there was, perhaps, something in the nature of science in the general sense of that term which made it a natural subject for women. Other chapters in this book have discussed the role of women as medical practitioners of one kind or another. Indeed, the ordinary role of mothers as nurse and doctor to their families, led the first Cartesian defender of the equality of the sexes, Poulain de la Barre, to observe that one proof that women's mental abilities were equal to those of men was the fact that, even without formal training, they acted as doctors to their households. There is no record of Anne Conway and Margaret Cavendish performing this function, but we may assume that as female heads of households, they were expected to perform such a role. They certainly both had knowledge of cures of one kind or another. What is certain, however, is the fact that medicine impinges on their theories in fundamental ways. Margaret Cavendish's later publications all culminate in discussions of human ailments and their remedies. And she notes of natural philosophy that 'above all it Instructs Men in the Rules and Arts of Physick'.[41] Anne Conway's theory of substance has affinities with the biological theory that underpinned the medical practice of her personal physician, Francis Mercury van Helmont. And, indeed, it was her own medical condition – her incurable disease – which was indirectly responsible for bringing her into contact with Helmontian and other medical theories.

Between them Margaret Cavendish and Anne Conway illustrate the dilemma of women engaging in pursuits not conventionally regarded as female: whether to go public and risk ridicule, which was the lot of Margaret Cavendish, or to pursue her interests privately and risk dropping altogether from view, as was the case with Anne Conway; a situation that prevailed until the twentieth century. Both Cavendish and Conway were able to engage with the scientific and philosophical ideas of their time. But the discussion was a one-way process. Although the extra-mural character of the new science enabled them to enter the debate, neither had a place in the new institutions of science that emerged in the period – one can be forgiven for suspecting that on Cavendish's visit to the Royal Society it was she who was the phenomenon under observation, not Boyle's demonstration of the weight of air! At all events it was an exceptional circumstance to have a woman visit the society. No women were invited to join. Nor did Conway or Cavendish have any followers elsewhere – although Conway's system impressed the German philosopher Leibniz.[42] Neither can, therefore, be said to have changed the course of science. This does not mean that their theories have no value. The history of science is not just about the winners, it is about everything that went on, including some of the theories which to us seem strange, irrational, even defunct, like alchemy. It is easy to forget that the scientific wisdom with which we are familiar today was less clear and obvious in its earliest beginnings. For twentieth-century consumers of scientific nostrums, acquiescent in purportedly rational scientism, Anne Conway's or Margaret Cavendish's writings can seem obscurely overburdened with non-scientific details. Approached from the other end, from the perspective of the confused quest for new explanatory theories of the universe, they do not seem so bizarre. (We should not forget that even Francis Bacon proposed investigating natural magic, divination and fascination (i.e. bewitchment) as part of his programme for the advancement of learning,[43] and that Isaac Newton devoted his enormous intellectual energy to cracking the secrets of the book of Revelation and investigating alchemy.)[44] Anne Conway and Margaret Cavendish have a place in the history of science every bit as much as Descartes, van Helmont and Charleton. Whatever we make of their theories, even if their numbers were few, women contributed to the revolution in scientific thinking in the seventeenth century.

Notes

1 On Charleton, see Sharp (1973). On J.B. van Helmont, see Pagel (1982); on F.M. van Helmont, Brown (1996). On More see Hutton (1992) and A. Hall (1990).

2 Cavendish (1676), p. 119; see Hall (1990), p. 41.

3 For the life of Cavendish, see her own *The True Relation of My Birth, Breeding and Life*, printed with her *The Life of the Thrice Noble, High and Puissant Prince William Cavendish, Duke, Marquess and Earl of Newcastle* (London, 1667); Grant (1957); Mendelson (1987). For Anne Conway's biography, see Hutton and Nicolson (1992).

4 *Ibid.*, Introduction.

5 This correspondence is printed in *ibid.*, letters 18, 19a, 19b, 22a, 24a.

6 Cavendish (1663), sig. b2^5.

7 This is evident from her *Philosophical Letters*, where she discusses the work of these men.

8 Jacquot (1952).

9 Cavendish (1663), 'To the Reader', sig. B.

10 It appeared as *Principia philosophiae antiquissimae et recentissimae* in an anonymous collection entitled *Opuscula philosophica*. The other two treatises in this collection were a Latin version of van Helmont's *Two Hundred Queries . . . Concerning the Doctrine of the Revolution of Human Souls* (which had been published in London in 1685) and *Philosophia vulgaris refutata* by Jean Gironnet.

11 Pepys (1970–83), 8:163 and 243.

12 For example Woolf (1935), pp. 91ff.

13 On Anne Conway and her doctors see Hutton (1996). Leibniz's copy of Anne Conway's book is held at the Niedersächsische Landesbibliothek, Hanover.

14 Anne Conway to Henry More, 26 January 1652/3, in *Conway Letters*, pp. 70–1.

15 'To the Two Most Famous Universities of England', Cavendish (1655a), sig. B2^v.

16 Pepys (1970–83), p. 243. On Cavendish and the Royal Society, see Mintz (1952) and Sarasohn (1984), Nicolson (1965), Ch. 3.

17 Nicolson (1965), Ch. 3.

18 *Ibid.*, 'An Epistle to the Reader', sig. a^v.

19 Cavendish (1666b).

20 'Of a Butterflie', Cavendish (1666a) pp. 26–7.

21 Cavendish (1663), sig. b2. One of her criticisms of microscopy is that it teaches us nothing useful.

22 Cavendish (1666a), p. 135. Also, p. 155, 'Nature is purely corporeal or material, and there is nothing that belongs to, or is part of Nature, which is not corporeal; so that nature or natural and corporeal are one and the same thing'.

23 Cavendish (1663), pp. 6–7.

24 Cavendish (1664), pp. 143–4.

25 Cavendish (1666), p. 66.

26 It is widely believed that Cavendish's philosophy is the antithesis of that of Hobbes, but I believe that there are greater affinities between them than is normally supposed. See my 'In Dialogue with Thomas Hobbes: Margaret Cavendish's Natural Philosophy'; *Women's Writing* (forthcoming).

27 On Digby, see Dobbs (1973, 1974).

28 In More (1659) and again in his *Enchiridion metaphysicum* (1671) he put forward his hypothesis of a '*Principium hylarchicum*' or 'Spirit of Nature' governing all the operations of the physical world. See Gabbey (1990) and Henry and Hutton (1990).

29 Cavendish (1664).

30 See Popkin (1990).

31 Conway (1996), p. 9. All quotations from Conway's *Principles of the Most Ancient and Modern Philosophy* are taken from this new translation by Allison Coudert and Taylor Corse.

32 See Hutton (1996).

33 Conway (1996), p. 64.

34 *Ibid.*

35 *Ibid.*, p. 67.

36 *Ibid.*, p. 58.

37 *Ibid.*, p. 58.

38 See Wilson (1995), pp. 202–5.

39 F.M. van Helmont (1694), p. 170.

40 Cavendish, *The World's Olio* (1671 edition).

41 Cavendish (1663), sig. 62.

42 For a discussion of the relationship between Leibniz's philosophy and Conway's see Brown (1990).

43 Bacon (1974), 2.8.3; 2.11.2 and 3.

44 On Newton and alchemy, see Dobbs (1982). On his apocalypticism, see Hutton (1994) and Iliffe (1994).

11

ASTRONOMY AND THE DOMESTIC SPHERE: MARGARET FLAMSTEED AND CAROLINE HERSCHEL AS ASSISTANT-ASTRONOMERS

Rob Iliffe and Frances Willmoth

Sir Maurice Meanwell: A pretty thing indeed, to see those long spectacles of yours, set on the Top of my House, for you to peep and tell how many Hackney Coaches are going in the Moon.
Lovewit: Oh the Illiterate Brute! thus to affront a Telescope.
Sir Maur: I am no Scholar, . . . but . . . so much common Sense has taught me, that all the Study and Philosophy of a Wife, should be to please her Husband, instruct her Children, have a Vigilant Eye over Domestick Affairs, keep a good Order in her Family, and stand as a Living Pattern of Virtue, and Discretion to all about her.[1]

Lady Reveller: Ridiculous Learning!
Alphiew [her companion]: Ridiculous, indeed, for Woman; Philosophy suits our Sex as Jack Boots would do.[2]

In the early modern period the variety of strategies open even to aristocratic women to appear as independent authors in astronomy or natural philosophy was extremely limited. Royal persons such as Queen Christina of Sweden or Princess Elizabeth of Bohemia were to some extent able to direct their own intellectual development and could command the attention of the major scholars of the day, but their scholarly attainments have conventionally been placed in the shadow of those of more brilliant men. In the case of Émilie le Tonnelier de Breteuil, the Marquise du Châtelet, for example, her story has usually been told (as Mary Terrall has remarked) in the light of Voltaire's, 'as if he were what made her interesting'. Nevertheless, although this is an accurate description of the situation which faced many women, the fact that the main centres of learning were exclusively male meant that women were invariably forced to receive tuition from, and hence remain close to men. As a character in a play written by Margaret Cavendish put it:

... that is the reason all women are fools; for women breeding up women, one fool breeding up another, and as long as that custom lasts there is no hopes of amendment, and ancient customs being a second nature, makes folly hereditary in that Sex, by reason their education is effeminate, and their times spent in pins, points and laces, their study only vain fashions, which breeds prodigality, pride and envie.[3]

Moreover the conventional wisdom that a woman's place was in the home was so prevalent in the early modern period that, with few exceptions, the education of women in mathematics and natural philosophy was invariably conceived as properly taking place either in the home or with a view to enhancing their domestic role. Within these confines, as other contributions to this volume show, women were capable of excelling in a wide range of scientific activities.

Individual women were occasionally able to circumvent these restrictions on their capacity to participate in intellectual life. In France, for example, women played a significant role in the salons that proliferated in the seventeenth century, and Londa Schiebinger points out that Pierre Richelet added the word 'académicienne' to his dictionary in the 1680s. In the eighteenth century, renowned salonnières such as Julie de l'Espinasse continued to wield a great deal of influence in creating the conditions for intellectual exchange despite the fact that famous men were now the centre of attention in the salons. Yet across Europe (with the possible exception of Italy) even the most gifted women were barred from entering academies, the disgraceful treatment of the astronomer Maria Kirch (von Winckelmann) by the Berlin Academy of Sciences being a prime example. Faced with this intransigent attitude from traditional bastions of male power, a number of individuals argued in the seventeenth century that women should set up their own academies of learning, though none of these schemes was ever implemented.[4]

That is not to say that women were universally prevented from gaining access to scholarship, and indeed in sixteenth-century Europe it became a commonplace in some circles that learning was an important activity for women. In part this was because scholarly achievement was seen as one of the useful and genteel accomplishments that would enhance a woman's marriage prospects at court, but it also fitted in with the humanist ideals for the education of women pioneered by Juan Luis Vives and Thomas More. Figures such as Joanna Lumley, who translated four of Isocrates' *Orations* from Greek to Latin, and Lady Jane Grey, whose solitariness and scholarly demeanour in reading Plato were recorded in Roger Ascham's *The Scholemaster* of 1570, were examples to women of their class. As for More's daughter Margaret Roper, when she showed interest in mathematics and astronomy in 1521 her father hired a tutor specially to instruct her in their pursuit, believing that what was conventionally taught only in the university liberal arts course (and hence only to men) should be available to all.[5]

DOMESTIC SCIENCE

For all classes of women, there was a strong presumption that wives should remain in a domestic setting even though they might be encouraged to learn mathematics or natural philosophy. In this volume Frances Harris has pointed to the way in which John Evelyn and his wife created a role for her which was conventionally domestic if not necessarily separate (see pp. 198–217 above). She gradually took over the authorship of the receipt book which contained the sort of relevant information usually pertinent to the woman's traditional role as housekeeper, and John reaffirmed that his wife would not renounce her economic duties when they took up residence in their utopian philosophical college. As Lynette Hunter also shows (pp. 89–107 above), noblewomen played a large role in disseminating and publishing information such as health and dietary receipts and remedies. However, female philosophical authors who encroached on what was seen as a male preserve tended, with few exceptions, to be ridiculed – unless they were especially demure or devout examples such as Anne Finch, Countess of Conway. Ironically, Conway died before she achieved authorship, and the structure of the published text arguably owes more to her admirers than to her own opinion.[6]

In seventeenth-century England, mathematics was also seen as useful for middle-class women who would be expected to look after the household accounts and who might go on to become head of the household if widowed. In a burgeoning and ambitious trading nation, this advice mirrored a simultaneous drive to increase the mathematical ability of males, but opinions varied regarding the extent to which mathematics was appropriate or relevant to a woman's education. The famous 'Sappho of Holland', Anna Maria van Schurman, published *De Ingenii Muliebris ad Doctrinam et Meliores Literas Aptitudine* in 1641, a work which was translated in 1659 as *The Learned Maid or Whether a Maid may be a Scholar*. Van Schurman argued that women should be allowed to study whatever they wanted, although she placed a strong emphasis on learning that was conducive to piety and to understanding scripture: 'The rest, i.e. *Mathematicks*, (to which is also referred *Musick*) *Poesie, Picture* and the like . . . may obtain the place of pretty Ornaments and ingenious Recreations.' In the late seventeenth century George Hickes urged that mathematics should play a major role in a woman's education, arguing that a genteel woman should learn the 'Four first great Rules of Arithmetic':

you may make good use of them, in teaching her thereby to keep your Accompts. This is indeed a troublesome Employment to a great many; but an Habit from her Childhood, joyn'd with the Easiness of keeping readily, by the help of these Rules, all sorts of Accompts, tho' never so intricate, will very much diminish this dislike. Now 'tis sufficiently known how much Exactness of Accompts conduces to the good Order in Families.

However, he also remarked that '*Natural Philosophy* seems not to be adapted to the Understanding of Women, or at least not to fall within the bounds of what concerns their Duty', and he warned that girls should 'beware of the Reputation of being *witty*.'[7]

The most significant call for women to take up the study of mathematics and natural philosophy came from Bathsua Makin, sister to the mathematician John Pell. In the early 1640s she was appointed tutor to Charles I's daughter Elizabeth, and taught her mathematics as well as Latin, Greek, Hebrew, French and Italian. In the 1650s she corresponded with van Schurman, and they shared an interest in anatomy and classical languages. In 1673 she published an essay on the education of women which was accompanied by a prospectus for a girls' school at Tottenham High Cross, run by Makin herself. She condemned a culture in which 'A Learned Woman is thought to be a Comet, that Bodes Mischief, when ever it appears', and pointed to women in the past who had been pre-eminent in learning. Although the number of women revered for their mathematical accomplishments was small, there were nevertheless some examples, such as the ill-fated Hypatia and 'A Lady of late' who had printed astronomical tables (the so-called 'Second Hypatia', Maria Cunitz – whose name Makin admitted to having forgotten). Among the questions addressed in her essay was the point that Solomon had made no mention of his wife's learning when he praised her merits. To this Makin replied:

> To buy wool and flax, to dye Scarlet and Purple, requires skill in Natural Philosophy. To consider a Field, the quantity and quality, requires knowledge in Geometry. To plant a vineyard, requires understanding in Husbandry. She could not merchandise without Arithmetic. She could not govern so great a family well without knowledge in Politics and Economics. She could not look well to the ways of her Household, except she understood Physic and Chirurgery.

However, Solomon's wife seemed little more than 'an honest, well-bred, ingenious, industrious Dutchwoman' whose accomplishments fell short of what was expected of the girls at the Tottenham Academy where, as Makin put it, 'those that think one language enough for a woman may forbear the languages and learn only *Experimental Philisophy*'.[8]

Even for as independent a writer as Bathsua Makin, the fundamental role of the housekeeper was the paramount consideration in justifying the purpose of education for women. Moreover, given the parlous state of most mathematical instruction for women at school, a great deal of tuition in that subject must have taken place in the home. A good example of the way in which a domestic educational relation was structured is given by Samuel Pepys in his *Diary*. In February 1662/3 he bought a pair of globes from Joseph Moxon for £3 10*s.* at which he pronounced himself 'well pleased, I buying them principally for my wife, who hath a mind to understand them – and I shall take pleasure to teach her'. However, it was not until October 1663 that Pepys, himself only recently schooled in the basics of multiplication, began the tuition: 'I began to enter my wife in Arithmetique, in order to her studying of the globes and she takes it very well – and I hope with great pleasure I shall bring her to understand many fine things'. On one evening, 1 November 1663, Pepys returned home, taught Elizabeth some subtraction, and had supper after which occurred 'another bout of Arithmetique with my wife'. Pepys took a great deal of pleasure in his wife's progress in November, and on 6 December he noted: 'she and I all the afternoon at Arithmetique: and she is come to do Addicion, Subtraccion and Multiplicacion very well – and so I purpose not to trouble her yet with Division, but to begin with the globes to her now.' After what was – according to Pepys – an idyllic tutorial relationship, Elizabeth ventured on to the topic of globes in January 1663/4. In the following years the Pepyses became avid consumers of the accoutrements of the new philosophy and purchased a telescope and a microscope, but, despite having Henry Power's *Experimental Philosophy* to hand, they found it difficult to see anything by means of the latter.[9]

OUTSIDE THE HOME

Notoriously, learned females who ventured outside their traditional domestic roles were variously classified as wonderful, monstrous, freakish or unnatural, and plays caricatured the recklessness that characterized such women's disregard for the well-being of the household economy. Laura Bassi was revered as a 'wonder' and compared to Minerva in 1730s Bologna, while Margaret Cavendish was condemned as outlandish by the likes of Mary Evelyn and Samuel Pepys when she dared to strut the philosophical stage in the 1660s. In Molière's influential *Les Femmes Savantes* of 1672, Cartesian-obsessed females were presented as mad and irresponsible, and a character neglected by his wife in this manner lamented: 'They want to write and become authors; no science is too deep for them. . . . They know the motions of the moon, the pole star, Venus, Saturn and Mars . . . and my food, which I need, is neglected.' Such attitudes persisted in virtually all areas in which learned females were discussed. In Alphonse de Vignoles' appreciative account of Maria Cunitz in 1721, for example, he felt obliged to defend her against the accusation that she had neglected her household duties and spent the entire day in bed, fatigued by her astronomical exertions:

Quand ils furent mariez, Mlle Cunitz s'appliqua tellement à l'Astronomie, qu'elle passoit la plûpart des nuits, à faire des Observations, ou à calculer, & prenoit le jour pour dormir: ce qui lui fit négliger ses affaires domestiques. Une vie si dérangée, pour une Femme, donna lieu aux plusieurs contes populaires, qu'on débita sur son sujet.

Another writer who urged that women were as capable as men at 'contemplation or speculative philosophy', Pierre Le Moyne, reassured his readers in 1660 that 'it is not my intention to call women to the colleges . . . to exchange their needles and wools for astrolabes and spheres. I respect the boundaries that separate us too well.'[10]

That gifted females could only be experienced by men as curiosities is well shown by attitudes to a brilliant young mathematician who attended the Dublin Philosophical Society in early 1685/6. Sir William Petty, first president of the society in 1683, produced a set of 'Rules' for its conduct among which was the recommendation that they 'do not contemn and neglect common triviall and cheap Expts and Observations; not contenting themselves without such as may surprize and astonish y^c vulgar'. Like its counterpart in London, the society enquired after all sorts of rare, wonderful and monstrous narratives and in January 1685/6 a Dublin meeting was regaled with a story of 'a woman lately dissected, who imagin'd herself for 3 years last past to be with Child, her right ovarium was as bigg as hogs bladder blown, and being opened it discharged above a pint of a discoloured liquor having much fat swimming upon it.' A fortnight later, when the discussion turned to inordinately long fastings, a somewhat typical story was told by a member of a 14-year-old girl, 'who lived near him in y^c county of Kildare, that was not observ'd to eat or drink for a twelvemonth, insomuch y^t her belly & gutts all shrunk up & clung together.'[11]

The gentlemen were given the opportunity the next week to witness at first hand what was clearly an unprecedented and extraordinary rarity, namely a gifted female mathematician who was to perform for them over the following meetings. On 1 February George Tollet, a professor of mathematics,

> brought a schollar of his, a girl not yet 11 years of age, who is to a prodigy skill'd in y^c Mathematicks; She was examin'd before y^c Soc: in y^c most difficult propositions of Euclid, w^{ch}, she demonstrated with wonderful readines. She extracts y^c square root of a number of 20 places by memory. She is to be examin'd at y^c next meeting therein & in Arithmetick, Algebra, Trigonometry & Astronomy.

The unnamed girl, 'Mr Tollet's Schollar', was duly interrogated two weeks later 'in Algebra, Mechanicks, the Theory of Musick, and Chronology or the Calendar', and it was noted that 'She answered in all with great readiness and judgment, & to admiration'. On 1 March 'Mr. Tollet's girl' – clearly now a great attraction – was examined by Tollet himself 'in Geography and the use of the Globes, a discourse and demonstration of a place between the Tropicks, where the shadow goes twice forward & twice backward in a day, as is said in scripture of Ahaz's dyall. . . '.[12]

Throughout the rest of March the girl was further examined in astronomy, especially 'the doctrine of Parallaxes and refraction,' and geography, 'particularly in what relates to the Latitudes and Longitudes of places', after which Tollet himself gave a paper on the 'extream improbability of ever attaining to an exact method of finding the longitude by the Heavenly Motions'. These extraordinary occasions were interspersed with discussion of a discourse by Jacob Sylvius about a 'horny girle' which took up the entire meeting of 22 March, and with the account of a boy who had been struck speechless for a year and who had 'a most greedy Canine appetite during his fitts' on 12 April (after which his mother 'gave the history of his conception and birth, wherein were some particulars odd enough'). However, the scholar was displayed for the last time on 19 April when she 'shew'd her skill in practicall musick upon the fiddle, wch was accompanied with a consert of excellent musick'.[13]

Although the mathematical talents of Tollet's 'girl' were extraordinary, women in general were about to participate in the culture of natural philosophy to an unprecedented extent. By the 1690s the popularity of experimental philosophy was providing another outlet for female interest in natural knowledge and in the early eighteenth century it became increasingly fashionable for ladies to attend public lectures or use philosophical instruments. Authors such as John Harris, who wrote *Astronomical Dialogues between a Gentleman and a Lady* in 1719, composed texts in a dialogue form which emphasized the conversational benefits that attended a lady who knew just enough natural philosophy to converse with males but not so much as to embarrass them. This genre catered for an expanding female public sphere which exerted increasing social and economic influence, but the new identity of the female experimental and natural philosopher was ridiculed as soon as it appeared. Such critiques drew upon the long-established depictions of the female philosopher mentioned above, although interest in the learned female natural philosopher became particularly prominent after Aphra Behn's translation of Fontenelle's *Entretiens sur la Pluralité des Mondes* in 1688.[14]

On 17 March 1690/1 the print entrepreneur John Dunton began a periodical called *The Athenian Gazette or Casuistical Mercury, Resolving all the most Nice and Curious Questions proposed by the Ingenious*; after two months the title was extended and the words 'of Either Sex' were added. The title changed once more to become *The Athenian Mercury*, although the journal continued to recognize that there was a sizeable female audience for the mathematics and natural philosophy which constituted its fare. *The Athenian Mercury* invited readers to submit questions to the three editors (in addition to Dunton) on any relevant subject, and on 23 May 1691 Dunton instituted a 'Ladies Day', claiming that 'Whereas the Questions we receive from the fair Sex are both pressing and numerous, we being willing to oblige 'em, as knowing they have a very strong party in the World, resolve to set apart the first Tuesday in every month to satisfie Questions of that Nature'. In defence of his publication of queries from women, Dunton claimed that females were as capable as males in improving natural philosophy and that their wit was 'conspicuous in their Loquacity and their Artifices, Intrigues and Dissimulations', while there had never in recorded history been a learned woman who was not equally chaste. In 1692 the editors created the Athenian Society, a body which published a work the same year entitled *The Young-Students-Library*. This book had as its frontispiece a depiction of fourteen readers questioning the editors of *The Athenian Mercury* across a table. One of these was a woman carrying a pet flea, an emblematic reference to a question submitted to the periodical the previous year in which a female reader had asked the editors 'Whether Fleas have stings, or whether they only suck or bite, when they draw blood from the body?' The success of Dunton's enterprise caused John Tipper to create the *Ladies' Diary* in 1704, although the level of mathematics required soon took it beyond the capacities of all but university-trained scholars.[15]

The only edition of the *Lady's Journal* (in October 1693) proclaimed 'That Women may apply themselves to the Liberal Arts and Sciences', and preached their superior mental abilities, arguing that 'their Forehead is generally high, rais'd and broad, which is the usual token of an ingenious and inventive person'. However, the same year, such pretensions of women to philosophical learning were satirized in Elkanah Settle's *New Athenian Comedy* (in which Dunton was lampooned as 'Jack Stuff, a subtile, ingenious, half Author, half Bookseller') and Thomas Wright's *The Female Vertuoso's*, which drew from Molière and from Thomas Shadwell's *The Virtuoso* of 1676. The role of the flea, an animal whose bulk was intended to indicate the scholarly attainments both of the new philosophy and of women in general, was reprised in both texts. In the first a prisoner asked the Athenians whether a louse was more noble than a flea, while in Wright's play a character called Miss Catchat taught a flea to sing and understand musical notes. Finally, in Susannah Centlivre's *The Basset-Table* of 1705, attention was centred on the dissection of a fly – which escaped, with farcical consequences.[16]

Although these plays catered for an audience which shared many of the prejudices against women's supposedly absurd predilection for the new philosophy, there is evidence that large numbers of accessible, vernacular books on mathematics and natural philosophy were being devoured by an increasingly literate female audience. The examples of Hickes and Makin – and there are many others – show that a familiarity with basic mathematics and natural philosophy was coming to be seen by a large number of commentators as a desideratum for young women. However, despite the tradition by which women were taught the art of remedies and dietary regimens, Makin was one of very few women who professed to want to teach or be able to teach other women mathematics. In most cases, as with those of Tollet and Pepys, direct tuition of whatever standard would invariably be undertaken by a male tutor.

The frontispiece from the *Young-Students-Library* (1692).

In the case of the two individuals whose experiences make up the remainder of this chapter, a male relative constituted the most significant avenue for learning astronomy. As Schiebinger has indicated, astronomical practice drew many of its codes of behaviour from the guild system in which a master trained apprentices, and both Margaret Flamsteed (wife to the First Astronomer Royal, John Flamsteed) and Caroline Herschel (sister to William, discoverer of Uranus in 1781) benefited from this situation. They both became astronomical assistants who were trained in the art by their male relative while retaining their primary role as housekeeper. Acting within the roles that were accepted by the vast majority of their contemporaries (including themselves), they nevertheless played a large part in facilitating the careers of their better-known relatives.[17]

MARGARET FLAMSTEED (C. 1670–1730)

Margaret Flamsteed was a daughter of the London lawyer Ralph Cooke and his wife Hester, and a granddaughter of the Ralph Cooke who was John Flamsteed's predecessor as rector of the Surrey parish of Burstow. Ralph Cooke senior, an Oxford MA and BD, was rector of the London parish of St Gabriel, Fenchurch Street from 1637 until a sequestration in 1643 or '44 (when he was succeeded there by the mathematician John Wallis). He was then permitted to retire to Burstow, where he had also been rector since 1637, remaining in undisturbed possession of that living and playing a leading role in diocesan affairs until his death at the age of seventy-eight.[18] His wife, whom he married at Burstow in 1639, was Susannah Coventry; as Margaret's will mentions 'the painted Armes' of the Coventry family, it is possible that this grandmother was a relative of Lord Keeper Thomas, 1st Baron Coventry. The younger Ralph Cooke was admitted to Gray's Inn in 1657, called to the Bar ten years later and to the Bench in 1685.[19] He accepted that last call in the following year and in the interim spent the substantial sum of £555 19s. 10d. on buying and refurbishing a house in Hatton Garden.[20] He married Hester Chamberlain in 1668; in later life, some time after his daughter Margaret's marriage, he became Treasurer of the Honourable Society of Gray's Inn and for two years held office as Dean of the Chapel.[21]

Lesley Murdin has suggested that when Margaret married the 46-year-old John Flamsteed, on 23 October 1692, she herself had reached forty,[22] but there is no room for doubt that Margaret (sometimes called Peg or Peggy) was the daughter of the younger Ralph Cooke and Hester Chamberlain. No certain record of her birth or baptism has yet been located, though the *International Genealogical Index* entry for a Margaret Cooke born in 1670 at Hackney appears plausible.[23] This would make her about twenty-two at the time of her marriage, and certainly no more than twenty-three. The disparity between Margaret's age and her husband's appears extreme, but could be taken simply to reflect an extreme case of a not uncommon situation: an analysis of ages on marriage among London's flourishing middle class has indicated that men in this group tended to marry later than their counterparts in other sections of the population, but often married wives who were comparatively young.[24] That is, they waited until their business or other sources of income appeared to be securely established, and could then undertake to support a young wife as readily as an older one. Flamsteed's official salary of £100 a year, haphazardly paid and depleted by the costs of running the Royal Observatory, was clearly insufficient for the support of a family and could only appear totally inadequate to the relatives of a prospective bride in the appropriate social class. Improvements in his circumstances came with his acquisition of the Burstow living in 1684, and after the death of his father in March 1688. The first call upon his inheritance was to pay for the mural arc, which he had failed to persuade the Ordnance Office to fund; this was built during 1688–9. Then, at last, he felt able to contemplate matrimony.

Murdin also cites the comment by Joseph Crosthwaite (in a letter to Abraham Sharp) that Flamsteed's will had given his widow, among other sums, 'about £50 per annum, which came by her', and concludes that she had not been much of a catch financially.[25] Although Crosthwaite's statement is technically correct, the will itself is more revealing. After leaving Margaret 'her Jewells and the Silver Plate with all the Households Goods and Linnen . . . her Lottery Ticketts and all the Annuall Product of them', it concludes:

> I give to her my said beloved Wife Margaret the Dividend or Interest arising from One thousand Pound Stock which I bought in the South Sea Company, for and during her Life As also an Annuity of Fifty Pounds a year on the 3700 Pounds a Weeke Haereditary Excise for and during her Life, And I do give her these Legacys in lieu of the Eleven hundred Pounds which was setled upon her by Marriage articles, and was in the hands of her uncle Mr Charles Chamberlin till the time of his decease, and then paid into mine.[26]

Margaret must therefore be regarded as reasonably well provided for, and she could also lay claim to some respectable family connections. It was for her uncle Charles Chamberlain that she transcribed Flamsteed's long letter on the causes of earthquakes in May 1693: 'the first peice she has done of this kind' according to Flamsteed's covering letter (and consequently the first that enables her hand to be securely identified).[27] The address of the recipient is given as 'Merchant at his house in Leaden hall street London'; he was briefly a City alderman, later a director of the newly founded Bank of England (in 1697–8 and 1703–5) and is also said to have been 'a staunch Whig'.[28] That he was a recipient of the earthquake theory may indicate that he took a particular interest in natural philosophical questions, or it may simply reflect the timing of the letters from the Reverend Andrew Glen at Turin that initially prompted Flamsteed to write on the subject. As a draft of Flamsteed's belated reply to Glen explains: 'I receaved your first in Surry where I was waiteing on a person I have since taken to my Wife your second came to hand as I married your third when I was makeing merry with my New relations doe not Censure me till you happen your selfe to be under the same happy Circumstances'.[29]

Although none of the surviving manuscript material in her hand can be shown to pre-date their marriage, she was clearly a well-educated young woman, literate and to some extent numerate, with the potential for taking an intelligent interest in her husband's pursuits and providing him with some practical assistance. Indeed, anyone lacking these characteristics might have been briefly attracted by a romantic idea of astronomy but is unlikely to have seriously considered accepting the unusual mode of life offered by residence at the Royal Observatory. The evidence for Margaret's study of mathematics and astronomy during the early years of her marriage is to be found in two notebooks and a batch of notes on loose sheets of paper, all preserved among her husband's papers in the archives of the Royal Greenwich Observatory (now at Cambridge University Library). The first notebook (RGO 1/67L) consists of twenty-six leaves, bound in a waste printed sheet headed 'The Beast of the Apocalypse' (now disbound for the purpose of conservation). The contents are almost wholly in her hand, with the exception of a few pages by Flamsteed's assistant Samuel Clowes, who seems to have decided to fill in some blank space after the rest was written. He dated one of his pages 27 August 1693, so it seems likely that Margaret's were written before this date, probably during the months immediately following her marriage.

The first few pages of the notebook contain standard geometrical definitions, axioms and theorems, with appropriate diagrams. Then there is a transcript of one of Flamsteed's accounts of the principles of optics, discussing the transmission, reflection and refraction of light, and the effects of various dispositions of plano-convex and double-convex lenses.[30] This is interrupted (before the examination of lenses) by two digressions or insertions, the first consisting of trigonometrical principles and theorems, the second of a single page headed 'projectile in uniforme' (supply 'motion'). This latter discusses the effect of gravitation on bodies orbiting the sun, and concludes that 'the greater disproportion their is between the Quantitie of attraction and the swiftness of the revolveing body the further from a circular motion and the more oblong and excentricall will the orbits be'. Towards the end of the notebook are further mathematical jottings on various subjects, including some in Margaret's hand on the circumferences, diameters and distances of the sun and moon.

The second notebook (RGO 1/68I, ff. 332ʳ–353ᵛ) was formerly bound with several others but has recently been restored to its original separate state. Its contents are entirely in Margaret's hand. After a page containing 'Mr Flamsteed new Table of Refractions', it launches into a detailed discussion of the geometry

page 99

$zy - xx + ax = 0$ Any Æquation given to find out the Fluxions of it, with the second Fluxions.

z, y, x in the first moment they begin to flow become oz, oy, ox in the second Moment they become $z + oz, y + oy, x + ox$

$z + oz$
$y + oy$

$x + ox$
$x + ox$

$ax + aox$

$yz + yoz + zoy + ooyz - xx + xox - xox - ooxx + ax + a$

$yz + zoy - xxox$

$yz + zy + oyz - 2xx - oxx$ / $y + oy, z + oz, x + ox$ be
/ by flowing
$yz + zy - 2xx + ax = 0$ / $y + oy; z + oz, x + ox$
the first fluxions

in order to find out the second, of the Æquation
$zy - xx + ax = 0$ haveing found out the first Fluxions
of that Æquation which is $yz + zy - 2xx + ax = 0$ proceed
according to the Æquation given
$yz + zy - 2xx + ax = 0$

$y + oy$ $y + oy$ $z + oz$
$z + oz$ $z + oz$ $y + oy$
$zy + zoy + yoz + oozy + zy + yoz + zoy + ooyz$

$2x + 2ox$
$x + ox$
$2xx + 2xox + 2xox + 2ooxx + ax + aox$

$zy + zoy + yoz + oozy + zy + yoz + zoy + ooyz - 2xx$
$- 2xox - 2xox - 2ooxx + ax + aox$ then subtractin
the given æquation there remains
$2oy + yoz + oozy + yoz + zoy + ooyz - 2xox - 2xox -$
$- 2ooxx + aox$ then dividing by o it is
$zy + yz + ozy + yz + zy + oyz - 2xx - 2xx + 2oxx$
$+ ax$ the making the little quantity o to vanish
$zy + yz + yz + zy - 2xx - 2xx + ax = 0$
$zy + 2yz + yz - 2xx - 2xx + ax = 0$

of the ellipsis, which leads to 'Kepler's Method of Calculating his Elliptical Æquations in the Theory of the Planets'. Three problems are examined, with the aid of appropriate diagrams, including that of finding earth–sun distances through observations of Mars (reminiscent of Flamsteed's early work investigating solar parallax through successive observations of that planet). Notes of a more purely mathematical kind, worked from the end of the book, concern cubes and the extracting of cube roots, a standard account of the geometrical propositions of Euclid and, extraordinarily, several pages of work on equations using Newtonian fluxions. This last skill was perhaps imparted by James Hodgson (Flamsteed's assistant from 1695 to 1702), whom Flamsteed describes as understanding such methods and who later published a book on the subject.[31]

The loose notes (RGO 1/69E, ff. 197^r–209^r) comprise four pages on 'Staticks or the Science of the force of Motion'; several more on 'Debates in the house of Lords concerning the Church of England being in danger' (1705 or later); a page on the astronomy and other features of China (probably derived from her husband's correspondence with James Pound); a page of notes on the tides, with a diagram; and several pages of theological discussion of the Fall, Redemption, Final Judgement, sin and sacrifice, citing Locke and another author on the distinction between matter and spirit and the nature of substance. Again, all these are in Margaret's hand except for a brief note by Flamsteed in the last section.

Margaret seems to have studied the mathematics relevant to astronomy in much the same way as the more competent of Flamsteed's paid assistants did. Most of the latter seem to have arrived at the Observatory as youths and bound themselves by seven-year indentures in the manner of apprentices; Flamsteed regretted that the training he supplied generally enabled them to move on to better-paid employment almost as soon as they were 'out of their time'. His numerous paying pupils were of similar age or older; one of them, incidentally, appears to have been the renowned Mary Astell, since a 'Mad[ame]: Astell' was noted by Flamsteed as having been present for approximately six months between September 1697 and February 1698.[32] Margaret's age at the time of her marriage was roughly equivalent to that of a fully trained assistant, with the advantage that any effort invested in training her would not go so swiftly to waste. But the question that remains to be considered is whether the skills she gained qualified her to join or replace the assistants in carrying out practical tasks requiring technical skills. The immediate impression given by the manuscript evidence is that it did not: she certainly acted as an amanuensis during daylight hours, copying letters for her husband, especially in his last years when his own hand became rather shaky and when she was sometimes writer as well as copyist; but her hand does not seem to appear in his observing notes. This is not conclusive evidence of her absence from the scene, however, as by the 1690s little of substance was recorded in Flamsteed's hand either:

whoever made the observation, the paid assistant was usually available to write down the details.

A few entries, in fact, reveal her occasional presence. The earliest dates from 23 March 1693, when Flamsteed's record of solar observations made that afternoon was annotated '*solus habui cum sponsa*' ('[these] I made alone with my betrothed').[33] Then a copy of a lunar observation made on 29 August 1694 is labelled '*Hac Observatio habita fuit a Clarissima Domina M. Flamsteed*' ('This observation was made by the most renowned Mrs M. Flamsteed').[34] On 13 August 1700 an observation of Jupiter's satellites was noted down in James Hodgson's hand with the comment '*Observavit JH. Adjuvante Domina Flamstedio*' ('JH observed this with the help of Mrs Flamsteed').[35] Help of a different kind is also indicated in a set of calculations in respect of Jupiter, probably made no earlier than 1705, where '*Clarissima Domina Margareta Flamsteed*' is said to have repeated a calculation and quantified an error.[36] The phrasing of all these notes suggests that her direct practical assistance was rare enough to warrant being carefully recorded; on the other hand, their spread over a long period suggests that they were not simply the result of a single burst of enthusiasm or token gesture.

Their rarity may reflect a lingering mistrust of a woman's capacities on the part of male observers, but was probably more directly caused by the demands of household duties – ensuring that her husband, his assistants, pupils and visitors were fed and well cared for – which meant that she could not often be spared for work at night. A comparison between her situation and that of Mary Evelyn, described by Frances Harris elsewhere in this volume (pp. 198–217), is instructive. As the Evelyns lived at Sayes Court, Deptford, about a mile and a half from the Royal Observatory, until 1694, it is actually possible that the two women met, and their husbands were certainly acquainted with one another.[37] Although Mary was of an older generation than Margaret their experiences were not dissimilar, and the engagement of both in household duties must not be assumed to have distanced them too far from their husbands' other concerns.

In Mary's case, Frances Harris describes how a blending of the domestic and intellectual spheres resulted first from John Evelyn's retreat to a 'retired' way of life and later from his horticultural interests. At the Observatory, too, an overlap occurred, for one similar and one contrasting reason: on the one hand its comparatively isolated position must have produced a sense of community among its few inhabitants and intensified the Flamsteeds' involvement with the lives of resident assistants and pupils; on the other, as an institution with well-publicized public functions, conspicuously placed in a spot that was easily accessible from the metropolis by river during the summer months, it attracted a continual stream of English and overseas visitors. A few of them were fellow astronomers, whose visits brought potential benefits and were welcomed; the rest were often simply of too high a social status to be excluded. In the event of Flamsteed's absence, they might be shown round by his assistant (who would probably have expected to be recompensed by a tip); Margaret, as the lady of the house, must have taken a substantial share in this duty.

In earlier years Flamsteed, with little spare cash and reliant upon a housekeeper, made a virtue of necessity, writing to Richard Towneley in 1682: 'May I not hope to see you here . . . you shall be welcome to a Philosophers treat a great deal of discourse and little victuailes [*sic*]'. Even after Margaret's arrival he did not entirely abandon the concept, as a letter to Dr Martin Lister in 1702 demonstrates: 'please therefore to let me know when you and your Lady will visit this place and her old acquaintance you shall find me at home and a philosophicall meale to enterteine you. that is I will not trouble my selfe to provide more for you then my own dinner. and what it wants in varietys shall be made out in hearty Welcome and free discourse . . . My wife gives her humble service to Madam Lister.'[38] Margaret was evidently a friend of this second Mrs Lister (Jane Cullen, the daughter of a London milliner),[39] and one suspects that, had the invitation been accepted, the meal would not have been a particularly frugal one.

Either way, the quality of the reception offered to visitors was recognized as an important enough matter to require comment. And Flamsteed's consciousness that a failure to entertain someone in the style expected could have unfortunate repercussions must have been heightened by the events of the mid-1680s described in two of his letters to William Molyneux. Molyneux had visited London in 1685 and had come to the Observatory with Halley; Flamsteed complained, in high dudgeon, about the subsequent circulation of an

account . . . of yours and your two freinds enterteinment here. which I will not excuse tho I am rallyed for it behind my back all over the towne. by their acquaintance. I must confesse I had treated Mr Molineux at another rate in other company. but I had enterteind one of them some hundreds of times freely here. and communicated my studies to him . . . but I found when hee invited me to his Quarters so rude and abusive a reception and such tricks put upon from abroad by him that . . . I can not forbeare useing meanes to make him sensible of his Ingratitude . . . but hee can doe me no injury and I truely pity him who has but one enterteinment to accuse me for that hee receved in your company. of the many hundreds hee has had at my house whilest I never was receaved but thrice by him and each time worse then slovenly.[40]

In the next letter he elaborated further: he had been told that one

Mr Dee . . . traduced me frequently in company affirmeing that I was a *single sould fellow*.[41] and that haveing invited some freinds downe to Greenwich I had treated them with a Cold Coast[42] of lambe: . . . some time before Mr

H[43] had asked mee if I knew Mr Dee. and told me hee abused me . . . and C B. had rallyed me for your enterteinment . . . but tis a dull toole. and will onely Injure themselves who of all Men liveing have the least Cause to complaine of me. for Enterteinment . . . E H dureing his fathers life was frequently my guest my study table and lod[g]eings were free to him and hee made mighty profession of freindship then and since has forced me thence to accept a bed at his house but my enterteinment was so rude and homely that I found his professions were onely superficiall thinges and therefore have since forborne to trouble him. twas on this account I plainely told him before hee thrust him selfe upon you as a companion hither that I would make no provision for him and for this reason I wrote *you had fared better without that company*.

Flamsteed undoubtedly recognized that Margaret could help to sustain the Observatory's public role and even to secure his own future as an astronomer by ensuring that no such criticisms could be levelled in future. She was aided in this by his niece (in effect adopted daughter) Ann Heming, who lived at the Observatory from September 1694 until 1706, and probably thereafter by her own sister Sarah Cooke. That she took on the task with enthusiasm is suggested by a comment in a letter to Flamsteed from his sometime assistant John Witty, who said that he had promised Mrs Flamsteed an account of his recent life as a tutor:

you will hear her read what it contain'd in my first memoir. . . . I suppose she will think it defective upon one account because I have not inserted a catalogue of all the dishes we have had to dinner and supper all the last month: but that charge I must beg to be reliev'd of, we had at least 434 in that time, a particular account of which wou'd take up so much space in one sheet that I shou'd have little room left to say any thing else.[44]

Thus, when her husband's friends and acquaintances concluded their letters by asking him to pass on their respects to his wife (and often also to Ann or Sarah), this was not merely an empty formality; it must on many occasions have been prompted by a memory of her role as hostess.

The teasing tone of Witty's remarks is echoed elsewhere, in a manner strongly reminiscent of the 'raillery' enjoyed or endured by Mary Evelyn by courtesy of her correspondent Ralph Bohun. The chief culprit in this case was Captain Henry Stanyan, a former pupil of Flamsteed's who had taken up employment as a tutor in a family travelling in Europe and sent back long accounts of his adventures in the Alps. On one occasion at least he addressed Mrs Flamsteed directly, writing from Berne on 14 July 1706:

To divert you Madam for a moment I send you the representation of the 13:th Total Eclipse [of the sun] since our Saviours Crucifiction. / Just so all things appeared at Zurich in Switzerland. The Castle on the Left hand the Scheme that resembles an Observatory is a strong ston building cituated in the Lake to cool Sinners in and where they put us for Adultery and fornication I was formerly thinking to have made some Observations there but for fear of being Confin'd during a Lunar Revolution to Bread and Water got me away to Berne where there is not that danger and where I drinke your health and the Doctors who am Madam Your most humble Servant H: Stanyan.[45]

The rest of his letters were directed to Flamsteed, but evidently on the assumption that they would be shown or read to Margaret. Thus in September 1706,

From Berne I went in our Own Coach as far as Thun, a pretty little Fortify'd Town. . . . There I mett my Company, We eate and dranke you may be sure; and also that your health and your Ladys was not forgot: For I had with me Mathematical men and Instruments, in order to take the hights of the Mountains, and draw their pictures where of I send you a Coppy; Nothing but Mr Flamsteed was our subject for a while, til I began your Ladys health, and told them, that That very Lady I mentioned was a well wisher to the Mathematicks, and understood them perfectly well, upon which her health went round with great devotion.[46]

On 12 October 1706 he had astronomical matters to report following a recent lunar eclipse:

I . . . shewed it to some Gentlemen and ladys that were curious in my 7 foot glass. . . . The Colledge and Library are just by me and I make all as convenient as I can, that one may be at ease and drink your health during our Observations. I had one Lady with me the night of the Eclips that would have pleased Madam Flamsteed she talked of nothing but Apogeums and peregiums Arctick and Antartick pole but very learnedly and was as well pleased with the constellations of the heavens as if she had placed them her self. Pray Sir give my most humble service to your good Lady and all our friends.[47]

Whatever Margaret thought of Stanyan's jovial jibes (and his possibly not unrelated habit of drinking healths at every opportunity), they now perform a useful service by corroborating the evidence of the observing books, making it clear that she continued at least to profess an interest in mathematical and astronomical studies over many years. If she did so despite the risks of being teased and patronized by the likes of Stanyan, it is probably safe to conclude that her commitment was genuine.

There is also evidence in Flamsteed's letters that she had some curiosity about an aspect of natural philosophy outside the sphere of astronomy. In December 1703 Stephen Gray reported: 'I have made some trial to grinde Microscopical Glasses in the Tooles you gave me they Performe very well and soe soon as I have an Opertunity I will send Madam Flamsteed some of them.'[48] If his attempts were successful, matters apparently went no further; five years later the completion of the project was entrusted to the young astronomer William Derham. On 9 September 1708 he wrote:

> I here send your Lady some of her Glasses set, in return of the favour of the Glasses she presented me with. I have set them as near as I could guess to fit her microscope, which if I had had by me, I might have better fitted. She should have rec[eive]d more, but I have sent her one of every sort she gave me, the plano-convexes, or double convexes being all ground upon only 2 or 3 Tools. I take them to be little, if at all inferiour to Wilsons; and if your Ladies Frame be commodious, you will find them perform very well. If she would have any more set, I shall be glad to be employed in her service. . . .[49]

Sadly, there seems to be no record of how the finished instrument was employed; its existence does, however, suggest that Margaret did not altogether share Mary Evelyn's view (admittedly expressed as a retort in the face of provocation) that the experiments of the 'Greshamites' were entirely 'unuseful and trifling' in comparison with duties within the family.

In another respect, too, Margaret's experience clearly diverged from Mary Evelyn's: when she committed herself to a task more obviously socially useful than astronomy or natural philosophy, it took her outside the walls of the Observatory. In 1700 she was one of the founders of Greenwich Girls' Charity School, a day-school designed to teach poor girls to read and say their catechism as well as to spin, knit, sew and other practical skills appropriate to their expected future as servants. It was run by an all-female committee, with the support of subscribers and the additional help of collections organized by the vicar of Greenwich, Dr Turner (for whom Flamsteed had once written a testimonial as a schoolmaster). Mrs Flamsteed was a subscriber from the start, and officially served as its treasurer from 1704 to 1718; she also acted as an auditor. These and other details were extracted by the nineteenth-century Astronomer Royal George Airy from a laudatory printed account of 1724, which noted that the institution's perfectly kept accounts were in Mrs Flamsteed's hand from the start. This was presumably because her colleagues felt she was the most reliably numerate among them.[50]

This experience perhaps helped prepare Margaret to deal confidently with the problems that eventually faced her as a widow. Flamsteed's will made her and his niece Ann Hodgson joint executrixes of his estate; he said he intended to supply a separate schedule making a disposition of his instruments, books and papers but no such document was ever found, with the result that custody of them remained with the executrixes. It was not unusual for women to be entrusted with legal and practical responsibilities of this nature: in the upper echelons of society widows could expect a sufficient financial provision at least to ensure their independence, while at a lower level their counterparts were allowed by the custom of the City and of guilds elsewhere to carry on their deceased husbands' businesses. In the book trade, at least, they often did so energetically and effectively, as recent studies by Maureen Bell have revealed.[51] Margaret was less fortunate in a number of respects: once the appointment of her husband's successor had been announced she had no option but to leave the Observatory, and then to meet a legal challenge from the Ordnance Office over the ownership of her husband's instruments.

Even while this battle was in progress, moves were underway towards completing Flamsteed's definitive edition of his star catalogue and observations in the three-volume *Historia Coelestis Britannica* (to supersede Halley's supposedly defective edition of 1712). When it finally appeared, in 1725, the signatories to the dedication were Mrs Flamsteed and James Hodgson; an extensive correspondence between Joseph Crosthwaite and Abraham Sharp (two former Observatory assistants who both helped with the work) reveals that Hodgson played only a minor supporting role. At an early stage, too, Crosthwaite reported that 'Mrs Flamsteed is resolved to have all the maps of the constellations of the zodiac engraved and drawn according to Mr Flamsteed's design' and that 'Sir James Thornhill and Mr Vandergucht, jun. dined with Mrs Flamsteed about a fortnight ago; at which time he promised to see all the maps well done'. This proved a slow and expensive business, but the *Atlas Coelestis* was finished in 1729, the year before Margaret's own death.[52] Crosthwaite then complained bitterly about the lack of a legacy to recompense him for his work, but some reason for this (if not a complete excuse) may be found in Mrs Flamsteed's own financial situation. Since the bulk of the money left her by Flamsteed had been invested in South Sea stock and he had died only a few months before the bursting of the South Sea Bubble, the chances are that she was less well off than she might have been and struggled to meet the unavoidable costs of the publishing venture. It is also possible that she was so absorbed by the task of vindicating and promoting her late husband's work that she simply failed to grasp that others might not be motivated by an equivalent degree of devotion.

Simply to achieve publication was not her only aim – she accompanied it with an energetic campaign against Halley's 1712 edition. She addressed a petition to the Lords Commissioners of the Treasury asking for custody of thirty-nine copies said to remain in their hands, on the grounds 'That the said Mrs Flamstead has . . . been at a very great expence in printing of 340 Copies of another part to perfect the aforementioned Book, without which the Petitioner is humbly of opinion it ought not to go abroad as a performance of her deceased husband's'; this was agreed provided that she first delivered the same number of copies of the corrected edition.[53] At a later date she tackled Dr Mather, Vice-Chancellor of Oxford, who had acknowledged receipt of a set of the 1725 volumes presented to the Bodleian, on the subject of a copy of Halley's edition which was said to remain there:

> I most humbly entreat You will please to order that single volume to be removed out of Your Public Library, the greatest part of which is nothing more than an Erronus Abrigment of Mr Flamsteed's Works. . . .
>   I beg Your pardon Reverend Sir, for giving You this trouble, and I persuade my self You will easily excuse me, when You consider that I am under an obligation not only to doe justice to the Memory of Mr Flamsteed, but alsoe to prevent the Worlds being imposed upon by a false Impression. / Reverend Sir / Your most Humble servant / Margaret Flamsteed.

In this instance she was less successful, although her protest was not altogether ignored: the letter survives because it was placed inside the front cover of the 1712 volume – which remained in public view on the shelf.[54]

The letter to Mather is neatly written in Margaret's own hand; its overall tone might be characterized as respectful but self-assured. It was probably copied from a preliminary draft, but there is no reason to doubt that it was her own composition. A hint of a similar self-assurance was displayed very soon after her marriage, when she transcribed Flamsteed's earthquake theory and boldly intervened in how it was conveyed to the public: he noted that 'the last paragraph she would needs omit as not Materiall tho I thought it most because I have covenanted in it not to suffer any copy of it to be conveyed to the presse. for I foresee it would draw a troublesome tribe of objectors upon me', and despite his protest it remained omitted.[55] Her confidence in her own judgement in such matters may have been encouraged by a knowledge that other contemporary English women were active participants in the book trade and increasingly in independent authorship, though Sarah Jinner, 'Student in Astrology', whose *Almanack or prognostication* appeared from the late 1650s, seems to have been the only one of them to venture anywhere near the field of astronomy.[56]

For a precise model for her own later activities it was necessary to look to Danzig, where Johannes Hevelius's second wife, Elizabeth, ensured that some of his most important works (*Uranographia*, 1687/90, and *Prodromus Astronomiae*, 1690) were published despite his death. It would not have been difficult for Margaret to identify with Elizabeth, who played a considerable part in the running of Hevelius's observatory, acted as hostess to visiting astronomers, and assisted in the making of observations; this last was illustrated in some of the engravings of *Machina coelestis pars prior* (1673), which Margaret must have seen among her

Portrait of Johannes and Elizabeth Hevelius observing with a sextant, from *Machina Coelestis pars prior* (Gdansk, 1673).

husband's books.[57] While following Elizabeth's example in printing and promoting Flamsteed's work after his death, she must have drawn confidence from the knowledge that this was one of the few ways in which a woman could engage in publishing and bring her own name before the learned world with virtually no risk of censure. By the end of the eighteenth century, the opportunities for certain women to appear in print were much greater, and Caroline Herschel's discoveries of comets and nebulae appeared in the *Philosophical Transactions*.

CAROLINE HERSCHEL (1750–1848)

Although Caroline Herschel was a sister and not a wife to the nominal head of her household, and her career derives from a later period than the other women in this chapter, her example is instructive since her role combined the duties both of a guild apprentice and of housekeeper. Indeed, this was exactly how Caroline presented herself. The most famous woman to have practised astronomy in Britain, she has received surprisingly cursory attention from recent historians. However, interest shown in her achievements by later members of her family means that a substantial amount of primary material relating to her career has been in the public domain for over a century. Detailed information exists about her astronomical schooling and although her earlier education was not as intensive as that of her older brothers, her father at least introduced her to a basic awareness of the heavenly bodies. A musician in the Hanoverian army, he was interested in astronomy and indeed all the sciences, and Caroline later recalled listening as a girl to discussions between her father and her brothers about the relative merits of Newton, Euler and Leibniz. Isaac Herschel, father to Caroline and William, spent a great deal of time teaching the latter natural philosophy and Caroline noted in a reminiscence: 'I remember his taking me on a clear frosty night into the street, to make me acquainted with several of the beautiful constellations, after we had been gazing at a comet which was then visible.'[58]

Not long after the outbreak of the Seven Years' War (1756–63), the French occupied Hanover and Caroline was forced to knit stockings for her brothers and to write letters on behalf of women to their soldier husbands who were held in a prisoner of war camp. Among these women, apparently, was her illiterate mother, who prevented Caroline from extending her intellectual interests beyond dressmaking when Isaac Herschel died in 1767. In 1772, however, Caroline's brothers Alexander and William, by then accomplished musicians in Bath, succeeded in persuading her to come to Britain by promising their mother to provide sufficient income to keep a servant in Caroline's stead. William discussed the constellations with her even as they travelled through Holland to reach England, and when she arrived at Bath he took her for English and arithmetic lessons during their 7 o'clock breakfasts: 'The remainder of the forenoon was chiefly spent at the harpsichord; shewing me the way how to practise singing with a gag in my mouth.' The mathematical lessons, called 'Little Lessons for Lina', went from basic geometry up to spherical trigonometry although at that point Caroline called a halt, saying that there was no point going any further.[59]

In April and May 1773 William increasingly concerned himself with optics and astronomy, and he pursued his interest in the latter by using his manual dexterity to help construct glasses and mirrors for telescopes. William's skill and labour in constructing such instruments was remarkable, but so was Caroline's devotion to the same enterprise. With her usual modest and self-deprecating irony, she recorded that in 1773 she was dismayed to see 'almost every room turned into a workshop' when her brother's music pupils vacated their premises:

A cabinet maker making a tube and stands of all descriptions in a handsome furnished drawing room. Alex putting up a huge turning machine (which in the Autumn he brought with him from Bristol) in a bedroom for turning patterns, grinding glasses and turning eye-pieces &c. . . . I had to amuse myself with making the tube of pasteboard for the glasses arrived from London, for at that time no optician had settled at Bath . . .

For the year 1775 she recorded that 'every leisure moment was eagerly snatched at for resuming some work which was in progress, without taking time for changing dress, and many a lace ruffle (which were then worn) was torn or bespattered by molten pitch, &c'. Caroline began to take up her whole time either copying music and practising her singing, or helping her brother to polish mirrors for his telescopes,

since by way of keeping him alive I was constantly obliged to feed him by putting the victuals into his mouth. This was once the case when, in order to finish a seven foot mirror, he had not taken his hands from it for sixteen hours together. . . . Generally I was obliged to read to him whilst he was at the turning lathe, or polishing mirrors, Don Quixote, Arabian Nights' Entertainment, the novels of Sterne, Fielding, &c; serving tea and supper without interrupting the work with which he was engaged . . . and sometimes lending a hand. I became in time as useful a member of the workshop as a boy might be to his master in the first year of his apprenticeship.[60]

In 1779 the Herschels moved to a residence not far from the fashionable Bath Literary and Philosophical Society and at the end of the year William was invited to join it by Sir William Watson. By now Herschel was already known to many of the astronomers of the day, and in the next few years he and Caroline – whose musical reputation had also already been established – turned their attention full-time to astronomy. This was helped by the discovery of Uranus (then called the Georgium Sidus in honour of the reigning monarch) in the middle of March 1781, a momentous event which earned William membership of the Royal Society and a royal salary of £200 per annum. Still he searched for more perfect and more powerful telescopes with which to scour the heavens for comets, stars and nebulae, and Caroline became his most valuable assistant. Their brother Alexander was also involved in these enquiries but according to his sister

> he wanted perseverance, and never liked to confine himself at home for many hours together. And so it happened that my brother William was obliged to make trial of my abilities in copying for him catalogues, tables, &c., and sometimes whole papers which were lent him for his perusal. . . . When I found that a hand was sometimes wanted when any particular measures were to be made with the lamp micrometer, &c., or a fire to be kept up, or a dish of coffee necessary during a long night's watching, I undertook with pleasure what others might have thought a hardship.

In 1781 Sir William Watson and the Herschels all pitched in to grind up dried horse dung to act as a mould for casting a 3 to 4-ft mirror in order to build a giant reflecting telescope. On this occasion, as with many others noted in her journals, the metal cracked.[61]

In the summer of 1782 the family moved to a large house in Datchet (near Windsor Castle) where telescopes could be erected more easily. While William returned periodically to Bath to arrange for equipment and materials to be delivered to their new address, or showed the king stars through a telescope set up at Windsor Castle, Caroline suddenly found herself with the opportunity to make her own observations:

> In my brother's absence from home, I was of course left solely to amuse myself with my own thoughts, which were anything but cheerful. I found I was to be trained for an assistant-astronomer, and by way of encouragement a telescope adapted for 'sweeping', consisting of a tube with two glasses, such as are commonly used in a 'finder', was given me. I was 'to sweep for comets', and I see by my journal that I began August 22nd 1782, to write down and describe all remarkable appearances I saw in my 'sweeps', which were horizontal. But it was not till the last two months of the same year that I felt the least encouragement to spend the star-light nights on a grass-plot covered with dew or hoar frost . . . I knew too little of the real heavens to be able to point at every object so as to find it again without losing too much time by consulting the Atlas.

Although she recorded that she gained satisfaction simply by helping her brother 'when he wanted another person, either to run to the clocks, write down a memorandum, fetch and carry instruments, or measure the ground with poles', she soon discovered nebulae which her brother had not seen or which were completely unknown to astronomy. In 1783 she turned to remeasuring double stars which had recently been catalogued by William, but by July she was again searching for comets, this time with the 'Newtonian small sweeper' with which William had presented her in recognition of her discoveries. However, although she found more nebulae in the autumn of 1783, her time was increasingly taken up assisting her brother's search for nebulae with his powerful 20-ft reflector, which he began using in October. In addition to this she noted: 'In my leisure hours I ground seven-foot and plain mirrors from rough to fining down, and was indulged with polishing and the last finishing of a very beautiful mirror for Sir William Watson.'[62]

In 1786 the Herschels moved (for the last time) to a residence in Slough. At this point, William had used up his savings but was granted £2,000 in order to proceed to the construction of his great 40-ft telescope (later supplemented by another grant of the same sum). At various points, there were forty workmen labouring at the same time to construct the foundations and structure of this instrument and their house became 'a complete workshop for making optical instruments'. In July 1786 William travelled to Göttingen to present the university with a 10-ft telescope which he had constructed himself, and Caroline was left to her own devices, cleaning the brass parts of the telescopes in the house and putting their recent correspondence in order. She dealt with the persistent stream of visitors lured by the prospect of viewing William's latest discoveries of new satellites orbiting Saturn and Georgium Sidus through his own telescope, calculated the positions of various nebulae and continued to 'sweep' the heavens for comets. In her journal for 1 and 2 August of that year she reported the initial sighting and then corroboration of the discovery of a new comet, an achievement which was published in the *Philosophical Transactions*. She was named Assistant Astronomer to the King and additionally was granted a salary of £50 per year in recognition of her work. In October 1787 she received £12 10s. as the first quarter of her payment and noted that this was the first money she had ever had in her life which she could spend freely on herself.[63]

When William married in 1788 he decided to take periodic holidays, a move which allowed Caroline to remain in charge of the house and instruments. She discovered a second comet in December 1788 and two more in early 1790, going on to find her eighth and final comet in August 1797. In addition to this work she continued as an amanuensis to William, and catalogued new nebulae as well as producing an index to Flamsteed's catalogue of stars (from the third volume of the 1725 *Historia Coelestis*). While the Herschels practised astronomy, brother and sister were usually mentioned in the same breath by correspondents such as Harry Englefield, Alexander Aubert, William Watson and the Astronomer Royal, Nevil Maskelyne. Remarkably, Caroline's work elicited none of the condescension experienced by women in the previous century. In 1793 Maskelyne visited her and saw her using a new and more powerful 5-ft sweeper built by her for William in 1791. Maskelyne described the instrument and its user as follows:

> The height of the eye-glass is altered but little in sweeping from the horizon to the zenith. This she does and down again in 6 or 8 minutes, & then moves the telescope a little forward in azimuth, & sweeps another portion of the heavens in like manner. She will thus sweep a quarter of the heavens in one night. The D^r has given her written instructions how to proceed, and she knows all the nebulae in the *Connoissance* [as listed by Messier] at sight, which he esteems necessary to distinguish new Comets that may appear from them. Thus you see, that wherever she sweeps in fine weather nothing can escape her.[64]

The astronomical community had genuine respect for Caroline Herschel's accomplishments, and she was honoured with awards in the early nineteenth century. Nevertheless, despite the work that she undertook on her own initiative, she never presented herself as more than an assistant to William's researches. She took pride in the fact that she looked after the household economy of the Herschel residence, and it was she who had to worry about the absurd price of food when they moved to Datchet in the aftermath of the discovery of Uranus. Indeed, she explicitly referred to her position as the 'housekeeper' in one of the very few references to William's marriage which survived her destruction of the journals containing passages relevant to this event. Although the Herschels became a renowned astronomical duo, Caroline arguably saw her role in their work as part of her household duties. Not even marriage could break this relationship, and Caroline remained close to her brother until he died in 1822. Later she recalled that she did nothing for her brother 'but what a well-trained puppy-dog would have done: that is to say, I did what he commanded me. I was a mere tool which *he* had the trouble of sharpening'. Yet the work she did was just what was required to make William's observations public, that is, to turn William's rough notes into robust and reliable knowledge. On the Royal Astronomical Society's presentation of a Gold Medal to her in 1828, James South, while mentioning her own achievements, remarked that 'she it was who arranged everything in a systematic order; and she it was who helped him to obtain an imperishable name'.[65]

The careers of Margaret Flamsteed and Caroline Herschel reveal the extent to which women were able and willing to participate in the scientific scene of the late seventeenth and eighteenth centuries, and point to the conditions under which they did so. There are strong resemblances between the two stories. Although Caroline Herschel's reputation stands far higher than Margaret Flamsteed's, they performed similar housekeeping roles in a conventional domestic situation as well as meeting the extraordinary demands placed upon them by the astronomical household. Each was fairly well educated by contemporary standards, although they both received additional training in mathematics and practical astronomy from male relations. In return they assisted in, encouraged and promoted the work of these men.

On the other hand, the differences are also revealing. Caroline Herschel was able to engage in the business of astronomy to a much greater extent than her predecessor, and she benefited greatly from the model of astronomical assistant bequeathed by the role of the craft apprentice. She participated in the actual construction of telescopes and progressed from that to become a highly skilled independent user of different varieties of the instrument. The constructional skill chiefly required in the seventeenth century for the production of angle-measuring devices was that of fine engraving, but there is no evidence that Margaret Flamsteed ever acquired this facility. Moreover, the major astronomical instruments of the seventeenth century generally required collaboration by at least two people for their effective use; by the late eighteenth century the changing nature of astronomy and the increasing power of telescopes meant that one person acting alone could make discoveries of significance. Finally, it should be noted that while Margaret Flamsteed's name appeared in print only in relation to her husband's work, Caroline Herschel was able to publish her own work in the *Philosophical Transactions*. Even then, however, such a publication was mediated by the male recipients of her letters, who facilitated her appearance on the page by communicating the information to the relevant body or journal.

Notes

1 Wright (1693), Act 3, p. 25.

2 Susannah Centlivre, *The Basset-Table* (1705), cited in Reynolds (1920), p. 391.

3 Terrall (1995), p. 283; Cavendish, 'Youth's Glory and Death's Banquet', in Cavendish (1662), I, i, 62, cited in Gagen (1954), p. 34.

4 Schiebinger (1989), pp. 23–35, esp. pp. 23 and 32; Terrall (1995), p. 285 (for the decreasing 'feminocentrism' of the salons by the 1730s); Goodman (1989); Schiebinger (1987), pp. 186–92 (for the contemporary claim that Kirch talked too much when visitors came to the Academy's observatory). For the salons' interest in Cartesianism after 1640 see Harth (1992), and for salons in general see Lougee (1976) and Goodman (1989). For criticism of a crude 'separate spheres' thesis see Daston (1992), Vickery (1993) and Jordanova (1993).

5 For academies see Schiebinger (1989), pp. 32–6. For the general education of women in the medieval period see Ferrante (1980), King (1980) and Schiebinger (1989), pp. 1–20. For Vives and the humanist interest in educating women see Watson (1912); for Lumley, Grey and Roper see Reynolds (1920), pp. 9–11; Phillips (1990), pp. 50–2; Ascham, *The Scholemaster* (1570), Bk 1 no. 7; Gagen (1954), pp. 13–15.

6 For Conway see Hutton (1992) and Conway (1996), pp. xxxviii–xxxix. For the place of women in the home see Amussen (1988).

7 For van Schurman see Phillips (1990), pp. 21–2 and Reynolds (1920), pp. 275–6 and for Hickes, see *ibid.* pp. 291–6. Hickes's translation of Fénélon's *Traité de l'Education des Filles* appeared under the heading *Instructions for the Education of a Daughter, by the Author of Telemachus. To which is added. A Small Tract of Instructions for the Conduct of Young Ladies of the Highest Rank. With Suitable devotions Annexed* (London 1688). The translator of van Schurman's *Learned Maid*, Clement Barksdale, published a proposal for an Oxford-style college for women (Barksdale, 1675), which would teach botany and experimental philosophy.

8 Makin (1673), pp. 35, 43. See also Reynolds (1920), pp. 276–82, Teague (1992) and Phillips (1990), pp. 33–40. Maria Cunitz's astronomical work was *Urania Propitia, sive Tabulae Astronomica, mire faciles* (1650), with a German edition published in the same year.

9 Pepys (1970–83), IV, pp. 302, 343–4, 360, 363–4, 403–6; V, pp. 8 and 241 (for the microscope); see also Reynolds (1920), pp. 86–7 for Elizabeth's education in drawing skills during 1665. Henry Power's *Experimental Philosophy* was published in 1663.

10 See Schiebinger (1989), pp. 216–63, 217–8; A. de Vignoles, 'Éloge de Madame Kirch l'occasion de laquelle on parle de quelques autres Femmes et d'un Paison Astronomes', *Bibliotèque Germanique*, 3 (1721), pp. 155–83, 163; P. Le Moyne, *La Gallerie des Femmes Fortes* (Leyden 1660), pp. 288–9, cited in Daston (1992), p. 227. See also Daston (1992), pp. 218–28 (for the domestic space) and pp. 228–30 (for women as prodigies). For Bassi see Findlen (1993); for Cavendish see Mendelson (1985), pp. 12–61 and Sarasohn (1984), pp. 289–307.

11 Gunther (1939), pp. 130, 182–3.

12 *Ibid.*, pp. 184–5. Tollet moved to England in the aftermath of the Glorious Revolution in 1689 and became a Commissioner for the Navy.

13 *Ibid.*, pp. 186–7, 188.

14 Fontenelle (1686) translated as Behn (1688); Terrall (1995), p. 293 and Spencer (1986). For the learned English metropolitan female culture between 1690 and 1720 see A. Wilson (1995), pp. 186–90, who points to evidence that the percentage of London women who could sign their name in 1730 (50%) had doubled in the previous half century. For French female interest in science in the eighteenth century see J. Peiffer (1991), pp. 196–222; for the English scene in the same period see Mullan (1993).

15 See Meyer (1955), pp. 49–60 and Perl (1979).

16 See Phillips (1990), p. 20; Phillips (1981), 283–92; Gagen (1954), pp. 55–7; Meyer (1955), pp. 95–7; Mullan (1993), p. 49 and Reynolds (1920), pp. 382–4.

17 Schiebinger (1987).

18 J. Foster, *Alumni Oxonienses*, part 1, vol. 1.

19 Information kindly supplied by the librarian of Gray's Inn.

20 A notebook recording this, the contents of his library and his accounts as his father's executor survives in the papers of the Royal Greenwich Observatory, at Cambridge University Library, as RGO 1/68K. His previous addresses, both close by in the same area of London, were 'In the Lady dafnetts house in Baldwins Gardens' (1670) (probably meaning a house let by the widow of Sir William Davenant the playwright) and 'in Leather Lane' (1682), according to the baptism records for his son Ralph and daughter Sarah in the registers of St Andrew Holborn, Guildhall Library, MS 6667/3 and 6667/5.

21 J. Foster and J. L. Chester, *London Marriage Licences, 1521–1869* (London, 1887), p. 323.

22 Murdin (1985).

23 *International Genealogy Index* (1992), London A1276, p. 33, 934. A branch of the Chamberlain family was also associated with Hackney, with a Hester the daughter of Thomas Chamberlain born there in 1658: *IGI* (1992), London A1262, p. 27, 391.

24 Earle (1989), pp. 180–5.

25 For the letter, dated 30 January 1719–20, see Francis Baily, *An Account of the Revd John Flamsteed* (London, 1835), p. 333.

26 London, Public Record Office, PROB 11/572. For Peter Earle's instructive discussion of marriage portions and jointures see Earle (1989), pp. 194–8.

27 See Flamsteed (1997), vol. 2, Letter 650.

28 Alfred B. Beaven, *The Aldermen of the City of London*, 2 vols (London, 1908, 1913); vol. 1, p. 177; vol. 2, pp. lvii, 115, 194.

29 27 Mar. 1693: RGO 1/36, ff. 64r–65r; reproduced in Flamsteed (1997), vol. 2, as Letter 647.

30 The original of this, written in 1691, is at RGO 1/44, ff. 21v–44r.

31 For Hodgson see the forthcoming article in the *DNB* by Frances Willmoth.

32 RGO 1/15, f.165r–166v. For Astell see Kinnaird (1979), pp. 53–75; Perry (1986). The identification of the person concerned as Mary Astell is plausible though not certain; it is also possible that the date of 14 February 1698, at which it is recorded 'she went hence', is Old Style, indicating the year 1698/9, in which case she actually remained with the Flamsteeds for a year and a half. However, none of this is corroborated by independent evidence.

33 RGO 1/15, f. 133r.

34 RGO 1/60, f. 84v; a heavily deleted note about the same observations occurs at f. 266r.

35 RGO 1/7, f. 86r.

36 RGO 1/58, f. 26r.

37 For instance, John Evelyn noted that on 1 August 1683: 'Came to see me Mr. Flamested the famous Astrologer from his Observatorie at Greenewich': Evelyn (1959) vol. 4, p. 333.

38 Flamsteed to Towneley and to Lister, 28 October and 11 July 1702: Flamsteed (1995, 1997), vol.1, p. 834 and 2, Letter 867. For a good account of the significance of food for the philosophical presentation of self see S. Shapin, 'The Philosopher's Chicken', introduction to Lawrence and Shapin (1997).

39 Dr Martin Lister's second wife was Jane Cullen of the parish of St Mildred's, Poultry (London), whom he married at St Stephen's Walbrook (London) in 1698: Geoffrey Keynes, *Dr Martin Lister, a Bibliography* (Godalming, 1981), p. 4; *IGI* (1992) A1286, p. 38,343. The tax list reproduced in D.V. Glass (ed.), *London Inhabitants within the Walls, 1695* (London Record Society, 2; Leicester, 1966), p. 78, indicates that she was the daughter of Abraham Cullen, a well-to-do milliner.

40 Letter of 4 November 1686, Letter 570 in Flamsteed (1995, 1997), vol.2.

41 Single-soled: 'of persons: poor, mean, of little account or worth' (*OED*), apparently deriving from the idea of soling one's shoes with a single layer of leather. *OED* lists no examples after 1640.

42 Coast: 'the side of the body . . . ; the part fortified by the ribs', 'the side of an animal, for cooking' (*OED*).

43 Edmond Halley; the first accounts of Flamsteed's complaints against him appear in Letters 569 and 570, both of 4 November 1686.

44 RGO 1/37, f. 145r,v, written on 5 September 1706.

45 *Ibid.*, f. 114r. The printed illustration he sent survives at RGO 1/69D, f. 256r.

46 *Ibid.*, ff. 118r–119v.

47 *Ibid.*, ff. 120r–121v.

48 *Ibid.*, ff. 9r–10r; letter of 26 December 1703.

49 RGO 1/36, f. 146r,v.

50 Airy's account survives at RGO 6/494, section 1 (his 'Correspondence with the Trustees of the Blue Coats Girls School' occupying this volume and 6/495). It was printed in 1867 in conjunction with an appeal for funds.

51 For women printers in seventeenth-century England see the studies by Bell (1988, 1989, 1992 and 1994).

52 Letters reproduced in Baily, *Account*, pp. 335, 343.

53 Published in *The Reliquary* 1 (1860–1), pp. 51–2.

54 Bodleian Library, Arch. A.b.1.

55 Flamsteed (1995, 1997), vol. 2, Letter 650.

56 Capp (1979).

57 *DSB* (Johannes Hevelius).

58 Schiebinger (1989), p. 260; Herschel (1876), pp. 7–8; Lubbock (1933), pp. 5–7; Ogilvie (1975), pp. 149–61, 150–1; Hoskin and Warner (1981), pp. 27–34.

59 Lubbock (1933), pp. 9–11, 47–50, 57; Ogilvie (1975), pp. 151–3.

60 Herschel (1876), pp. 35–8.

61 Lubbock (1933), pp. 72–5, 87–90; Herschel (1876), pp. 39–45. William believed that there was life on the moon.

62 Hoskin and Warner (1981), pp. 27–8; Ogilvie (1975), pp. 153–4; Herschel (1876), pp. 52–4 and 56; Lubbock (1933), pp. 133–39 and 150–2. The atlas was Flamsteed's *Atlas Coelestis*.

63 Lubbock (1933), pp. 143–5, 152–3 and 171–2; Herschel (1876), pp. 56–61 and 64–5; Ogilvie (1976), pp. 154–5; C. Herschel (1787), pp. 1–5.

64 Hoskin and Warner (1981), pp. 29–31; Ogilvie (1975), pp. 155–6. Charles Messier was a French astronomer renowned for his tables of nebulae (and from whose name they now get their 'M' prefix) and for his ability to find or 'ferret' out comets from the night sky.

65 Lubbock (1933), p. 173; Ogilvie (1975), p. 150 (for the South citation).

BIBLIOGRAPHY

PRIMARY SOURCES

Agrippa, Henry Cornelius (1569). *Of the Vanietie of the Artes and Sciences*, tr. J. Sanford. London.

——(1670). *Female Pre-eminence*. London. Reprinted in Bornstein (1980).

Alexis of Piemont (1562). *The Secrets of the Reuerend Maister Alexis of Piemont*, tr. W. Warde. London: Rouland Hall.

Annals of the Royal College of Physicians (1518–1710), vols 1–7. London: transcript/typescript (1953–7).

Astell, M. (1694, 3rd edn 1696). *A Serious Proposal to the Ladies, for the Advancement of their True and Greatest Interest. By a Lover of her Sex*. London: R. Wilkin.

Athenian Mercury, The (1690–7).

Aubrey, J. (1898). *Brief Lives*, ed. A. Clark. Oxford: Clarendon Press.

—— (1949). *Aubrey's Brief Lives*, ed. Oliver Lawson Dick. London: Secker & Warburg.

—— (1969). *Aubrey's Natural History of Wiltshire (1685)*. New York: Augustus M. Kelley.

—— (1982). *Brief Lives*, ed. Richard Barber. Woodbridge: Boydell Press.

Bacon, Francis (1854). *The Works*. London: H.G. Bohn.

—— (1884). *The Moral and Historical Works of Lord Bacon*. London.

—— (1974). *The Advancement of Learning and New Atlantis*. ed. A. Johnston. Oxford: Clarendon Press.

Baker, G. (1599). *The Practise of the New and Old Phyisicke*. London: by Peter Shore.

Banister, Richard (1621). *An Appendant Part of a Treatise of One Hundreth and Thirteene Diseases of the Eyes and Eyelids*. London: by William Jones.

Barksdale, C. (1675). *A Letter Touching a Colledge of Maids; or a Virgin Society*. London.

Batman, Stephen (1577). *The Golden Booke of the Leaden Gods*. London.

Baxter, Nathaniel (1606). *Sir Philip Sydneys Ourania, that is, Endimions Song and Tragedie, Containing all Philosophie*. London: Edward White.

Behn, Aphra (tr.) (1688). *The Theory or System of Several New Inhabited Worlds Lately Discover'd and Pleasantly Describ'd in Five Nights Conversation*. London.

Beier, A.L. (1985). *Masterless Men: The Vagrancy Problem in England 1560–1640*. London: Methuen.

Bèze, Theodore de (1581). *The Psalmes of David, truly opened and explained by paraphrasis, according to the right sense of everie Psalme*, tr. Anthony Gilby. London: H. Denham.

The Bible and Holy Scriptures. Geneva, 1560 (1969) facsimile. Madison: University of Wisconsin Press.

Boke of keruynge, The (1508) The English Experience 298. Amsterdam and New York: Theatrvm Orbis Terrarvm Ltd. 1971.

Book of Cookery (1500). London: R. Pynson.

[A Book of Engraved Lace Patterns] (1605). *STC* 15116.

Booke of Curious and Strange Inuentions, called the first part of Needleworkes (1596). London: William Barley.

Boorde, Andrew (1542). *A Compendious Regyment or a Dyetary of Helth*. London: Robert Wyer.

Boyle, Robert (1655). *An Invitation to a Free and Generous Communication of Secrets and Receipts in Physick*, in Hartlib (1655).

—— (1663). *Some Considerations touching the Usefulnesse of Experimental Naturall Philosophy*. Oxford: by Henry Hall for Richard Davis.

—— (1692). *Medicinal Experiments or a Collection of Choice Remedies for the most part Simple and Easily Prepared*. London: for Sam Smith.

—— (1744). *The Works of the Honourable Robert Boyle*, ed. T. Birch. 5 vols, London. London: T. Birch.

—— (1991). *The Early Essays and Ethics of Robert Boyle*, ed. J. Horwood. Carbondale: Southern Illinois University Press.

Breton, Nicholas (1879, rep. 1966). *The Works in Verse and Prose of Nicholas Breton*, ed. Alexander Grosart. New York: AMS Press.

Browne, Thomas (1977). *Sir Thomas Browne: The Major Works* , ed. C.A. Patrides. New York: Penguin.

Bullein, William (1562). *Bulwark of Defence against all Sickness*. London.

Buttes, Henry (1599). *Dyets Dry Dinner*. London: for William Wood.

Calvin, John (1571). *The Psalms of David and Others. With M. John Calvins Commentaries*, tr. Arthur Golding. London: H. Middleton.

Cartari, Vincenzo (1580). *Gli imagini degli dii degli antichi*. Venice.

Cavendish, Margaret (1655a), *Philosophical and Physical Opinions*. London: J. Martin and J. Allestrye.

—— (1655b). *The World's Olio*. London: J. Allestrye.

—— (1662). *Playes*. London: A. Warren for J. Martyn, J. Allestrye and T. Dicas.

—— (1663). *Philosophical and Physical Opinions*, 2nd edn. London: William Wilson.

—— (1664). *Philosophical Letters*. London: William Wilson.

—— (1666a). *Observations upon Experimental Philosophy*. London: A. Maxwell.

—— (1666b). *The Description of a New World, Called the Blazing World*. London: A. Maxwell.

—— (1667). *The Life of the Thrice Noble, High and Puissant Prince William Cavendish, Duke, Marquess and Earl of Newcastle*. London: A. Maxwell.

—— (1676). *Letters and Poems in Honour of the Incomparable Princess, Margaret Duchess of Newcastle*. London.

—— (1668a). *Grounds of Natural Philosophy*. London

—— (1668b). *Observations upon Experimental philosophy: to which is added the description of a new blazing world*. London: by A. Maxwell.

—— (1872). *The Lives of Wm Cavendishe, Duke of Newcastle, and of His Wife, Margaret Duchess of Newcastle*, ed. Mark A. Lower. London: John Russell Smith.

Celleor, Elizabeth, *see* Cellier, Elizabeth.

Cellier, E. (1687). *A Scheme for the Foundation of a Royal Hospital . . . for the Maintenance of a Corporation of Skillful Midwives and such Foundlings, or, Exposed Children as shall be Admitted therein*. London.

—— (1688) *A Letter to Dr. —— An Answer to his Queries, concerning the Colledg of Midwives; Together with the Scheme for a Cradle Hospital, for Exposed Children*. [London].

Chamberlain, John (1979). *The Letters of John Chamberlain*, ed. Norman Egbert McClure. Westport, CT: Greenwood Press. First published 1939.

Charleton, Walter (1652). *The Darknes of Atheism Dispelled by the Light of Nature, a Physico-Theological Treatise*. London.

—— 1654. *Physiologia Epicuro- Gassendo- Charltoniana.* London.

——.1657. *The Immortality of the Human Soul.* London. Facsimilie edition, with introduction by J. M. Armistead. New York, NY: AMS Press, 1985.

Cicero (1956). *De Natura Deorum,* tr. H. Rackham. Cambridge, MA: Harvard University Press.

Clarendon, *see* Hyde.

Clifford, Anne (1990). *The Diaries of Lady Anne Clifford,* ed. D. Clifford. Stroud: Alan Sutton.

—— (n.d.). *The Diary of Lady Anne Clifford,* ed. Vita Sackville-West. New York: George H. Doran.

A Closet for Ladies and Gentlewomen, Or, The Art of preseruing, Conseruing, and Candying (1608). London: Arthur Iohnson.

Cockayne, Sir Aston (1658). *Small Poems of Divers Sorts.* London: Wil Godbid.

Comenius, J.A. (1651). *Naturall Philosophie Reformed by Divine Light or a synopsis of Physics.*

Conway, Anne (1690). *Principia philosophiae antiquissimae et recentissimae* in *Opuscula philosophica.* Amsterdam.

—— (1996). *The Principles of the Most Ancient and Modern Philosophy,* tr. Allison Coudert and Taylor Corse. Cambridge: Cambridge University Press.

Cunitz, Maria (1650). *Urania Propitia, sive Tabulae Astronomica, mire faciles.* Oels.

Daniel, Samuel (1594). *Delia and Rosamond Augmented. Cleopatra.* London: Simon Waterson.

Dawson, T. (1588). *The Good Housewives Treasurie.* London.

—— (1596). *The Good Huswifes Iewell.* London: J. Wolfe & E. White.

Dee, John (1842). *The Private Diary of Dr John Dee,* ed. James Orchard Halliwell. London: Camden Society.

De Serres, O. (1607). *The Perfect Vse of Silk-wormes.* The English Experience 345. Amsterdam and New York: Theatrvm Orbis Terrarvm Ltd, 1971.

Digby, K. (1654). *A Treatise of Adhering to God,* tr. A. Magnus. London: printed for Henry Herringman.

—— (1675). *Choice and Experimental Receipts in Physick and Chirugery.* London: by Andrew Clark for Henry Brome. 1657.

——(1677). *The Closet of the Eminently Learned Sir Kenelm Digby Kt. Opened.* London: H.C. for H. Brome.

—— (1682). *Chymicall Secrets: A choice collection of rare secrets and experiments in philosophy. as also rare and unheard of Medicines, menstruums and alkahests; with the true secret of volatilizating the fixt salt of tartar . . . hitherto kept secret since his dicease, but now published for the good and benefit of the Publick, by George Hartman.* London: for the Author sold by William Cooper and Henry Faithorne and John Kersley.

Drayton, Michael (1931). *Works,* ed. J. William Hebel. Oxford: Basil Blackwell.

Dryden, J. (1958). *The Poems of John Dryden,* ed. James Kinsley. Oxford: Clarendon Press.

Elyot, T. (1595). *The Castell of Health.* London: The Widow Orwin.

Evelyn, John (1656). *An Essay on the First Book of T. Lucretius Carus De Rerum Natura.* London.

—— (1859). *Diary and Correspondence of John Evelyn,* ed. William Bray. London: Bohn.

—— (1939). *The Life of Mrs Godolphin,* ed. H. Sampson. London and New York: OUP.

—— (1959). *The Diary of John Evelyn,* ed. Esmond de Beer. Oxford: OUP.

—— (1995). *The Writings of John Evelyn,* ed. Guy de la Bedoyere. Woodbridge: Boydell.

Fénelon, François de Salignac de La Mothe (1688). *Instructions for the Education of a Daughter by the Author of Telemachus. To which is added a Small Tract of Instuctions for the Conduct of Young Ladies of the Highest Rank. With Suitable Devotions Annexed,* tr. G. Hickes. London.

Fitzherbert, J. (1598). *Booke of Husbandrie*. Repr. Amsterdam and New York: Theatrvm Orbis Terrarvm Ltd., 1979.

Flamsteed, John (1997). *The Correspondence of John Flamsteed, the First Astronomer Royal*, ed. Eric G. Forbes, Lesley Murdin and Frances Willmoth. Bristol and Philadelphia: IOP Publishing.

Fontenelle, B. (1686). *Entretiens sur la Pluralité des Mondes*. Paris.

Forbes, E.G. (*et al.* eds) (1995); *see* Flamsteed, John.

Fraunce, Abraham (1592). *The Third Part of the Countesse of Pembrokes Ivychurch*. London: Thomas Woodcocke.

Gager, William (1592). *Ulysses Redux: Tragoedia Nova*. Oxford: Joseph Barnes.

Galabin, A.L. (1904). *A Manual of Midwifery*. 6th edn. London: Churchill.

Gassendi, Pierre (1657). *The Mirrour of True Nobility and Gentility Being the Life of the Renowned Claudius Fabricius*. London.

Gerard, John (1597). *The Herball or Generall Historie of Plantes*. London: J. Norton.

Giovio, Paolo (1585). *The Worthy Tract of Paulus Iouius, contayning a Discourse of Rare Inuentions, both Militarie and Amorous called Imprese*. tr. Samuel Daniel. London. Facsimilie edition (1976) with *Dialogo dell' Imprese* (1659), introduced by N.K. Farmer. Delmar, NY: Scholars, Facsimilies and Reprints.

—— (1559) *Dialogo dell'imprese*. Lyons.

Giraldi, L.G. (1548). *De diis gentium*. Basel.

Good Huswiues Hand-maid, for Cookerie in her Kitchin, The (1588). London: R. Jones.

Greer, Germaine *et al.* (eds) (1988). *Kissing the Rod: An Anthology of Seventeenth-Century Women's Verse*. New York: Noonday Press.

Grey, E. (1653). *The Choice Manual of Rare and Select Secrets in Physick and chyrurgery*. London: G.D.

—— (1671). *A True Gentlewomans Delight where is contained all Manner of Cookery*. London: Printed by A. M. for Margaret Shears.

Guillemeau, J. (1612). *Child-birth Or, the Happy Deliverie of Women*. London: J. Hatfield.

Gunther, R.T. (ed.) (1939). *Dr Plot and the Correspondence of the Philosophical Society of Oxford*, in *Early Science in Oxford*. 15 vols, vol. 12. Oxford.

Harris, J. (1719). *Astronomical Dialogues between a Gentleman and a Lady*. London.

Hartlib, S. (1655). *Chymical, Medicinal and Chyrugical Addresses made to Samuel Hartlib Esq*. London.

Harvey, William (1981). *Disputations Touching the Generation of Animals*, tr. Gweneth Whitteridge. Oxford: Basil Blackwell.

Helmont, Francis Mercury van (1694). *The Divine Being and its Attributes*. Amsterdam.

Here Beginneth the Seynge of Urynes (1550). London: John Waley.

Herschel, Caroline (1787). 'An Account of a New Comet in a Letter from Miss Caroline Herschel to Charles Blagden, M.D., Sec. R.S.', *Philosophical Transactions of the Royal Society of London*, 77: 1–5.

Herschel, Mrs J. (ed.) (1876). *Memoir and Correspondence of Caroline Herschel*.

Hevelius, J. (1673). *Machina coelestis*. Danzig.

—— (1690). *Prodromus Astronomiae*. Danzig.

Hill, T. (1577). *The Gardeners Labyrinth*. London: Henry Bynneman.

Hoby, M. (1930). *Diary of Lady Margaret Hoby 1599–1605*, ed. D. Meads. London: Routledge.

Holden, M. (1688, 1689). *The Woman's Almanack*. London: J. Millet.

Hooke, Robert (1665). *Micrographia: or Some Physiological Descriptions of Minute Bodies Made by Magnifying Glasses with Observations and Enquiries thereupon*. London: J. Martyn and J. Allestrye.

Howard, Alethea (1655). *Natura Exenterata*. London: H. Twiford.

Howard, Thomas, Earl of Arundel (1969). *The Life and Correspondence and Collections of Thomas Howard, Earl of Arundel*, ed. M. Hervey. New York: Kraus, 1st edn 1921.

—— (1980). 'Cookery Books: a Cabinet of Rare Devices and Conceits', *Petits Propos Culinaires*, 5 (May).

—— (1986). 'Sweet Secrets: From occasional receipt to specialised books' in C. Wilson (ed.) (1986).

—— (forthcoming). *Cambridge Bibliography of English Literature*, 3rd edn: 1500–1700.

Hutchinson, Lucy (1817). *On the Principles of the Christian Religion. Addressed to her Daughter*, ed. Julius Hutchinson. London: Hurst, Rees, Orme and Browne.

—— (1973). *Memoirs of the Life of Colonel Hutchinson, with the Fragment of an Autobiography of Mrs. Hutchinson*, ed. James Sutherland. New York: Oxford University Press.

—— (1996). *Lucy Hutchinson's Translation of Lucretius*, ed. H. de Quehen. London: Duckworth.

Hutton, Sarah and Marjorie Nicholson (eds) (1992). *The Conway Letters*. Oxford: Clarendon Press.

Hyde, Edward, Earl of Clarendon (1888). *The History of the Rebellion and Civil Wars in England, begun in the Year 1641*, ed. W. Dunn Macray. Oxford: Clarendon Press.

Josselin, Ralph (1976). *The Diary of Ralph Josselin 1616–1683*, ed. A. MacFarlane. *British Academy Records of Social and Economic History*, New Series, 3.

Kircher, Athanasius (1654). *Oedipi Aegyptiace*. Rome.

Ladies Companion, or a Table furnished with sundry sorts of Pies and Tarts, Gracefull at a Feast, with many receipts. By Persons of Quality whose names are mentioned (1653/4). London: W. Bentley.

Ladies Diary, The (1704–1840).

Lalande, J. de (1786). *Astronomie des dames*. Paris.

Lanyer, Aemilia (1993). *The Poems of Aemilia Lanyer: Salve Deus Rex Judaeorum*, ed. Susanne Woods. Oxford: Oxford University Press.

Lawson, W. (1618). *A New Orchard and Garden*. London: B. Alsop.

Le Roy, Louis (1594). *Of the Interchangeable Course or Variety of Things in the Whole World*, tr. R. Ashley. London: C. Yetsweirt.

Lucretius (1714). *Lucretius Carus, of the Nature of Things*, tr. Thomas Creech. London.

Lynche, Richard (1599). *The Fountaine of Ancient Fiction*. London.

M., T. (1599). *The Silkwormes, and their Flies*. London: V.S.

Makin, Bathsua (1673). *An Essay to Revive the Antient Education of Gentlewomen*. London.

—— (1989). 'An Essay to Revive the Antient Education of Gentlewomen', ed. Frances Teague in Wilson and Warnke (eds) (1989).

Markham, G. (1614). *Cheape and Good Husbandry*. Amsterdam and New York: Theatrvm Orbis Terrarvm Ltd., 1969.

—— (1615a). *The English Huswife*. London: for Roger Jackson.

—— (1615b). *Countrey Contentments*. Amsterdam and New York: Theatrvm Orbis Terrarvm Ltd. 1973.

—— (1986). *The English Housewife* (1615), ed. Michael R. Best. Montreal: McGill-Queen's University Press.

Ménage, G. (1690). *Historia mulierum philosopharum*. Lyons.

——— (1984). *The History of Women Philosophers*, tr. B. Zedler. Lanham.

Meres, Francis (1598). *Palladis Tamia*. London.

Meurdrac, M. (1674). *La Chymie charitable et facile, en faveur des dames*. Paris.

Moffet, Thomas (1599). *The Silkwormes and their Flies: Lively described in verse, by T.M. a Countrie Farmar, and an Apprentice in Physicke*. London: Nicholas Ling.

——— (1655). *Health's Improvement*. London.

——— (1940). *Nobilis or a View of the Life and Death of a Sidney and Lessus Lugubris*, ed. Virgil B. Heltzel and Hoyt H. Hudson. San Marino: Huntingdon Library.

Moore, Dorothy (forthcoming). *The Letters of Dorothy Moore 1641–1646*, ed. L. Hunter.

More, Henry (1653). *An Antidote Against Atheism*. London.

——— (1659). *Of the Immortality of the Soul*. London.

——— (1671). *Enchiridion Metaphysicum*. London.

——— (1878). *The Complete Poems of Dr. Henry More (1614–1687)*, ed. Alexander B. Grosart. Edinburgh: Edinburgh University Press.

Mouffet, *see* Moffet.

Murrel, Iohn. (1617). *A Daily Exercise for Ladies and Gentlewomen*. London: Widow Helme.

Newton, Isaac (1936). *Sir Isaac Newton's Principles of Natural Philosophy*, tr. A. Motte, revised with notes by F. Cajori. Berkeley and Los Angeles: UCLA Press.

North, Sir Thomas (1888). *The Morall Philosophies of Doni*, ed. J. Jacob. London, 1st edn 1570.

Oldenburg, H. (1965–86). *Correspondence*, ed. and tr. A. Rupert Hall and Marie Boas Hall. Madison: University of Wisconsin Press.

Ortelius, Abraham (1610). *Theatrvm Orbis Terrarvm*. London: J. Norton.

Papin, D. (1687). *A Continuation of the New Digester of Bones*. London: by J. Streater.

Parkinson, J. (1629). *Paradisi in Sole, Paradisus Terrestris*. London.

Partridge, D. (1694). *The Woman's Almanack*.

Partridge, J. (1595). *The Widdowes Treasure*. London: I. Roberts.

Pepys, Samuel (1970–83). *The Diary of Samuel Pepys*, ed. R. Latham and W. Matthews, 11 vols. London: Bell.

Petty, William (1963). *The Economic Writings of Sir William Petty*, ed. C.H. Hull. 2 vols. New York: Augustus M. Kelley.

Peyton, Thomas (1620). *The Glasse of Time in the Two First Ages*. London.

Pisan, Christine de (1521). *The Boke of the Cyte of Ladyes*.

Platt, Sir Hugh (1602). *Delights for Ladies, to adorne their Persons, Tables, Closets and Distillatories*. London: Peter Short.

——— (1595) *The Jewell House of Art and Nature*. London: P. Short.

Porta, J. (1669). *Natural Magick . . . wherein are set forth all the riches and delights of the natural sciences*. London: for John Wright.

Ripa, Cesare (1603). *Iconologia overo descritione di diversi imagini cauate dall'antichita*. Rome.

Roesslin, E. (1598). *The Birth of Mankinde, otherwyse named the Womans Booke*, tr. T. Raynalde. London: Richarde Watkins.

Ross, Alexander (1648). *Mystagogus Poeticus or the Muses Interpreter*. London. 1647.

Ruthven (1639). *The Ladies Cabinet*. London: for Richard Meighen.

Schurman, Anna Maria van (1659). *The Learned Maid,: or whether a Maid may be a Scholar? A Logick Exercise*, tr. Clement Barksdale from *De Ingeniis Muliebris ad Doctrinam et Meliores Literas Aptitudina* (1641).

Schurmann, Anna Maria von; see Schurman, Anna Maria van.

Sermon, William (1671). *The Ladies Companion or the English Midwife*. London.

Sharp, Jane (1671). *The Midwives Book. Or the whole art of midwifry*. London: Simon Miller.

Sharpe, J. (1996). *Instruments of Darkness: Witchcraft in England 1550–1750*. London: Hamish Hamilton.

Sherburne, Edward (1961). *The Poems and Translations of Sir Edward Sherburne (1616–1702) excluding Seneca and Manilius*, ed. F. J. Van Beeck. Assen: Royal Van Gorcum.

Sidney, Mary (forthcoming). *Collected Works of Mary Sidney Herbert, Countess of Pembroke*, ed. Margaret P. Hannay, Noel J. Kinnamon and Michael G. Brennan. Oxford: Clarendon Press.

Sidney, Philip and Sidney, Mary (1963). *The Psalms of Sir Philip Sidney and the Countess of Pembroke*, ed. J.C.A. Rathmell. New York: New York University Press.

Smith, John (1979). *John Smith the Cambridge Platonist: Select Discourses (1660)* facsimile with an introduction by C.A. Patrides. Delmar, NY: Scholars' Facsimiles & Reprints.

Spratt, Thomas (1667). *The History of the Royal Society*, London.

Stallenge, W. (1609). *Instrvtions for the Increasing of Mulberrie Trees, and the Breeding of Silke-wormes, for the making of Silke in this Kingdome*. London: E. Edgar.

Stuart, Henrietta Maria (1655). *The Queens Closet Opened*, ed. W.M. London: for Nathaniel Brooke

Sweeper, Walter (1622). *Israels Redemption by Christ wherin is confuted the Arminian Universall Redemption*. London: William Jones.

Talbot, A. *See* Howard, Alethea.

Tasso, Torquato (1973). *Discourses on the Heroic Poem*, tr. with notes Mariella Cavalchini and Irene Samuel. Oxford: Clarendon Press.

Thornton, Alice (1873). *The Autobiography of Mrs. Alice Thornton, of East Newton, C. York*, ed. C. Jackson. Surtees Society Publications, vol. 62.

Triumphs of Female Wit, In some Pindarick Odes. Or, the Emulation together with an Answer to an Objector against Female Ingenuity, and Capacity of Learning. Also, a Preface to the Masculine Sex. By a Young Lady (1683).

Turner, William (1551). *New Herball*. London.

Tusser, T. (1580). *Five Hundred Points of Good Husbandry*, ed. G. Griegson. Oxford: Oxford University Press, 1984.

Vigon, J. (1543). *The Most Excellent Workes of Chirurgerye*. London.

Whiteman, Anne, with Clapinson, Mary (1986). *The Compton Census of 1676: a Critical Edition*. London: British Academy, and Oxford: Oxford University Press.

Wilkins, John (1649). *A Discourse concerning the Beauty of Providence*. London.

Willis, T. (1684). *Pharmaceutice Rationalis (Part 1): Or an exercitation of the operations of medicines in humane bodies*. London: for T. Dring, C. Harper and J. Leigh.

Willughby, Percival (1863). *Observations in Midwifery. As also the country midwife's opusculum or vade mecum*, ed. Henry Blenkinsop. Facsimile reprint, ed. John L. Thornton, Wakefield: S.R. Publishers, 1972.

Wolveridge, James (1671). *Speculum Matricis*. London.

Wood, Owen (1639). *An Alphabetical Book of Physicall Secrets, For all those Diseases that are most predominant and dangerous (curable by Art) in the Body of Man*. London: John Norton.

Woolf, Virginia (1935). *A Room of One's Own*. London: Hogarth Press. (1st edn 1929).

Woolley, H. (1664). *The Gentlewoman's Companion or, a Guide to the Female Sex*. London: A. Maxwell.

—— (1675). *The Accomplish'd Lady's Delight*.

Wright, T. (1693). *The Female Virtuoso's*. London.

Wrightson, K. (1982). *English Society 1580–1680*. New Brunswick, NY: Rutgers University Press.

Wroth, Mary (1988). *Lady Mary Wroth's Love's Victory. The Penshurst Manuscript*, ed. Michael G. Brennan. London: Roxburghe Club.

SECONDARY SOURCES

Abir-Am, P. and Outram, D. (eds) (1987). *Uneasy Careers and Intimate Lives*. New Brunswick, NJ: Rutgers University Press.

Aers, D. (ed.) (1992). *Culture and History 1350–1600*. New York: Harvester Wheatsheaf.

Åkerman, S. (1991). *Queen Christina of Sweden and Her Circle: The Transformation of a Seventeenth-Century Philosophical Libertine*. Leiden: Brill.

Alcoff, Linda and Potter, Elizabeth (1993). *Feminist Epistemologies*. London: Routledge.

Amussen, S.D. (1988). *An Ordered Society: Gender and Class in Early Modern England*. Oxford: Oxford University Press.

Anglin, J.P. (1980). 'The Expansion of Literacy: Opportunities for the Study of the Three Rs in the London Diocese of Elizabeth I', *Guildhall Studies in London History*, 3, 63–74.

Archer, I.W. (1991). *The Pursuit of Stability: Social Relations in Elizabethan London*. Cambridge: Cambridge University Press.

Aveling, J.H. (1872). *English Midwives: Their History and Prospects*. London: Churchill.

—— (1882). *The Chamberlens and the Midwifery Forceps: Memorials of the Family and an Essay on the Invention of the Instrument*. London: Churchill.

Badinter, E. (1983). *Emilie, Emilie: L'ambition féminine au XVIIIième siècle*. Paris.

Bainton, R.H. (1980). 'Learned Women in the Europe of the Sixteenth Century' in Labalme (1980).

Barbour, Reid (1993). 'The Early Stuart Epicure', *English Literary Renaissance*, 23, 170–200.

Baumann, Greg (ed.) (1986). *The Written Word; Literacy in Transition*. Oxford: Clarendon Press.

Beier, A.L. (1985). *Masterless Men: The Vagrancy Problem in England 1560–1640*. London: Methuen.

Beier, A.L. and Finlay, R. (eds) (1986). *London 1500–1700: the Making of the Metropolis*. London: Longman.

Beier, L. McCray (1987). *Sufferers and Healers: The Experience of Illness in Seventeenth-Century England*. London: Routledge & Kegan Paul.

Bell, Maureen (1988). 'Mary Westwood, Quaker Publisher', *Publishing History*, 23, 5–66.

—— (1989). 'Hannah Allen and the Development of a Puritan Publishing Business, 1646–51', *Publishing History*, 26: 5–66.

—— (1992). 'Elizabeth Calvert and the "Confederates"', *Publishing History*, 32: 5–50.

—— (1994). '"Her Usual Practices". The Later Career of Elizabeth Calvert', *Publishing History*, 35, 5–64.

Benjamin, A., Canto, G. and Christie, J. (1987). *The Figural and the Literal: Problems of Language in the History of Science and Philosophy, 1630–1800*. Manchester: Manchester University Press.

Benjamin, M. (ed.) (1993). *A Question of Identity: Women, Science and Literature*. New Brunswick, NJ: Rutgers University Press.

Bennett, H.S. (1952). *English Books & Readers 1475–1557*. Cambridge: Cambridge University Press.

—— (1965). *English Books & Readers 1558–1603*. Cambridge: Cambridge University Press.

Bennett, J.M. (1991). 'Misogyny, Popular Culture, and Women's Work', *History Workshop Journal*, 31, 166–88.

—— (1992). 'Medieval Women, Modern Women: Across the Great Divide' in Aers (1992), pp. 147–75.

Berkowitz, D. (1988). *John Selden's Formative Years*. London: Folger Books.

Berman, R. (1989). 'From Aristotle's Dualism to Materialist Dialectics: Feminist Transformation of Science and Society' in Bordo and Jaggar (1989).

Bing, Gertrude (1937). 'Nugae circa veritatem', *Journal of the Warburg and Courtauld Institutes*, 1, 304–12.

Binneveld, H. and Dekker, R. (eds) (1992). *Curing and Insuring: Essays on Illness in Past Times*. Hilversum: Verloren.

Birch, U. (1909). *Anna von Schurman: Artist, Scholar, Saint*. London: Longmans.

Blain, Virginia, Grundy, Isobel and Clements, Patricia (eds) (1990). *The Feminist Companion to Literature in English*. New Haven, Conn.: Yale University Press.

Bordo, Susan (1987). *The Flight to Objectivity. Essays on Cartesianism and Culture*. Albany, NY: SUNY Press.

Bordo, S. and Jaggar, A. (1989). *Gender/Body, Knowledge. Feminist Reconstructions of Being and Knowing*. New Brunswick, NJ: Rutgers University Press.

Bornstein, D. (ed.) (1980). *The Feminist Controversy of the Renaissance*. Delmar, NY: Scholars' Facsimile Reprints.

Boss, Bernice and Boss, Jeffrey (1983). 'Ignorant Midwives – a Further Rejoinder', *Bulletin of the Society for the Social History of Medicine*, 33.

Boxer, M. and Quataert, J. (eds) (1987). *Connecting Spheres: Women in the Western World, 1500 to the Present*. New York and Oxford: OUP.

Bradford, G. (1969). *Elizabethan Women*. Freeport, NY: Books for Libraries Press.

Brears, P. (1991). 'Rare Conceits and Strange Delights' in C.A. Wilson (1991).

—— (1996). 'Behind the Green Baize Door: the Architecture of Food Preparation' in C. A. Wilson (ed.) (1996).

Brennan, M. (1988). *Literary Patronage in the English Renaissance*. London: Routledge.

—— (1991). 'The Medicean Dukes', *Notes and Queries*, 38, pt 4.

Bridenthal, R., Koonz, C. and Stuard, S. (eds) (1987). *Becoming Visible: Women in European History*, 2nd edn. Boston: Houghton Mifflin.

Brink, J.R. (ed.) (1980). *Female Scholars: A Tradition of Learned Women before 1800*. Montreal: Eden.

Brockliss, Laurence (1990) 'Copernicus in the University: the French Experience' in Henry and Hutton (1990), pp. 190–213.

Brown, Stuart (1990). 'Leibniz and Henry More's Cabalistic Circle' in Hutton (1990).

—— (1996). 'F.M. van Helmont: his Philosophical Connections and the Reception of his Later Cabalistic Philosophy' in *Studies in Seventeenth-Century Philosophy*, ed. M.A. Stewart. Oxford: OUP.

Burke, Sean (1992). *The Death and Return of the Author: Criticism and Subjectivity in Barthes, Foucault and Derrida*. Edinburgh: Edinburgh University Press.

Burnby, J. (1983). 'The Herbwomen of the London Markets', *Pharmaceutical Historian*, 13, pp. 5–6.

Bynum, W.F. and Porter, R. (eds) (1985). *William Hunter and the Varieties of Man-Midwifery*. Cambridge: Cambridge University Press.

Camden, C.C. (1975). *The Elizabethan Woman*. Maroneck, NY: Paul P. Appel.

Campbell, M. (1983). *The English Yeoman under Elizabeth and the Early Stuarts*. London: Merlin.

Cantor, G. (1989). 'The Rhetoric of Experiment' in Gooding *et al.* (1989).

Capp, Bernard (1979). *Astrology and the Popular Press. English Almanacs 1500–1800*. London and Boston: Faber.

Chadwick, W. and de Courtivron, I. (eds) (1993). *Significant Others. Creativity and Intimate Partnership*. London: Thames and Hudson.

Charles, L. and Duffin, L. (eds) (1985). *Women and Work in Pre-Industrial England*. London: Croom Helm.

Chastel, A. (1959). *Art et Humanisme à Florence au Temps de Laurent le Magnifique*. Paris: PUF.

Christie, J. (1987). 'Introduction: Rhetoric and Writing in Early Modern Philosophy and Science' in Benjamin *et al.* (1987).

Clark, A. (1919, reprinted 1982). *Working Life of Women in the Seventeenth Century*. London: G. Routledge & Sons.

Clark, P. (1976). 'The Ownership of Books in England 1560–1640: The Example of Some Kentish Townsfolk' in Stone (ed.) (1976).

Clericuzio, A. and Rattansi, P. (1994). *Alchemy and Chemistry in the Sixteenth and Seventeenth Centuries*. Dordrecht: Kluwer.

Cook, H.J. (1985). 'Against Common Right and Reason: the College of Physicians versus Dr Thomas Bonham', *American Journal of Legal History*, 29, 301–22.

—— (1986). *The Decline of the Old Medical Regime in Stuart London*. Ithaca and London: Cornell University Press.

Crawford, P. (1984). 'Printed Advertisements for Women Medical Practitioners', *Bulletin of the Society for the Social History of Medicine*, 35.

—— (1985). 'Women's Published Writings 1600–1700' in Prior (1985).

Cressy, D. (1980). *Literacy and the Social Order, Reading and Writing in Tudor and Stuart England*. Cambridge: Cambridge University Press.

Cunningham, A. and Grell, O. (eds) (1996). *Religio Medici*. London: Variorum.

Dale, M.K. (1932–4). 'The London Silkwomen of the Fifteenth Century', *Economic History Review*, 4, 43–55.

Daniel, Samuel (1594). *Delia and Rosamond Augmented. Cleopatra*. London: Simon Waterson.

Daston, L. (1992). 'The Naturalized Female Intellect', *Science in Context*, 5, 209–35.

Daumas, M. (1972). *Scientific Instruments of the Seventeenth and Eighteenth Centuries and their Makers*, tr. and ed. M. Holbrook. London: Batsford.

David, E. (1979a). 'A True Gentlewoman's Delight' in *Petits Propos Culinaires*, pp. 43–53. London: Prospect Books.

—— (1979b). 'The Harvest of Cold Months'. *ibid.*, pp. 9–16.

Davis, Natalie Zemon (1982). 'Women in the Crafts in Sixteenth-Century Lyon', *Feminist Studies*, 8, 47–80.

Dear, P. (1991a). *The Literary Structure of Scientific Argument: Historical Studies*. Philadelphia: University of Pennsylvania Press.

—— (1991b). 'Narratives, Anecdotes, and Experiments: Turning experience into science in the seventeeth-century' in Dear (1991a).

De Blécourt, W. (1992). 'Cunning Women, from Healers to Fortune Tellers' in Binneveld and Dekker (eds) (1992).

Debus, A. (1970). *Science and Education in the Seventeenth Century: The Webster-Ward Debate*. New York: Elsevier.

—— (ed.) (1974). *Medicine in Seventeenth-Century England*. London: University of California Press.

Demisch, H. (1977). *Die Sphinx. Geschichte ihrer Darstellung von den Anfangen bis zur Gegenwart*. Stuttgart: Urachhaus.

De Quehen, Hugh (1996). 'Ease and Flow in Lucy Hutchinson's Lucretius', *Studies in Philology*, 93, pp. 288–303.

Dixon, L.S. (1995). *Perilous Chastity: Women and Illness in Pre-Enlightenment Art and Medicine*. Ithaca, NY and London: Cornell University Press.

Dobbs, B.J.T. (1973 and 1974). 'Studies in the Natural Philosophy of Sir Kenelm Digby', *Ambix*, 18, 1–25; 20, 143–63; 21, 1–28.

—— (1982). *The Foundations of Newton's Alchemy*. Cambridge: Cambridge University Press.

Dongen, J.A. van (1967). *De Zieke Mens in Beeldende Kunst*. Delft: Mycofarm.

Donnison, Jean (1977). *Midwives and Medical Men: a History of Inter-Professional Rivalries and Women's Rights*. London: Heinemann.

Durant, D. (1977). *Bess of Hardwick*. London: Weidenfeld & Nicolson.

Eamon, W. (1994). *Science and the Secrets of Nature: Books of Secrets in Medieval and Early Modern Culture*. Princeton, NJ: Princeton University Press.

Earle, Peter (1989). *The Making of the English Middle Class. Business, Society and Family Life in London, 1660-1730*. London: Methuen.

Eccles, Audrey (1982). *Obstetrics and Gynecology in Tudor and Stuart England*. Kent, OH: Kent State University Press.

Ehrenpreis, I. and Halsband, R. (1969). *The Lady of Letters in the Eighteenth Century*. (William Andrews Clark Library Seminar Papers). Los Angeles: University of California Press.

Ehrman, E. (1986). *Mme. du Châtelet: Scientist, Philosopher, and Feminist of the Enlightenment*. Leamington Spa: Berg.

Estes, L.L. (1983). 'The Medical Origins of the European Witch Craze: A Hypothesis', *Journal of Social History*, 17, 271–84.

Evelyn, Helen (1915). *The History of the Evelyn Family*. London: E. Nash.

Evenden, Doreen (1993). 'Mothers and their Midwives in Seventeenth-Century London' in Marland (ed.) (1993), pp. 9–26.

Everett, B. (1972). '*Romeo and Juliet*: the Nurse's Story', *Critical Quarterly*, 14, 129–39.

Ezell, M.M. (1984). *The Patriarch's Wife: Literary Evidence and the History of the Family*. Chapel Hill: University of North Carolina Press.

Farrington, B. (1970). *The Philosophy of Francis Bacon. An Essay on its Development from 1603 to 1609, with New Translations of Fundamental Texts*. Liverpool: Liverpool University Press.

Fattori, Marta (1980). *Lessico del Novum Organum di Francesco Bacone*. 2 vols. Rome: Ateneo & Bizzari.

Ferrante, J. (1980). 'The Education of Women in the Middle Ages in Theory, Fact and Fantasy' in Labalme (ed.) (1980).

Fildes, Valerie (ed.) (1990). *Women as Mothers in Pre-Industrial England. Essays in Memory of Dorothy McLaren*. London: Routledge.

Findlen, P. (1993). 'Science as a Career in Enlightenment Italy: The Strategies of Laura Bassi', *Isis*, 84, 441–69.

Finlay, R. (1981). *Population and Metropolis: the Demography of London 1580–1650*. Cambridge: Cambridge University Press.

Fisken, Beth Wynne (1985). 'Mary Sidney's Psalmes: Education and Wisdom' in Hannay (ed.) (1985), pp. 166–83.

Fleischmann, Wolfgang Bernard (1960). 'Lucretius Carus, Titus' in *Catalogus translationum et commentariorum*, ed. P.O. Kristeller and F.E. Kranz. Washington DC: Catholic University of America Press.

Force, J.E. and Popkin, R.H. (eds) (1994). *The Books of Nature and Scripture*. Dordrecht: Kluwer.

Fraser, Antonia (1984). *The Weaker Vessel: Woman's Lot in Seventeenth-century England*. London: Weidenfeld & Nicolson. (Pbk edn, London: Methuen, 1985.)

Fraser, F. (1987). *The English Gentlewoman*. London: Barrie and Jenkins.

Furnivall, F.J. (1868). *Early English Meals and Manners*. London: Early English Text Society O.S. 32.

Gabbey, Alan (1990). 'Henry More and the Limits of Mechanism' in Hutton (ed.) (1990).

Gagen, Jean (1954). *The New Woman: Her Emergence in English Drama 1660–1730*. New York: Twayne Publishers.

George, M. (1988). *Women in the First Capitalist Society: Experiences in Seventeenth-Century England*. Urbana: University of Illinois Press.

Getz, F. (1991). *Healing and Society in Medieval England: A Middle English Translation of the Pharmaceutical Writings of Gilbertus Anglicus*. Madison: University of Wisconsin Press.

Goldberg, P.J.P (1992). *Women, Work and Life Cycle in a Medieval Economy: Women in York and Yorkshire c.1300–1520*. Oxford: Clarendon Press.

Golinski, J. (1992). *Science as Public Culture: Chemistry and Enlightenment in Britain 1760–1820*. Cambridge: Cambridge University Press.

Gooding, D., Pinch, T. and Schaffer, S. (eds) (1989). *The Uses of Experiment: Studies in the Natural Sciences*. Cambridge: Cambridge University Press.

Goodman, D. (1989). 'Enlightenment Salons: the Convergence of Female and Philosophic Ambitions', *Eighteenth Century Studies*, 22, 329–50.

Goody, J. (ed.) (1968). *Literacy in Traditional Societies*. Cambridge: Cambridge University Press.

Gordon, Donald (1939). 'Veritas filia temporis, Hadrianus Junius and Geoffrey Whitney', *Journal of the Warburg and Courtauld Institutes*, 3, 228–40.

Grafton, Anthony and Jardine, Lisa (1986). *From Humanism to Humanities*. Cambridge: CUP.

Grant, D. (1957). *Margaret the First. A Biography of Margaret Cavendish, Duchess of Newcastle, 1623–1673*. London: Rupert Hart Davis.

Grant, Edward (1981). *Much Ado About Nothing: Theories of Space and Vacuum from the Middle Ages to the Scientific Revolution*. Cambridge: Cambridge University Press.

Greaves, Richard L. (1990). *The Puritan Revolution and Educational Thought: Background for Reform*. New Brunswick, NJ: Rutgers University Press.

Green, I. (1979). 'The Education of Women in the Reformation', *History of Education Quarterly*, 19, 93–116.

Gregory, A. (1991). 'Witchcraft, Politics and "Good Neighbourhood" in Seventeenth-Century Rye', *Past and Present*, 133, 31–66.

Griffiths, P. (1996). *Youth and Authority: Formative Experiences in England 1560–1640*. Oxford: Clarendon Press.

Haase-Dubose, D. and Viennot, E. (eds) (1991). *Femmes et Pouvoirs sous l'Ancien Régime*. Paris.

Hall, A.R. (1983). *The Revolution in Science, 1500–1750*. Harlow: Longman.

—— (1990a). *Henry More. Magic, Religion and Experiment*. Oxford: Basil Blackwell.

—— (1990b). 'Henry More and the Scientific Revolution' in Hutton (ed.) (1990).

Hanlon, J. (1965). 'These be but Women' in *From the Renaissance to the Counter-Reformation*, ed. C. Carter. New York: Random House.

Hannay, Margaret P. (ed.) (1985). *Silent but for the Word: Tudor Women as Patrons, Translators, and Writers of Religious Works*. Kent, OH: Kent State University Press.

—— (1990). *Philip's Phoenix: Mary Sidney, Countess of Pembroke*. New York: OUP.

—— (1994). '"House-confined Maids": The Presentation of Woman's Role in the Psalmes of the Countess of Pembroke', *English Literary Renaissance*, 24, 20–35.

Harding, Sandra (1986). *The Science Question in Feminism*. Ithaca, NY: Cornell University Press.

—— (1991). *Whose Science? Whose Knowledge? Thinking from Women's Lives*. Milton Keynes: Open University Press.

Harley, David N. (1993). 'Provincial Midwives in England: Lancashire and Cheshire, 1660-1760' in Marland (1993), pp. 27–48.

Harrison, Charles Trawick (1934). 'The Ancient Atomists and English Literature of the Seventeenth Century', *Harvard Studies in Classical Philology*, 45, 1–79.

Harth, E. (1992). *Cartesian Women: Versions and Subversions of Rational Discourse in the Old Regime*. Ithaca, NY: Cornell University Press.

Healy, Thomas and Sawday, Jonathan (eds) (1990). *Literature and the English Civil War*. Cambridge: Cambridge University Press.

Hekman, Susan (1990). *Gender and Knowledge. Elements of a Postmodern Feminism*. Oxford: Basil Blackwell.

Henry, John (1990). 'Henry More versus Robert Boyle: the Spirit of Nature and the Nature of Providence' in Henry and Hutton (1990), pp. 55–76.

—— (1992). 'The Scientific Revolution in England' in Porter and Teich (1992).

Henry, J. and Hutton, S. (eds) (1990). *New Perspectives on Renaissance Thought: Essays in the History of Science, Education and Philosophy*. London: Duckworth.

Hesse, Mary (1980). 'The Explanatory Function of Metaphor' in *Revolutions and Reconstructions in the Philosophy of Science*. Brighton: Harvester.

Hirsch, R. (1975). *Printing, Selling and Reading 1450–1550*. Wiesbaden: Otto Harrossowitz.

Hiscock, W.G. (1951). *John Evelyn and Mrs Godolphin*. London: MacMillan.

—— (1955). *John Evelyn and his Family Circle*. London: Routledge & Kegan Paul.

Hitchcock, James (1967). 'A Sixteenth-Century Midwife's License', *Bulletin of the History of Medicine*, 41, 75–6.

Hobby, Elaine (1988). *Virtue of Necessity. English Women's Writing 1649–1688*. London: Virago.

Hodgkin, K. (1985). 'The Diary of Anne Clifford: a Study of Class and Gender in the Seventeenth Century', *History Workshop*, 19.

Hoffman, Ann (1977). *Lives of the Tudor Age.* New York: Barnes & Noble.

Hogrefe, P. (1975). *Tudor Women: Commoners and Queens.* Ames: Iowa State University Press.

—— (1977). *Women of Action in Tudor England.* Ames: Iowa State University Press.

Holmes, C. (1993). 'Women: Witnesses and Witches', *Past and Present*, 140, 45–78.

Holmes, F. (1991). 'Argument and Narrative in Scientific Writing' in Dear (1991a).

Holmes, Martin (1975). *Proud Northern Lady: Lady Anne Clifford, 1590–1676.* Chichester: Phillimore.

Hoppen, K. (1970). *The Common Scientist in the Seventeenth Century: A Study of the Dublin Philosophical Society 1683–1708.* London: Routledge & Kegan Paul.

Horsley, R.A. (1979). 'Who were the Witches? The Social Roles of the Accused in the European Witch Trials', *Journal of Interdisciplinary History*, 9, 698–715.

Hoskin, M. and Warner, B. (1981). 'Caroline Herschel's Comet Sweepers', *Journal for the History of Astronomy*, 12, 27–34.

Houghton, Walter E. (1942). 'The English Virtuoso in the Seventeenth Century', *Journal of the History of Ideas*, 3, 51–73, 190–219.

Houlbrooke, R.A. (1988). 'Women's Social Life and Common Action in England from the Fifteenth Century to the Eve of the Civil War', *Continuity and Change*, 171–89.

Houston, R.A. (1988). *Literacy in Early Modern Europe.* New York: Longman.

Howarth, D. (1985). *Lord Arundel and his Circle.* London: Yale University Press.

Hufton, O. (1995). *The Prospect Before Her: A History of Women in Western Europe, Vol. I: 1500–1800.* London: Harper Collins.

Hull, S. (1982). *Chaste, Silent and Obedient; English Books for Women 1475–1640.* San Marino: Huntington.

Hunter, L. (1980). 'Cookery Books: a Cabinet of Rare Devices and Conceits', *Petits propos culinaires*, 5 (May).

—— (1991). 'Sweet Secrets: From Occasional Receipt to Specialised Books' in C. A. Wilson (1991).

—— (forthcoming). 'Household Books' in *Cambridge Bibliography of English Literature*, 3rd edn: *1500–1700.*

Hunter, M. (1975). *John Aubrey and the Realm of Learning.* New York: Science History Publications.

—— (1981). *Science and Society in Restoration England.* Cambridge: Cambridge University Press.

—— (1989). 'Hooke's Possessions at his Death: a Hitherto Unknown Inventory' in *Robert Hooke: New Studies*, ed. M. Hunter and S. Schaffer. Woodbridge: Boydell Press.

—— (1994). *Robert Boyle Reconsidered.* Cambridge: Cambridge University Press.

—— (1995). 'John Evelyn in the 1650s: a Virtuoso in Quest of a Role' in *Science and the Shape of Orthodoxy.* Woodbridge: Boydell Press.

Hurd-Mead, Kate Campbell (1937). *A History of Women in Medicine.* Haddam, CT: Haddam Press, Rpt Boston: Longwood Press, 1979.

Hutton, Sarah (ed.) (1990). *Henry More (1618–1687): Tercentenary Studies.* Dordrecht: Kluwer.

—— (1993). 'Between Platonism and Enlightenment: Damaris Cudworth, Lady Masham, and John Locke', *British Journal for the History of Philosophy*, 1, 29–54.

—— (1994). 'More, Newton and the Language of Biblical Prophecy' in Force and Popkin (1994).

—— (1996). 'Of Physic and Philosophy: Anne Conway, Francis Mercury van Helmont and Seventeenth-Century Medicine' in Cunningham and Grell (1996).

Hutton, Sarah and Nicolson, Marjorie (eds) (1992). *The Conway Letters*. Oxford: Clarendon Press.

Iliffe, R. (1994). '"Making a Shew": Apocalptic Hermeneutics and the Sociology of Christian Idolatry in the Work of Isaac Newton and Henry More' in Force and Popkin (1994).

Ingram, M. (1994). '"Scolding Women Cucked or Washed": A Crisis in Gender Relations in Early Modern England' in Kermode and Walker (eds) (1994), pp. 48–80.

Irwin, J.L. (1980). 'Anna Maria von Schurman: the Star of Utrecht' in Brink (1980), pp. 86–100.

Isler, H. (1968). *Thomas Willis 1621–1675, Doctor and Scientist*. London: Hafner.

Iwasaki, S. (1958). 'Veritas filia temporis and Shakespeare', *English Literary Renaissance*, 3, 472–93.

Jacob, J.R. (1977). *Robert Boyle and the English Revolution: A Study in Social and Intellectual Change*. New York: Burt Franklin.

Jacobus, M., Keller, E. and Shuttleworth, S. (eds) (1990). *Body Politics: Women and the Discourses of Science*. London and New York: Routledge.

Jacquot, Jean (1952). 'Sir Charles Cavendish and His Learned Friends: A Contribution to the History of Scientific Relations between England and the Continent in the Earlier Part of the Seventeenth Century', *Annals of Science*, 8, 13–27 and 175–91.

James, F. (ed.) (1989). *The Development of the Laboratory*. London: Macmillan.

Jardine, Lisa (1974). *Francis Bacon. Discovery and the Art of Discourse*. Cambridge: Cambridge University Press.

Jeffers, R. (1967). *The Friends of John Gerard 1545–1612*. Falls Village, CT: Herb Grower Press.

Johns, A. (1991). 'History, Science, and the History of the Book: The Making of Natural Philosophy in Early Modern England', *Publishing History*, 30, 5–30.

Jones, Howard (1989). *The Epicurean Tradition*. New York: Routledge.

Jordanova, L. (1989). *Sexual Visions: Images of Gender in Science and Medicine between the Eighteenth and Twentieth Centuries*. London: Harvester Wheatsheaf.

—— (1993). 'Gender and the Historiography of Science', *British Journal for the History of Science*, 26, 469–83.

Kanner, B. (ed.) (1979). *The Women of England, from Anglo-Saxon Times to the Present*. Hamden, CT: Archon Books.

Kaplan, B. (1993). '*Divulging of Useful Truths in Physick*': *The Medical Agenda of Robert Boyle*. London: Johns Hopkins University Press.

Kargon, Robert Hugh (1966). *Atomism in England from Hariot to Newton*. Oxford: Clarendon Press.

Keeble, N.H. (1990). '"The colonel's shadow": Lucy Hutchinson, Women's Writing and the Civil War' in Healy and Sawday (1990), pp. 227–47.

Keller, Evelyn Fox (1983). *A Feeling for the Organism. The Life and Work of Barbara McClintock*. New York: Freeman.

—— (1985). *Reflections on Gender and Science*. New Haven, CT: Yale University Press.

—— (1995). 'Mrs Jane Sharp: Midwifery and the Critique of Medical Knowledge in Seventeenth-Century England', *Women's Writing*, 2, 101–11.

Keller, Evelyn Fox and Longino, Helen (eds) (1996). *Feminism and Science*. Oxford: Oxford University Press.

Kelly-Gadol, J. (1987). 'Did Women Have a Renaissance?' in Bridenthal *et al.* (1987).

Kermode, J. and Walker, G. (eds) (1994). *Women, Crime and the Courts in Early Modern England*. London: UCL Press.

Kettering, S. (1989). 'The Patronage Power of Early Modern French Noblewomen', *Historical Journal*, 32, 817–41.

King, M. (1980). '"Book-lined cells": Women and Humanism in the Early Renaissance' in Labalme (1980), pp. 66–90.

Kinnaird, J. (1979). 'Mary Astell and the Conservative Contribution to English Feminism', *Journal of British Studies*, 19, 53–75.

Kroll, Richard W.F. (1991). *The Material Word: Literate Culture in the Restoration and Early Eighteenth Century*. Baltimore, MD: Johns Hopkins University Press.

Kroll, R.W.F. *et al.* (eds) (1992). *Philosophy, Science, and Religion in England, 1640–1700*. Cambridge: Cambridge University Press.

Labalme, P.H. (ed.) (1980). *Beyond their Sex. Learned Women of the European Past*. New York: New York University Press.

Lamb, Mary Ellen (1976). 'The Countess of Pembroke's Patronage', unpublished PhD dissertation, Columbia University.

——— (1985). 'The Cooke Sisters: Attitudes Toward Learned Women in the Renaissance' in Hannay (1985).

——— (1992). 'The Agency of the Split Subject: Lady Anne Clifford and the Uses of Reading', *English Literary Renaissance*, 22, 362–66.

Laqueur, T. (1976). 'The Cultural Origins of Popular Literacy in England, 1500–1850', *Oxford Review of Education*, 2, 255–75.

Lawrence, C. and Shapin, S. (eds) (1997). *Science Incarnate: the Presentation of Scholarly Self*. Chicago: Chicago University Press.

Le Doeuff, Michèle (1989). *The Philosophical Imaginary*. London: Athlone.

Leeuwen, Henry G. van (1963). *The Problem of Certainty in English Thought, 1630–1690*. The Hague: Nijhoff.

Levy, F.J. (1982). 'How Information Spread among the Gentry, 1550–1640', *Journal of British Studies*, 21, 11–34.

Lewalski, Barbara Keifer (1993). *Writing Women in Jacobean England*. Cambridge, MA: Harvard University Press.

Leyden, W. von (1958). 'Antiquity and Authority', *Journal of the History of Ideas*, 19, 472–3.

Lloyd, Genevieve (1992). *The Man of Reason*. London: Routledge. First published 1983.

Longino, Helen (1993). 'Subjects, Power and Knowledge: Description and Prescription in Feminist Philosophies of Science' in Alcoff and Potter (1993).

Loudon, I.S.L. (ed.) (1997). *Western Medicine: an Illustrated History*. Oxford and New York: OUP.

Lougee, C. (1976). *'Le paradis des femmes': Women, Salons and Social Stratification in 17th-century France*. Princeton, NJ: Princeton University Press.

Lubbock, C.A. (ed.) (1933). *The Herschel Chronicle. The Life Story of William Herschel and His Sister Caroline Herschel*. Cambridge: Cambridge University Press.

McAdoo, Henry R. (1965). *The Spirit of Anglicanism: A Survey of Anglican Theological Method in the Seventeenth Century*. New York: Charles Scribner.

MacDonald, M. (ed.) (1991). *Witchcraft and Hysteria in Elizabethan London: Edward Jorden and the Mary Glover Case*. London: Routledge.

MacLean, A. (1972). *Humanism and the Rise of Science in Tudor England*. London: Heinemann.

MacLean, Ian (1980). *The Renaissance Notion of Woman*. Cambridge: Cambridge University Press.

McMullen, N. (1977). 'The Education of English Gentlewomen, 1540–1640', *History of Education*, 6, 87–101.

Maddison, R. (1969). *The Life of the Hon Robert Boyle*. London: Taylor & Francis.

Man, Paul de (1983). *Blindness and Insight: Essays in the Rhetoric of Contemporary Criticism*. Minneapolis, MN: Minnesota University Press. (First published 1971.)

Marland, Hilary (ed.) (1993). *The Art of Midwifery: Early Modern Midwives in Europe*. London: Routledge.

—— (1996). '"Stately and Dignified, Kindly and God-fearing": Midwives, Age and Status in the Netherlands in the Eighteenth Century' in Marland and Pelling (1996), pp. 271–305.

Marland, H. and Pelling, M. (eds) (1996). *The Task of Healing: Medicine, Religion and Gender in England and the Netherlands 1450–1800*. Rotterdam: Erasmus Publishing.

Martin, Julian (1991). *Francis Bacon, the State, and the Reform of Natural Philosophy*. Cambridge: Cambridge University Press.

Masek, R. (1979). 'Women in the Age of Transition: 1485–1714' in Kanner (1979).

Mayo, Thomas Franklin (1934). *Epicurus in England (1650–1725)*. Dallas, TX: Southwest Press.

Mendelson, Sara Heller (1985). 'Stuart Women's Diaries and Occasional Memoirs' in Prior (1985).

—— (1987). *The Mental World of Stuart Women: Three Studies*. Brighton: Harvester.

Merchant, Carolyn (1980). *The Death of Nature: Women, Ecology and the Scientific Revolution*. San Francisco, CA: Harper & Row.

Meyer, Gerald Dennis (1955). *The Scientific Lady in England, 1650–1760: An Account of Her Rise, with Emphasis on the Major Roles of the Telescope and Microscope*. Berkeley, CA: University of California Press.

Mintz, Samuel (1952). 'The Duchess of Newcastle's Visit to the Royal Society', *Journal of English and Germanic Philology*, 51, 168–76.

Monter, W. (1969a). 'Law, Medicine and the Acceptance of Witchcraft' in Monter (ed.) (1969), pp. 55–71.

—— (1969b). *European Witchcraft*. New York: John Wiley & Sons.

—— (1987). 'Protestant Wives, Catholic Saints, and the Devil's Handmaid: Women in the Age of Reformations' in Bridenthal *et al.* (1987), pp. 203–19.

Mullan, J. (1993). 'Gendered Knowledge, Gendered Minds: Women and Newton, 1690–1760' in Benjamin (1993).

Munro, Hugh (1858). 'Mrs Lucie Hutchinson's Translation of Lucretius', *Journal of Classical and Sacred Philology*, 4, 121–39.

Murdin, L. (1985). *Under Newton's Shadow. Astronomical Practices in the Seventeenth Century*. Bristol and Boston: Hilger.

Nagy, D. Evenden (1988). *Popular Medicine in Seventeenth-Century England*. Bowling Green: Bowling Green State University Popular Press.

Narveson, Katherine (1989). 'The Source for Lucy Hutchinson's *On Theology*', *Notes & Queries*, 234, 40–1.

Nicolson, Marjorie (1965). *Pepys' Diary and the New Science*. Charlottesville, VA: University Press of Virginia.

Noble, D. (1992). *A World without Women: The Christian Clerical Culture of Western Science*. New York: Knopf.

Nutton, V. and Porter, R. (eds) (1995). *The History of Medical Education in Britain*. Amsterdam: Rodopi.

Ogilvie, M.B. (1975). 'Caroline Herschel's Contributions to Astronomy', *Annals of Science*, 32, 149–61.

O'Keefe, K.O. (1990). *Visible Song; Transitional Literacy in Old English Verse*. Cambridge: Cambridge University Press.

Ong, W.J. (1971). *Rhetoric, Romance, and Technology: Studies in the Interaction of Expression and Culture*. Ithaca, NY: Cornell University Press.

—— (1982). *Orality and Literacy; the Technologizing of the Word*. London: Methuen.

Osen, Lynn (1974). *Women in Mathematics*. Cambridge, Mass: MIT Press.

Osler, Margaret J. (ed.) (1991). *Atoms, Pneuma, and Tranquillity: Epicurean and Stoic Themes in European Thought*. Cambridge: Cambridge University Press.

Otten, Charlotte F. (ed.) (1992). *English Women's Voices 1540–1700*. Miami FL: Florida University Press.

Pagel, Walter (1982). *Joan Baptista van Helmont, Reformer of Science and Medicine*. Cambridge: Cambridge University Press.

Parry, Graham (1994). 'John Evelyn as Hortulan Saint' in *Culture and Cultivation in Early Modern England*, ed. M. Leslie and T. Raylor. Leicester: Leicester University Press, pp. 130–50.

Pelling, M. (1982). 'Tradition and Diversity: Medical Practice in Norwich 1550–1640' in *Scienze credenze occulte livelli di cultura*, Istituto Nazionale di Studi sul Rinascimento. Florence: Olschki, pp. 159–71.

—— (1986). 'Appearance and Reality: Barber-Surgeons, the Body and Disease' in Beier and Finlay (1986), pp. 82–112.

—— (1987). 'Medical Practice in Early Modern England: Trade or Profession?' in Prest (1987), pp. 90–128.

—— (1988). 'Child Health as a Social Value in Early Modern England', *Social History of Medicine*, 1, 135–64.

—— (1991). 'Old Age, Poverty and Disability in Early Modern Norwich: Work, Remarriage and Other Expedients' in Pelling and Smith (1991), pp. 74–101.

—— (1994). 'Apprenticeship, Health and Social Cohesion in Early Modern London', *History Workshop Journal*, 37, 33–56.

—— (1995a). 'Knowledge Common and Acquired: the Education of Unlicensed Medical Practitioners in Early Modern London' in Nutton and Porter (1995), pp. 250–79.

—— (1995b). 'The Women of the Family? Speculations around Early Modern British Physicians', *Social History of Medicine*, 7, 383–401.

—— (1996a). 'Compromised by Gender: the Role of the Male Medical Practitioner in Early Modern England' in Marland and Pelling (1996), pp. 101–33.

—— (1996b). 'The Body's Extremities: Feet, Gender and the Iconography of Healing in Seventeenth-Century Sources' in Marland and Pelling (1996), pp. 221–51.

—— (1997). 'Unofficial and Unorthodox Medicine' in Loudon (ed.) (1997).

—— (forthcoming a). 'Older Women: Household, Caring and Other Occupations in the Late Sixteenth-Century Town' in Pelling (forthcoming c), pp. 264–76.

—— (forthcoming b). 'Nurses and Nursekeepers: Problems of Identification in the Early Modern Period' in Marland and Pelling.

—— (forthcoming c). *Poverty, Medicine and Urban Society in England 1500–1700*. London: Longman.

—— (forthcoming d). *The Strength of the Opposition: the College of Physicians and Irregular Medical Practice in Early Modern London*.

Pelling, M. and Smith, R.M. (eds) (1991). *Life, Death, and the Elderly: Historical Perspectives*. London and New York: Routledge.

Pelling, M. and Webster, C. (1979). 'Medical Practitioners' in Webster (1979).

Pepys, Samuel (1970–83). *The Diary of Samuel Pepys*. ed. R. Latham and W. Matthews, 11 vols. London: Bell.

Pérez-Ramos, Antonio (1986). *Francis Bacon's Idea of Science and the Maker's Knowledge Tradition*. Oxford: Clarendon Press.

Perl, J. (1979). 'The Ladies' Diary or Woman's Almanack, 1704–1841', *Historia Mathematica*, 6, 36–53.

Perry, R. (1986). *The Celebrated Mary Astell. An Early English Feminist*. Chicago and London: University of Chicago Press.

Pfeiffer, J. (1991). L'engouement des femmes pour les sciences au XVIIIième siècle' in D. Haase-Dubosc and E. Viennot (eds) (1991).

Phillips, Patricia (1981). 'The Lady's Journal (1693)', *Studia Neophilologica*, 53, 283–92.

—— (1990). *The Scientific Lady: A Social History of Woman's Scientific Interests, 1520–1918*. New York: St. Martin's Press.

Pollard, A.W. and Redgrave, G.R. (1976–86). *A Short-title Catalogue of Books printed in England, Scotland, & Ireland and of English Books Printed Abroad 1475–1640* (2nd edn, 2 vols, eds W.A. Jackson, F.S. Ferguson, K.F. Panzer). London: Bibliographical Society.

Pollock, L. (1989). '"Teach her to live under obedience": the Making of Women in the Upper Ranks of Early Modern England', *Continuity and Change*, 4, 231–58.

—— (1993). *With Faith and Physic: the Life of a Tudor Gentlewoman, Lady Grace Mildmay 1552–1620*. London: Collins and Brown (1993).

Pope-Hennessy, U. (1909). *See* Birch, Una.

Popkin, Richard H. (1979). *The History of Scepticism from Erasmus to Spinoza*. Berkeley, CA: University of California Press.

—— (1990). 'The Spiritualistic Cosmologies of Anne Conway and Henry More' in Hutton (1990).

Porter, R. (1989). 'The Early Royal Society and the Spread of Medical Knowledge' in Wear and French (1989).

Porter, Roy and Teich, Mikulas (eds) (1992). *The Scientific Revolution in National Context*. Cambridge: Cambridge University Press.

Prest, W. (ed.) (1987). *The Professions in Early Modern England*. London: Croom Helm.

Prior, M. (ed.) (1985). *Women in English Society 1500–1800*. London: Methuen.

Pumfrey, Stephen, Rossi, Paolo and Slawinski, Maurice (eds) (1991). *Science, Culture and Popular Belief in Renaissance Europe*. Manchester: Manchester University Press.

Purkiss, D. (1995). 'Women's Stories of Witchcraft in Early Modern England: the House, the Body, the Child', *Gender and History*, 7, 408–32.

Rawcliffe, C. (1995). *Medicine and Society in Later Medieval England*. Stroud: Alan Sutton.

Rawson, M. (1910). *Bess of Hardwick and her Circle*. London: Hutchinson & Co.

Real, Hermann Josef (1970). *Untersuchungen zur Lukrez-Übersetzung von Thomas Creech*. Berlin.

Rebière, A. (1897). *Les Femmes dans la science*, 2nd edn. Paris.

Rees, Graham (1975). 'Francis Bacon's Semi-Paracelsan Cosmology', *Ambix*, 22, 161–73.

—— (1977). 'The Fate of Bacon's Cosmology in the Late Seventeenth Century', *Ambix*, 24, 27–38.

Reynolds, Myra (1920). *The Learned Lady in England, 1650–1760*. New York: Houghton Mifflin.

Roberts, Josephine (1983). 'The Huntington Library Manuscript of Lady Mary Wroth's Play, *Loves Victorie*', *Huntington Library Quarterly*, 46, 156–74.

Roberts, M. (1985). '"Words they are Women, and Deeds they are Men": Images of Work and Gender in Early Modern England' in Charles and Duffin (1985), pp. 122–80.

Roper, L. (1989). *The Holy Household: Women and Morals in Reformation Augsburg*. Oxford: Clarendon Press.

—— (1994). *Oedipus and the Devil: Witchcraft, Sexuality and Religion in Early Modern Europe*. London and New York: Routledge.

Rose, Hilary (1994). *Love, Power and Knowledge. Towards a Feminist Transformation of the Sciences*. Cambridge: Polity.

Rosenthal, E. (1971). 'Plus ultra, non plus ultra and the Columnar Device of Emperor Charles V', *Journal of the Warburg and Courtauld Institutes*, 34, 204–28.

—— (1973). 'The Invention of the Columnar Device of the Emperor Charles V at the Court of Burgundy in Flanders in 1510', *Journal of the Warburg and Courtauld Institutes*, 36, 198–230.

Rowbotham, Sheila (1973). *Hidden from History. Rediscovering Women in History from the Seventeenth Century to the Present*. London: Pluto Press.

Rowse, A. (1993). *Four Caroline Portraits*. London: Duckworth.

Salgado, G. (1977). *The Elizabethan Underworld*. London: Dent.

Sarasohn, Lisa T. (1984). 'A Science Turned Upside Down: Feminism and the Natural Philosophy of Margaret Cavendish', *Huntington Library Quarterly*, 47, 289–307.

Sargent, R. (1995). *The Diffident Naturalist: Robert Boyle and the Philosophy of Experiment*. London: University of Chicago Press.

Sawyer, R. (1988–9). '"Strangely Handled in all her Lyms": Witchcraft and Healing in Jacobean England', *Journal of Social History*, 22, 461–85.

Sayre, Anne (1975). *Rosalind Franklin and DNA*. New York: Norton.

Schama, S. (1988). *The Embarrassment of Riches: An Interpretation of Dutch Culture in the Golden Age*. n.pl.: Fontana.

Schiebinger, Londa (1987). 'Maria Winkelmann at the Berlin Academy: a Turning Point for Women in Science', *Isis*, 77, 174–200.

—— (1988). 'Feminist Icons: the Face of Early Modern Science', *Critical Inquiry*, 4, 661–91.

—— (1989). *The Mind Has No Sex?: Women in the Origins of Modern Science*. Cambridge, MA: Harvard University Press.

Schleiner, L. (1994). *Tudor and Stuart Women Writers*. Bloomington, IN: Indiana University Press.

Schmitt, Charles B. (1983). *Aristotle and the Renaissance*. Cambridge, MA: Harvard University Press.

Schofield, R.S. (1968). 'The Measurement of Literacy in Pre-industrial England' in Goody (1968).

Shapin, Steven (1988). 'The House of Experiment in Seventeenth-Century England', *Isis*, 79, 373–404.

—— (1991). '"A Scholar and a Gentleman": The Problematic Identity of the Scientific Practitioner in Early Modern England', *History of Science*, 29, 278–327.

—— (1994). *A Social History of Truth*. Chicago, IL: University of Chicago Press.

Shapiro, B. (1969). *John Wilkins, 1614–1672: An Intellectual Biography*. Berkeley, CA: University of California Press.

—— (1983). *Probability and Certainty in Seventeenth Century England*. Princeton, NJ: Princeton University Press.

—— (1991). 'Early Modern Intellectual Life: Humanism, Religion and Science in Seventeenth-Century England', *History of Science*, 29, 45–71.

Sharp, L. (1973). 'Walter Charleton's Early Life, 1620–1659, and Relationship to Natural Philosophy in Mid-Seventeenth-Century England', *Annals of Science*, 30, 311–43.

Sharpe, J. (1996). *Instruments of Darkness: Witchcraft in England 1550–1750*. London: Hamish Hamilton.

Siraisi, N. (1990). 'Medicine, Physiology and Anatomy in Early Sixteenth-Century Critiques of the Arts and Sciences' in Henry and Hutton (1990), pp. 214–29.

Simon, J. (1966). *Education and Society in Tudor England*. Cambridge: Cambridge University Press.

Slack, P. (1979). 'Mirrors of Health and Treasures of Poor Men: The Uses of the Vernacular Medical Literature of Tudor England' in Webster (1979b), pp. 237–73.

Slive, S. (1995). *Dutch Painting 1600–1800*. New Haven, CT and London: Yale University Press.

Smith, Hilda (1982). *Reason's Disciples: Seventeenth-Century English Feminists*. London: University of Illinois Press.

—— and Cardinale, Susan (1990). *Women and Literature of the Seventeenth Century. An Annotated Bibliography Based on Wing's Short Title Catalogue*. New York: Greenwood Press.

Sommerville, Margaret (1995). *Sex and Subjection: Attitudes to Women in Early-Modern Society*. London: Edward Arnold.

Spencer, Herbert (1927). *The History of British Midwifery from 1650–1800*. London: John Bale, Sons and Danielson.

Spencer, J. (1986). *The Rise of the Woman Novelist from Aphra Behn to Jane Austen*. Oxford: Basil Blackwell.

Spender, Dale (1982). *Women of Ideas and What Men Have Done to Them from Aphra Behn to Adrienne Rich*. London: Routledge & Kegan Paul.

Stallings, W. (1979). 'Ice Cream and Water Ices in 17th and 18th Century England', *Petits Propos Culinaires*, Supp. to 3 (Autumn).

Steadman, John M. (1971). 'Beyond Hercules: Bacon and the Scientist as Hero', *Studies in the Literary Imagination*, 4, 3–48.

Stearns, P.N. (1980). 'Old Women: Some Historical Observations', *Journal of Family History*, 5, 44–57.

Stone, L. (ed.) (1964). 'The Educational Revolution in England, 1560–1640', *Past & Present*, 28, 41–80.

—— (ed.) (1976). *Schooling and Society*. Baltimore, MD: Johns Hopkins University Press.

Sutton, P. (ed.) (1984). *Masters of Seventeenth-Century Dutch Genre Painting*. Philadelphia, PA: Philadelphia Museum of Art.

—— (1990). *Northern European Paintings in the Philadelphia Museum of Art*. Philadelphia, PA: Philadelphia Museum of Art.

Taton, R. (1969). 'Mme. du Châtelet, traductrice de Newton', *Archives internationales d'Histoire des Sciences*, 22, 185–210.

Tawney, R.H. and Power, E. (eds) (1953). *Tudor Economic Documents*, 3 vols. London: Longmans, Green.

Teague, Frances (1992). 'The Identity of Bathsua Makin', *Biography*, 16, 1–17.

Tebeaux, Elizabeth (1990). 'Books of Secrets – Authors and their Perception of Audience in Procedure Writing of the English Renaissance', *Issues in Writing*, 3, 41–67.

Terrall, M. (1994). 'Gendered Spaces, Gendered Audiences: Inside and Outside the Paris Academy of Sciences', *Configurations*, 2, 207–32.

—— (1995). 'Émilie du Châtelet and the Gendering of Science', *History of Science*, 33, 283–310.

Thomas, K. (1976). *Age and Authority in Early Modern England*. London: British Academy.

—— (1986). 'The Meaning of Literacy in Early Modern England' in Baumann (1986).

Tiles, Mary (1986). 'Mathesis and the Masculine Birth of Time', *International Studies in the Philosophy of Science: Dubrovnik Papers*, 1, 16–35.

Todd, B.A. (1985). 'The Remarrying Widow: a Stereotype Reconsidered' in Prior (1985).

Tuana, Nancy (ed.) (1989). *Feminism and Science*. Bloomington, IN: Indiana University Press.

Turnbull, G. (1947). *Hartlib, Dury and Comenius*. London: Hodder & Stoughton.

Unwin, G. (1927). 'Medieval Guilds and Education' in *Studies in Economic History: the Collected Papers of George Unwin*, ed. R.H. Tawney. London: Macmillan.

Verney, F. (1970). *Memoirs of the Verney Family*. New York and London: Barnes and Noble.

Vickers, Brian (1968). *Francis Bacon and Renaissance Prose*. Cambridge: Cambridge University Press.

Vickery, A. (1993). 'Golden Age to Separate Spheres? A Review of the Categories and Chronology of English Women's History', *Historical Journal*, 36, 383–414.

Wade, I.O. (1941). *Voltaire and Madame du Châtelet: an Essay on the Intellectual Activity at Cirey*. Princeton, NJ: Princeton University Press.

Waller, G. (1993). *The Sidney Family Romance: Mary Wroth, William Herbert and the Early Modern Construction of Gender*. Detroit, IL: Wayne State University Press.

Warburg, Ingrid (1937). *Lucy Hutchinson: Das Bild einer Puritanerin*. Hamburg.

Warner, Marina (1995). *From the Beast to the Blonde: On Fairy Tales and Their Tellers*. London: Vintage.

Warnicke, Retha (1983). *Women of the English Renaissance and Reformation*. London: Greenwood.

—— (1989). 'Lady Mildmay's Journal: A Study in Autobiography and Meditation in Reformation England', *Sixteenth Century Journal*, 20, 55–68.

Watson, F. (ed.) (1912). *Vives and the Renaissance Education of Women*. London: Edward Arnold.

Wear, A. (1989). 'Medical Practice in Late Seventeenth- and Early Eighteenth-Century England: Continuity and Union' in Wear and French (1989).

Wear, A. and French, R. (eds) (1989). *The Medical Revolution of the Seventeenth Century*. Cambridge: Cambridge University Press.

Webster, C. (1970). *Samuel Hartlib and the Advancement of Learning*. Cambridge: Cambridge University Press.

—— (1975). *The Great Instauration: Science, Medicine and Reform 1626–1660*. London: Duckworth.

—— (1979a). 'Alchemical and Paracelsian Medicine' in Webster (1979b), pp. 301–4.

—— (1979b). *Health, Medicine and Mortality in the Sixteenth Century*. Cambridge: Cambridge University Press.

—— (1982). *From Paracelsus to Newton: Magic and the Making of Modern Science*. Cambridge: Cambridge University Press.

Weigall, Rachel (1911). 'An Elizabethan Gentlewoman. The Journal of Lady Mildmay, circa 1570–1617', *Quarterly Review* 215, pp. 119–138.

Weiss, Samuel (1955). 'Dating Mrs Hutchinson's Translation of Lucretius', *Notes & Queries*, 200.

Whiteman, Anne with Clapinson, Mary (1986). *The Compton Census of 1676: a Critical Edition*. London: British Academy, and Oxford: Oxford University Press.

Wiesner, M.E. (1986). *Working Women in Renaissance Germany*. New Brunswick, NJ: Rutgers University Press.

—— (1993). *Women and Gender in Early Modern Europe*. Cambridge: Cambridge University Press.

Willen, D. (1992). 'Godly Women in Early Modern England', *Journal of Ecclesiastical History*, 43, 4.

Williams, E. (1959). *Bess of Hardwick*. London: Longmans, Green.

Wilson, Adrian (1982). 'Childbirth in Seventeenth- and Eighteenth-Century England', unpublished D.Phil. thesis, University of Sussex.

—— (1985). 'William Hunter and the Varieties of Man-Midwifery' in Bynum and Porter (eds) (1985), pp. 343–69.

—— (1990). 'The Ceremony of Childbirth and its Interpretation' in Fildes (ed.) (1990), pp. 68–107.

—— (1995). *The Making of Man-Midwifery: Childbirth in England, 1660-1770*. London: UCL Press.

—— (forthcoming). *A Safe Deliverance: Childbirth in Seventeenth-Century England*. London: UCL Press.

Wilson, C. (1995). *The Invisible World. Early Modern Philosophy and the Invention of the Microscope*. Princeton, NJ: Princeton University Press.

Wilson, C.A. (1986). *Banquetting Stuffe*. Edinburgh: Edinburgh University Press.

—— (ed.) (1991a). *Banquetting Stuffe*. Edinburgh: Edinburgh U.P.

—— (ed.) (1991b). *Waste Not, Want Not*. Edinburgh: Edinburgh U.P.

—— (1996). *Skills and Equipment for Provisioning the Country House, 1700–1900*. Stroud: Alan Sutton.

Wilson, F.P. (1927). *The Plague in Shakespeare's London*. Oxford: Clarendon Press.

Wilson, Katherina M. and Warnke, Frank J. (eds) (1989). *Women Writers of the Seventeenth Century*. Athens, GA: University of Georgia Press.

Wing, D. (1945). *Catalogue of Books Printed in England, Scotland, Ireland, Wales and British America and of English Books Printed in other Countries, 1641–1700*. New York: Columbia University Press. *Early English Books 1641–1700*. University Microfilms Incorporated. Ann Arbor, 1990. 9 vols.

Wittkower, R. (1937). 'Chance, Time and Virtue', *Journal of the Warburg and Courtauld Institutes*, 1, 249–63.

Woolf, Virginia (1935). *A Room of One's Own*. London: Hogarth Press. 1st edn, 1929.

Wright, L.B. (1931). 'The Reading of Renaissance English Women', *Studies in Philology*, 28, 139–56.

—— (1958). *Middle-class Culture in Elizabethan England*. Ithaca, NY: Cornell University Press.

Wrightson, K. (1982). *English Society 1580–1680*. New Brunswick, NY: Rutgers University Press.

Wrigley, E.A. and R.S. Schofield (1981). *The Population History of England 1541–1871*. London: Edward Arnold.

Wyman, A.L. (1984). 'The Surgeoness: the Female Practitioner of Surgery, 1400–1800', *Medical History*, 28, 22–41.

Yates, Frances (1964). *Giordano Bruno and the Hermetic Tradition*. London: George Routledge & Sons.

Zilboorg, G. (1935). *The Medical Man and the Witch during the Renaissance*. Baltimore, MD: Johns Hopkins University Press.

INDEX